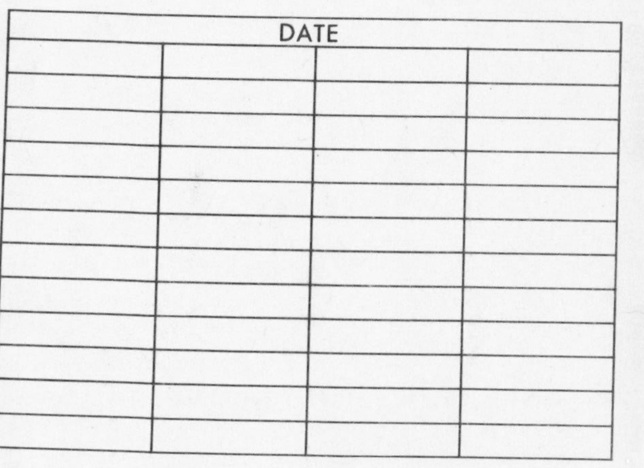

SKITS, COMEDIES AND FARCES
for
TEEN-AGERS

Skits, Comedies and Farces for Teen-agers

A collection of humorous one-act royalty-free plays for all occasions

Edited by

A. S. Burack

Publishers PLAYS, INC. *Boston*

CAUTION

NOTICE FOR AMATEUR PRODUCTION

These plays may be produced by schools, clubs, and similar amateur groups without payment of a royalty fee.

NOTICE FOR PROFESSIONAL PRODUCTION

For any form of non-amateur presentation (professional stage, radio or television), permission must be obtained in writing from the publisher. Inquiries should be addressed to PLAYS, INC., 8 Arlington Street, Boston, Massachusetts 02116.

Library of Congress Catalog Card Number: 79–110497
International Standard Book Number: 0–8238–0001–6

MANUFACTURED IN THE UNITED STATES OF AMERICA

Contents

Skits

Comedies and Farces

good

SKITS, COMEDIES AND FARCES for TEEN-AGERS

The Whites of Their Eyes

by Frank Willment

Characters

POLLY WENDEL, *director of "The Pageant of Freedom"*
BARNEY, *owner of a costume store*
MR. KRICK, *owner of the theater*
DUSTY
DON
SKIPPER
SPIKE
HARRY
SHORTY
TIM
JILL
CINDY
MIDGE
APRIL
DOODLES
DORIS
CHRISTY
PAM
PENNY
(DUSTY through PENNY: *cast of the Pageant*)

TIME: *Evening, three days before opening night.*
SETTING: *The stage of Mr. Krick's theater.*
AT RISE: *The stage is bare, except for a few red and white*

streamers, which a few members of the pageant cast are putting up at the back, supervised by APRIL. SHORTY *and* HARRY *are working on a record player, which is on a table at left.* SKIPPER *is talking on the phone, which is also on the table.* DOODLES *is sewing an American flag at right, and the rest of the cast is grouped at center, standing or sitting on the floor.*

JILL: Polly or no Polly, we'd better get this rehearsal started. It's only three days before opening night, and we need lots of practice if we want "The Pageant of Freedom" to be a success.

SPIKE: I'll say we need practice! Some of us still don't know all our lines. The scenery isn't up, either.

APRIL (*Coming forward with a roll of green crepe paper*): We may never get the scenery up. Who brought the green crepe paper? How can I make a patriotic display out of red, white, and *green* crepe paper?

DOODLES: Never mind that, April. I'm worried about the costumes. We don't have them yet.

CINDY: Where *are* the costumes? How can we put on "The Pageant of Freedom" without costumes? What's holding Polly up?

SKIPPER (*Hanging up phone and joining group at center*): I just talked to Polly's mother. Polly's bringing the costumes with her. She went over to Barney's Costume Shop to talk the deal over with Barney himself.

MIDGE: She should be here by now. We'll never be ready by Saturday night at this rate. Polly's the director and she should be here.

DON: We're about twenty minutes late already!

POLLY (*Entering from left, waving a script*): Sorry to be late. Hi, everybody! (*She comes to center.*) Let's get rolling! Time's a-wastin'! (BARNEY, *his arms full of cos-*

tume boxes, enters, follows POLLY *center and puts down his packages.*)

HARRY: It's about time you got here, Polly. (*All the members of the cast gather around* POLLY.)

APRIL: Did you get the costumes?

POLLY: You bet I did, April. Say, I want you all to meet Mr. Barney. He's the sole owner of Barney's Better Costume Shop, Incorporated. In these boxes we have everything we need for our pageant from Pocahontas' feathers to General Grant's beard!

DOODLES: Well, let's try them on. Do you have my Betsy Ross dress? (*She starts to open one of the boxes, when* BARNEY *stops her.*)

BARNEY: Hold on, hold on! Not so fast! First there's a little matter of fifty dollars.

DORIS: Fifty dollars? What for?

BARNEY: What for? What for? For renting the costumes, of course. That's what for. You think maybe I'm in this business for my health? I have a slogan. I made it up myself. It's "No Cash—No Costumes."

CHRISTY: But we gave Polly ten dollars for a down payment.

SHORTY: And we can give you the rest on opening night.

BARNEY: Opening night may be closing night. I operate on a cash-and-carry basis. You pay cash or I carry out the costumes.

POLLY (*Pleading*): Where's all your patriotism? This is a patriotic play. We wrote it ourselves. It's called "The Pageant of Freedom." Why, did you know that right on this stage we are going to show Washington crossing the Delaware, the Boston Tea Party and Paul Revere's ride?

JILL: Paul Revere can't warn the farmers without a costume.

BARNEY: Pay the fifty dollars, and Paul Revere can warn the British in Barney's best.

PAM: Paul Revere didn't warn the British. He warned the Minutemen.

BARNEY: That's between you and Paul Revere. Tell him to warn anyone he wants, *after* I have my money.

POLLY: I appeal to your patriotic spirit. Think of our glorious past— "Don't Give Up the Ship!" "Remember the Alamo."

BARNEY: I remember better the last time I got stuck. Now, I have a motto, too. It's "In God We Trust—All Others Pay Cash."

POLLY (*Gesturing dramatically*): Think of the glories we will show on this stage in three short days! Patrick Henry, decked out in Barney's best, will cry out the immortal words—"Give me liberty or give me death!"

BARNEY: Give me my fifty bucks or the costumes go back!

TIM: Can't we at least try them on for size?

BARNEY: Don't worry, they'll fit. I guarantee it.

PENNY: Have faith in us, Mr. Barney. Washington couldn't pay the troops at Valley Forge, but they stayed through a long, hard winter.

BARNEY: Not in Barney's costumes, they didn't.

MIDGE: But our country was built by those heroes at Valley Forge.

BARNEY: I have my own hero.

CINDY: Who? John D. Rockefeller?

BARNEY: No, Jack Benny.

SPIKE: No cash, no costumes?

BARNEY: No cash, no costumes!

POLLY (*With resignation*): All right, Mr. Barney. You can wait over there with your precious costumes. (*Points to left*) Maybe something will turn up. (BARNEY *gathers up his boxes and puts them on the floor at left, then stands guard over them with arms folded.*) Let's get on with the rehearsal, kids. We'll start with the Paul Revere scene.

Places, everyone. (HARRY *goes to record player at left, as* SHORTY *and* DUSTY *go off right.*) Paul Revere, you come on from the right. (SKIPPER *goes off right.*) Minutemen, take your places. (*Other boys gather down left with girls.*) Get the record player started, Harry. (*He starts a record of patriotic music.*) Ready, everyone? (*Cast nods, and the sound of hoofbeats is heard from off right.*)

SPIKE (*Cupping hand to ear*): Hark! I hear the hoofbeats of a horse!

DON: Perhaps it is tidings of the British!

SKIPPER (*From off right*): Whoa! (*Hoofbeats continue.*) Whoa! (*Hoofbeats continue.*) I said, "Whoa!" (SKIPPER *strides on stage and goes to* POLLY.) Polly, will you tell Shorty to stop the hoofbeats when I say "Whoa"? How can Paul Revere enter when his horse is galloping away?

POLLY (*Calling off right*): Watch your cues, Shorty.

SHORTY (*Coming in from right*): O.K., O.K., but Skipper is just trying to shorten my part. (*Exits*)

POLLY: Go out and come in again, Skipper. (SKIPPER *exits, and hoofbeats start.*)

SKIPPER (*Off right*): Whoa! (*Hoofbeats stop, and* SKIPPER *rushes in, shouting to group down left.*) To arms! To arms! The Redcoats are coming!

BARNEY (*From left, where he has been watching*): Not in Barney's costumes, they aren't.

HARRY: Get your rifles, men. We will march on Concord Bridge, *now!*

DUSTY (*Rushing in from right*): Don't fire until you see the whites of their eyes!

POLLY: Hold it! Hold it! Dusty, you don't come in yet. That line is in the next scene.

DUSTY: It sounded like my cue, Polly. I come out when somebody shouts "Now!"

POLLY: Not this *now,* Dusty, the next *now.*

DUSTY: Oh, the next *now.* Now I have it. (*He goes off right.*)

POLLY: All right, kids. That's straightened out. Back to work. (*They take their places again.*)

DOODLES: Do your duty, my brave boys. Our hearts are with you as you ride to battle.

TIM: And what will you do, Betsy Ross, while we are gone?

DOODLES: I will make flags for our new nation. (*She unfolds a modern American flag and holds it up.*)

POLLY: Hold it, Doodles! There were only thirteen colonies in Betsy Ross's time. You can't hold up a flag with fifty stars!

DOODLES: Well, where am I going to get one with thirteen stars?

PAM: Oh, let's get on with the rehearsal or we'll be here all night!

POLLY: Places, everyone. Let's take it from the Betsy Ross speech.

DOODLES: I will make flags for our new nation (*Holds up flag*) but with thirteen stars instead of fifty like this one.

SPIKE: Farewell, Betsy, we will go meet the British *now!*

DUSTY (*Rushing on*): Don't fire until you see the whites of their eyes!

POLLY: Not now, Dusty. You came in too soon, again!

DUSTY: You said the next *now.*

POLLY: I didn't mean this *now* now. I meant the next *now.* Now, do you know which *now?*

DUSTY: I thought this *now* was the next *now.* Now I don't know which *now* is *now* and which *now* is not *now.*

POLLY: You'd better go backstage and study your lines, Dusty. (DUSTY *leaves.*) Let's get back to the play. Where were we?

SPIKE: I had just said: "Farewell, Betsy, we will go to meet the British—*right away!*"

SKIPPER: I must mount my trusty steed and warn the other Minutemen! Farewell! (*Hoofbeats start offstage. Turning to* POLLY.) Polly, will you tell that mixed-up sound effects man to let me get on my horse before it gallops away?

SHORTY (*Coming on stage*): All right, all right. I'll hold up the hoofbeats until you get offstage. Don't be such a crab about it. (*Exits.*)

SKIPPER (*Taking his place again*): Farewell! (*He runs off right, and hoofbeats start.* SPIKE *lines up Minutemen, who pick up broomsticks from pile at left and carry them like rifles.* SPIKE *calls out orders, and they march around stage in a disorganized fashion, as the girls wave in farewell.*)

POLLY: Not so bad. Not good, but not too bad. (SHORTY *and* SKIPPER *re-enter.*) O.K., let's do the scene about Washington and his men at Valley Forge.

PENNY: Polly, I just thought of something. Why couldn't all the girls make candy and sell it during this scene?

POLLY: Sell candy during the Valley Forge scene?

PENNY: Yes, we could call it Valley Fudge.

DORIS: We could dress as colonial ladies and sell it in the aisles.

BARNEY: No, you couldn't. Not until Barney gets his fifty bucks. I want it *now!*

DUSTY (*Running in*): Don't fire until you see the whites of their eyes!

POLLY: Not yet, Dusty!

DUSTY: Somebody said "Now!"

POLLY: Wait until *I* say *now*. Don't worry about other *nows*. Come out and shout your line when I say *now*. O.K.?

DUSTY: When you say *now*. Now I know which *now*. (*He goes offstage again.*)

POLLY: Everyone take his place. (*Looking at script, as*

girls watch scene) It's a bleak, cold winter at Valley Forge. A group of soldiers are huddling around a fire—huddle over there, boys—(*She points down left and the boys form a semicircle around an imaginary fire.*) George Washington enters from the left.

DON (*Warming hands over imaginary fire*): It has been a long hard winter indeed.

TIM: If only our noble leader has been able to get supplies.

HARRY (*Pointing off left*): Here comes General Washington through the woods. (*All rise and face left, standing at attention.*)

BOYS (*Saluting*): Hail, General Washington! (MR. KRICK, *a middle-aged man in topcoat and derby, enters.*)

MR. KRICK: Where's Polly Wendel? I want to see Polly Wendel!

TIM: Who are you? You're not General Washington!

MR. KRICK: Of course I'm not General Washington! I'm Oliver J. Krick, the owner of this theater, and I want to see Polly Wendel!

POLLY (*Coming to center to meet him*): Here I am, Mr. Krick. Don't get excited.

MR. KRICK: Polly, where's the fifty dollars rent for this theater? You promised to pay me three days ago.

POLLY: Well, you see—

BARNEY: *Another* fifty dollars? You'll have to wait your turn, buddy. (*Pointing behind him*) The line forms on the left.

JILL: What's this all about? I thought you had paid the theater rent, Polly.

POLLY: Well, I meant to, but—

MIDGE: Didn't we have enough money from the advance sale to pay the rent?

POLLY: We had to use that money for properties, advertising and other things, Midge.

MR. KRICK: Am I to understand that you can't pay? Out! Out! Everybody out!

POLLY: Whoa! Hold your horses, Mr. Krick! You'll get your money on opening night.

MR. KRICK: There'll be no opening night if I don't get my money.

CINDY: Have a heart, Mr. Krick. "The Pageant of Freedom" is bound to be a big success.

MR. KRICK: No money, no theater.

CHRISTY: No money, no theater, no costumes. Let's change the name to "The Pageant of Failure."

POLLY: Where's your American spirit, Mr. Krick? Suppose the men who owned the boats had refused to let Washington cross the Delaware until they had been paid for. Where would America be today?

MR. KRICK: They weren't my boats.

APRIL: A lucky thing! If they had been your boats, Washington would have had to swim.

PAM: Think of Washington, Jefferson, Benjamin Franklin!

MR. KRICK: I'd rather think of King Midas. He had the right idea!

POLLY: Well, we just can't pay you *now*.

DUSTY (*Rushing on stage*): Don't fire until you see the whites of their eyes!

POLLY: Oh, Dusty! You're wrong again!

DUSTY: But you said to come in when you said *now,* and I heard you say *now*.

POLLY: Listen, Dusty. When it's your turn I'll shout *now*.

DUSTY: O.K. I'll be backstage. Shout it good and loud so I'll know. (DUSTY *goes offstage*.)

POLLY: Mr. Krick, won't you let us finish the rehearsal? If you'll wait with Mr. Barney, we can talk things over when the rehearsal has ended.

MR. KRICK: I'll give you ten minutes to think of something,

and it had better be good. (*He goes to wait with* BARNEY.)

DORIS: Let's face it. The pageant is off. We can't possibly raise one hundred dollars quickly enough to pay for the costumes and rent.

JILL: But we can't call it off. We've sold 172 tickets, and Polly has spent the money. We have to give a show!

SKIPPER: Where? Out on the sidewalk? I don't think the mayor would give us a permit.

MIDGE: This looks like the end of the line. What do we do now?

PENNY: I had an uncle once who couldn't pay his debts.

PAM: What did he do?

PENNY: He went into bankruptcy.

CHRISTY: Well, we're bankrupt, and at our age, too!

APRIL: Now, look. Things can't be that bad! Remember the spirit of our forefathers. That's what we're putting on this whole pageant for—to show their determination and perseverance.

DOODLES: That's the way to talk—"Remember the Alamo", Davy Crockett and Jim Bowie and the rest. They didn't give up when things looked blackest!

DORIS: And, if I remember my history, none of them got out of the Alamo alive, did they? (*All are silent for a moment. Suddenly the phone rings.*)

MIDGE: Answer the phone, Polly. It's probably another creditor wanting money.

POLLY: (*Answering the phone*): Polly Wendel speaking. Do you want Mr. Krick? (*Pause*) You just want to speak to whoever answers the phone? Who is this? (*Pause*) You are what? Hold on a sec—(*Puts hand over receiver and speaks to others*) Hey, kids, it's a quiz program. They want me to answer some fool question for one hundred dollars. (*Suddenly*) *A hundred dollars!* (*Into phone*) Did you say one hundred dollars? Of course I know the answer. What's the question? (*Pause*) What did the Colonial commander say at the Battle of Bunker Hill? How long do I have? (*Pause*) Thirty seconds? (*To the others*) Here's our chance to make the hundred dollars we need! I have to answer this question in thirty seconds. What did the Colonial commander say at the Battle of Bunker Hill? Quick!

HARRY: Don't give up the ship?

CINDY: No, silly. What would a ship be doing on Bunker Hill?

POLLY: Don't argue! It's something famous. Keep shouting things at me. I'll know it when I hear it.

SHORTY: We have met the enemy and they are ours?

JILL: Lafayette, we are here?

SKIPPER: I have just begun to fight?

CHRISTY: Taxation without representation is tyranny?

DON: You may fire when ready, Gridley?

APRIL: Life, liberty and the pursuit of happiness?

TIM: A penny saved is a penny earned?

MIDGE: Fourscore and seven years ago?

SHORTY: Remember Pearl Harbor?

POLLY: No, no, it's none of those!

DORIS: I could go home and look it up in my history book.

POLLY: Time is running out! I need the answer *now!* Now, do you hear me? *Now!*

DUSTY (*Rushing onstage*): Don't fire until you see the whites of their eyes!

POLLY: That's it! That's it!

DUSTY: What's it? (*Others watch* POLLY *anxiously and pay no attention to* DUSTY, *who shrugs and goes off again.*)

POLLY (*Into phone*): Don't fire until you see the whites of their eyes! Am I right? (*Pause*) I am? I've won the hundred dollars? Golly, that's great! Say, mister, when do I get the money? (*Pause*) You'll put it in the mail tonight? Gee, thanks! Thanks a million! I mean, thanks a hundred! You've just saved our lives, that's all! (*Pause*) Send it to Polly Wendel at Krick Theater. Goodbye, now, and thanks again! (*She hangs up the phone, and cast crowds around her.*)

SPIKE: Did we get it, Polly? Did we really win the hundred bucks?

POLLY: We sure did—thanks to Dusty! (*To* BARNEY *and* MR. KRICK) Gentlemen, your money is in the mail!

BARNEY: That's good enough for me. (*Indicating boxes*) Here are your costumes, Polly.

MR. KRICK: The theater is yours, Polly. Best of luck with the show. I'll see you on opening night. Goodbye, everybody.

BARNEY: I have to be going along, too. Goodbye, and good luck. (BARNEY *and* MR. KRICK *leave as all call "Goodbye."*)

POLLY: Now that we have settled the minor details, let's start the rehearsal. Everybody in places—right *now!*

DUSTY (*Rushing onstage again*): Don't fire until—

ALL: Oh, no! (*All laugh as curtain falls.*)

THE END

The Case of the Frustrated Corpse

by Ruth Wallace

Characters

CORPSE
MAID
WIFE
DETECTIVE

SETTING: *A living room furnished with sofa, table and chairs. A sofa diagonally faces audience on one side of the stage, with the entrance to room on opposite side.*

AT RISE: CORPSE *is stretched out on sofa with dagger prominently shown sticking up out of his chest. There is no action for several seconds. Then,* CORPSE *slowly sits up and props himself up on one elbow to talk to audience.*

CORPSE: Life is full of little surprises, isn't it? I really wasn't prepared for this, but then, who is? I might as well make the best of it and enjoy all the excitement when they discover my body. Of course, *I* know who did it, but I'm not in the best of positions to name the culprit, don't you agree? So, I'll just lie back and watch —oh, oh, excuse me, someone is about to discover my body. (CORPSE *resumes prone position as* MAID *enters.* MAID *dusts and straightens room, completely ignoring body, and walks offstage.* CORPSE *props himself up on elbow.*) You know, I couldn't get her to pay any attention to me when I was alive, either. Oh, here comes my sweet wife. Poor thing! I hate to think of her grief when she finds me. (CORPSE *resumes prone position as* WIFE *enters.*)

WIFE (*Takes one look at* CORPSE): Well! ! Of all the lazy, good-for-nothing loafers! Just when I wanted you to run some errands for me! I never can depend on you for anything! (*Exits*)

CORPSE (*Sitting up again*): Isn't she sweet? Such grief, such devotion. (*Quickly lies down as* WIFE *re-enters*)

WIFE: And get your feet off the sofa! (*Pushes feet off and exits*)

CORPSE (*Sitting up*): Some people just don't like to show their feelings openly. Just wait—she won't let this crime go unsolved. I was always the most important thing in the world to her! (CORPSE *lies back, as* WIFE *enters with* DETECTIVE, *dressed in trench coat and carrying a suitcase.*)

WIFE: Right this way, Inspector. Oh, I do hope you can solve this crime.

DETECTIVE: Now, don't you worry, madam. Leave everything to me. I've never failed to solve any crime I've worked on.

WIFE: Really? How many cases have you had?

DETECTIVE: This is my first one. Now, let's get down to business. (DETECTIVE *puts suitcase on table and begins to open it.*)

WIFE: What do you have there?

DETECTIVE: Clues, madam, clues. You can't solve crimes without clues.

WIFE: You mean you bring clues with you? I thought you found them at the scene of the crime.

DETECTIVE: Ah, that's what an ordinary detective would do. But what happens when he can't find any clues? He can't solve the crime! I am always prepared. (*Taps forehead*) I use my head. (CORPSE *rises and speaks to audience.*

Other characters freeze in position whenever CORPSE *talks.*)

CORPSE: Something tells me we're not going to get very far. I wish they'd pay a little attention to me—after all, the body ought to have some importance in this case. (CORPSE *lies down.*)

DETECTIVE (*Taking clues out of suitcase. These can be exaggerated cardboard cutouts, large enough to be recognized by audience.*): Now let's see what we have here. Aha! Footprints—I thought so!

WIFE: What does that tell you?

DETECTIVE: Nothing yet, but footprints are always important. Look! (*Holds up fingerprint cutouts*) Fingerprints, too! I think I'm going to need some assistance—there are a great many clues here.

WIFE: I'll get the maid. She can help. (*Exits and immediately re-enters with* MAID)

DETECTIVE: What were *you* doing about eight o'clock last night? Better still, what are you doing about eight o'clock tonight?

CORPSE (*As all action stops*): I'm beginning to lose confidence in this guy.

DETECTIVE (*To* MAID): Here, you hold these clues. (*Takes out each clue in turn and hands it to* MAID, *who holds it up for audience to see, then puts it on table.*) Ah-h-h, poison—a perfumed handkerchief—What's this? A long blonde hair! Ah-h, the plot thickens.

CORPSE (*To audience*): What plot?

WIFE: What do all these clues mean? Oh, you must solve this mystery. It's the most important thing in the world to me!

CORPSE (*To audience*): What did I tell you?

DETECTIVE (*As he continues to take clues from suitcase*): A gun! A lipstick-stained glass! . . . Now, wait. Some of these clues are from another case I'm working on.

WIFE: You don't seem to be getting anywhere.

CORPSE: Did you get that feeling, too?

DETECTIVE: The next step is to retrace all the action leading to the crime. Tell me exactly what happened.

WIFE: I just can't think straight. I'm too upset.

MAID: I remember, madam. The last time I saw you, you were all dressed up to go out, sitting on the sofa there (*Pointing at body*) with Mr.—

WIFE (*Interrupting hurriedly*): *All* the details aren't necessary.

CORPSE (*To audience*): What's been going on behind my back?

DETECTIVE: Have you looked at the sofa?

CORPSE: It's about time somebody paid attention to the sofa. (DETECTIVE *walks to sofa, rolls* CORPSE *over, reaches down into sofa cushions and dramatically pulls out long strand of pearls.*)

DETECTIVE: Here we are, madam! The mystery of the missing jewels is solved!

WIFE: Oh, my pearls! You've found them! How wonderful! I couldn't live without them—they're the most important thing in the world to me! And they were right here all the time!

CORPSE: I'm right here, too, you know. (WIFE *exits, clutching pearls happily.*)

DETECTIVE (*Sweeps clues from table into suitcase, closes suitcase, turns to* MAID): Now, young lady, isn't there some detective work I can do for you? (*Takes* MAID *by arm and both exit.*)

CORPSE (*Sits up, looks around at empty room, turns to audience*): Sooner or later, somebody's going to sit on this sofa. (*Drums fingers, looks off into space with worried expression as curtain falls.*)

THE END

Professor Countdown Takes Off

by Polly Lewis Bradley

Characters

PROFESSOR COUNTDOWN
JAMES, *his chauffeur*
MRS. FLITTER
MISS STERLING
LADIES

SCENE 1

SETTING: *A road.*

AT RISE: JAMES *and* PROFESSOR COUNTDOWN *are seated in chairs, as if they were riding in a car.* JAMES *pretends to hold a steering wheel, as if he were driving. He wears a chauffeur's uniform.* PROFESSOR COUNTDOWN *is behind and slightly to the right of* JAMES. *They sway backwards and forwards, with the motion of the "car," as* JAMES *"steers." Suddenly* JAMES *puts his foot on the imaginary "brake," and the "car" comes to an abrupt halt. Both* JAMES *and* PROFESSOR COUNTDOWN *lurch forward in their seats at the same moment.*

PROFESSOR (*As he straightens up in his seat*): I say, James, you might try driving a little more smoothly.

JAMES (*Turning in his seat and looking at* PROFESSOR): I'm sorry, Professor Countdown. The brakes have just been fixed, and they're still pretty tight. And that light turned red very fast.

PROFESSOR: I see. Well, try to calculate the margin of error, so you can do better next time. You interrupted my train of thought just as I was trying to deduce how a rocket's guidance system can be shielded from the effect of the Van Allen Radiation Belt. The secondary gamma radiation might prove most harmful.

JAMES: I'm very sorry, sir. Is there anything I could do to help you?

PROFESSOR (*Ironically*): You might try giving my speech at the Ladies' Luncheon League today. I could use the time to think.

JAMES (*Laughing*): That's not quite in my line, sir.

PROFESSOR: No, but I certainly wish it were. I'm sick and tired of giving speeches. I've given hundreds of them.

JAMES: Yes, and I guess I must have listened almost as many times.

PROFESSOR: I imagine you're as sick of hearing them as I am of giving them.

JAMES: Oh, no, sir, I always enjoy them. I almost know one or two of them by memory.

PROFESSOR: You do? (*He thinks a moment.*) Say, I'll bet you do at that. James, I have a wonderful idea! You really *can* give my speech for me.

JAMES (*Startled*): What's that, sir?

PROFESSOR: But of course! You know it as well as I do.

JAMES: But, sir, what do I know about science?

PROFESSOR: You don't need to know anything about science. You know my speech. And after all, the ladies in the Luncheon League aren't scientists either. They'll never suspect.

JAMES: Well, sir, I don't know.

PROFESSOR: Think of the challenge, James.

JAMES: I'd like to help you out, sir, but I'd rather face

twenty taxis in the five o'clock rush than a bunch of curious ladies.

PROFESSOR: It will be just the same standard speech you've heard many times.

JAMES: Which speech were you planning to give, sir? Is it the "Wonders of Outer Space" speech, or the "Joy of Research" speech.

PROFESSOR: I had in mind the "Wonders of Outer Space."

JAMES: That's my favorite. I often dream of chauffeuring a spaceship. Come to think of it, I'll bet I could give your speech at that.

PROFESSOR: Of course you can. You'll have no trouble at all.

JAMES: O.K., why not? I'll give it a try, sir.

PROFESSOR: Wonderful! Wonderful! Now if you'll just stop at the next turnout, we'll change clothes and trade places.

JAMES: Very well, sir.

PROFESSOR: And James, the light has been green for some time now. You may drive on.

JAMES: Yes, sir. (*He turns around and begins to "drive." They lurch along in silence for a few moments, then the* PROFESSOR *leans forward and points toward the right, so that* JAMES *can see him.*)

PROFESSOR: There's a good spot.

JAMES: Yes, sir. (*He "steers" toward right and stops. Both lurch forward.* JAMES *pulls up the "emergency brake," gets out of "car," and opens "door" for* PROFESSOR COUNTDOWN, *who steps out.*)

PROFESSOR (*As they start to trade coats and hats*): Once we've changed clothes, no one will suspect. It's lucky we're both about the same size. None of the ladies will know a thing.

JAMES: I hope not, sir.

PROFESSOR: Don't worry, James. I don't see how anything

can happen. (*After* JAMES *has put on suit coat and Homburg*) You look excellent, James. Go look at yourself in the rearview mirror. (JAMES *and* PROFESSOR *go around to the left side of "car" and* JAMES *looks in "mirror."*)

JAMES: Oh, my goodness, Professor, this will never work! I forgot all about your mustache. That would give me away in a minute. Everyone knows about Professor Countdown's elegant mustache.

PROFESSOR: True, true.

JAMES (*Starting to take off* PROFESSOR'S *coat*): It's too bad, sir.

PROFESSOR (*Holding out his hand to stop* JAMES): Don't take that coat off, James. It hurts me to tell you, but my wife hates mustaches. I think they give a man dignity, but she refuses to kiss me unless I'm clean-shaven. Therefore I wear this only at the laboratory. (*He takes off fake mustache and hands it to* JAMES.)

JAMES: Why, Professor, I never suspected.

PROFESSOR: And here is some mustache glue. (*He takes a small tube of glue from the pocket of the coat which* JAMES *is wearing.* JAMES *puts on mustache. Both look in mirror.*)

JAMES: Why, I look just like you, sir.

PROFESSOR: Excellent! Excellent!

JAMES: I even feel like you, sir. (*He straightens up and puts on an expression of dignity and wisdom.*) As I was telling my colleagues the other day, I'm terribly worried about those secondary gamma gamma gamma radiation effects.

PROFESSOR: James, I can see that you'll do a superb job. Why, perhaps you can give all my speeches for me!

JAMES: Now, let's not get carried away, sir.

PROFESSOR (*Waving his chauffeur's hat*): What freedom! Here, let me help you into the car. (*He opens rear "door" for* JAMES, *who enters "car" and sits down. Then the* PROFESSOR *gets into the driver's seat, pushes in the "emergency brake," and starts the "car" with a jerk as they lurch backwards. They "drive" a few moments, then the* PROFESSOR *applies the "brake" suddenly and they lurch forward.*)

JAMES: I say, Professor Countdown, you might try driving a little more smoothly.

PROFESSOR (*Looking back at* JAMES): You're right—these brakes are a little tight.

JAMES: You should have no trouble calculating the margin of error.

PROFESSOR: You're not supposed to be giving my speeches yet. Wait until the luncheon. By the way, you'd better call me James. It would be unfortunate if we gave ourselves away with a slip of the tongue.

JAMES: Yes, sir. Oh, James, the light has been green for some time now. You may drive on.

PROFESSOR: Yes, sir. (*They "drive" away as the curtains close.*)

* * *

SCENE 2

TIME: *An hour later.*

SETTING: *The meeting of the Ladies' Luncheon League.*

AT RISE: *At right sit a group of* LADIES, *and behind them stands* PROFESSOR COUNTDOWN, *in his chauffeur's uniform, deeply immersed in thought. At left are a speaker's stand and two chairs.* MRS. FLITTER *is sitting on one of the chairs.* JAMES *is at the speaker's stand, and is almost through speaking.*

JAMES: Now, the future lies before us. We will travel to the stars, and nothing can keep us from this otherworldly destiny. We will learn the promise of the planets, the secret of the solar system, the glory of the galaxy. (*Applause*)

In my work, I often sit thinking of empty space. But remember, ladies, each of us has a role in the future of science. Those of you who are not professional scientists can help the advance of science by realizing its importance and thinking of its progress. You, too, as you do the dishes or make the beds, can think about empty space. You, too, can be way out of this world.

In closing, dear ladies, let me make a few comments about my profession. You may think the greatest work is to be a scientist—but no, I admire most the daring astronauts who will take these spaceships aloft—we might call them the chauffeurs of outer space. Yes, in the future, chauffeurs will be recognized as great leaders, as the finest and noblest of men. They will have the title they deserve—in fact, they will be known as "Man's Best Friend." (*Applause*)

Thank you, ladies, for your attention. (*He bows as the* LADIES *applaud.* MRS. FLITTER *comes forward and* JAMES *sits down.*)

MRS. FLITTER: Thank you, Professor Countdown, for your inspiring speech. I'm thrilled that such a marvelous scientist as you could take time out to speak to poor little us. All of us were overjoyed to know about the wonders of outer space, and I'm sure we have all made a vow to ourselves to spend more time thinking about empty space. And now, we will have our question period.

JAMES (*Worried*): Question period? This is unexpected. . . . Is this the usual thing?

MRS. FLITTER: No, Professor, it isn't. But we have an unusual visitor in our audience.

JAMES (*Uneasily*): You do? (*He wipes his brow.*)

MRS. FLITTER: Yes, we have with us today as a special guest Miss Sterling, the science editor of the *Daily City Trib-*

une, who has come especially to hear your speech. I think she may have a question to ask you. Miss Sterling?

MISS STERLING (*Rising*): Yes, I do have one, Mrs. Flitter.

MRS. FLITTER: I'm sure the Professor would just love to answer your question. (*She sits and* JAMES *comes forward, looking extremely uneasy.*)

MISS STERLING: Professor Countdown, in the light of Einstein's Theory of Relativity, how do you think the parameter time affects the life expectancy of those traveling in a spaceship, when the vehicle's velocity is approaching the speed of light? (*She sits.*)

JAMES (*Panicky*): Well—madam—that's an excellent question. Yes, a very fine question. It's a matter of great importance, and something we scientists have often worried about. (*Stalling*) Yes, indeed, I've often discussed it with other scientists. We've talked about it many times, far into the night. Many is the time we've said to each other, "I wonder what the real truth of the matter is." (*Unhappily*) Yes, what is the real truth? What *is* the answer? (*He looks at the* PROFESSOR *desperately. Then he suddenly brightens.*) Yes, it seems like a difficult question. But in reality, Miss Sterling, it's not difficult at all. In fact, it's so simple that even my chauffeur could answer it. James! (PROFESSOR *comes forward.*) Will you answer the lady's question?

PROFESSOR: Certainly, sir. I'd be glad to. Some authorities say that due to the Lorentz time contraction at these velocities, the spaceship's occupants, upon returning to earth, will find that their contemporaries have aged considerably more than they have. However, I personally believe that this time contraction is purely a relative matter and does not affect biological processes.

MRS. FLITTER (*To* PROFESSOR, *as he returns to his place behind the* LADIES): Thank you. (*To* MISS STERLING) Miss Sterling, does that answer your question?

MISS STERLING: I believe so. And you do agree with your chauffeur's opinion, don't you, Professor Countdown?

JAMES: Oh, absolutely, absolutely! The matter is quite obvious.

MRS. FLITTER: Professor, let me thank you again for coming here today. You have proved that your great reputation is fully deserved—you are so wise that even your chauffeur knows more than the man in the street. Now, we're going to have tea and cookies in the social hall, and I hope you'll come along.

JAMES: Of course. I'd be delighted. (*The* LADIES *all exit, and* JAMES *starts to follow them. As he passes the* PROFESSOR, *he stops a moment.*) You handled that very well, James. Now, you may wait outside in the car while I have my tea.

PROFESSOR (*As* JAMES *exits*): Lucky there was time for only one question! (*Quick curtain*)

THE END

Man in the Red Suit

by Bill Moessenger

Characters

ARBO GLOG, *a Martian astronaut*
MOTHER GLOG
PRESIDENT OF MARS
TWO MARTIAN SPACE SUIT CHECKERS
OTHER MARTIANS
MR. KRINGLEHOFFER
MRS. KRINGLEHOFFER
NICHOLAS, *12* } *the Kringlehoffers' children*
HOLLY, *10* } *the Kringlehoffers' children*
YULE, *9, a boy* } *the Kringlehoffers' children*
NOEL, *7, a girl* } *the Kringlehoffers' children*
NEARSIGHTED EARTHMAN
LADY
TINY SON
FIVE CAROLERS
TV ANNOUNCER

BEFORE RISE: TV ANNOUNCER *may enter and stand before curtain, or may speak from offstage.*

TV ANNOUNCER: This is MBC. I repeat, this is MBC preparing to report on the Earth shot. In just a few minutes our cameras will bring you live coverage of the first flight to the Earth. Stay tuned to MBC—the Mars Broadcasting Company. . . . (TV ANNOUNCER *exits as the curtain rises.*)

SCENE 1

SETTING: *The planet Mars. A small table with "hypno-ray gun" on it is at one side of stage.*

AT RISE: *The* PRESIDENT OF MARS, *who holds a red cap with a white tassel on it, is addressing* ARBO GLOG. GLOG *wears red suit with white trim and has white hair.* OTHER MARTIANS, *some of whom also have white hair, are gathered about.*

PRESIDENT OF MARS: As the President of Mars, I award you, Arbo Glog, the order of the red cap. (*He places red cap on* GLOG'S *head.*) Since you will be the first Martian to rocket to the planet Earth, I would like personally to offer my congratulations. (*He shakes* GLOG'S *hand.* MOTHER GLOG *runs on, carrying parcels.*)

MOTHER GLOG (*Running to* GLOG): My son, my son! (*Handing him package*) You forgot your toothbrush.

GLOG (*Taking toothbrush and stuffing it into his space suit; embarrassed*): Mother!

MOTHER GLOG (*Handing him more parcels*): And take along this toothpaste, and this box of cookies, cakes and all your favorite desserts. (*He puts packages into pockets of his space suit.* MOTHER GLOG *hands him large teddy bear.*) And don't forget your teddy bear. You've never gone away without it.

GLOG (*Taking teddy bear*): Mother! You know I wouldn't have forgotten. All astronauts always carry teddy bears as good luck charms—you know that. And besides, we're on MBC television right now.

MOTHER GLOG: We are? Oh, my! (*She fixes her hair, and pretends to be looking into camera; waving*) Yoo hoo!

(*Turns back to* GLOG) And you forgot your electric razor. (*She hands him razor.*)

GLOG: Now, I'll be all right, Mother. Don't you worry.

MARTIANS (*Cheering*): Hurrah! Hurrah! Hip, hip, hurray!

GLOG (*To his mother*): They're all cheering for me. See?

MARTIANS (*Cheering*): Hurray for Arbo Glog! (*Singing*)
For he's a jolly good fellow,
For he's a jolly good fellow,
For he's a jolly good fellow,
(*Pointing upward*)
He'll soon be in the sky.

MOTHER GLOG (*Crying loudly*): Oh, my little boy! You've never gone this far away from home before.

GLOG: Now, Mother, it's not *that* far away!

MOTHER GLOG: It's 49,000,000 miles. That's far enough! (*Suddenly*) Did you bring your rain boots?

GLOG: Well—

MOTHER GLOG: You *must* bring your rain boots! Earth is such a damp place. Three quarters of it is oceans, rivers, and lakes. And it gets cold this time of year. (*She begins to cry.*) And you'll be all by yourself—away from home—on a strange planet. Without a mother to make you hot chocolate on cold damp nights!

GLOG: Now, now, Mother!

PRESIDENT OF MARS: Now, now, madam!

1ST MARTIAN: Now, now, little lady! (MOTHER GLOG *stops crying.*)

GLOG (*Patting her on the back*): There, there. . . . (Two SPACE SUIT CHECKERS *enter.*)

1ST CHECKER: We must check your space suit before you blast off.

2ND CHECKER: We have to be sure that there are no leaks in it.

GLOG: Certainly. (*They check the suit and empty all pockets.*)

1st Checker: Everything's fine—shipshape.

2nd Checker: Top shape!

Both (*Making an O.K. sign with their thumbs and forefingers*): A-O.K. (*They exit as* Glog *carefully replaces packages in his suit. He keeps electric razor in his hand.*)

President of Mars (*Looking at his watch*): Mr. Glog, it is twenty seconds before blast-off time.

Glog: Oh, my! I'd better get inside.

President of Mars (*Handing ray gun to* Glog): This is your hypno-ray gun. It may be very useful to you. (Glog *puts his electric shaver down on table as the* President *hands him the ray gun.*)

Mother Glog: Are you sure you have everything?

Glog: Yes, Mother! I have everything. I have to go now. Bye! (*He runs offstage.*)

Mother Glog (*Sadly*): 'Bye, son.

All: 10, 9, 8, 7, 6, 5, 4, 3, 2, 1, 0—Blast off! (*All raise their arms and look skyward*) Whooooo! (*Calling*) Good luck! Good luck, Arbo Glog!

Mother Glog (*Looking at table and picking up shaver*): Oh, my! He has forgotten his electric shaver! (*She holds the shaver in her hand and raises it skyward. She shrugs her shoulders.*)

CURTAIN

* * *

Scene 2

Time: *Christmas Eve.*

Before Rise: Five Carolers *enter, standing in front of curtain.*

1st Caroler: This is the first time I've ever gone caroling

on Christmas Eve. Don't you think we should practice first?

2ND CAROLER: Good idea! Which song do you want to try?

3RD CAROLER: How about "Jolly Old St. Nicholas"? (*They nod in agreement and sing carol.*)

4TH CAROLER: Well, what house should we go to first?

5TH CAROLER: Let's go to the Kringlehoffers'. (5TH CAROLER *gestures to others, who follow him off. The curtain rises.*)

* * *

SETTING: *The stage is divided: stage left is the Kringlehoffer living room. A table with pile of envelopes on it is by the front door; a Christmas tree stands in one part of the room. Stage right is the yard outside the house.*

AT RISE: MRS. KRINGLEHOFFER *enters and takes envelopes from table.*

MRS. KRINGLEHOFFER: Look at all these Christmas cards! (*She leafs through them.*) Some for Mr. Kringlehoffer and me, some for Yule and Holly, and all these for Noel. Just think—Noel will be seven years old tomorrow—Christmas Day. And she still believes in Santa Claus. If only she could always believe! (*Calling*) The mail's here, everybody. (MR. KRINGLEHOFFER, NICHOLAS, HOLLY, YULE, *and* NOEL *enter.* MRS. KRINGLEHOFFER *sorts cards and hands some to* MR. KRINGLEHOFFER.) These are all cards for Mr. and Mrs. Kringlehoffer and family. (*To* NOEL) Noel, these are for you. (*To* YULE) These are yours, Yule.

NOEL *and* YULE: Thanks, Mama.

YULE (*To* HOLLY, *looking at a large card*): Boy! Look at that one.

NOEL: It would be wonderful if I could see the real genuine Santa Claus this Christmas Eve.

NICHOLAS: Don't count on it, kid.

MRS. KRINGLEHOFFER: I think you have some mail, too, Nicholas.

MR. KRINGLEHOFFER (*Handing cards to* HOLLY): Holly, these are yours.

HOLLY: Thanks, Papa.

MR. KRINGLEHOFFER (*Handing cards to* NICHOLAS): Nicholas, here is your mail. (*Sound of rocket is heard from offstage.*)

NICHOLAS: What was that? (*The* KRINGLEHOFFERS *freeze and hold positions as action shifts to stage right, outside the house. If desired, lights may dim stage left and come up on stage right.* GLOG *enters right; he now has long white beard and a large stomach.*)

GLOG: At last this trip is over. (*Looking offstage right*) I thought I'd never land that rocket, with all those trees around. (*He looks about; stroking his beard*) I should have listened to Mama. I forgot my electric shaver. (*Holding out beard*) Look at this beard! I've traveled 49,000,000 miles without a shave. I must look a mess. And with all those cookies and cakes I ate (*Holding his stomach*), I must have gained fifteen pounds. (*Looking about*) My, my, my, my. So this is the planet Earth. (*He looks at the* KRINGLEHOFFER *house.*) Why, this must be an Earth dwelling. (*He looks in the window.*) And those must be Earth people. They look amazingly Martian! (*He touches each part of his body as he names it.*) They have one nose, two eyes, one mouth! Two ears! Amazing! Amazing! Why, they might have a language of their own. I must find out more about these people before I go back to Mars. They may not understand my language, but perhaps I can learn some of the important words in *their* language. (GLOG *freezes, and the* KRINGLEHOFFER *home comes to life again.*)

MR. KRINGLEHOFFER: What *was* that noise?

MRS. KRINGLEHOFFER: I heard it, too! It sounded like a jet.

NICHOLAS (*Looking out to stage right*): Well, there's nothing outside except a sidewalk Santa Claus. (*They all look right, and hold positions as the curtain falls.*)

* * *

SCENE 3

TIME: *A short while later.*

SETTING: *This scene may be played before the curtain.* GLOG, *carrying his hypno-ray gun, enters and paces back and forth.*

GLOG: Now, if I can meet an Earthman and communicate with him, I may make some important discoveries about the Earth people's language. (*He paces again, looking down at the ground.* NEARSIGHTED EARTHMAN, *wearing glasses, enters looking up at the sky.*)

EARTHMAN: Oh, my, I think it might snow! I think it might snow yet. (GLOG *and* EARTHMAN *bump into each other.* EARTHMAN *falls to ground; his glasses fall off and he holds them in his hand.*)

GLOG (*Aside*): I certainly hope this man understands Martian. (*To* EARTHMAN, *as* GLOG *tries to help him up.*) Gleeps porgle nards snerp!

EARTHMAN (*Rising*): I beg your pardon!

GLOG: Porgle nards snerp, gleeps noggle gleep snoz! (EARTHMAN *puts on his glasses.*)

EARTHMAN: Oh, it's you. (*He smiles and pats* GLOG *on the stomach.*) Ho, ho, ho. Merry Christmas! (EARTHMAN *exits left.* LADY *and* TINY SON *enter right.* GLOG *stands still, thinking, with his hypno-ray gun held muzzle upward.*)

GLOG (*Puzzled*): Ho, ho! Merry Christmas! Ho, ho, ho! Merry Christmas!

TINY SON (*Aside, to* LADY): Mommy! Mommy! Santa Claus! Santa Claus!

LADY: I see him. (SON *whispers in her ear.*) All right, I'll drop some money in so the poor children can have a merry Christmas.

GLOG: Ho, ho, ho! Merry Christmas! (LADY *holds* SON'S *hand; as she passes* GLOG *she drops some change into the muzzle of his gun.*)

LADY: Merry Christmas!

GLOG (*Smiling*): Ho, ho, ho! Merry Christmas! (LADY *and* SON *exit, as the* CAROLERS *enter.*)

1ST CAROLER: We're almost there. The Kringlehoffers live right around the corner.

GLOG: Ho, ho, ho! Merry Christmas!

CAROLERS: Merry Christmas! (*They group together and sing to* GLOG)

We wish you a merry Christmas,
We wish you a merry Christmas,
We wish you a merry Christmas,
And a happy New Year!

(CAROLERS *bow to* GLOG.) Merry Christmas! (*They exit.*)

GLOG (*Still somewhat bewildered*): How wonderfully simple it is to talk with Earthmen and gain their trust and understanding. (*He exits.*)

* * *

SCENE 4

TIME: *Later on that night.*

SETTING: *The same as Scene 2.*

AT RISE: NICHOLAS, HOLLY, YULE, *and* NOEL *are decorating the Christmas tree.*

NICHOLAS: Just a few more hours and it will be Christmas.

(MRS. KRINGLEHOFFER *enters, carrying tray with cups.*)

MRS. KRINGLEHOFFER: I've brought hot chocolate for everyone.

ALL (*Ad lib*): Great! Yum, yum! Thanks, Mom. (*Etc.*) (*Children each take a cup of chocolate.*)

NOEL: Maybe we should leave a cup for Santa Claus.

NICHOLAS (*Sarcastically*): Why? Do you think you'll see Santa Claus tonight?

NOEL: I don't know, but I'd be very happy if I did.

NICHOLAS: Well, I'm twelve years old, and I've never seen the real Santa Claus. I don't even believe in him anymore. When you're my age, you won't believe in him either.

MRS. KRINGLEHOFFER: Why don't you drink your hot chocolate, Nicholas. (NICHOLAS *sips his hot chocolate as others continue to decorate tree.*)

NOEL: Nicholas. . . .

NICHOLAS: Yes?

NOEL: If you ever saw the real Santa Claus, and you were really, really sure that it was the real one and only Santa Claus, would you still believe in him?

NICHOLAS: If he did something to *prove* he was Santa Claus, I guess so . . . sure, but you don't want to be fooled by any old man in a red suit!

NOEL: Maybe I'll be luckier than you. Maybe I'll see the *real* Santa Claus, and then I'll *always* believe in him. (MR. KRINGLEHOFFER *enters, carrying a string of Christmas tree lights.*)

NICHOLAS: Don't count on it, kid.

MR. KRINGLEHOFFER: A *kid* is a baby goat.

NICHOLAS: All right, I know, Dad.

MR. KRINGLEHOFFER (*Looking at his watch*): Say, does anybody realize that it's midnight?

MRS. KRINGLEHOFFER: Twelve o'clock? I don't believe the children have ever been up this late before.

NOEL: Oh, Mommy! It's Christmas now. It's Christmas!

MR. KRINGLEHOFFER: You certainly sound happy.

NOEL: Only one thing could make me happier.

MR. KRINGLEHOFFER: I'll bet I know what it is.

NOEL: I can't tell you what it is, because I'm wishing for it, and if I tell you my wish, it won't come true.

MRS. KRINGLEHOFFER: Come, children. We'd all better get some sleep. (*Surveying the Christmas tree*) I think we've all done a beautiful job on the Christmas tree.

MR. KRINGLEHOFFER: You know, I think it's one of the prettiest trees we've ever had. (*To children*) Come along, children, it's time to go to bed.

NOEL (*As other children follow* MR. KRINGLEHOFFER): I just want to put one more piece of tinsel on the tree. (*She picks up tinsel.*)

MR. KRINGLEHOFFER: All right, Noel. And then hurry along to bed. (*All except* NOEL *exit.* NOEL *puts tinsel on tree and holds position, as* GLOG, *carrying teddy bear, enters from right. If desired, lights may dim on stage left and come up on right.*)

GLOG (*To audience*): It's time for me to leave now. What an experience this planet has been! (*He holds up teddy bear.*) Teddy bear, you've brought me so much good luck on this trip, maybe I'll leave you here as a present to this planet and its people. (*He puts teddy bear on front step of the* KRINGLEHOFFERS' *house. As he does so, lights may come up on left, and* NOEL *goes to window, gazing out toward stage right.* GLOG *turns and starts to exit right.*)

NOEL (*Looking out window*): I think there's someone there. (*She runs to open front door and looks outside.*)

GLOG (*Turning back and waving*): Ho, ho, ho! Merry Christmas! (*He exits and* NOEL *continues to watch, as sound of rocket taking off is heard.* GLOG*'s voice is heard above the noise.*) Ho, ho, ho! Merry Christmas! (NOEL *looks skyward and waves goodbye. She sees teddy bear on the steps, picks it up, and re-enters the house very happily.*)

MRS. KRINGLEHOFFER (*Entering left*): Noel! I thought you were coming right to bed!

NOEL: Mother, I saw Santa Claus! The *real* Santa Claus!

MRS. KRINGLEHOFFER (*Calmly*): Good. Now come along to bed.

NOEL: And he waved goodbye and said, "Merry Christmas," and rode away in a rocket ship.

MRS. KRINGLEHOFFER: But Santa drives a sleigh, dear—with eight reindeer.

NOEL: But he was in a rocket, Mother, and I saw it, and he rode straight up like a shooting star going back to heaven.

MRS. KRINGLEHOFFER: You were probably asleep and dreaming, dear.

NOEL: But look at what Santa left me. (*She shows her mother the teddy bear.*)

MRS. KRINGLEHOFFER: What a strange teddy bear. . . . I've never seen one like it before.

NOEL (*Aside*): Nicholas wanted proof of Santa Claus. Maybe this will convince him. (*To her mother*) Mother, are there Santa Clauses on other planets?

MRS. KRINGLEHOFFER: I don't know, dear. Maybe there are. (NOEL *takes her mother's hand, and both exit left as the curtain falls. There is a brief pause, and then* GLOG *enters right, in front of curtain, as* PRESIDENT OF MARS, *carrying large book, enters left.*)

GLOG: Ho, ho, ho! Merry Christmas!

PRESIDENT OF MARS: Arbo Glog, welcome back to Mars.

GLOG: Ho, ho, ho! Merry Christmas!

PRESIDENT OF MARS: I beg your pardon! Why do you keep saying that?

GLOG: There are people on Earth who look just like you

and me. They say those same words over and over again.

PRESIDENT OF MARS: Well, what do they mean?

GLOG: I don't know. No one explained it to me. But saying "Ho, ho, ho! Merry Christmas!" seems to give great pleasure to the Earth people.

PRESIDENT OF MARS: We must solve the mystery of this "Ho, ho, ho!" Another trip must be planned. (*He consults large book.*) My book of astronomical calculations says that such a trip would be possible in exactly 364 days. Let's see . . . that would be December 24, 19— (*Insert next year's date*). (PRESIDENT OF MARS *smartly closes book, tucks it under his arm, and walks off left, followed by* GLOG.)

THE END

No Garden This Year

by Paul S. McCoy

Characters

WILBUR
CARRIE, *his wife*
DAN, *their neighbor*

TIME: *Saturday afternoon in early spring.*
SETTING: *The living room of Wilbur's home.*
AT RISE: WILBUR *enters, carrying a golf club and a golf ball. He moves to center, and places ball on floor. As he grips club and prepares to putt, he suddenly realizes he has nothing into which he can drop the ball. He straightens up, glances impatiently around the room. With a sudden smile, he sees a vase, which he picks up and places on its side, on the floor. He moves back and brings the club up to the ball. As he swings the club, there is a loud knock on the door. He jumps violently. The club barely strikes the ball, which rolls upstage, well away from the vase. Grumbling,* WILBUR *picks up vase, replaces it on table. Again there is a knock at the door.*

WILBUR (*Loudly*): All right! I'm coming! (*He moves upstage, opens door. At doorway stands* DAN, *who carries several seed catalogues.*) Dan, my old pal!
DAN: Hello, Wilbur.

WILBUR (*Grasping* DAN'S *arm, pulls him through doorway*): Bounce on in here! (WILBUR *enthusiastically escorts* DAN *into the room.*)

DAN (*Hesitantly*): Is it all right? (*He removes his hat.*)

WILBUR: Of course, it's all right! (*Grins*) That knock on the door threw me for a minute. Company on Saturday afternoon always annoys me.

DAN (*Humbly*): I'm sorry, Wilbur. I guess I shouldn't have come.

WILBUR (*Heartily*): *You're* not company, Dan. (*He gives* DAN *a vigorous but friendly slap on the back.* DAN *almost loses his balance.*) My next-door neighbor is welcome in this house day or night!

DAN: I thought perhaps you were busy.

WILBUR: Busy? (*Chuckles*) Yes, I'm busy—doing exactly as I please for a change.

DAN (*Startled*): As you please?

WILBUR (*Nodding*): Cast your eyes on this, Dan. (WILBUR *retrieves the golf ball. With a flourish he moves back, places ball on floor.*)

DAN (*Watches* WILBUR *in horrified fascination*): Wilbur, you're *not* playing golf!

WILBUR (*Unconcerned*): Just a few practice shots around the house. A man must unkink his muscles before he heads for the course. (WILBUR *swings his putter with gusto.*)

DAN (*Still amazed*): Wilbur, I just can't believe it.

WILBUR: Believe what?

DAN: I mean—my goodness, doesn't your wife object?

WILBUR: Carrie? (*Laughs loudly*) What a quaint idea!

DAN: She always has a Saturday schedule worked out for you.

WILBUR: Carrie isn't home this afternoon. If she were, I'd *still* be in spring training. (*Again he swings the club.*)

DAN: Wilbur, I hate to mention it—but this isn't like you.

WILBUR (*With confidence*): Dan, you old slave, I'm a changed man.

DAN (*Uneasily*): I declare, I believe you are.

WILBUR: I'm happy and relaxed. I'm as free as a juke box without a coin slot. I'm king of my— (*Breaks off*) Sit down, Dan—sit down. (*He indicates chair.*) You look done in.

DAN (*Sitting down*): I'm afraid I am. I've been assisting the little woman today—as usual. (*Seed catalogues are on* DAN'S *knees.*)

WILBUR (*Grinning broadly*): Poor old downtrodden Dan! Always at work.

DAN: The little woman thinks—

WILBUR (*Cutting in*): Dan, gaze at your old buddy. Do *I* look done in?

DAN (*Hesitantly*): No.

WILBUR: Exactly. (*As he swings the golf club*) What would *your* wife say if she saw *you* toying with a new golf club?

DAN (*Greatly pained*): Wilbur—please! Let's not even discuss it. There's enough trouble in the world as it is.

WILBUR (*Triumphantly*): I'm just smart—just smart, Dan. (*Using the putter,* WILBUR *lightly knocks the golf ball to left of stage.*)

DAN (*Jumping to his feet*): Be careful! (*Catalogues fall to floor.* WILBUR *turns to* DAN. DAN *drops to his knees, nervously begins to pick up the scattered catalogues.* WILBUR *takes a step toward* DAN. DAN *looks up apologetically.*) Forgive me, Wilbur—just a slight accident.

WILBUR (*Pointing to catalogues*): What do you have there?

DAN (*Indicating catalogues*): These? (DAN *rises.*)

WILBUR: Don't tell me your wife sent you out to sell magazine subscriptions.

DAN (*Smiling weakly*): No. Not yet, anyway. These are seed catalogues. (DAN *again sits in chair.*)

WILBUR: Seed catalogues?

DAN (*Nodding*): It's about time to think of our spring gardens, Wilbur. My wife—(*Hastily*) My *dear* wife insists I plant a garden, as usual. (*Smiles with effort.*) Of course I'm overjoyed, as usual.

WILBUR (*Dryly*): Yeah.

DAN: You always raise quite a variety of vegetables yourself, Wilbur. So the little woman decided—(*Quickly corrects himself*) So *I* decided we might send in an order together this year.

WILBUR (*Skeptically*): You did, did you?

DAN: That's why I brought over the catalogues. Since we'll both be cultivating in our back yards again, the little woman suggested that—

WILBUR (*Breaking in*): Listen, junior, I have news for you.

DAN: Really? (*With a sad little sigh*) That's what the little woman always has—news for me. (*Places catalogues on floor at his side*)

WILBUR (*Expansively*): Dan, my boy, it's time you learned the facts of life. (*After an impressive pause*) Namely, that I am not raising a garden this year.

DAN (*Shocked*): Wilbur!

WILBUR: I'm not even planting one stupid radish seed.

DAN (*Amazed*): Not raising a garden? (*With sudden alarm*) Wilbur, you're sick!

WILBUR: Not sick. Just smart.

DAN: How could you possibly convince Carrie?

WILBUR: Dan, my little eggplant, you just don't know how to manage your wife.

DAN: A man isn't supposed to—to manage his wife. (*He sinks back into chair.*) I think there's something about it in the wedding ceremony.

WILBUR: Nonsense! (*Significantly*) Of course you mustn't let a wife know what's really behind your actions. If you're clever enough, you can handle any situation.

DAN (*Flatly*): I tried to handle a situation once—unfortunately.

WILBUR: I did a bit of deep thinking. Then I went into action. (*He takes another happy swing with his club.*) No, I'm not ordering seeds this year—not a dime's worth.

DAN (*After a pause*): Wilbur—

WILBUR: Yes?

DAN (*A bit breathlessly*): How did you do it? I mean, in the past you've always planted a garden for Carrie.

WILBUR: My innocent little pal, it was really quite simple.

DAN: Simple?

WILBUR (*Nods*): I merely gave away my garden tools.

DAN (*Shocked*): You gave away your garden tools?

WILBUR: I gave them to Mr. Sweetberry, the man who deals in second-hand stuff.

DAN: Mr. Sweetberry? (*Amazed*) Wilbur, you didn't!

WILBUR (*Shrugging*): Oh, yes, I did.

DAN: But Carrie? What did you tell Carrie?

WILBUR (*Facing* DAN): I explained to her that I had no garden tools. (*Grins*) I said that sometime last fall I'd lent them to you.

DAN (*Jumping up*): What!

WILBUR: I also told Carrie I couldn't get them back because the junk man hauled them away when he was cleaning out your garage this spring.

DAN: Wilbur—no!

WILBUR (*Easily*): It was a most convincing story.

DAN (*Almost speechless*): You told your wife it was *my* fault? (*Starts to protest*) Now see here, Wilbur—

WILBUR (*With a grin*): I said you were such a loyal and friendly neighbor that I couldn't think of asking you to replace them.

DAN (*Angrily*): You know very well that I didn't lose them.

WILBUR (*Raising his golf club for silence*): Enough, my boy! (DAN *sputters, but* WILBUR *remains calm and self-*

assured.) I also pointed out to Carrie that the cost of new tools would amount to far more than the value of a garden. Carrie agreed with me. (WILBUR *breaks into a happy chant to the tune of "Farmer in the Dell."*)

So we're having no garden this year!
We're having no garden this year!
My scheme has worked, oh, Carrie dear,
We're having no garden this year!

(*He dances, swinging his golf club in rhythm.*)

DAN (*Shouting*): Stop it! Stop it! (*He rushes to* WILBUR, *snatches golf club from him.* WILBUR *slowly subsides.* DAN *marches grimly to chair. He leans the club against side of chair.*)

WILBUR (*Grinning*): Sorry, old chap. I suppose I *am* breaking your heart. Can you blame me for being carried away?

DAN: I've never heard of such a thing!

WILBUR (*Tapping his head significantly*): Brains, my comrade. That's what it takes—brains.

DAN: If I'd even *think* of doing such a thing to *my* little woman— (*He breaks off with a shudder.*)

WILBUR: I know. You'd better go right on making a garden, Dan. You're simply not the clever and aggressive type.

DAN (*Still stunned*): To think—Mr. Sweetberry has your garden tools!

WILBUR: Not only that, but I gave them to him. *Gave* them to him, mind you. (WILBUR *sinks into chair. He stretches contentedly.*) Best investment I ever made. Carrie's satisfied—and I'm free from garden tools and puny seeds. (*Grins*) I can hear that golf course calling me already.

DAN (*Stubbornly*): I still think it—it's unconstitutional or something.

WILBUR (*With dramatic self-assurance*): You ought to let

me work these things out for you. I don't believe you realize how fortunate you are—having a next-door neighbor with such shattering intelligence. By the way, Dan, remind me to give you my autograph sometime.

DAN (*Sinking into chair*): I just don't know how you do it.

WILBUR: I'll think of you often this spring, old boy, while I'm relaxing on the golf course and you're weeding the carrots. (*The door opens.* CARRIE *breezes into the room.*)

CARRIE (*To* WILBUR): Wilbur!

WILBUR (*Rises, smiling*): Carrie, my dear.

CARRIE (*To* DAN, *as she trots down center*): Dan! How nice to see you.

DAN (*To* CARRIE): I just dropped by to—to— (*He breaks off.*)

CARRIE (*Questioningly*): To—what?

DAN: It doesn't matter now.

CARRIE (*Looking closely at* DAN): Dan, is something wrong? You *do* have a strange look.

DAN: I think it's a slight case of envy.

CARRIE (*To* WILBUR): Darling, I've had the most exciting afternoon.

WILBUR (*With confidence*): So have I, pet. Since we're not raising a garden this year, I've been getting a bit of exercise with an old pal of mine.

CARRIE (*Studying* WILBUR): You *do* need exercise, don't you, Wilbur?

WILBUR (*Heartily*): Absolutely! A man shouldn't get flabby, especially in the spring.

CARRIE (*Enthusiastically*): That's exactly why I did it, Wilbur.

WILBUR: Did what, honey? (CARRIE *goes quickly to* WILBUR *and hands him her purse.*)

CARRIE: Wait right here, Wilbur. (WILBUR *holds purse and looks puzzled, as* CARRIE *hurries to door.*)

WILBUR (*Suddenly*): Hey, where are you going? (CARRIE

does not answer. She exits. After a brief pause, she reappears. In her hands are a rake, a hoe and a spading fork. Obviously, they have been used.)

CARRIE (*Proudly displaying tools*): See, Wilbur?

WILBUR (*With a horrified gasp*): Carrie!

CARRIE: These are for you—a rake, a hoe and a spade. (*She thrusts tools into* WILBUR'S *hand. Now* WILBUR *holds the tools and* CARRIE'S *purse.* CARRIE *beams at* WILBUR. WILBUR *gazes at* CARRIE *in horror.*) Isn't it terribly exciting? (*She turns to* DAN.) You'll have to excuse us, Dan. This is a little matter just between Wilbur and me. (DAN *is speechless.* CARRIE *smiles at* DAN.)

WILBUR: Carrie!

CARRIE: Yes, dear?

WILBUR (*With effort*): Where did you get these?

CARRIE: They look exactly like your old ones, don't they? Of course they've been used, but I got them at a marvelous bargain.

WILBUR: A bargain?

CARRIE (*Nods*): From Mr. Sweetberry, the second-hand dealer.

WILBUR (*Explosively*): What?

DAN: Mr. Sweetberry?

CARRIE: I don't know where he picked them up, darling, but think what they would have cost new. (*Excitedly*) That's not all, Wilbur. (*She turns, steps through door, and stoops, still visible to audience. She picks up a hatbox which has been just out of sight, then straightens and steps through doorway.*) With the money I saved, I bought myself the most adorable new hat! (WILBUR *collapses into chair, as* DAN *breaks into hilarious laughter.* CARRIE *watches in confused silence as the curtain quickly falls.*)

THE END

Ariadne Exposed

by E. M. Nightingale

Characters

MINOS, *King of Crete*
PICUNUS, *Minister of Finance*
ARIADNE, *daughter of Minos*
THESEUS, *a Greek hostage*
SOPORUS, *Court Chamberlain*

TIME: *Long ago.*

SETTING: *The throne room of Minos' palace in Crete.*

AT RISE: MINOS *is sitting at a table, scowling at a chessboard.* PICUNUS *enters center, carrying a large stack of clay tablets.*

MINOS (*Looking up*): Don't tell me you've more bills there, Picunus! If this keeps up, we'll have to float another bond issue. A fine Minister of Finance you turned out to be!

PICUNUS: On the contrary, Your Majesty, this helps to bolster the national economy. Clay was up three points yesterday.

MINOS (*Rising*): What has my daughter been spending money for this time?

PICUNUS: The Princess Ariadne had a yachting party. Admiral Parkos said he enjoyed himself immensely.

MINOS: *Admiral Parkos?* Since when has he been associating with the younger set?

PICUNUS: She borrowed the royal fleet. I suppose she had to invite him.

MINOS (*Smacking his forehead*): Tell me, Picunus, what am I going to do with that child? She has no more appreciation of money than a politician.

PICUNUS (*Setting tablets on bench at right*): I'd say she needs the restraining influence of a husband.

MINOS: The *what?* Only a bachelor could make such an asinine statement. Besides, I can no longer provide a dowry for my daughter sufficient to kindle the flame of desire in a suitor's eye.

PICUNUS: Someone might marry Ariadne for love.

MINOS: This is *not* the age of miracles. But I have to do something with her. (ARIADNE *enters, center, carrying a metal mirror with a long handle. She is loaded with baubles and bangles.*)

ARIADNE: Oh, Father, I'm told the Greek hostages have arrived: seven youths and seven maidens. (*She looks at herself in mirror.*)

MINOS: Did you lock up the silverware?

ARIADNE (*Still admiring herself*): I couldn't find any.

MINOS (*Scowling at* PICUNUS, *who shrugs*): I'm beginning to wonder if Crete really won that war with Greece. Those Greeks are too smart. Every year I have fourteen more mouths to feed, fourteen more bodies to bed down —and the Greeks have fourteen fewer. I'm running a regular boarding house here. It's driving me to bankruptcy!

PICUNUS: Only thirteen, Your Majesty. The treaty specifies one of them must meet the Minotaur, and the Minotaur always wins.

MINOS (*Gloomily*): It's still fourteen, if he can escape the bull. (*Suddenly brightening*) Of course, if he does escape, then *all* the hostages go home and I can have a little peace. That's specified in the treaty, too.

PICUNUS: You forget that he who safely leaves the arena must next find his way out of the Labyrinth. None have yet succeeded.

MINOS (*Shaking his head*): Which reminds me, that place needs airing out. Listen, Picunus, is there any reason why we can't call off this whole Minotaur business? You saw the grain bill last month for that beast. (*Sighs*) I wish I could trade places with a certain feed and fuel merchant.

ARIADNE: Why, Father, how can you possibly speak of such a thing? I've bought a block of seats for a theater party and my guests are already arriving.

MINOS: There goes my gold plate.

PICUNUS: Besides, the god who lives in the bull would be angry.

MINOS: Just what makes you believe the bull actually contains a god? I could certainly think of a better place to hole up in.

PICUNUS: The priestesses say it does.

MINOS: The priestesses may be wrong.

PICUNUS: Granted, but it's not politically expedient to say so.

MINOS: I wish the god had picked a cow instead. We could at least have gotten some milk. (SOPORUS *enters center with* THESEUS. SOPORUS *stops and bows.* ARIADNE *stares at* THESEUS *with frank interest.*)

SOPORUS (*Approaching* MINOS): I bring the leader of the Greek hostages, Your Majesty, he who is to meet the Minotaur.

MINOS: Hmph! He probably hasn't eaten in a week. Come forward, boy, and let me look at you. (THESEUS *just stands and smiles at* ARIADNE.) I said, come forward. What's wrong with children nowadays? They've absolutely no manners. (THESEUS *moves to stand before* MINOS.) Don't you bow to a king? Show a little respect there. What's your name?

THESEUS: I am Theseus, son of King Aegeus of Athens.

MINOS: You mean to tell me the king sent his own son? What have *you* been doing?

THESEUS: Preparing myself for accomplishing the mission of freeing my fellow hostages.

MINOS (*Sighing*): A pleasant thought, but you haven't a chance.

THESEUS: On the contrary, I shall succeed.

MINOS: Why are you so sure?

THESEUS: Because I'm the epitome of Greek manhood. (*He swells his chest, fists clenched at his side, and looks at* ARIADNE, *who sighs and smiles.*) At the age of ten, I won a scholarship to the Attica School of Physical Culture. The city fathers put me on the Athenian training table when I was only twelve. The length and breadth of Greece, you'll find my endorsement on athletic equipment.

MINOS (*Nodding happily*): You may fit the bill. But remember, even if you kill the Minotaur, you still have to get out of the Labyrinth. Every man who has ever entered it has been lost.

THESEUS: I won't be. My father has often marveled how one in such a fog as I always finds his way home.

MINOS (*To* PICUNUS): Sounds promising, doesn't he?

PICUNUS: Even better than those ten percent Egyptian debentures.

SOPORUS: I'm sorry, but he won't do. (*The others look at him in shocked surprise.*)

MINOS: I'd like to know why not.

SOPORUS: Why, Your Majesty, this fellow's whole background smacks of professionalism. The treaty specifically states those who meet the Minotaur must be acceptable to the Amateur Athletic Union.

MINOS *and* PICUNUS (*Together*): Oh? (*They look at each other in consternation.*)

ARIADNE: But we don't have to dig up his past. That's scandalmongering.

MINOS: And very poor taste.

SOPORUS: I beg to differ with Your Majesty. It's a matter of national honor. We must abide by all the provisions. The contracting parties at the peace negotiations agreed, in paragraph two of subsection six, title "Hostages," that a participant is required to be in good standing with the Union. Your grandfather had that clause inserted as he knew that a professional stood too great a chance to pass the test of the Minotaur, and Crete would lose its supply of hostages. Your grandfather was an astute politician.

MINOS: My grandfather was a fool! Since his day we've been collecting Greek hostages like debts. You can't turn around any more without bumping into a Greek. (ARIADNE *begins to move languorously about, striking poses with the mirror as* THESEUS *watches her.*)

PICUNUS: I believe the entire discussion to be unnecessary. The present status of Theseus is that of amateur.

MINOS: You're right, Picunus. And the contest starts at noon.

SOPORUS: There are enough members of the Union, here to attend the festivities, for me to have them call an emergency meeting before noon and hold a vote on this man's eligibility.

MINOS: You wouldn't do that, would you?

SOPORUS: Yes, Your Majesty, I fear I must. I have a duty to Crete higher than my duty to you.

MINOS (*Aside*): These blasted patriots! (*He thinks for a moment, then smiles grimly.*) Very well, Soporus, go call your meeting, but before you do, find the Captain of the Guard and tell him to see me at the main gate in five minutes. (SOPORUS *bows and exits center. To* ARIADNE) What are you flouncing about for?

ARIADNE (*Indicating* THESEUS *with her mirror*): He's a man, isn't he?

MINOS: Mm-m. What do you think, Picunus? (*He watches* THESEUS *thoughtfully.*)

PICUNUS: Assuming he or one of the other Greeks passes the test?

MINOS: Don't worry, I've a feeling he's going to pass it.

PICUNUS: In that case, she could do worse—but not much. These minor royalty are as thick as flies on a dead fish. On the other hand, they come cheap. I suppose we could fix him up with some sort of sinecure.

MINOS: Absolutely not! If any sinecure is being handed out around here, *I'm* getting it. (*Eyes* THESEUS *and* ARIADNE) No, I can see he lacks the proper qualifications. I wouldn't consider giving my daughter's hand in marriage to an ex-hostage.

ARIADNE: You mean I can't have him even if he becomes a free man?

MINOS: No! Not even then! Forget him. I forbid you to entertain any ideas about marrying a Greek.

ARIADNE: Oh, you do, do you?

MINOS: Yes, I do. You'd have to be a long way from Crete before it would be safe to take him for a husband.

ARIADNE: Well!

THESEUS: It seems to me I might be consulted on the matter.

MINOS: Nobody is asking your opinion! (*To* PICUNUS) Come on, I want to see that captain.

PICUNUS (*Indicating* THESEUS): What about him?

MINOS: He can't escape. (*To* ARIADNE) While we're gone, you might inform the hostage as to how he is to perform in the arena. (*To* THESEUS) And you mind your manners.

THESEUS: I assure Your Majesty, I'll do nothing your daughter won't like.

MINOS (*Rubbing his chin*): Yes. (*Exits center with* PICUNUS)

ARIADNE: Now to begin with, you must realize the Minotaur is a very large bull, a product of forced feeding.

THESEUS: I am not impressed.

ARIADNE: And when he charges you, you must place one hand on a horn and vault over his back.

THESEUS: Do I carry arms?

ARIADNE: Don't be silly! That would spoil the fun. If and when you've accomplished the feat, a door will be opened and you'll be allowed to escape.

THESEUS: Can I be sure of that?

ARIADNE: Of course. We Cretans are good sports. (*Smiles*) Yes, I really think you'll succeed. (*She walks about, thinking aloud.*) But the Labyrinth worries me. It's much more difficult than you imagine. I'll have to contrive some means to assure your finding the way out.

THESEUS (*Suspiciously, as he moves a few steps away from her*): Why are you so interested in me? You must remember your father's warning. He doesn't want you to marry me.

ARIADNE: That's reason enough. Of all the presumption! Imagine, trying to tell me, his daughter, whom I can't marry! I'm not a child.

THESEUS: A most obvious fact. So I gather you'd like to marry me provided your father objects.

ARIADNE: Maybe. Of course you're rather poor. Not that money is a necessity, but being a princess and all, I'm used to having lots of little luxuries.

THESEUS: Admittedly, my family is land poor. However, property values are rising in Athens, and all the oracles predict a boom. (*He goes to her and takes her hand, then drops to one knee.*) Harken, O beautiful Ariadne, I can't live without you . . . and that's the truth. Determine some means for me to escape the Labyrinth and we'll fly to Greece. Apollo will light our way by day and Artemis by night. Poseidon will calm the waves as we sail over the water to a life of bliss, wafted on the wind of your father's fury.

ARIADNE (*Doubtfully*): I might get seasick.

THESEUS: But think how livid your father will be.

ARIADNE (*Thoughtfully*): He will be terribly annoyed. (*Gazing into* THESEUS' *eyes.*) The strangest things can create love, can't they? (*Thinks*) Yes, I'll do it! It will serve him right!

THESEUS: Ah, my one and only! (*Rises and kisses her*)

ARIADNE: Oh! (*Steps back*)

THESEUS: What's the matter?

ARIADNE: I just thought that if Soporus has you barred, one of the other Greek hostages will have to take your place.

THESEUS (*Worried*): And he wouldn't stand a chance against the Minotaur.

ARIADNE: Oh, Theseus, then you'd have to remain a hostage and I couldn't get even with Father. (*Lays her head on his shoulder*) I can't bear the thought. (MINOS *enters center with* PICUNUS. *He carries a ball of twine on a spindle. The end of the twine has been caught offstage, so it unwinds behind him as he walks down center to* ARIADNE *and* THESEUS.)

MINOS: What's going on here, Ariadne? I told you to leave that man alone.

ARIADNE (*Smiling slyly at* THESEUS; *then remembering*): Oh, is the Amateur Athletic Union going to meet?

MINOS: It is not.

ARIADNE: Why?

MINOS: Soporus won't be able to find a quorum. My Captain of the Guard is in the process of shoving its members over the cliff.

ARIADNE: Then everything will be fine! Father, what are you doing with that twine? It's unraveling behind you.

MINOS: Why, so it is. Careless of me. I took it from the royal stores to tie up my bills. Really should have taken rope. (*Studies twine*) You know, any of you could find out exactly where I've been by following this back to the beginning. Interesting thought, isn't it? My exact route.

ARIADNE (*Indifferently*): Yes . . . (*Realization dawns suddenly.*) Yes, indeed!

MINOS (*Handing her the spindle*): Do me a favor and wind it up.

ARIADNE: Gladly. (*She goes up center to exit and gives* THESEUS *a knowing look.*) I'll see you at the arena. (*She waves the spindle at* THESEUS, *then exits, rewinding twine.* SOPORUS *enters and bows to* MINOS.)

MINOS: Tell me, Soporus, are you going to have your meeting?

SOPORUS: Alas, no, not a single member of the Union seems to be available. It's as though they had all been unavoidably detained somewhere.

MINOS (*Aside*): An astute observation. (*Louder*) Well, what do you want now?

SOPORUS: The time approaches for the hostage to meet the Minotaur.

MINOS: Good, prepare him for the arena. (*To* THESEUS) May the gods protect you, but I don't wish to lay eyes on you again. *Ever.*

THESEUS (*Bowing*): I can assure Your Majesty that wish will be fulfilled. (*Exits center with* SOPORUS)

MINOS (*Rubbing his hands*): This will be one time a Greek doesn't beat me. And Picunus, I want you to remove the guard from the hostages' ship and see that it's well supplied with food and water.

PICUNUS (*Bowing*): Yes, Your Majesty. Genius! Thinking of the twine was the work of a genius! (*Beaming*) With both the hostages and Ariadne gone I even foresee a balanced budget! Just wait until this tale of your sagacity spreads through the island! You'll *really* be respected.

MINOS: Don't you dare breathe a word of it to anyone! If Ariadne ever found out, she'd come home just to spite me. (*Thoughtfully*) No, the thought saddens me, but history will never record what a truly capable monarch I was, and no one will ever know the true story of Ariadne and Theseus. (*Curtain*)

THE END

Is There Life on Other Planets?

by Marion Lane

Characters

HEAD SCIENTIST
FIVE SCIENTISTS

SETTING: *A conference room.*

AT RISE: *The* HEAD SCIENTIST *and the* FIVE SCIENTISTS *are seated at a conference table with their backs to the audience.*

HEAD SCIENTIST (*Rising, with back to audience*): Gentlemen, gentlemen. Please come to order. I have called you here today to make an important announcement. I am sorry to tell you that after exhaustive studies, we have come to the conclusion that there cannot possibly be any life on the planet nearest us.

1ST SCIENTIST: But what about the changes in color from white to green that have been observed on the planet's surface? Don't these indicate weather changes and some kind of atmosphere?

HEAD SCIENTIST: All tests show that there is some atmosphere on the planet, but it is not enough to sustain life as we know it.

2ND SCIENTIST: Then how do you account for the ditches or canals which have been seen with our telescopes?

HEAD SCIENTIST: Latest viewings indicate that these are merely natural ground formations, and there is no proof whatever that they are made by any living beings.

3RD SCIENTIST: Then we must conclude that the flying saucer stories are all hoaxes?

HEAD SCIENTIST: No, of course not. Most of these sightings have perfectly logical, scientific explanations, and the rest are the direct result of mass hysteria.

4TH SCIENTIST: Then all the strange sounds picked up on radio receivers come from our own transmitters or are produced by atmospheric pressures?

HEAD SCIENTIST: I'm afraid so.

5TH SCIENTIST: I, for one, am extremely disappointed. I've always been sure we had neighbors on other planets, or at least on the one nearest to us. Perhaps not life as we know it, but some kind of intelligent life, totally unknown to us.

HEAD SCIENTIST: Gentlemen, I am going to adjourn this meeting. I can see no point in discussing this matter further. The tests have been so conclusive that any intelligent person must accept the fact that there is no life on—

ALL (*Turning to audience to reveal weird masks or make-up*): Earth! (*Curtain*)

THE END

Snow White and Friends

by Val Cheatham

Characters

NARRATOR	WOODSMAN
QUEEN	DOC
SNOW WHITE	DOPEY
MIRROR	

SCENE 1

SETTING: *The Queen's throne room.*

AT RISE: MIRROR *is placed near throne.* NARRATOR *enters and addresses the audience.*

NARRATOR: The story you are about to see is true—every bit of it. Well, most of it. (*Pauses*) Some of it is true. A little bit, anyway. This story is about a little girl who, just overnight, grew up and became beautiful. Her name is Snow White, which gives you a clue to the time and setting. As the scene opens, we see the wicked Queen. (QUEEN *enters, yawns, wanders to throne, and sits.*) She has just banished three knights, dispossessed four rich merchants, beheaded two commoners, and now is looking for more fun things to do. Having found no one around, she turns to her faithful Magic Mirror. (QUEEN *goes to* MIRROR.) And with that, dear audience,

I take my leave, but I will return before the next scene, to fill you in on all the circumstances surrounding the plot, the detailed settings, the various intrigues, and all the other jazz that's about to happen. (NARRATOR *exits.*)

QUEEN: Tell me, Mirror, am I not still the most lovely and desirable creature that ever lived?

MIRROR:

To hear the things I have to say,
You must ask the proper way.

QUEEN: Oh, good heavens! You and your ridiculous rhymes! When are you going to give up the idea that you're some kind of Edgar Allan Poe and just be a plain old looking glass?

MIRROR:

A looking glass is all I can be,
When you forget to question me.

QUEEN: Oh, all right! All right!
Mirror, mirror on the wall,
Who's the fairest of them all?

MIRROR:

Raven hair as soft as silk,
Eyes so bright and blue,
Blushing sunshine in her cheeks,
A heart so kind and true;
The radiance of her tender smile,
The countenance of a saint;
All these things of loveliness—
Too bad—*you* it ain't!

QUEEN: Your jokes are even worse than your grammar.

MIRROR:

There are some things, O my Queen,
Of which I joke a lot,
But where your beauty is concerned,
You *know* I kid you not!

QUEEN: What? For someone to be lovelier than I is out of

the question. It's treason! It's even very bad manners! Tell me who it is!

MIRROR:

A lovely sight—
Young Snow White.

QUEEN: Snow White? You're putting me on. She's just a little girl, an adolescent, a mere child!

MIRROR:

Once a child was our Snow White.
But she grew up—just overnight.

QUEEN: I can't have this. She must be eliminated. I'll hail the knights! I'll summon the guard!

MIRROR:

No, no! My dear Queen,
You don't want attention.
This foul deed must come to pass
Without your slightest mention.
Call in some obscure person,
From a far-off, wooded plain.
Have him rid you of this girl,
Then send him back again.

QUEEN: Very good! Sometimes you're worth every penny I spend on polish. (*Calling offstage*) Summon the Woodsman from his far-off, wooded plain.

WOODSMAN (*Entering immediately*): You summoned?

QUEEN: Yes. What kept you? I have a little chore for you.

WOODSMAN: Chopping down trees?

QUEEN: Well, it's a kind of chopping.

WOODSMAN: Name it, O Queen! It shall be done.

QUEEN: You see, there's this girl who thinks she's more beautiful than I. She's not, of course, but if she keeps saying she is, someone will think my subjects do not always deal in the truth, as does their Sovereign Queen.

WOODSMAN: Perish the thought.

QUEEN: No, not the thought—it's Snow White who must perish.

WOODSMAN: Snow White? Little Snow White? But she's just a child. . . . a little child!

QUEEN: That was yesterday. She grew up—just overnight.

WOODSMAN: You realize that disposing of girls is not really my line of work.

QUEEN: Silence! You have a choice between two heads.

WOODSMAN: Two? One was plenty!

QUEEN: A choice between two, Woodsman. Yours or the girl's. Well?

WOODSMAN: Very well, my Queen. (*Bows and leaves*)

QUEEN: Heh, heh, heh! (*To* MIRROR) How about that, Mirror-mirror-on-the-wall? (*Curtain*)

* * *

SCENE 2

SETTING: *The forest. A stump is down center.*

AT RISE: NARRATOR *enters and sits on stump.*

NARRATOR: As we say in the theatre, the plot thickens. What will happen to young Snow White, who grew up overnight and became beautiful? Can the wicked Queen make it hot enough to melt the snowy beauty of Snow White? We'll find out in the second scene. Here are the Woodsman and Snow White in the forest. (WOODSMAN *and* SNOW WHITE *enter.*) Snow White is unaware of the Queen's evil intentions. She thinks that the Woodsman has brought her into the forest to broaden her knowledge of conservation and to show her the natural resources of their fair country. (NARRATOR *exits and* WOODSMAN *and* SNOW WHITE *come down center as the* WOODSMAN *points out trees to her.*)

WOODSMAN: And this, Snow White, is a fir tree of the genus *Abies*. It is a coniferous pine that yields lumber and resins.

SNOW WHITE: Oh! How very interesting.

WOODSMAN: And now, if you will bend over this stump, you can see what's over here.

SNOW WHITE (*Bending over stump and looking off*): Way over here?

WOODSMAN: Yes. (*Prepares ax*) That's it. Now hold it. (*He hesitates, then drops ax.*) I can't do it! I just can't do it!

SNOW WHITE: Can't do what, Mr. Woodsman?

WOODSMAN: The Queen's dirty work. She sent me out here to get rid of you because you are more beautiful than she is.

SNOW WHITE: Me? Beautiful? Why, only yesterday they were calling me the Ugly Duckling.

WOODSMAN (*Gloomily*): That was yesterday. (*Brightening*) Look, I'll tell you what. You stay here in the woods and I'll go back and tell the Queen you're dead.

SNOW WHITE: Will that be safe for you, Mr. Woodsman?

WOODSMAN: I'll be all right. The Queen's getting old. It won't be too long before many girls will be more beautiful than she is, and you'll be able to come back.

SNOW WHITE: Whatever you say, Mr. Woodsman.

WOODSMAN: Don't call me "Mr. Woodsman." My name is Boswell Smith.

SNOW WHITE: Whatever you say, Mr. Boswell Smith.

WOODSMAN: No! Not "Mr."—just Boswell—Boswell!

SNOW WHITE: Whatever you say, Boswell-Boswell.

WOODSMAN (*Shrugging*): Whatever *you* say, Snow White. Now I must go. Be careful in the woods. (*Exits*)

SNOW WHITE (*Waving*): Thank you and goodbye. Now, which way shall I go? (*Looking off right*) That sign over there says, "To Grandma's House." That's the wrong story. If I remember correctly, I'm supposed to find some dwarfs who'll take care of me.

DOC *and* DOPEY (*Chanting off left*): Hi-ho, hi-ho. (*They enter.*)

DOC: Man, it's like off to work we go.

SNOW WHITE: Oh! Who are you?

DOC (*To* DOPEY *as he sees* SNOW WHITE): Cease and desist, we've found the skin man.

DOPEY: Groovy. (*They go up to* SNOW WHITE *and look at her closely.*)

DOC: Say, Dopey, dig that crazy costume he's wearing.

SNOW WHITE (*Looking around*): He?

DOPEY: Like yeah, man.

DOC: Hey, Dad, where are your sticks?

SNOW WHITE: Sticks?

DOC: Skin-tappers, pace-setters, the 2–4's. How can you make your skins cry without your beaters?

DOPEY: Like, yeah, man.

SNOW WHITE: Beaters? Skins? I don't know what you're talking about!

DOC: You know, Dopey, like I have a feeling this cat's not our man.

DOPEY: I don't even think it is a man, Doc.

DOC: Yeah? (*Walks around* SNOW WHITE) Yeah! It's all that long hair. I thought it was a boy.

SNOW WHITE: I'm Snow White. I'm looking for some dwarfs.

DOC: Dwarfs! That's us! You must be that skin man!

SNOW WHITE: What's a skin man?

DOC: That's a drummer. (*To* DOPEY) We're not only playing in different keys, but one of us is like playing the wrong tune. Communicate, Dopey.

DOPEY: O.K., Doc. (*To* SNOW WHITE) You are Snow White—we are the Dwarfs.

SNOW WHITE: You don't look like dwarfs to me. Aren't dwarfs supposed to be little men?

DOC: We grew up. Even Peter Pan must be an old man by now.

SNOW WHITE: All I know is that I'm supposed to meet the Seven Dwarfs and they will take me home and help me.

DOPEY: That's our *name:* "The Seven Dwarfs—Littlest Band with the Biggest Beat." He's Doc, and I'm Dopey.

DOC: So, like, who put you on to us?

SNOW WHITE: Nobody. It's just the way the story goes: The Wicked Queen wants me eliminated because she thinks I am more beautiful than she is.

DOC: The Queen! Now, why didn't you say so? Anyone on the Queen's list can't be that square. Are you sure you can't play drums?

SNOW WHITE: I'm sure. (*Crying*) Oh-h-h, why does the Queen hate me so?

DOPEY: Cool it, kid. The Queen doesn't like us either.

DOC: The Dwarfs had three discs on the top ten and were slated for TV and personal appearances all over the kingdom. But the Queen fixed that.

DOPEY: We were getting to be more popular than the Queen.

SNOW WHITE: Did she try to kill you?

DOC: No. She like sentenced us to a new kind of "wild" life. (*Indicates surroundings*) Now we blast for the creatures of the forest . . . the sparrows and the blue jays.

DOPEY: The Queen said our playing was for the birds.

DOC: Are you *sure* you're not a drummer?

SNOW WHITE: I'm really quite certain. Now, can't we go? It's getting dark.

DOC: Say, maybe the little lady's a go-go dancer.

SNOW WHITE: Absolutely not! However, I did sing in the church choir.

DOC: Man, that's it! A singer! Now, that could give our

sound some real class. (*They start to exit together.*) Let's hear you try a few bars of "I Dream of Queenie with the Light Brown Throne." Start at the beginning and give it all you've got. (*They exit as curtains close.*)

* * *

SCENE 3

SETTING: *The Queen's throne room.*

AT RISE: MIRROR *is beside throne.* NARRATOR *enters.*

NARRATOR: For the next scene we go back to visit the Queen and her magic mirror. If you recall, it was the mirror that started this whole mess in the first place, by telling the Queen that Snow White had grown up overnight, and had become more beautiful than she. Now you *know* that a mirror with a mouth like that is going to snitch on the Woodsman. What will happen? Will Snow White remain in the forest and sing lead for the Dwarf Combo? Will the woodchopping Woodsman be caught and given a taste of his own chopping? Or, will he escape to the woods and become the new drummer for the Seven Dwarfs, the Littlest Band with the Biggest Beat? Anticipate no longer. (*He indicates* QUEEN, *who has just entered, then* NARRATOR *exits.*)

QUEEN: Ho-hum, another day, another ten thousand dollars. I wonder who that brilliant monarch was who discovered taxes. It certainly makes being a queen tolerable. (*Looks in* MIRROR) What is this? A wrinkle? Oh, no! I'm getting old! It's all this worrying I've been doing about Snow White. I wonder if I could tax people for giving me wrinkles? Oh, wait! It's only a hair brushed across my cheek. What a relief! (*Pauses to admire herself*) What a doll I am. There can never be anyone to equal my great beauty. Isn't that right, Mirror?

MIRROR:
To hear the things I have to say,
You must ask the proper way.

QUEEN: Oh, brother! One of these days, one of these days —*pow!*

MIRROR:
Just remember if you do,
It's seven years' bad luck for you.

QUEEN: Don't push me! Sometimes I think it would be worth it.

MIRROR:
Let's hear your question one more time,
And, if you please, recite in rhyme.

QUEEN: All right, all right. (*Hastily*)
Mirror-mirror-on-the-wall,
Who's-the fairest-of-them-all?
Now, hurry up and tell me.

MIRROR:
Sometimes you go too far, my Queen.
My patience can be spent.
You can always be replaced by
An elected president.

QUEEN: Quit stalling. Now, get on with it!

MIRROR:
I'll get on with it, my dear.
But you won't like what you will hear.

QUEEN: Just stick with facts, and never mind the opinions.

MIRROR:
Raven hair as soft as silk,
Eyes so bright and blue,
Blushing sunshine in her cheeks,
A heart so kind and true;
The radiance of her tender smile—

QUEEN (*Interrupting*): Wait a dogbone minute! You're not going to give me that Snow White routine again, are you? Get with it. Remember? The Woodsman? (*Chops imaginary ax.*)

MIRROR:

Snow White is very much alive,
Our lovely heroine.
The tender-hearted Woodsman was
Too kind to do her in.
She's taken refuge with some dwarfs,
Who helped her in her plight.
Now she's singing groovy tunes
With the go-go band each night.

QUEEN: Snow White is still alive! That chicken-hearted Woodsman! Those crazy dwarfs. I'm their Queen! Where's all the respect for Her Royal Majesty? The dignity of the Traditional Monarchy? What's a queen to do when her subjects don't obey her?

MIRROR:

Beauty is not meant to be
One's only goal in life.
It's courage, faith, and goodness
That can take life's toil and strife.
These things will stay right with you.
They can't be bought or sold.
Beauty withers with the years,
And, face it, Queen—you're old.

QUEEN: You stupid old mirror! You just say that because you're not as pretty as I am.

MIRROR:

I just reflect what faces me;
I think Snow White should be left free.

QUEEN: Do your reflecting somewhere else. I must do some thinking. Let's see now. I must get rid of Snow White myself. Certainly can't trust men to do anything. (*Paces back and forth*) I know! I'll poison her. I'll take this nice, big, red, juicy (*Pulls banana from pocket*)—banana? Oh, well, one thing will work as well as another. Heh, heh, heh! An apple a day keeps the doctor away—a banana brings the undertaker. Ha! Ha! Ha! (*To* MIRROR) How about that, Mirror-mirror-on-the-wall? (*Curtain*)

* * *

SCENE 4

SETTING: *The forest.*

AT RISE: NARRATOR *enters.*

NARRATOR: Well, there you have it—everything but the finale. As this scene opens, the Queen has disguised herself as an ugly, old woman. (QUEEN *enters*) And now . . . (*Sees* QUEEN) Say, I thought you were supposed to be an ugly, old woman.

QUEEN: Heaven knows I tried, but it's very hard to disguise this great beauty of mine.

NARRATOR (*Shrugging*): Whatever you say, Queen. The Queen has disguised herself as a *beautiful* old woman and has brought the poisoned banana to give to Snow White, hoping she will eat it and drop dead. (*He exits.*)

QUEEN: Oh, Snow White—where are you? Yoo-hoo! Come out, come out, wherever you are! (SNOW WHITE *enters.*)

SNOW WHITE: Were you calling me?

QUEEN: Yes. You're such a cute little thing and do such a marvelous job singing with the band, I want you to have this banana. (*Offers it to her*)

SNOW WHITE: No, thank you. You've been to the club to hear me?

QUEEN: Yes, I've been to the club. I used to do some singing myself. Here, have a banana.

SNOW WHITE (*Taking banana*): You're a little old to be a go-go girl, aren't you?

QUEEN: It was back in the Golden Era of Big Bands. We used to jitterbug to the boogie-woogie.

SNOW WHITE: Jitterbug? Boogie-woogie? My, you don't look *that* old! (*Hands back banana*) I really don't care for this banana.

QUEEN: But it's such a beauty and I *do* want you to have it. (*Gives banana back to her*)

SNOW WHITE: Well, all right. But I still don't like bananas.

QUEEN (*Smiling*): This one is . . . different. (SNOW WHITE *peels it and takes bite, then she drops to floor.*) Heh, heh, heh! Let's see you sing now! Ha, ha, ha!

DOC (*Entering with* DOPEY): Hey, Granny-o, what's all the giggling about?

QUEEN: Well, hello! Who are you?

DOC: Doc Dwarf, leader of the coolest sound this side of the Ming Dynasty.

QUEEN: Cool sound? You sell noisy refrigerators?

DOC: No, Ancient Square One. The Seven Dwarfs, Gonest Go-Go Group in the Kingdom.

QUEEN: The Dwarfs!

DOPEY: You know our music?

QUEEN: I've heard it (*To* DOC), but I sure didn't know it was led by such a handsome, mature gentleman.

DOC: You're kind of cute yourself. What say we split this scene and get acquainted? (*Takes apple from pocket*) Would you care for this juicy, red fruit?

QUEEN: A pleasure, Mr. Dwarf. (*Accepts apple, starts to eat. They exit.*)

DOPEY: Hey, like what about me? (*Shrugs, turns and sees* SNOW WHITE *still on floor*) Holy Hullabaloo! What's wrong with Snow White?

WOODSMAN (*Entering*): She is waiting for me!

DOPEY: Like that?

WOODSMAN: Sure, it's an old story. The Queen just gave her a poisoned banana, and I'm the Prince with the remedy that will get her back on her feet in no time. Let's see—(*Searches pockets, finds bottle*) Toad Turner. No, that's not it. (*Takes out another bottle*) Here it is! Anti-Banana. (*Passes bottle under* SNOW WHITE'S *nose*)

SNOW WHITE (*Sitting up abruptly*): Whew! What's that smell? It must be my Prince. (*Rubs eyes*) Wait, you're not the Prince—you're the Woodsman.

WOODSMAN: Wrong! I am the Prince disguised as a Woodsman to escape from the Queen. But that's all ended now.

SNOW WHITE: Is she dead?

WOODSMAN: No, better than that. Doc just gave her a Boy Scout Apple.

SNOW WHITE: What's a Boy Scout Apple?

WOODSMAN: One bite, and it will make her trustworthy, loyal, helpful, cheerful, thrifty, brave, clean, reverent. Also, she will feel like doing a good deed every day! (*Curtain*)

THE END

Teen and Twenty

by John Dorand

Characters

TOM WAINE
ALICE WAINE
MIKE WAINE, *their junior high son*
JENNIFER WAINE, *their high school daughter*
DORA BARKLEY } *friends*
PETER KENDALL }
CAM MCCONNELL, *a college student*
MRS. PRENTICE, *a friend of Mrs. Waine's*
MADGE PRENTICE, *her daughter*

TIME: *Midday on a Saturday.*
SETTING: *The Waine living room.*
AT RISE: MRS. ALICE WAINE *is arranging flowers in a bowl on the coffee table at center.* JENNIFER *enters from right and seems distraught.*

JENNIFER (*Crossing to* MRS. WAINE): Mother!
ALICE: Yes, Jennifer.
JENNIFER (*Angrily*): Mother! How long am I going to have to share my room with that—that female Fagin?
ALICE (*Shocked*): Be quiet, for goodness' sake! What if Madge should hear you? How do you think she'd feel?

JENNIFER: Who cares? Mother, do you know what she's done this time?

ALICE (*Sighing*): No, dear. But tell me, what has Madge done now?

JENNIFER: She's only taken my new gray skirt, that's all—the skirt I was saving to wear to the senior play tryouts next week. And if things turn out as usual, she'll probably return it smeared with ink stains, splattered with cocoa spots, and smudged with lipstick. Mother, I am growing to dislike that girl!

ALICE (*Laughing*): Aren't you making a great deal out of nothing, dear? How do you know she took it? Perhaps if you looked—

JENNIFER: She left a note. Let me quote: "Dearest Jenny—Forgive me for taking your lovely skirt, but everything I have is simply filthy, and I do want to look my best today. Love, Madge." End quote. And she knows that I loathe being called Jenny.

ALICE: I think it's sort of—of *cozy*.

JENNIFER: Exactly. Mother, you haven't answered my question. How *long* is Madge going to be here?

ALICE (*Vaguely*). I really don't know, dear. Her mother is still busy settling Madge's grandfather's estate. Sometimes those things drag on forever.

JENNIFER: Let's hope her grandfather left Madge enough to get *my* clothes dry-cleaned!

ALICE: I'm afraid Madge is just like her mother. Grace always borrowed my clothes when we roomed together at college. She never seemed to like her own things.

JENNIFER (*Flopping onto sofa*): Oh, Madge is big about that! She adores her own things, and when they're no longer wearable—well, then she adores my things! That girl just can't lose.

ALICE (*Moving around the room, tidying*): Try to be patient, Jennifer.

JENNIFER: Sure! I only hope my wardrobe holds out.

ALICE: Why don't you wear your pink cotton to the try-outs, dear? You look lovely in pink.

JENNIFER: Absolutely not! The character I'm reading isn't a pink part. Shakespeare calls for something more somber.

ALICE: What is the senior play this year?

JENNIFER: Well, Miss Wiggins gave us a choice between *The Barretts of Wimpole Street* and *Romeo and Juliet.*

ALICE: And the class chose *Romeo and Juliet*! How lovely!

JENNIFER: No. The class voted for *A Streetcar Named Desire,* but Miss Wiggins turned pale and whispered something about tremendous royalties, so we settled for *Romeo and Juliet.*

ALICE (*Amused*): Well, I should think so! *A Streetcar Named Desire,* indeed! I suppose you're trying out for the part of *Juliet?*

JENNIFER: No. Miss Wiggins said my voice isn't right. Anyway, Juliet has too many lines, and with the condition my geometry's in, I'd never find time to memorize them.

ALICE: That's wise, Jennifer. What part are you trying out for?

JENNIFER: Juliet's nurse. She's the only other decent female character in the play.

ALICE: Would you like me to help you with your lines? I used to be considered rather a good actress in my time—er, when I was younger, that is.

JENNIFER (*Laughing*): No, thanks, Mother! Dora's coming over later to read the lines with me.

ALICE: Is there something wrong with Dora, Jennifer?

JENNIFER (*Rearranging flowers in the bowl*): Nothing more than usual. Why?

ALICE: Do stop fussing with those flowers. It's just that she seems so—well, so *abrupt* and detached lately.

JENNIFER: Poor Dora! Last week the gang saw a revival of

an early Barbara Stanwyck movie—one in which she played a hard-headed business executive, and ever since, Dora has imagined herself to be the dedicated career-type girl. She'll get over it.

ALICE: Gracious! You girls.

JENNIFER: Now, Mother, please—not that tired old bit about teenagers! After all, if Madge is an example of the *older girl,* I consider the teen-ager the best of the bargain!

ALICE (*Giving up*): Tsk! Tsk!

JENNIFER: To change the subject, when is Dad going to bring home that new fellow from the office?

ALICE: Oh, the college boy?

JENNIFER (*Patiently*): Mother, sweet—if he's in college, he is not a boy!

ALICE (*Wisely*): I know, dear. I suspect your father might ask him to dinner tonight. But I thought that you had a date with Pete Kendall this evening?

JENNIFER: Oh, I don't know. I think Pete and I need a change from each other. (MIKE *enters from left. He carries a baseball bat and mitt.*)

MIKE: Hi, Mom. What's this about a change, Jenny, ole girl? I like your nose just the way it is. Why resort to plastic surgery? We can't all be beautiful! (*He plunks himself into an armchair.*)

JENNIFER: Did you hear him, Mother? Did you hear him? Did you? *Nobody* called me Jenny until Madge started, and now even my own brother has taken up the cry! I hate that name. (*Looks at* MIKE) And for your absolute edification, Babe Ruth, I have never considered changing my facial features. It so happens that my nose is one of my strongest attractions.

MIKE (*Looking at her closely*): Sure! You and Jimmy Durante!

ALICE: That's enough, children. And Mike, you needn't

be so funny. Jennifer and I were talking about Pete Kendall.

MIKE (*Selecting a candy from a dish on the coffee table*): That so? What's Kendall been up to now? I just saw him down at the tennis courts. He said he might drop by later this afternoon.

JENNIFER: How condescending of him, I'm sure. He didn't by any chance, mention the purpose of this probable visitation?

MIKE (*Unconcernedly*): Nah! He was deep in conversation with Madge.

JENNIFER (*Gasping*): Madge, Mother, did you hear what Mike said? Did you hear? Pete was deep in conversation with *Madge!*

ALICE: I'm not deaf, Jennifer. Of course I heard him. But don't jump to hasty conclusions.

JENNIFER: Hasty! There's certainly nothing hasty about our Madge. She's had her eyes on Pete Kendall since the day she arrived—but she's gone too far this time!

MIKE: Gosh, you'd think I'd exploded a bomb or something!

ALICE: Tact was never your strong point, Mike.

JENNIFER (*Dramatizing the situation, she moves to center*): No, Mother, no—don't say anything to him. It's time someone told me the truth.

MIKE (*Perplexed*): Say, Mom, is she trying out for another play or something again?

ALICE: As a matter of fact, she is. (*Rises*) But I advise you not to heckle your sister right now. I'd better take stock of the refrigerator in case your father does bring that boy—er, young man, home tonight. I'll need you to help me pretty soon, Jennifer, and I don't want you to be nasty to Madge. She may not be here much longer, and we must remember that she *is* our guest. I'm quite sure that everything will work out all right. (*She exits right.*)

JENNIFER (*Heavily*): I wish I could share Mother's bright outlook on matters concerning our guest, and my clothes and former friends!

MIKE: You must have quite a case on Pete Kendall to make so much fuss. Yes, indeedy, that boy must be number one man in your life!

JENNIFER (*Bristling*): He's no such thing! It's only that it makes me so mad that the poor man's Cleopatra can get away with murder. And just because she's a guest in our house—and practically a permanent one at that—there's nothing I can do!

MIKE: Aw, heck, Jennifer—she was only talking to the guy.

JENNIFER: That's enough! No wonder she wanted my gray skirt today—and that note about wanting to look her very best—of *all* the nerve!

MIKE: She did look pretty sharp.

JENNIFER (*Hopelessly*): You—my own brother! Why, you're no better than that Kendall character. I'm going to my room. If I can't be nasty to Madge Prentice, at least I can think about the nasty things I could say to her—if I were allowed to be nasty to her—not that I'd even demean myself to be nasty to her! (*She exits right.*)

MIKE (*Shaking his head*): Boy! It's getting so a fellow learns more about his family every day. Now who could have thought a simple little remark would have set off an explosion like that! (*Rises and props his baseball bat against the telephone table next to the sofa. He puts his mitt on the table, then crosses to the bookcase left and hunts through books.*) Wonder what happened to my *Startling Space Comics*. Don't tell me Madge has started borrowing those, too? (*Doorbell rings. He starts for door, left.*) I wouldn't put it past her to trade my comic books for perfume or something. That would be good. (*Doorbell rings again.*) Two *Startling Space Comics* for one bottle of *Sinful Moment*! (*He opens door.*) Hi, Dora.

Come on in. (DORA *enters. She is a bright, intense young lady, with a severe hair style. She wears horn-rimmed glasses, which she removes frequently to emphasize conversational points.*)

DORA: Hello, Mike. (*She looks at his baseball uniform critically.*) I see you're still engaging in America's favorite sport.

MIKE: What do you mean?

DORA: Baseball, Mike—baseball!

MIKE: Oh, sure. That's right, it is, isn't it? What've you been doing with yourself? (*They sit on the sofa.*)

DORA: A little of this—a little of that. I've been spending quite a bit of time with John Keats.

MIKE: Yeah? Don't think I know him. Does he live around here?

DORA: He's been dead for a hundred and thirty years, Mike!

MIKE: Oh, then I guess I wouldn't know him. What'd he do?

DORA: Good heavens! He wrote poetry. What do you read, anyway?

MIKE: Who, me? Give me a good book about mountain-climbing, a mystery or a sports story—or better yet, *Startling Space Comics*—that is, if it hasn't been exchanged for cologne.

DORA: I beg your pardon?

MIKE: Never mind, Dora, old girl. I'll call Jennifer for you. (*Crosses to stage right*) Jennifer! Jennifer! Dora's here.

DORA: All right. (*To herself*) Now what does a copy of *Startling Space Comics* have to do with cologne?

JENNIFER (*Offstage*): I'm coming.

MIKE: Guess I'll go see what Mom found in the refrigerator. You'd better be careful of what you say to sis. She's having Madge-trouble again. I'll see you. (*Exits right*)

DORA: O.K. (*Makes herself comfortable on sofa. Takes a*

magazine from table. She reads aloud to herself.) Hm-m-m! "*Life* Goes to a Reducing Farm."

JENNIFER (*Entering door right*): Hi, Dora!

DORA: Hi, Jen! Just reading about life on a reducing farm.

JENNIFER (*Aghast*): Dora!

DORA (*Startled*): Now what! My goodness, Jennifer, you needn't take it personally! What's the matter with you?

JENNIFER (*Crossing to bookcase*): Oh, Dora, everything! You know how I detest being called anything but Jennifer. Madge started it; she called me Jenny. Then, my own brother took it up, and now you. *Jenny*—ugh! What a name!

DORA: Sorry. A moment of rashness. I'll remember from now on. I feel the same about my name. But what can you do with *Dora?* Speaking of *the girl*—what's with you and Madge? Mike mentioned a little tension in the atmosphere.

JENNIFER: That's what's the matter with me in one word—Madge. Honestly, Dora, I've always considered myself level-headed, calm and fair—

DORA (*Becoming the lady executive listening to an employee's complaint*): Of course, dear. I've always given you credit for those qualities, too. But what *precisely* has Madge done?

JENNIFER (*Frantically*): Done! *Done*! She just *is,* that's all! Dora, you don't *know*. She's gone through every last garment I own—even, mind you, the Indian *sari* I wore last New Year's Eve. She discovered it in the storage closet and said it would make a divine evening stole. That's what she had on last Saturday night.

DORA: So that's what she had hanging around her neck! I thought your Mother had given her that tablecloth your aunt brought back from Europe. Jim said that when he helped her take it off at the movies, he got entangled in it and missed twenty minutes of the feature picture!

JENNIFER: But that's not all, Dora. I've just learned that Madge has her eye on Pete. Mike said they were on the tennis court together this morning.

DORA: Pete. Pete Kendall? *Your* Pete! Well, I'd say that was going a bit too far—even for a guest.

JENNIFER: I really have no claim on Pete Kendall, Dora. He's a free agent. It's just—just the injustice of it. Mother won't allow me to say a word to Madge, and Dad—I just can't understand Dad. He treats her as though she were the neighborhood Elizabeth Taylor. Whatever Madge has—and she certainly must have something—it eludes me.

DORA: Jennifer, we've got to do something. Why, if she finds she can get her own way this easily, it might affect her whole life! It's up to us to save Madge Prentice from herself.

JENNIFER: You don't understand, Dora! Madge is our guest. That's just Mother's point! I can't say or do anything.

DORA: Maybe *you* can't, but *I* can.

JENNIFER: What's the use, Dora? What could you possibly say to Madge?

DORA: Don't worry about me. I'll think of something. Say, weren't we supposed to rehearse the play this afternoon?

JENNIFER: Let me get my *Romeo and Juliet.* (*Selecting a volume from the bookcase, she crosses and gives it to* DORA) It's Act III, Scene 2—about page 200, I think. Heavens, the tryouts are next week! I'd better do some studying if I want the part.

DORA (*Looking for the correct page*): Don't worry. All the others are reading for the leads. You're smart. You're sure to be in the play.

JENNIFER: Let's hope!

DORA: Here's the place. Where'll we begin?

JENNIFER: Read that part about the storm—where Juliet learns that Romeo has been banished.

DORA (*Adjusting her spectacles and searching for the line*): Mm-m! Yes,—here we are. O.K. I'll read Juliet's lines. Sure you won't need the play?

JENNIFER: I need it all right, but I'd better do without it.

DORA (*Launching into the role*):
"What storm is this that blows so contrary?
Is Romeo slaughter'd, and is Tybalt dead?
My dear-loved cousin, and my dearer lord?
Then, dreadful trumpet, sound the general doom!
For who is living, if those two are gone?"

JENNIFER (*Assuming the slightly quavering voice of an elderly woman, the Nurse*):
Tybalt is gone, and Romeo banished;
Romeo, that kill'd him, he is banished."

DORA (*Her voice achieving depth and color, so that even* JENNIFER *listens to her attentively*.): "O God! did Romeo's hand shed Tybalt's blood?"

JENNIFER: Ah, ah—oh, darn! What's the line, Dora?

DORA: "It did, it—"

JENNIFER: Never mind, I have it. (*Slipping back into character*) "It did, it did; alas the day, it did."

DORA (*Meeting the spirit of the lines*):
"O serpent heart, hid with a flowering face!
Did ever dragon keep so fair a cave?
Beautiful tyrant! fiend angelical!
Dove-feather'd raven! wolvish-ravening lamb!"
(*She is interrupted by* JENNIFER.)

JENNIFER: Golly, Dora. You're good! Say, why don't you try out for Juliet?

DORA (*Embarrassed*): Oh, you know me. I'd fall off the balcony or lose my wig or something. Besides, half the girls in school are dying to play Juliet. I wouldn't stand a chance.

JENNIFER: Don't be silly. Why, most of the girls can't read, let alone memorize and act! Miss Wiggins says that herself. And your grades are tops! Come on, why don't you?

DORA: Well, we'll see. Hadn't we better get on with your lines?

JENNIFER: O.K. (*Crosses over to her to consult the book*) Let's do this part.

DORA: "Speakest thou from thy heart?"

JENNIFER: "And from my soul too; else beshrew them both."

DORA: "Amen!"

JENNIFER: "What!" (TOM WAINE *enters quietly left on this speech. He remains silent until* DORA *has finished reading. The girls are not aware of his presence.*)

DORA:

"Well, thou hast comforted me marvellous much.
Go in, and tell my lady I am gone,
Having displeased my father, to Lawrence' cell,
To make confession, and to be absolved."

TOM: What's this about displeasing your father, Dora? (*He crosses to telephone table and sets his briefcase on it.*)

JENNIFER (*Turning to him*): Oh, Daddy! We didn't hear you come in. We were rehearsing my lines for the senior play tryouts.

DORA: Yes, Mr. Waine. It was Juliet who displeased her father.

TOM: Oh, ho! Yes, I seem to remember something of the story. (*Lifts two or three pieces of mail from the table and sorts through them*) Where's your mother, Jennifer?

JENNIFER: She went out to the kitchen ages ago. She's probably on the patio now. We're going to eat outside tonight. Weren't you bringing someone home to dinner, Dad?

TOM: Cam McConnell? He'll be along shortly. He had to

finish some work, so I came on ahead. I want you and your brother on your best behavior while he's here, too. He might not be used to family cross fire.

JENNIFER: Really, Dad! You act as though I were uncivilized. I assure you I'll know how to behave in front of Mr. McConnell. Although, I can't speak for Mike—or Madge!

TOM: I think Madge will know how to act.

JENNIFER (*Seething*): What did I tell you, Dora. My father prefers a house guest to his own daughter.

TOM: Now, now, Jennifer. I just meant that Madge is a bit older and—

JENNIFER (*Sharply*): *Quite* a bit older, I believe.

DORA (*Changing the subject*): Er—who's this Mr. McConnell, Jennifer? Someone I might know?

JENNIFER: No. He's a student from the University. He's working part time in Dad's office.

TOM: Which reminds me—if we're eating outside, I'd better get started on the fire. Just make Cam at home when he arrives, Jennifer. Bring him outside. (*He exits right.*)

JENNIFER (*Upset*): Dora, why do I do it? Every time someone mentions that girl's name I simply go to pieces. I can just feel my hair standing on end and my flesh goes all tingly and clammy and cold.

DORA: That's right. I felt the same way the first time I saw a black widow spider.

JENNIFER: Oh, be serious! I don't want to feel this way.

DORA: Well, seriously, then—I think you're letting this reaction you have to Madge get the best of you. But I'll speak to her.

JENNIFER: About that—I don't know, Dora. Maybe we'd better leave well enough alone. She'll probably be joining her mother soon anyway.

DORA: I'm not going to hurt the girl, dear. The correct word at the right time is what I have in mind! I just want to be *helpful,* Jennifer.

JENNIFER (*Wryly*): Yes, I know! Helpful—oh, gosh! I was supposed to help Mother. Dora, I'll go see what she wants me to do. Do you mind waiting a minute or two? We can finish the scene when I'm through.

DORA: Go along. (JENNIFER *exits door right, and* DORA *again takes up the play. Her back is to door left. Near the end of her speech the doorbell sounds but she is oblivious to its ringing and reads on.*)

"What's Montague? it is nor hand, nor foot,
Nor arm, nor face, nor any other part
Belonging to a man. O, be some other name!
What's in a name? that which we call a rose
By any other name would smell as sweet;
So Romeo would, were he not Romeo call'd,
Retain that dear perfection which he owes
Without that title: Romeo, doff thy name;
And for that name, which is no part of thee,
Take all myself." (CAM MCCONNELL *enters while* DORA *is reading. He is a tall, well-built youth about 21 years old. His voice has authority.*)

CAM (*As Romeo answering his Juliet*):

"I take thee at thy word:
Call me but love, and I'll be new baptized;
Henceforth I never will be Romeo."

(*Startled,* DORA *turns and sees* CAM. *She continues the scene.*)

DORA:

"What man art thou, that, thus bescreen'd in night,
So stumblest on my counsel?"

CAM (*Crossing to stage center opposite* DORA):

"By a name
I know not how to tell thee who I am:

My name, dear saint, is hateful to myself,
Because it is an enemy to thee;
Had I it written, I would tear the word."

DORA (*Breaking the mood*): I didn't hear you come in. You must be—ah, Mr. McConnell.

CAM: Cam will do. You're Jennifer?

DORA: No, I'm not. Jennifer's helping her mother. I'm Dora Barkley, her best friend.

CAM: That was a pretty good reading you were giving. I suppose you're in a school play.

DORA: No. Jennifer and I have been going over her lines. She's trying out for the part of the Nurse next week. I was just helping her with her lines. You—you weren't bad yourself. Say, you spoke those lines from memory! (*She removes her spectacles and sets them and the book on a shelf in the bookcase.*)

CAM (*Laughing*): Yes! Didn't think I could do it either. I played Romeo in the sophomore production last year. Hardest thing I ever did. The fencing wasn't so bad—but those tights! And I lost my wig during the balcony scene.

DORA (*Joining in laughter*): You didn't! But that's what would happen to me if—well, that's the sort of thing that I might do. (TOM, ALICE *and* JENNIFER *enter from right.*)

ALICE: Dora, did someone ring? (*Sees* CAM *and lets* TOM *continue.*)

TOM: Glad to see you, Cam. I guess you and Dora have already met. This is Mrs. Waine and my daughter, Jennifer. Cam McConnell. (*They all exchange greetings.*) Why don't you stay for dinner, Dora? Those steaks are mighty tempting.

DORA: No, thanks, Mr. Waine. I have to get home. We're having guests, too.

TOM: Well, Alice, what do you say about going out to the summer house? It's a lot cooler out there.

ALICE: All right.

CAM: Fine, Mr. Waine. I'm happy to have met you, Dora. I think *you* ought to try out for that play. You're good. Coming, Jennifer?

JENNIFER: I'll be along in a minute. (CAM, TOM *and* ALICE *exit.*) I must say that was fast work, Dora! He talked to you as though you'd been friends forever. And whatever happened to Dora Barkley, this year's calculating, impersonal career woman? (DORA *sits on the sofa with a faraway look in her eye, paying no attention to* JENNIFER'S *good-natured ribbing.*)

DORA (*Suddenly*): Jennifer! I've got it! I know how to put Madge Prentice in her place. It's foolproof.

JENNIFER (*Warily*): Oh, dear. The dreaded moment. I thought you'd forgotten all about that. You might as well tell me the worst, though.

DORA: Get Cam McConnell to take you to the Summer Serenade dance next Friday. You can ask him—it's that kind of dance, but Madge won't know it. And think of the blow to her pride when she finds you're going with a college man! She'll be positively paralyzed with envy. He'll almost have to accept since he's working for your father.

JENNIFER (*Doubtfully*): I don't know. He seems too nice a fellow to drag into my problems. Why make him a tool of destruction?

DORA: Get with it, girl. He won't have to drop a bomb on anyone! All you're asking him to do is spend a pleasant evening with a lovely girl. He probably doesn't know anyone else in town. You'll be doing him a favor.

JENNIFER: Do you think it would work? It is just the sort of thing Madge would die over. She thinks she's so sophisticated.

DORA: Of course, Pete might not like the idea.

JENNIFER: That would hardly enter into *my* considerations.

DORA: Then what's to stop you?

JENNIFER: Dora, I'll do it! I can hardly wait to see her face.

DORA (*Looking at her watch*): I have to run now. Why don't you call me later tonight, and we'll talk about it?

JENNIFER: O.K., and thanks loads, Dora. (*Smiling*) I've got a feeling this is going to work. (JENNIFER *accompanies* DORA *to the door, left. She disappears for a moment, and when she returns she tidies the room a bit, then exits.* MIKE *enters right, after a pause. He begins looking for his comic books again and is visibly irked that he can't find them.*)

MIKE: Boy, that beats everything! (*Looks under sofa cushions*) I didn't suppose they'd be here. Let's see now. If I were a lost *Startling Space Comics* book, where would I be? (*Doorbell rings.*) Aw, what the heck—(*Crosses to door, left*) might as well count them lost! (*Disappears from view while answering the door, then re-enters with* PETE KENDALL, *an energetic high school boy*)

PETE: Hiya, Mike! You all alone?

MIKE: No, the others are out in the summer house. I'll get Jennifer for you.

PETE: No. Never mind. I wanted to talk to you.

MIKE (*Surprised*): Me! What do you want to talk to me about?

PETE (*Embarrassed*): Well—it's like this—you see, I—

MIKE (*Slouching down onto the sofa*): Say! I'll bet you need some advice. That right, Kendall, old boy? Well, you've come to the right man. Yes, sir, your choice was a good one. They all come around to old Mike sooner or later! And from what I've seen and heard today, believe me, I don't know of one person in this town—no, sir!—

not *one* person who needs ole Mike's advice more than Pete Kendall!

PETE (*Seating himself on the other end of the sofa*): And just what do you mean by that, fellow?

MIKE: Well—er, gosh! When I told Jennifer about you and Madge—

PETE (*Jumping to his feet*): When you *what?*

MIKE (*Gulping*): When I told Jennifer that I'd seen you and Madge on the tennis court this morning—you remember, you were talking—

PETE (*Sinking to the sofa, a wounded animal*): Oh! Oh, no!

MIKE (*Peering at him closely*): What's the matter, Pete?

PETE (*Rising and pacing the floor*): You—you vacuum! What did you want to tell Jennifer about that for—of all the—and that probably clinches the whole deal!

MIKE: Say, Pete—I'm sorry if I let the cat out of the bag, but—

PETE: There wasn't any cat *in* the bag!

MIKE: You'd better tell Jennifer that, because she was plenty burned up. (*Blandly*) You know she thinks quite a bit of you.

PETE (*Painfully wounded again, he sits on sofa*): Oh! It's fate, Mike. All the forces of the universe are pressing me down. Every little atom is working against me. (*Pitifully*) I haven't got a chance. It's fate.

MIKE (*Reminiscently*): You know, there was a situation like that in last month's *Startling Space*. This scientist was trying his best to—

PETE: Oh, blast your scientist!

MIKE: That's what happened! Hey, you must have read that issue!

PETE: Cut the clowning, Mike. I'm in trouble—real trouble!

MIKE: Well, as I said, you've come to the right man for advice. Now what is this problem?

PETE: This is confidential. Understand? Do you think you can keep it to yourself?

MIKE (*Hurt*): My lips are sealed! Ray guns couldn't tear your secret from me.

PETE: I don't know about ray guns, but just don't blab!

MIKE (*Impatiently*): Come on, man, give!

PETE: It's like this: you saw Madge and me talking this morning. Well, she cornered me about the Summer Serenade dance, you know, the dance next week. The girls can invite the fellows, if they want. Or vice versa. It doesn't matter. Anyway, Madge asked me to go with her and—and she twisted my words all around. I tried to tell her I was sure Jennifer would ask me—or I'd ask Jennifer—but by the time I could say anything, well—Madge thinks I'm going to the dance with her. There's one girl who can talk and talk and talk!

MIKE (*Awed*): You're right, Pete. You have a problem.

PETE: *That* I know. I want you to help me get out of it.

MIKE: That's a pretty big order. What can I do?

PETE: You live here. Talk to Madge. Explain to Jennifer. Make Madge see that she doesn't want to go to that dance with me. After all, I'm younger than she is. Say, how old is she, anyway?

MIKE: Huh? Madge? Oh, she's older than anyone, I guess.

PETE: Older than anyone! I don't know as I'd say that!

MIKE: I didn't mean it that way. She's older than anyone you and Jennifer go around with. I don't know—maybe she's as old as twenty. She's pretty well preserved, though.

PETE: Yeah, and I might as well be preserved—in vinegar—if Jennifer ever finds out about what's happened! I just have to find a way out of that mix-up! I'm counting on you, Mike.

MIKE: I'll see what I can do, Pete. Who knows? I might solve the whole problem for you!

PETE: Do your best, Mike. (JENNIFER *and* CAM *enter the room from door right.* JENNIFER *stops short when she sees* PETE. CAM *crosses to left and stands near the bookcase.*)

JENNIFER: Mother thought she heard the doorbell ring, Mike. (*To* PETE) *You!* Here! But I forgot—Madge probably invited you! Mike, will you tell Madge's guest that she isn't home yet. Come along, Cam. We don't want to interrupt anything personal. They usually have a lot to talk about.

PETE: You've got it all wrong, Jennifer. Honestly, there's nothing—

JENNIFER: I really don't care to hear about it. Besides, you're embarrassing my guest. Oh, you haven't met each other yet, have you? Cam, this is a friend, a *former* friend of mine, Peter Kendall. Cam McConnell, a *university* man.

PETE (*Sadly*): Hello!

CAM (*Crossing to him, extending his hand*): Hi! Glad to meet you, Kendall! (*They shake hands.*)

JENNIFER: Let's go back outside, Cam. There's something I want to ask you. I do hope you haven't anything planned for next Friday night. There's going to be a dance, and I thought you— (*They start to exit right.*)

PETE (*Anticipating her next words*): Jennifer! You wouldn't do that, would you? Aw, Jennifer, you have everything twisted around.

JENNIFER (*Turning at door to face him*): *I* have everything twisted! Well, that is news! It seems to me that—

MIKE: Give him a chance to explain, sis!

CAM: Sure. Perhaps Mike and I had better leave you two alone for awhile.

JENNIFER: Not at all. There's nothing to discuss. I wouldn't think of leaving *my* guest alone.

PETE: Oh, for Pete's sake!

JENNIFER: Hm-m! Always thinking of yourself.

MIKE (*Impulsively*): Why don't you two let up? Just because Madge corners Pete into asking her to the Summer Serenade dance next Friday night, Jennifer, it doesn't mean that he—(*Realizing his error*) Oh, man—*man!* That does it. (*Slides onto sofa*) I've had it.

JENNIFER: So! That's what you were up to with Madge Prentice this morning!

CAM (*Astounded*): Madge Prentice!

PETE (*At his most sinister*): Mike, old man, Mike Waine! I'd like a few words with you outside. You—you (*Approaching him*) microphone-mouthed monster, you!

JENNIFER (*Planting herself in front of a cowering* MIKE): How dare you insult my little brother! I think, Peter Kendall, it's time you left.

PETE: Oh! Those atoms—they're swirling all around me. I'm being engulfed by fate. (*He stands a broken figure.*)

CAM: Say, did someone mention Madge Prentice's name? (*As he asks the question, there is a flurry of motion at left.* MADGE PRENTICE *enters.*)

MADGE (*Breathlessly*): Hello, everyone! My goodness, I'm late. Did I hear someone ask about Madge Prentice? (*Spies* CAM) It isn't! It can't be! I don't believe it! But it is—Cam McConnell! What in the world!

CAM (*Smiling*): Hi, there, Madge. Yes, it's really me. Why, I haven't seen you since—since the freshman prom!

MADGE (*Crossing to him*): That's right, Cam. It's been just ages.

JENNIFER (*Overwhelmed*): You two know each other?

MADGE: Do we!

CAM: I'll say!

JENNIFER: But—but—

MADGE: Jennifer, you darling, why didn't you tell me you were inviting one of my old friends to dinner? But that's just like you. Considerate. Always so sweet to me. Oh, Cam, I've loads to tell you (*Pauses*), but I'm boring everyone. The gossip can keep until later.

PETE (*Taking advantage of his opportunity*): No—no—not at all. You and McConnell just talk and visit. I'll take Jennifer outside.

JENNIFER (*Furiously*): You will not!

MIKE: Aw, Jennifer—

PETE: *You* were just leaving, weren't you, Mike? Outside, I mean. Now!

MIKE (*Remembering*): Yeah, that's right. I sure was—things to do, you know. I'd better go right now. (*Exits quickly right*)

MADGE: Oh, heavens. I must change for dinner. We can talk later, Cam. You are staying?

CAM: Sure thing.

MADGE: Wait a minute! How marvelous! The Summer Serenade dance—next Friday night. Pete, don't go away. I want to talk to you! Are you going to be in town, Cam?

CAM: I think so.

JENNIFER: Now, really, Madge!

MADGE: I have the most marvelous idea. Let's make it a double date. Pete can take you, Jennifer, and I'll go with Cam!

JENNIFER (*Angry*): Well, really—of all the—

CAM: It's up to you people.

PETE (*Gratefully*): You know, Madge's idea sounds pretty good to me.

JENNIFER: Not to me, it doesn't. Just what makes you think I want to go any place with Pete Kendall, Madge? You certainly are able to slip your escorts on and off like a glove! Besides, I intended to ask Cam—

CAM (*Innocently*): Now, look—

MADGE: But this is so much nicer, dear. I know that Pete would rather—

JENNIFER: Frankly, I don't care what you or Pete would rather do. As far as I'm concerned, Madge Prentice, you can go to that dance with—with the Maharajah of Timbuktu. I'm sure you could talk him into it. Pete can—oh, I don't care *what* Pete does. As for me, I'm going to my room. Good night! (*She rushes out door right, almost colliding with* TOM *and* ALICE *as they are entering.*)

ALICE: Gracious, we could hear your voices in the summer house.

TOM: And from the expressions on your faces, I'd say there had been a few words exchanged—and not all of them pleasant ones!

PETE: It's all my fault, Mr. Waine.

CAM (*Cutting in*): I must have said the wrong thing.

MADGE (*Interrupting*): Oh, dear, I'm sorry—

TOM (*Raising his hands*): Whoa, wait a minute! What is all this? (*Doorbell rings.*) Who can that be? (*Starts for door, left*)

ALICE: Never mind, Tom. I'll get it. (*Crosses left and exits for a moment*)

TOM: Now, as I was saying, what happened in here?

MADGE: Oh, Mr. Waine, it's my fault. I guess I'll never learn to mind my own business. You see, I've had the feeling lately that, well—that Jennifer has resented me. I wanted to make up for whatever I'd done.

ALICE (*Re-entering from left, preceded by* DORA): It's Dora. She forgot her glasses.

DORA: Goodness, yes. I don't know how I'll find them since I can't see very well without them.

TOM: We'll help you look for them. (*Everyone searches.*)

CAM (*At bookcase*): Are these yours? You probably set

them on the shelf when you finished reading. (*Gives them to her*)

DORA (*Putting them on*): I remember. That's just what I did do. I hope I didn't interrupt anything, but our guests couldn't come and I had some homework to do, so—

ALICE: Not at all, Dora. You're perfectly welcome. It's only that Jennifer seems a little upset. She went to her room.

DORA (*Glancing at* MADGE): Oh, is there anything I can do?

MADGE: Dora Barkley, don't you look at me that way. I know just what you're thinking and it's not true!

TOM: Girls—girls! Let's get to the bottom of this calmly.

CAM: Say, Dora, I don't think we're needed in here. How about coming out to the patio with me? Someone had better have a look at that fire.

DORA (*Pleased*): I'd love to. (*As they start to exit at right*) And perhaps you can tell me some more about *Romeo and Juliet*. I've been thinking about what you and Jennifer said, and, you know, I just might—(*They exit.*)

MADGE (*Looking after them*): That's an interesting development.

TOM: Now, please, what *did* happen in here?

PETE: I guess it's really all my fault, Mr. Waine. You see, Jennifer's upset because she thinks I asked Madge to go to the Summer Serenade dance with me.

MADGE (*Surprised*): Pete Kendall! How on earth did she get an idea like that?

PETE: What do you mean, how did she get an idea like that? What other idea was she to get? You did talk me into taking you, didn't you? My gosh, you beat around the bush enough this morning, but I knew what you wanted, I guess!

MADGE (*Laughing*): Oh, Pete! You are hopeless. No wonder Jennifer wanted a change from you!

PETE: What do you mean, a change from me? You have a nerve!

MADGE: And no wonder she's annoyed with me. I certainly don't blame her.

TOM: Please! I can follow only every other word of this conversation. (*Doorbell rings.*) Ye gods! This might as well be the White House on Inauguration Day!

ALICE (*Crossing to door, left*): Temper, temper, Tom! (*She exits for a moment.*)

PETE (*Glaring at* MADGE): Do you mean to say that you don't want to go to that dance with me?

MADGE: Of course not! Do you think I want to be responsible for a break between you and Jennifer? If you weren't so dense, you would have realized that I wasn't *beating around the bush,* as you put it, this morning. I was trying—very subtly—to inform you that Jennifer would really be delighted to go with you—no matter what she said.

PETE (*Sinking into the nearest chair*): Oh! Oh! How dumb can a guy be? Now what'll I say to Jennifer?

ALICE (*Re-entering with* GRACE PRENTICE, *who is carrying a dress box under her arm*): We have another guest, folks!

MADGE: Mother! (*Runs across to her and hugs her*)

TOM: Glad to see you, Grace. Why didn't you let us know you were coming? I'd have met you at the station.

GRACE: That's nice of you, Tom. But I couldn't impose on you and Alice any longer. The lawyers finally settled your grandfather's estate, Madge, but I have to rush right back to New York to sign some legal papers. (*To* TOM *and* ALICE) I decided to pick up some personal things, take Madge off your hands, and we'd fly to New York together.

MADGE (*Excited*): You don't mean it, Mother! New York! How fabulous!

GRACE: The plane leaves later tonight. You'd better get your packing done.

MADGE: I'll do it right now. Oh, Mr. and Mrs. Waine, you've been wonderful, and I hope that you don't think I'm not appreciative of all you've done to make my visit here a happy one.

ALICE: We understand, dear.

MADGE: I do feel just awful about Jennifer, though. Goodness, she must think all sorts of things about me!

PETE (*Moaning from his chair*): Oh!

MADGE (*Noticing dress box under her mother's arm*): Is that what I think it is, Mother?

GRACE: It is. (*She gives the box to* MADGE.)

MADGE: I know what I'll do. I'll take this right up to Jennifer, and I'll just explain everything to her. I can at least do that. (JENNIFER *enters.*)

JENNIFER (*Quietly*): You needn't explain anything to me, Madge. Mother and Dad, and even Dora were right. I've acted like a silly child. Suspicious and hateful and nasty! I guess I've been sort of—well, jealous. Dashing out of here was the final silliness. You and Cam can hardly be blamed for knowing each other. I guess if Pete wants to ask you to the dance it's his business.

PETE: But I didn't, Jennifer! It's all a misunderstanding.

MADGE: Jennifer, it has been a misunderstanding. Pete intended to take you to the dance all along. I just poked my nose in where it didn't belong.

GRACE: That sounds familiar.

JENNIFER: I should have let you explain before I lost my temper.

PETE (*Crossing to her*): Does that mean I'm forgiven?

JENNIFER: I guess there's nothing to forgive, Pete. If there is, I'm the one to be forgiven.

MADGE (*Giving dress box to* JENNIFER): This is for you. I wrote Mother and asked her to bring it from New York.

I hope it will make up for all the times I've worn your clothes, but, you see, I didn't bring many with me, and your friends always dress so well that I didn't want to disgrace you by wearing the same old thing all the time.

ALICE: It seems there's a reason for everything, isn't there, Jennifer?

JENNIFER (*Lifting a lovely dress from the box*): I don't know what to say, Madge. It seems that I've had everything wrong from the beginning. The dress is simply lovely. Thank you, Mrs. Prentice—and Madge.

GRACE: That's all right, Jennifer. I know how Madge goes through a wardrobe. You probably need a new dress. (CAM *and* DORA *enter from door right.*)

CAM: I don't know about you people, but we're ready.

TOM: Alice! These kids must be famished. Grace, you and Madge are staying for dinner, then we'll drive you to the airport. Pete and Dora, you call your parents, you're staying, too.

DORA: I don't know if I should. Jennifer, you're going to be awfully mad at me. Cam asked *me* to the dance, and I accepted! What's everyone looking at me like that for?

JENNIFER (*Laughing*): It's all right, Dora. Cam couldn't have chosen a better date. Pete and I'll make it a foursome.

DORA (*Puzzled*): We must have missed something, Cam.

MADGE: My mother's here, and I'm leaving for New York with her tonight.

DORA: Now, I get it.

CAM: Uh—huh! And, guess what, Dora has agreed to try out for the play. I'm going to coach her.

DORA: Maybe we should be rehearsing *All's Well*. . . .

MIKE (*Peeking around door, right*): Anybody mind if I come in?

PETE (*Genially*): Not at all, Mike—not at all! You come right in. We'd *like* you to come in.

MIKE (*Doubtfully*): Yeah? Well, maybe. (*Crossing to his father*) Say, Dad, did you start the barbecue fire with some of these? (*He holds up several tattered comic book pages.*)

TOM: Yes, I think I did, son. Why?

MIKE (*Philosophically*): Oh, nothing. Better a steak than cologne, if you know what I mean.

ALICE: I'm afraid we don't, Mike. But you can tell us all about it after we've had a good dinner. Come on, everyone, this will have to be a cooperative effort! (*They all exit door right, laughing and talking, as the curtain falls.*)

THE END

Miss Frankenstein

by Helen Louise Miller

Characters

MONSTER OF CEREMONIES
MR. BEELZEBUB
DR. JEKYLL-MR. HYDE
FRANKENSTEIN
MADAME SCAREMELLI
MISS SHROUDSBURG
MISS TOMBSTONE TERRITORY
MISS VAMPIRE VILLAGE
MISS SWAMPLAND
MISS DISTRICT OF GHOULUMBIA
MISS MUMMEAPOLIS
MISS BLOODY BLUFFS
MISS HAUNTSVILLE
MISS WITCH OF WITCHITA
GIRL } *volunteers from audience*
BOY }
TWO USHERS
STAGEHAND
SELECTED MEMBERS OF THE AUDIENCE

SETTING: *The stage of the Hauntatorium, in Panic City, set for the finals of the Miss Frankenstein Contest.*

AT RISE: MR. BEELZEBUB, DR. JEKYLL-MR. HYDE, *and*

FRANKENSTEIN *are seated on one side of the stage. On the other side, the* MONSTER OF CEREMONIES *is at a microphone.*

M.C.: Good evening, fellow Goblins and Hobgoblins! Welcome to the second annual Miss Frankenstein Contest. This is the night we've all been waiting for. In just a short time, here on the great stage of the Hauntatorium in Panic City, we will witness the crowning of Miss Frankenstein of (*Insert year*).

We've all had a wonderful time these past few days in Panic City, where we have all been royally entertained by the spectacle of the most gruesome, the most hideous, the most diabolically gifted specimens of female ugliness ever to be assembled under one roof. The semi-finalists who will appear before you this evening are unquestionably the most frightening array of female spirits it has ever been our privilege to introduce.

But before you meet these eight lucky unlovelies, I wish to present our distinguished judges. We will ask each of them to rise so you may see for yourselves the monsters who have given so unstintingly of their time and talent in this difficult task of selecting Miss Frankenstein of (*Insert year*).

First, let us present the chairman of the judges, a gentleman who needs no introduction—the distinguished patron of the lost—the one and only Mr. Beelzebub himself! (MR. BEELZEBUB, *in devil costume, rises, and acknowledges applause by clasping his hands over his head and shaking them at audience.* NOTE: SELECTED MEMBERS OF THE AUDIENCE *begin the applause for each judge as introduced.*) Our second judge is no less distinguished in his own field of horror literature . . . that famed split personality, the demoniacal Dr. Jekyll and Mr. Hyde! (DR. JEKYLL-MR. HYDE, *dressed as* JEKYLL *in opera hat and cloak, rises and bows politely to audience. He then quickly removes hat, dons a shaggy wig, inserts a pair of protruding, tusklike wax teeth, and gives a long, maniacal laugh.*) And for our third and last judge, we have chosen one whose qualifications for the job at hand spring from his own experience. I give you that well-known literary creation, and beloved star of stage, screen, and television. . . . the original Frankenstein Monster! (FRANKENSTEIN *rises, bows.* SELECTED MEMBERS OF THE AUDIENCE *shout "Speech!"* M.C. *raises his hand for quiet.*) There's no way out, Frank. You'll just have to step to the mike and say a few words. (FRANKENSTEIN *goes to microphone.*)

FRANKENSTEIN: My fellow Monsters, and sister Hags and Harridans, greetings! I am overwhelmed by this ovation. The credit for all this, you know, belongs not to myself, but to my designer and creator, the brilliant young student for whom I am erroneously named. When Mary Shelley wrote her famous novel more than a hundred years ago, little did she know that by destroying her hero she would create a thousand monsters who have added to the delicious terrors, tremors and traumas of the entire human race. This evening we stand on the threshold of a new age in sorcery. This evening we will see the Frankenstein Crown bestowed on the female monster most worthy of this classic name. No one could have worn this diabolical diadem with greater horror than our winner of last year, Miss Witch of Witchita, but this evening a new Weirdy will take her place on this stage, and in your hearts. And to speed that exciting moment, I say . . . on with the show! (*Returns to seat*)

M.C.: Thank you, Frank. And now, if Madame Scaremelli will join me at the microphone to describe the gowns of the semi-finalists, we are ready to begin. (MADAME SCAREMELLI *enters, and joins* M.C.)

MME. SCAREMELLI: First, let me say how absolutely spine-chilling it is to be here on this occasion to describe the frightful fashions which I am sure will start a new trend in graveyard attire from coast to coast. The judges really have my sympathy in the all but impossible task of scoring the contestants in this costume category.

M.C.: Thank you, Mme. Scaremelli. Now, without further ado, we proudly present our first contestant . . . Miss Shroudsburg! (*To appropriate musical accompaniment, such as "The Funeral March,"* MISS SHROUDSBURG *enters right, advances to center of stage, pauses, displays her attire in typical model fashion, as* MME. SCAREMELLI *comments on her dress.* NOTE: *The contestants appearing later model their dresses in the same manner.*)

MME. SCAREMELLI: Miss Shroudsburg is wearing a lovely white sheath with long, flowing sleeves, artfully slit to display her skeleton arms and bony shoulders. This full-length shroud falls full and free from the shoulders and its simplicity is broken only by patches of mold in muted tones of gray and green. Miss Shroudsburg's headdress is classical in style with a single bandage supporting the jaw muscles, a truly delightful touch, reminiscent of the bubonic plague era. The whole creation is simple but elegant in cut and design, and Miss Shroudsburg looks as fresh as if she had just stepped out of her own mausoleum. (MISS SHROUDSBURG *exits left, to applause.* NOTE: SELECTED MEMBERS OF THE AUDIENCE *begin the applause for each contestant as she leaves the stage.*)

M.C.: The next aspirant for the Frankenstein Crown is Miss Tombstone Territory! (*She enters, repeats modeling routine.*)

MME. SCAREMELLI: Here we have a three-dimensional effect, as Miss Tombstone Territory parades across the stage in an exact replica of a grave marker, *circa* 1800. Fashioned of marbleized white paper over lightweight cardboard construction, the tombstone completely covers the contestant from her head to her knees. This dramatic treatment of the shift is truly unusual, and we think an extra round of applause should go to Miss Tombstone Territory for her ability to walk across the stage without tumbling into the footlights. (*Contestant exits.*)

M.C.: I told you we would have our share of thrills tonight, and this is only the beginning, folks. Next in the spotlight . . . Miss Vampire Village! (*She enters.*)

MME. SCAREMELLI: Miss Vampire Village is wearing a dramatic black velvet sheath with enormous batlike wings attached to her wrists to give her a peculiar floating motion, as she weaves and twists her way across the stage. The bat motif is repeated in the close-fitting hood which serves to accentuate her most outstanding feature—the long, pointed fangs protruding from her upper jaw. (*Contestant exits.*)

M.C.: And now, from the Haunted Hills and Hollows of the Old South . . . Miss Swampland! (*She enters.*)

MME. SCAREMELLI: Miss Swampland is the very picture of old Okefenokee itself, the haunt of the alligator, the snake and the lizard. Her gown is of basic bark cloth, and her slender legs and feet are encased in a dark red, hairy fabric, suggestive of cypress roots. Her arms are festooned with flowing draperies of Spanish moss and her headdress bears the Swampland family crest, the head of an alligator. Coiled about her throat is a charming necklace of two deadly water moccasins. This is altogether as striking a costume as one might hope to see. (*Contestant exits.*)

M.C.: Now our next semi-finalist . . . Miss District of Ghoulumbia! (*She enters.*)

MME. SCAREMELLI: I cannot find words to describe the creation worn by Miss District of Ghoulumbia. The basic one-piece skeleton coverall is girdled by a wire frame from which are suspended six skulls, souvenirs of this intrepid graverobber. Over one shoulder she carries the tools of her trade, a silver pick and shovel, and slung over the other shoulder is a large gunny sack from which protrudes the head of her most recent victim. (*Contestant exits.*)

M.C.: Our next contestant is Miss Mummeapolis! (*She enters.*)

MME. SCAREMELLI: From ancient Egypt comes Miss Mummeapolis, in the classic costume of the dead Pharaohs. Swathed from head to foot in ceremonial wrappings turned brown from centuries of entombment in the pyramids, she gropes her way across the stage with sightless eyes. We can well imagine the shriveled face and withered limbs beneath these ancient burial wrappings. Truly, Miss Mummeapolis claims to be the best-dressed mummy of the centuries. (*Contestant exits.*)

M.C.: Our next contestant . . . Miss Bloody Bluffs! (*She enters.*)

MME. SCAREMELLI: Here, the American Indian motif takes over, for a traditional ensemble of buckskin, beads and blanket. The supernatural element, however, is immediately apparent in the headdress, which consists of a brilliantly feathered arrow stuck directly through the contestant's cranium. In her right hand Miss Bloody Bluffs carries a most interesting accessory, a scalp, which looks, to our unpracticed eye, as if it had just come off the nearest paleface. (*Contestant exits.*)

M.C.: And now, the last of our semi-finalists . . . Miss Hauntsville, U.S.A.! (*She enters.*)

MME. SCAREMELLI: Miss Hauntsville is wearing the traditional ghostly garments associated with Haunts the world over. Her gown, however, is richly ornamented with a black skull and crossbone design, and her accessories consist of a double girdle of chains extending well below the hemline and trailing along behind her. The highlight of this spectral ensemble, which is equally suited to castle or cottage, is the illuminated headdress. A flashlight, cunningly concealed in the cowl neckline, gives an unearthly glow to Miss Hauntsville's well-modeled skeleton face. (*Contestant exits.*) And now, Mr. Monster of Ceremonies, I turn the microphone over to you.

M.C.: Thank you, Mme. Scaremelli. Well, folks, what do you say to a great big hand for this little lady who has done such a fabulous job on these spooky fashions? (*She exits to applause.*) And now for the talent part of our program. Our first contestant in the talent category is Miss Tombstone Territory. Miss Tombstone Territory is known and beloved by followers of cowboy movies the world over. A native of Graveyard Gulch, she has played hostess to such desperadoes as Jesse James, Wild Bill Hickok, and Billy the Kid. I give you Miss Tombstone Territory. (*Contestant enters, does tap dance and exits to applause.*) Next in our talented line-up is Miss Vampire Village, a sophomore at Grave City College where she is majoring in Dio-Chemistry. She will demonstrate her skill in this field by performing an experiment whereby she changes water into blood. (MISS VAMPIRE VILLAGE *enters.* STAGEHAND *carries on a table, two beakers of colorless liquid, and an empty beaker, then exits. With much ceremony, she pours the two liquids together into the empty beaker, producing a red liquid. She holds up beaker, then exits to applause.* NOTE: *Directions for experiment may be found in books of magic, or red food coloring may be used.* STAGEHAND *removes the table.*) Wonderful! Our third performing artist is that darling of the Deep South, Miss Swampland. (MISS SWAMPLAND *enters with large, stuffed snake and performs a snake dance to weird, oriental music, then exits.* M.C. *wipes his forehead.*) I don't mind telling you, I am glad Miss Swampland and her pet have withdrawn to a safe distance. Next, the lovely Miss Shroudsburg, a recent graduate of Old Scratch Academy and presently enrolled at Casket Conservatory, will favor us with a musical selection. (MISS SHROUDSBURG *enters, performs vocal or instrumental solo of an appropriate song, such as "That Old Black Magic," then exits.*) Our next contestant asks for the cooperation of the audience. May I have two volunteers, please? (GIRL *and* BOY, *seated in audience, rise and come to the stage.*) Ah, I see we have a young lady and a gentleman. Our next performer, endowed with the mystic powers of the supernatural, will conduct an experiment in hypnotism . . . Miss Hauntsville! (*She enters, carrying a hand mirror.*)

MISS HAUNTSVILLE: I must ask for absolute quiet while I conduct my experiment. As you know, I have seen neither of these young people before, but I shall ask both of them to gaze into my magic mirror and subject their minds and their wills to my controlling force. (*With much hocus-pocus and flashing of the mirror, she succeeds in reducing the volunteers to rigid automatons. To* GIRL) Step forward, young lady, and tell us your name.

GIRL (*In high, piping voice*): I am (*Insert name of volunteer*).

MISS HAUNTSVILLE: How old are you?

GIRL: Thirteen.

MISS HAUNTSVILLE: When next you speak, you will be ninety-nine years old and afflicted with rheumatism. You will ask me to rub your aches and pains away. Speak.

GIRL (*In high, cracked voice, as she bends almost double*): O-o-oh! Please, please, Miss Hauntsville, rub my right shoulder. (*As she does so*) O-o-oh, that feels good. O-o-oh, I have a pain in my back. (MISS HAUNTSVILLE *rubs her back.*) Ah! That's so much better. Ouch, ouch! I have a terrible cramp in my right leg. Please make it go away. And my neck is killing me! O-oh!

MISS HAUNTSVILLE (*Rapidly passing her hands in front of the* GIRL'*s face*): You will wake up now, and be yourself again. (GIRL *seems to awaken suddenly, stands straight.*) Well, how do you feel?

GIRL (*Puzzled*): Fine, thank you.

MISS HAUNTSVILLE: No aches or pains?

GIRL (*Laughing*): Of course not!

MISS HAUNTSVILLE: I'm glad to hear that. Now, our young gentleman. Step forward, please. (BOY *goes to her.*) How old are you?

BOY: Fourteen.

MISS HAUNTSVILLE: When I clap my hands three times, you are four years old and you are having a temper tantrum. (*She claps three times, and the* BOY *stamps his feet, cries, throws himself on the floor, kicks, howls, etc.*) That's enough. When I clap my hand three times, you will be yourself again, but when I cough, you will go over and kick the Monster of Ceremonies in the shins until I sneeze. (*She claps her hands.*)

BOY: When do we start the big act? When do you hypnotize me?

MISS HAUNTSVILLE: I'm sorry, young man. I have such a bad cold that I can't perform my act. (*She begins to cough.* BOY *runs over to* M.C. *and starts kicking him in the shins. She sneezes, and he stops.*)

BOY: This is a gyp. I thought I was going to be hypnotized.

MISS HAUNTSVILLE: Better luck next time. Thank you very much for your cooperation. You may be seated. (*The volunteers return to their seats in the audience.*)

M.C.: How about a big hand for Miss Hauntsville? (*She exits to applause.*) Our next contestant is Miss Bloody Bluffs. (*She enters, followed by* STAGEHAND *carrying tar-*

get, bow, and suction cup arrows.) Miss Bloody Bluffs will demonstrate the uncanny skill which made her the monster of Bloody Bluffs' Massacre. (*She gives a demonstration of target practice, then exits.* STAGEHAND *removes target.*)

The variety of talent which shows up at these contests never ceases to amaze me, and I am sure you will enjoy our next contestant, Miss District of Ghoulumbia. She will introduce us to the secret society of Ghouls Anonymous by presenting the theme song and ritual of that royal order, "Ghoula, Ghoula." (MISS DISTRICT OF GHOULUMBIA *enters.*)

MISS DISTRICT OF GHOULUMBIA (*Singing to the tune of "Boola, Boola"*):

Ghoula-Ghoula, Ghoula-Ghoula,
Ghoula-Ghoula, Ghoula-Ghoula,
When I meet my love so true-la,
He will be my Ghoula-goo! (*She exits to applause.*)

M.C.: After that romantic number, we will have a change of pace with Miss Mummeapolis and her mind-reading act. Two ushers are already stationed in our audience to challenge Miss Mummeapolis with articles they borrowed from our guests. (*Calling*) Miss Mummeapolis? (*She enters.*)

MISS MUMMEAPOLIS: I am ready.

M.C.: Since Miss Mummeapolis is already blindfolded, we can dispense with that ceremony.

1ST USHER (*From audience, standing beside* 1ST SELECTED MEMBER OF THE AUDIENCE): I have a lady, Miss Mummeapolis. (*Holding up watch*) Can you identify this object?

MISS MUMMEAPOLIS: I think I hear a faint ticking. Is it a watch?

1ST USHER: It is. (*To lady*) Thank you, madam.

2ND USHER (*With* 2ND MEMBER OF AUDIENCE): I have a

gentleman, Miss Mummeapolis. (*Holds up a wallet*) What am I holding in my hand?

MISS MUMMEAPOLIS: I am not sure. I get the feeling of some sort of animal—a cow, or maybe a pig—or even an ostrich. Could it be something made of leather? A wallet, for instance?

2ND USHER: Correct. It is a wallet. (*To man*) Thank you, sir.

1ST USHER (*With* 3RD MEMBER OF AUDIENCE, *holding up a scarf*): I have a lady, Miss Mummeapolis. What am I holding up?

MISS MUMMEAPOLIS: I get the feeling of something light and filmy, something soft and silky like fur, but lighter than fur, more like silk. I should say it is a scarf.

1ST USHER: Correct. (*To lady*) Thank you, madam.

M.C.: I am sorry to interrupt this fascinating demonstration of your skill, Miss Mummeapolis, but we must proceed. (*She exits.* M.C. *steps to the front of the stage, and the curtains close behind him.*) Since we have reached the end of our talent show, we are ready for the final act of our Panic City Pageant with the selection of Miss Frankenstein for (*Insert year*). While our judges retire to confer on their selection of the four fatal finalists, we proudly present our present wearer of the Frankenstein Crown, Miss Witch of Wichita. (*She enters, wearing a crown and a long silver cloak, and carrying a large jack-o'-lantern.*)

MISS WITCH OF WITCHITA: Before I transfer my royal robes and golden crown to one of the fantastic creatures we have met this evening, I would like to tell you what this wonderful year as Miss Frankenstein has meant to me. I have flown over every corner of the globe, scaring the wits out of hundreds of thousands of men, women, and children. I have swooped over the chimney pots of London, I have circled the rooftops of Paris, I have peered through the windows of castles and rattled my bony fingers over the doorways of cottages. I have swirled through dust storms on the Sahara, and slithered through the ice fields of the frozen North. But everywhere I have met with the same reception—shrieks of terror. You have no idea how much this has meant to me and how much it will mean to my successor. In these days of atomic missiles and the hydrogen bomb, it is good to know that people are still afraid of a good old-fashioned spook. When I go back to Witchita, I promise you I will never forget this wonderful year and all you wonderful, wonderful haunts and horrors who have made it possible. I thank you. (*She exits, to applause.*)

M.C.: Wonderful, isn't she? And now, folks, we approach that thrilling, chilling moment we have all been waiting for. When the curtains open, you will behold Miss Frankenstein upon her throne ready to transfer her crown and jack-o'-lantern to this year's winner . . . one of the four finalists whose names are being chosen at this very minute by our judges. (*Lights flicker.*) And there is our signal that we are ready to begin. (*Curtains open on throne with* MISS WITCH OF WITCHITA *in place. Four chairs are arranged at one side of the stage. The judges stand on the other side.*) Mr. Beelzebub will make his report.

MR. BEELZEBUB: Let me say first that this has been a most terrifying experience. To select four finalists from this array of horrible talent is no small task, but we have done our best. I will ask Dr. Jekyll-Mr. Hyde to announce the names of the finalists.

JEKYLL-HYDE (*As* JEKYLL): Please, please, I must know which I am to be. I cannot speak for both of me.

MR. BEELZEBUB: I think your Mr. Hyde personality would be more fitting.

JEKYLL-HYDE (*Putting on wig and adjusting teeth, as*

HYDE): Very well. I'm really more comfortable this way. Our first finalist—Miss Tombstone Territory. (*She enters.*) Our second finalist, Miss Vampire Village. (*She enters.*) Number three in our final line-up—Miss Swampland. (*She enters.*) And finally, number four—Miss Shroudsburg. (*She enters.*) I am sure your applause will tell us you approve our selections. (*Applause*)

M.C.: There's no doubt about it. The audience is with you one hundred percent. But before we make our Miss Frankenstein award, our contestants must face still another hurdle—the Question and Answer Quiz. Frankenstein himself holds the giant skull which contains the questions. Are you ready, Frank?

FRANKENSTEIN (*Stepping forward with skull container which holds four slips of paper*): I am quite ready. Mr. Hyde and Mr. Beelzebub will step into the wings where they will do their final judging. I will score my own ballot as we proceed. (*Judges move to wings.*) I will now ask each of our contestants to choose a question at random. Read your questions carefully and take plenty of time before you answer. First, Miss Tombstone Territory. (*She steps forward and selects question.*)

MISS TOMBSTONE TERRITORY: My question is: "In your opinion, what is the gravest problem a modern ghost or goblin must face in our present-day society?" (*Pause*) Well, I think the gravest problem a ghost has to face today is the problem of housing. With all the modern buildings going up and the scarcity of mansions, castles, and private estates, it's hard for a ghost to find a good place to haunt. If I am selected as Miss Frankenstein, I will use my influence to try to preserve all the houses I can find with suitable cellars, attics, secret staircases, and hidden rooms. "Better Housing for Haunts" will be my slogan. (*Applause*)

FRANKENSTEIN: Excellent! Excellent! And now, Miss Vampire Village will select her question.

MISS VAMPIRE VILLAGE (*Selecting question and reading*): "Do you feel that movies and television are helping or harming your profession?" (*Pause*) This is a hard question to answer. In one way, the movies and television are helping the professional haunts by giving us new ideas for horror techniques. I must say I have benefited personally from watching Bela Lugosi on the screen, and the few times that I have gone to a midnight horror show, I confess I was scared right out of my wits. But on the other hand, these productions are making the general public so accustomed to blood and gore that they are becoming harder and harder to scare. Only last week, when I flew into the bedroom of a teen-ager, I had a terrible time convincing her she was not watching a late, late, late show. All in all, I would say it's about fifty-fifty —for us and against us. (*Applause*)

FRANKENSTEIN: A very good answer to a very difficult question. It leaves us right where we were before we asked it. Miss Swampland, there are only two questions left. Which will you choose?

MISS SWAMPLAND (*Takes paper from skull and reads*): "What is your opinion of higher education for spooks?" (*Pause*) Oh, I'm all for education—the higher the better. My own studies at the Institute of Advanced Spookology have undoubtedly helped me in my career, and I would advise every aspiring Spook to be at least a Seminary Graduate. Some of my young friends at Cemetery Seminary and Satan Seminary are doing extremely well and plan to go on to Scorpion Academy or Gallows Institute. No specter of today can hope to be successful without at least a year of higher education. (*Applause*)

FRANKENSTEIN: Most commendable, most commendable,

indeed. Now, my dear Miss Shroudsburg, this final question is for you. Would you like me to read it?

MISS SHROUDSBURG: Oh, please do. I'm so nervous.

FRANKENSTEIN (*Reading question*): "When you get married, who will be the boss—you or your husband?"

MISS SHROUDSBURG (*Coyly*): Well, that depends on the husband. If he were the strong, masterful type, like you or like any one of the other two marvelous judges, I would never attempt to boss. But if he were just a spineless spirit with no will of his own, well, then, maybe it would be a different story.

FRANKENSTEIN: I am sure the judges have taken careful note of your answer, Miss Shroudsburg, and now, back to our Monster of Ceremonies. (FRANKENSTEIN *joins other judges in wings.*)

M.C.: What a display of wit and intelligence we have witnessed here this evening! Any one of these four Weirdies might wear the Frankenstein Crown with honor, but alas, only one will be chosen. In just a moment, the judges will return with the big, black envelope which will decide this tremendous issue. As you know, the first three names to be read will constitute the Court of Honor, and the fourth name will be that of our new Miss Frankenstein. Aha! Here is the envelope. (*The three judges enter, bow.* MR. BEELZEBUB *hands a big, black envelope to the* M.C.) My fingers are all thumbs. You must excuse me. (*Fumbles*) At last the seal is broken, and our first Lady-in-Waiting . . . Miss Swampland! (*She takes her place beside the throne.*) Our second Lady-in-Waiting . . . Miss Tombstone Territory. (*She goes to throne.*) Listen! Can you hear the heartbeats of the two remaining contestants? (*Sound of hoofbeats is heard.*) And now, our third runner-up is . . . Miss Shroudsburg! (*She goes to her place.* MISS VAMPIRE

VILLAGE *gives a screech of joy.* M.C. *takes her by the hand.*) And here she is, Miss Vampire Village . . . our new Miss Frankenstein! (*Fanfare, cheers, and applause. She begins to cry.* M.C. *hands her a big, black handkerchief.* MISS WITCH OF WITCHITA *rises, hands jack-o'-lantern to* MISS SWAMPLAND, *then descends from throne.* MISS TOMBSTONE TERRITORY *and* MISS SHROUDSBURG *remove her cloak*)

MISS WITCH OF WITCHITA: Congratulations, Miss Vampire Village! You are even more horrible than I dared to imagine.

MISS VAMPIRE VILLAGE (*Sniffling into handkerchief*): Oh, dear, everyone has been so wonderful! I can't believe it!

MISS WITCH OF WITCHITA: Your royal robe! (*She steps aside as* MISS TOMBSTONE TERRITORY *and* MISS SHROUDSBURG *fasten cloak on* MISS VAMPIRE VILLAGE.) Your golden orb! (MISS SWAMPLAND *hands jack-o'-lantern to her.*) And now, the most royal symbol of all—the crown. (*She removes crown from her own head and places it on* MISS VAMPIRE VILLAGE.) I hereby crown you Miss Frankenstein of (*Insert year*). (*Cheers and fanfare. Attendants line up beside* MISS VAMPIRE VILLAGE *as the curtains close.*)

THE END

Yes, Yes, A Thousand Times Yes!

by Claire Boiko

Characters

NELL SWEETINGOOD
GRANNY SWEETINGOOD
MISS HANNAH
PRISS, MINNIE, SARAH LOU — *members of sewing circle*
HARRY STRONGBORE, *hero presumptive*
MONTAGUE ELEGANT, *overseer of villains*
RODNEY X. URBANE, *apprentice villain*
DEPUTY HENCH

SCENE 1

TIME: *The Good Old Days.*

SETTING: *The threadbare parlor of the poor-but-honest Sweetingood home. A cabinet is up left, bare except for a cookie jar and a box of crackers. Beside the cabinet is a bucket with a dipper and a small sign,* DON'T WASTE WATER. *Samplers on walls read,* WASTE NOT, WANT NOT; HOME, HUMBLE HOME, *etc. A door is up right, and a window with chicken feed sacks for curtains is up center.*

AT RISE: PRISS, MINNIE, SARAH LOU, *and* NELL *are grouped around bare kitchen table down left, sewing.* GRANNY *sits up right in a rocker, knitting with a ball of twine.* MISS HANNAH *goes to each girl, looking over her stitching. When she comes to* NELL, NELL *hides sewing from her.*

MINNIE (*Squinting at* GRANNY): Granny, what are you knitting for the poor-little-orphans? I never saw wool that stiff before.

GRANNY: Why, Minnie, I'm knitting a nice warm sweater for the poor-little-orphans. But it struck me that wool is mighty expensive this year, so I unraveled me a burlap sack. I'm knitting with burlap. A penny saved . . .

GIRLS (*Dutifully*): Is a penny earned.

MISS HANNAH: Isn't that the truth? Just think of all the money we saved making these aprons for the poor-little-orphans out of old tablecloths. Look at Priss's apron. Neat, I call it. Let's have a look at the rest of the aprons. Hold them up, girls. (*Girls display identical white aprons, except for* NELL, *who looks down at her lap.*) Nell child, show us your apron. (NELL *shakes her head.* PRISS *pulls the apron from* NELL*'s lap, where she has been hiding it.*)

PRISS: She is hiding it, Miss Hannah, and I know *why.* (PRISS *holds up the apron. All gasp.* GRANNY *hides her eyes. The apron is made of white organdy and lace with pink and blue ribbons and embroidery.*)

ALL: Oooh.

MISS HANNAH: Sakes' alive. It's all organdy. *Organdy*—at a dollar a yard!

GRANNY (*Rocking back in distress*): Oh, the expense of it. Satin ribbons! I declare, you'll be the ruination of me, Nell!

SARAH LOU: She didn't sew it for a poor-little-orphan at all. She sewed it for her own glory. She's going to sell it.

NELL (*Spunkily*): I am not either going to sell it. It's for my very own poor-little-orphan.

MINNIE: You're going to give *that* to an orphan? Why, the poor-little-orphan will stick out from all the rest like a butterfly in a moth closet.

GRANNY: I don't know what's got into the girl. French knots! Lace!

MISS HANNAH: It's our duty to take care of the poor, but I don't know about organdy.

NELL: Please, Miss Hannah. Put it into the box with the others. It would be a treat to see the poor-little-orphan's face when she picks it out from all those old tablecloths.

PRISS (*Making a face*): I hope she'll be duly grateful.

NELL: Shucks, I don't care how grateful she is. Just the shine on her face would be enough. Wish I had a little pearl comb to put in the pocket, and a cunning gold locket and . . .

GRANNY: Stop! Stop! These are poor-little-orphans, not your kith and kin from Kansas City. Now, Nell, serve some refreshments for the girls.

ALL (*Looking at each other and grimacing*): Refreshments?

PRISS (*Cautiously*): Same as we had last time, Granny Sweetingood?

GRANNY: To be sure. Well water and sody crackers. (*Girls rise in unison and move toward door.*)

PRISS: Didn't I hear the bell in the valley? I'd best be getting home.

MINNIE: Me, too. I have choir practice, and sody crackers always take the edge off my voice.

SARAH LOU: My mamma needs me to dust the parlor.

MISS HANNAH (*Putting all the aprons away in a box*): I do appreciate the thought, Mrs. Sweetingood, but these aprons have to be packed up directly. (*She quickly puts lid on the box*)

GRANNY: If you won't have the sody crackers this month,

I'll just hold onto them, and we'll have them next month.

NELL: Oh, girls, I was hoping you'd stay and help me entertain my betrothed, Marshal Harry Strongbore.

PRISS: Harry Strongbore, town marshal and professional hero, is coming here? I wish you'd told us before you mentioned the sody crackers.

SARAH LOU: Harry Strongbore. (*She sighs*) And you're engaged to him. Some girls have all the luck.

MINNIE: Harry Strongbore. (*She giggles.*) Let's run down to meet him. Maybe we'll see a bear and he'll save one of us. (*The three girls exit up right.* MISS HANNAH *puts the box under her arm.*)

MISS HANNAH: Harry Strongbore. A marshal and a hog man. His pa was a hog man, too. Why, Nell, soon you'll be Mrs. Nell Sweetingood Strongbore. Where are you having the wedding?

NELL: Harry figures to have it in the apple orchard. So's to save money. He reckons the folks can pick their own apples for the wedding supper, and we'll save on the cake and vittles. He's powerful prudent, Harry is.

GRANNY (*Rocking happily*): He's a pure genius at thrift. Such a good man. Just keeps a-saving money and a-rescuing people the livelong day.

MISS HANNAH: Well, I'd best be trotting along. Maybe I'll get a chance to shake hands with him. He's so handsome. Goodbye, Mrs. Sweetingood. Goodbye, Nell. (*She exits up right.*)

NELL: Goodbye, Miss Hannah. (*She dusts the table, looking at the window, center.*) Granny, I've been thinking. Now it's spring, why don't I put up some nice new curtains?

GRANNY (*Alarmed*): New curtains? What's the matter with the ones we have? We've only had them five years. You can't be too hasty-mouthed, Nell. You have to study about the curtains some.

NELL: I have. I've been studying about them for four years, ten months and twenty-one days. (*The door up right opens.* HARRY STRONGBORE *poses in doorway, grinning.*)

HARRY: Yoo-hoo. I have arrived.

GRANNY (*Fluttering*): He's here. You come right on in, Harry. Nell, isn't he a sight for sore eyes?

NELL (*Matter-of-factly*): He comes every day, Granny. Hello, Harry.

HARRY (*Entering and posing again*): Nell! My betrothed. (*He holds his hands behind his back.*) I'll bet you don't know what I brought for you.

NELL (*Hopefully*): Flowers? I had a hankering for flowers today, Harry.

HARRY: Better than that. Come on, Granny, over to the table. I want you to see this, too. (*He picks up* GRANNY, *rocker and all, and brings her to the table.* NELL *crosses slowly down left and sits left of the table.* HARRY *brings out a folder of press clippings labeled* HARRY STRONGBORE—PRESS CLIPPINGS.)

GRANNY: Press clippings! More of your wonderful rescues. Look, Nell.

NELL (*Resigned*): I'm looking, Granny. Seems to me that's all I ever do—look at Harry.

HARRY: Now these are yesterday's rescues. I had a good day yesterday. Press coverage as far north as Kansas City. Here I am in profile. (*He demonstrates, turning his face.*) Now this one doesn't do me justice. I rescued Abigail Hickenlooper from a Brahma bull and she kept clinging to me, grateful-like. She covered up half my face. (NELL *looks away, disappointed.*)

GRANNY (*Sharply*): Nell, you're not paying proper regard to the pictures.

NELL: Oh, they're nice. Real nice. So were the ones last week. And the week before. But—could I speak my mind, Harry?

HARRY (*Magnanimously*): You go right ahead, Nell.

NELL: Well, it's about where we're going to live after we're married, Harry. Over in the valley I saw such a cunning little white clapboard house. There were roses climbing up the walls to beat the band. I figured, with my egg money we could afford that little house.

GRANNY: Spend your egg money on a frivolous house with no-account roses crawling all over it? Scandalous!

HARRY (*Patting* NELL*'s hand patronizingly*): Now, now. We're going to keep all our money in the bank, Nell. For the hog farm. It takes a heap of money to feed twenty thousand hogs.

GRANNY: That's a pretty thought—twenty thousand hogs! And you'll know each one by name, won't you, Harry?

HARRY: I'll make it my business to, Granny.

NELL: But where'll we live, Harry?

HARRY: Shucks, I wanted to keep it a secret. (NELL *brightens.*) But Granny knows how fond you are of this house, so she's offered to let us live here for ten or fifteen years, till we pay for the hog farm.

NELL (*Dismayed*): Here?

GRANNY: I knew she'd be overjoyed. And I've put up a whole carton of sody crackers for the jolly evenings around the candle.

HARRY: Right, Granny. Think of all the happy times we're going to have—Nell, and me, and Granny and the press clippings. (*There is a knock at the door.*) I expect that's Deputy Hench. I told him to notify me if anything began to commence down in the valley. Come in, Deputy. (DEPUTY HENCH *enters, chewing a straw. He removes his hat.*)

HENCH (*Removing the straw from his mouth and drawl-*

ing): Howdy, Mrs. Sweetingood, Nell. I just came up from the valley because Harry told me as how I was to come up here if anything transpired down yonder.

HARRY: Well?

HENCH: Well. You know the laundry.

HARRY: Yes.

HENCH: I didn't say which laundry, so you can't know the laundry I mean. You know Ma Bailey's laundry on the other side of the street from Ah Woo's laundry?

HARRY: Get on with it. I know every laundry in town. There are only two.

HENCH: Yes, well, I was passing Ma Bailey's laundry and she hollered for me. Know what she told me?

HARRY: What did she tell you?

HENCH: She told me your shirts are not done.

HARRY: You came up here to tell me my shirts are not done?

HENCH: But I left them there a month ago. But that's not what I was going to tell you. After I passed the laundry, I was hot from walking, and I stopped at Doc Haines' drug store for a sarsaparilla, and you know what I found out?

HARRY: No. Wait—is Doc sick again?

HENCH: Of course not! But I found out that Doc Haines cheats. He doesn't use sarsaparilla in his soda water. He uses birch bark.

HARRY: Deputy, I am a busy man.

HENCH: I just thought you ought to know what goes on in this valley. Then I moseyed over to the bank, and, Marshal, it's a shame!

HARRY: What is?

HENCH: The pens are all dry. They don't give you any ink to speak of. I figured to write a letter with the free pens, but I couldn't get ink for love nor money. Oh, yes. The bank manager was all tied up in his office. Seems as how

Montague Elegant, Overseer of Villains, is back in town. And he has a new apprentice villain, Rodney X. Urbane.

HARRY (*Rising and posing*): Say no more, Deputy Hench. You did your duty. Now get back to town. Take the shortcut, and let the newspapers know that I'm appearing at the bank in exactly ten minutes. That'll give me time to change into my white chaps and silver spurs. (HENCH *puts on his hat and tips it to the ladies, exiting up right.*) Nell, Granny, my duty calls me. It's not that I don't appreciate your company, but yonder, in the valley, is a bank manager all tied up. He needs me, ladies. He needs me.

GRANNY: Oh, how noble. Just trot yourself off. Don't stand on ceremony.

HARRY (*Posing at door*): Farewell. (*He exits.*)

GRANNY: Well, I hope you thank your lucky stars for a feller like that. It's not every man who averages three rescues a day and can run a hog farm, too.

NELL: I expect so, Granny. Everybody tells me I'm lucky. Maybe if they tell me long enough, pretty soon I'll begin to feel lucky.

GRANNY: Are you feeling poorly?

NELL: No, ma'am. It's just that after Harry leaves, I feel so—numb.

GRANNY: Feel like you've been kicked in the head?

NELL: Yes, ma'am.

GRANNY (*Chuckling*): Why, child, that's love. Now, I reckon it's time for us to gather the watercress for supper. You know what we'll have with our watercress salad?

NELL: What, Granny?

GRANNY: We'll split us a fat hummingbird. Come on, Nell. (*They exit right.* MONTAGUE ELEGANT *enters stealthily from left. He turns and beckons to* RODNEY X. URBANE, *who attempts to enter stealthily, but trips on his cane. He carries book, candy, and bouquet.*)

ELEGANT: Here, Urbane. Give me the cane. You obviously can't manage it.

URBANE: Sorry. My feet keep getting tangled up. (*He looks around distastefully.*) I say, Elegant, this place doesn't look at all promising. Did you say there's money here?

ELEGANT (*Laughing richly*): Heh, heh. Little does the owner know. This property is rolling in money. Acres of green, green money.

URBANE: All I saw was acres of watercress.

ELEGANT: That's it! Watercress. Do you know what the government just found out about watercress? Properly distilled, watercress juice will propel a new horseless carriage at the astonishing speed of thirty-five miles per hour. Now do you understand?

URBANE: My mind boggles.

ELEGANT: Don't say that. Never boggle. Ogle, but do not boggle.

URBANE: Ogle. But do not boggle. Yes, I have it.

ELEGANT: Suppose we review the mission, step by step. Operation: Deed. Do you have your handbook open for reference? (URBANE *nods, shows him a book*) Step One?

URBANE: Bribery. I bribe the owner of the property.

ELEGANT: What bribes did you bring along?

URBANE: Flowers and chocolates.

ELEGANT: Good, Now, since the fair owner of this property is a maiden pure in heart, she will refuse your goodies (*He demonstrates.*) with a sigh and with face averted—so. Next?

URBANE: I offer her a life of luxury.

ELEGANT: To which she will cry, "Heaven forbid!" They never vary from the text. Next?

URBANE: I threaten. (*He scowls.*)

ELEGANT (*Stepping back and examining* URBANE): Very nice scowl. You have good eyebrows for this sort of thing. Now, let me see you leer. Give us the advanced leer. URBANE *twitches his mustache and tries to leer. He sneezes.*)

URBANE (*Apologetically*): I always seem to sneeze when I leer.

ELEGANT: Well, some of us have it; some don't. However, it is at this point that some of you apprentice villains boggle. The fair maiden gets to you. Don't soften. Be resolute. Outsneer her tears. Outsnarl her pleas. But have a certain style—a flair. (*He twirls his cape.*) Work up to a climax. Don't throw the buzz saw at her first. Begin with something small—like tying her to a chair. Above all, don't boggle.

URBANE: I won't. I won't boggle.

ELEGANT (*Patting him on the back*): Good chap. Except for that unfortunate leer, you have the makings of a first-class villain. Now, Rodney X. Urbane, I shall retire and leave the field to you. (*He bows and tips his hat.*)

URBANE (*Alarmed*): I say, Elegant, you're going to leave me alone? With a strange girl?

ELEGANT: Of course. This is where we separate the meanies from the boys. Farewell, Urbane! (*He exits left.*)

URBANE (*Crossing after him*): But, dash it all, I'm not ready. (NELL *appears at the door up right, with a basket of watercress over her arm. She watches* URBANE, *who is standing with his back to her. She puts the basket down on the table.*)

NELL: Howdy, stranger. (URBANE *jumps, and whirls around.*)

URBANE: Oh! You startled me. (*Aside*) What now? (*He squints at his book.*) Flowers. (*He presents the bouquet to* NELL.) Pray accept these flowers, my lovely creature. (NELL *grabs them without hesitation.*)

NELL (*Inhaling deeply*): Well, thank *you*. I had a powerful hankering for flowers today. (*She admires him*) My, aren't you elegant!

URBANE (*Tipping his hat*): Actually, I'm Urbane. Rodney X. Urbane. An impresario of the ipso facto. Businessman to you, my dear. Have a chocolate. (*He offers her a box of candy.*)

NELL: Thank *you*. This is a real fine way to do business. (*She takes a candy.*)

URBANE: Suppose we get down to brass tacks. I have examined what you laughingly call your land, and I find it to be totally worthless. Heh, heh. (*He coughs.*) I never could cackle properly. However, I thought I might do you a favor. I'll take this worthless land off your hands for twenty dollars. How about that, eh? (*He tries to leer and begins to sneeze.* NELL *helpfully pinches his nose.*)

NELL: There. Granny showed me how to stop a sneeze. Better now? (URBANE *nods sheepishly.*) To tell you the truth, Mr. Urbane, you wouldn't want our land. There's nothing on it but watercress. It's worthless.

URBANE: Don't argue with me. I tell you this land is worthless. Think of it—with twenty dollars you could go clear to Kansas City. (NELL *nods.*) You don't like that, eh? You could buy a Paris dress. (NELL *nods.*) You could even buy a rabbit-trimmed cloak. Am I correct? (NELL *nods.*) Don't argue with me!

NELL: I wasn't going to.

URBANE: Why not? The handbook specifically states that at this particular point you, the fair maiden, argue angrily. When you don't argue angrily, I get all upset. You ought to be saying, "What, leave my humble but happy home? Never!"

NELL: But shucks, if I had my druthers, I'd leave here in a minute flat. I'd rather live in a white clapboard house with roses climbing to beat the band.

URBANE (*Trying a new tactic*): Why didn't you say so? I can take you away from all this! (*He twirls his cape, which falls off.*)

NELL: All what?

URBANE (*Hissing at her, as he wags his finger in her face enticingly*): Sell me your land, me proud beauty, and I will see that you have a mansion with a front and a back porch. Crystal chandeliers. Oriental rugs. Rich purple drapes. Heh, heh. (*He coughs.*)

NELL (*Excitedly*): Purple drapes! Land sakes. That's even better than a little white house. But shouldn't we get acquainted before you declare yourself? (*She curtsies.*) Howdy. My name is Nell Sweetingood. I'm grandchild to Granny Sweetingood, and I'm most nearly seventeen. I can cook chicken with dumplings, and sew shirts, and I use a flat-iron real well.

URBANE (*Taken aback*): Aren't you going to scream virtuously?

NELL: I don't think so.

URBANE: But I want your land. Give me the deed to your land or I'll abduct you to yon sawmill. The buzz saw will do my convincing for me.

NELL (*Puzzled*): Buzz saw?

URBANE (*Snapping his fingers in vexation*): Drat! I spoiled the climax. Forget what I said about the buzz saw. (*He takes a rope from his pocket.*) Now, my proud beauty!

NELL: Oh, you do say the nicest things. Harry never calls me pretty names. (*She gazes adoringly at* URBANE.)

URBANE (*Winding the rope around* NELL): How do you tie a girl up? They should give us Boy Scout training before they send us out on a mission. Imperious demoiselle, I have you at my mercy!

NELL (*Aside*): He's speaking French. What an educated feller. The only language Harry knows is hog calling.

URBANE (*Looking at the messy rope job*): Miss Nell, would

you be so kind as to sit down? I have to finish tying you up. (*He puts a chair under her.* NELL *sits down obligingly*)

NELL: Anything to make your job easier. Are you practicing for a rodeo?

URBANE (*Tying a final knot*): There. Now you are as helpless as a kitten.

NELL: My, it certainly is tight, Mr. Urbane.

URBANE: Too tight? I'll loosen it a little. Dash it all, I'm most frightfully sorry. (*Adjusts rope*) Is that better? (NELL *nods.*) Now! I have you in my power. (*He rubs his hands.*) You will do as I command, or I'll fling your helpless screaming form across the merciless steel rails of the Atchison, Topeka and the Sante Fe. (*Acting out his words*) Listen. Do you hear the distant thunder of the locomotive, far down the tracks? Makes you think a little, doesn't it? What's that? Ah, the shrill whistle of an oncoming monster hurtling toward you. A split second more and then . . . farewell, little Nell. Heh, heh, heh. (*He coughs.*)

NELL: Mr. Urbane, you sure tell a peach of a story!

URBANE: You aren't impressed? You didn't turn a hair. All right, listen. How's this? (*Gesturing*) You are high, high on a precipice, on a single ledge. Below you are jagged rocks, and a foaming sea. In the distance a construction company is blasting the cliff. At my command they light a certain fuse. The precipice disappears in a cloud of dust, and off the cliff hurtles a small, slight form. Down, down, down into the foaming sea. (URBANE *begins to cry.*) Farewell, Miss Nell. Oh! Horrible! How could I have done such a thing! Forgive me, Miss Nell. Don't cry.

NELL: I'm not crying. You are.

URBANE: I know. Don't tell anyone, I beg you. It's my fatal flaw. I have a tender heart. I can't even stand mousetraps. Oh, drat it all, keep your deed. I'll go. I shall never darken your door again. (*He stalks to the door up right.*)

NELL: Don't go, Mr. Urbane. If you want that deed so badly, you can have it. It's in yonder cookie jar.

URBANE (*Crossing to cabinet, and taking out the deed*): You *are* a sport. I say, would you mind doing me just one more small favor? Would you scream a little?

NELL: Scream? Whatever for? I haven't enjoyed a visit so much since the Fuller Brush man dropped by with a sample of vegetable brushes.

URBANE (*Downcast*): The fact is, Miss Nell, I'm a perishing failure at my profession. I do have my pride. A modest scream would let my compatriot, Mr. Elegant, know that I have succeeded at my mission.

NELL: Oh, a victory yell. Why, to be sure. Anything to oblige. (*She shouts loudly. Instantly* HARRY STRONGBORE *crashes through the door, followed by* DEPUTY HENCH *with a flash camera, and* GRANNY *cowering behind them.*)

HARRY (*Striking a pose*): Nell! Poor little Nell! (*He unties her, while* HENCH *tries to focus the camera.* NELL *is furious.*)

NELL: Help! Don't you dare touch me, Harry Strongbore. Help, Rodney X. Urbane! Help! (HARRY *puts her over his shoulder.*)

URBANE (*Putting up his fists*): Unhand that maiden, Marshal. (*He wrestles* NELL *away from* HARRY, *and puts her over his shoulder.*)

HARRY: Curse you, Rodney X. Urbane!

GRANNY (*Putting her hands over her ears*): Harry, watch your language! (HARRY *grabs* NELL *and tucks her under his arm, kicking. He poses.*)

HARRY: Deputy, do your duty. Shoot me! (*He mugs as* HENCH *shoots a flash picture.*)

HENCH: Got you. That was a good one, Harry. Now your left side. (HARRY *turns his profile.* HENCH *takes another picture.* NELL *squirms free and stands, hands on hips, between* HARRY *and* URBANE.)

HARRY: Nell, what has been going on betwixt this cut-rate villain and yourself?

URBANE (*Going down on his knees*): Miss Nell. I kneel before you. I offer you my heart, my soul, my chocolates.

HARRY: Don't listen to him, Nell. He hasn't got a hog to his name.

URBANE: I ask you once again. Miss Nell, Miss Nell, me proud beauty . . . marry me!

NELL (*Grabbing his hand*): Yes, yes, a thousand times yes! (HARRY'*s mouth drops open.* GRANNY *groans.*)

HENCH (*Brightly*): Close your mouth, Harry. (*He shoots another picture.*) There. I'd surely give a heap to see how that one develops!

CURTAIN

* * *

SCENE 2

TIME: *Five years later.*

SETTING: *The interior of Granny's house, with a few changes. The table is covered with a lace tablecloth, and holds a silver tea service and candles. A fancy sampler on wall reads,* HOME, LAVISH HOME, *and there is a large group picture on the wall right with girls in organdy aprons and boys in top hats and capes. The windows are hung with purple drapes.*

AT RISE: NELL, *in a rich gown, and* URBANE, *in dressing gown and cravat, are seated at table.* NELL *hands* URBANE *a dish of bonbons.*

NELL: One chocolate, Rodney, or two?

URBANE: Two, my treasure. (*There is a knock at door.* NELL, *blowing a kiss to* URBANE, *opens the door.* MONTAGUE ELEGANT *enters.*)

ELEGANT: Greetings, Urbane.

URBANE (*Rising*): Montague Elegant, my old overseer. Come in, please. Won't you sit down?

ELEGANT: No, thank you very much, Urbane. This will only take a minute. We like to follow our apprentices' progress. Frankly, Urbane, we've lost track of you down at Local 13. What happened?

URBANE: I don't know how to tell you. I had a fatal flaw. Don't be offended, Elegant, but I went straight.

ELEGANT (*Reeling back*): Appalling! You didn't.

NELL (*Proudly*): He did.

URBANE: I owe it all to little Nell. (*Embraces* NELL)

ELEGANT (*Horrified*): You're not—!

NELL: We are. (*Showing hand with wedding band*)

ELEGANT (*Pointing to picture on the wall*): And those?

NELL: Those are the poor-little-orphans. We adopted the whole home.

URBANE (*Twirling his moustache*): You can't just take one. It's not fair to the rest. Besides, they're *rich*-little-orphans now.

NELL: Rodney cornered the whole watercress market. He's watercress king.

URBANE: Frankly, old chap, I boggled when I should have ogled.

ELEGANT: Frightful. How can I tell the cads down at Local 13 one of the bunch went good? What can I tell the new apprentice villains? How can I point with pride to a scene like this? (URBANE *and* NELL *sit down, and hold hands across the table, gazing into each other's eyes.*)

URBANE: My treasure! (*The curtain begins to close*)

NELL: My hero!

ELEGANT: Ghastly! He's permanently boggled himself! It's a fate worse than death. (*Curtain*)

THE END

Junior Prom

by Charles F. Wilde

Characters

SUSAN WOODFORD
EDDIE REVELL
MYRNA HAYES
ROBERT FRENCH
MARILYN STONE
ROCKY BLAKE
} *high school students*

HOWARD CROSBY, *principal of Malden Forks High School*
MRS. CROSBY, *his wife*

SETTING: *The trophy room of Malden Forks High School.*

AT RISE: SUSAN WOODFORD *enters, followed by* EDDIE REVELL. *They are both in evening dress.* SUSAN *is in one of the highest dudgeons ever dudgeoned.*

SUSAN (*Upon entering*): Eddie, how could you! Of all the stupid, dumb, weakling things to do! (*She flounces downstage, flops on settee and smoothes her evening gown. She opens her evening bag, removes handkerchief and rubs viciously at dress. The bag is left lying on settee.* EDDIE, *much dejected, follows, miserable but still somewhat defiant.*)

EDDIE: O.K., O.K., so it was stupid, so I'm a weakling . . . so what . . .

SUSAN (*Almost screaming*): So what! Why . . . why . . . I've never been so embarrassed, never in all my life so degraded . . . so *humiliated!*

EDDIE: Aw, you women are always getting humiliated. You never seem happy unless you're playing the martyr. (*He flops into chair at right.*)

SUSAN (*Rising*): Martyr! (*She walks upstage and back in her fury.*) *Martyr!* You mean to insinuate that I'm playing martyr because of what happened out there?

EDDIE: O.K., O.K., so you're not a martyr . . . that's that.

SUSAN (*Bending over him*): And that's all you can say, is it, Mr. Revell?

EDDIE: What else can I say? We're dancing . . . I drop you . . . (*Shrugs it off.*)

SUSAN (*Hardly able to keep her hands off him*): You drop me . . . *You drop me!!* You . . . you . . . you oaf!

EDDIE: You didn't hit the floor, did you?

SUSAN: Eddie Revell, I could kill you!

EDDIE: Boy, you certainly hit the ceiling, though! (*Laughing.*)

SUSAN: Don't you dare laugh at me . . . you . . . you clumsy Frankenstein, you!

EDDIE: Now I'm Frankenstein. Ye gods . . . what can a man do?

SUSAN: Everybody looking . . . especially that Myrna Hayes . . .

EDDIE: She's not so bad. Anyway, she's not always knocking herself out on the dance floor.

SUSAN: If you were a gentleman you wouldn't say that!

EDDIE: If you'd dance like normal people, we wouldn't have fallen. And besides, this prom is no place for that way-out stuff.

SUSAN: I'll dance any way I like, Eddie Revell, at a prom or anywhere else.

EDDIE: O.K. Then you'll have to take the consequences.

SUSAN: I'll find somebody who can dance.

EDDIE: Get Rocky Blake. He has more twists than a dislocated pretzel.

SUSAN: I'll get whom I please. (*She starts for the door, but just then* MR. *and* MRS. CROSBY *enter.* SUSAN *turns back.*)

CROSBY: Hello, Susan . . . Eddie.

SUSAN *and* EDDIE: Hello . . . Mr. Crosby . . . Mrs. Crosby. (EDDIE *rises.*)

MRS. CROSBY: Hello, Susan. Lovely dance, isn't it?

SUSAN: Uh . . . yes.

CROSBY: Have you two been on the floor yet?

EDDIE (*Meaningfully*): We certainly have been on the floor.

MRS. CROSBY (*Noticing* SUSAN *rubbing her dress*): What's the matter, Susan?

SUSAN: Oh . . . I got a spot on my dress somehow . . . it won't come off.

MRS. CROSBY (*Crossing*): Let me see. (*Examining dress*) What a shame! Don't rub it. You'll only spoil the fabric. (*To* MR. CROSBY) Howard . . .

CROSBY: Yes, dear.

MRS. CROSBY: May I have your keys? I'll take Susan down to the homemaking room. There's some cleaning fluid there.

CROSBY: Of course. (*Hands her his keys*)

MRS. CROSBY: Thank you. Come on, Susan, and we'll have that spot out in no time. (*They exit.*)

EDDIE (*Slumping into settee*): Women . . . phooey!

CROSBY (*Joining him*): Well, Eddie, you sound a bit cynical.

EDDIE: Cynical. Yeah . . . that's me.

CROSBY: Trouble with Susan?

EDDIE: Yeah . . . as usual.

CROSBY: What about?

EDDIE: She doesn't like my footwork.

CROSBY: Footwork? You mean your dancing?

EDDIE: If you call it that. Gosh, Mr. Crosby, women can certainly get your goat. All they want to do is the very latest dances. They aren't satisfied with ordinary dancing.

CROSBY: I see. . . .

EDDIE: The trouble is that Susan knows all the new steps and I don't—I'm just not with it when it comes to dancing.

CROSBY: It's really too bad to have it worry you.

EDDIE: *I'm* not worried, it's just Susan. As soon as we get on the dance floor and the drummers start their weird routine—

CROSBY: I don't follow you, Eddie.

EDDIE (*Laughing*): The licorice sticks—I mean the clarinets . . . anyway, as soon as they start, Susan says, "Oh, Eddie, that really sends me!"

CROSBY: Sends?

EDDIE: Yes, sends. She was sent, all right—right to the floor! (*Laughing*) She tried this new dance, and that did it. The next thing I knew, Susan was practically on the floor, and she pulled me down with her. Boy, was I embarrassed.

CROSBY (*Laughing*): And Susan? Was that how she got the spot on her dress?

EDDIE: Yes, and I'll never hear the end of it.

CROSBY: She'll get over it. They always do. Now, Eddie, why don't you go and drown your sorrows in a glass of punch. When Susan comes back, everything will be all right. Mrs. Crosby will see to that. Go on, now.

EDDIE (*Rising*): O.K. . . . Won't you come along and have something?

CROSBY: No, thanks. I'll stay here until the ladies get back.

EDDIE: O.K. (*Exits.* MR. CROSBY *goes to desk, picks up magazine and moves upstage left to easy chair among palms. He has no sooner settled down when* MYRNA

HAYES *and* ROBERT FRENCH *enter.* MYRNA *is highly amused.*)

MYRNA (*Upon entering*): Honestly, Bob, I thought I'd die.

ROBERT: It really did me good to see Eddie flat on his face for once. (*They come downstage and sit on settee.*)

MYRNA: Eddie? Huh . . . Susan, you mean . . . the little cat . . . running around in last year's dress. You'd think the school couldn't get along without her. She gives me a pain . . .

ROBERT: . . . the same pain she gives me. Tried to tell me how to make the punch. (MYRNA *sees* SUSAN's *evening bag on settee. Picks it up, looks it over, puts it down*) I told her where to get off. I said, "Listen, Lady Susan, I made punch when you were still imbibing your baby formulas. Beat it."

MYRNA: What did she say?

ROBERT: What could she say? Nothing. She just disappeared. (*Coming closer to* MYRNA) But, listen, baby, let's not talk about those two drips. Let's talk about you (*Closing in*) . . . or better yet, let's not talk.

MYRNA (*Snuggling up*): Let's not, honey. (*Their heads come together, but before they can kiss,* MR. CROSBY *rises and comes downstage.*)

CROSBY: Hello, Robert . . . Myrna.

ROBERT *and* MYRNA (*Moving apart,* ROBERT *rising*): Hello, Mr. Crosby.

CROSBY: Having a good time?

ROBERT: Yeah . . . great . . . great time.

MYRNA: We . . . we just came in here for a minute.

CROSBY: I see.

ROBERT: Well . . . guess we'd better be getting back, eh, Myrna?

MYRNA: Uh . . . yes . . . well . . . nice seeing you, Mr. Crosby.

CROSBY: Nice seeing *you.*

MYRNA: Goodbye.

CROSBY: Goodbye. (*They exit.* MR. CROSBY *returns to his corner just as* ROCKY BLAKE *and* MARILYN STONE *enter. She is limping, one shoe off, leaning on* ROCKY's *shoulder.* ROCKY *has one of her shoes in his hand. He guides her to settee. She puts her bag next to* SUSAN's. ROCKY *chews gum vigorously throughout conversation.*)

ROCKY: Here, sit down. I'll see if I can get this heel back on. (*Examines shoe and heel.*)

CROSBY (*Coming downstage*): Hello, Rocky . . . Marilyn.

ROCKY *and* MARILYN: Oh, hello, Mr. Crosby.

CROSBY: Trouble?

ROCKY: I'm afraid so. Marilyn lost a heel out there. I guess the music got too wild.

MARILYN: The music! You mean you did. Honestly, Mr. Crosby, you'd think I was a sack of oats or something, the way he throws me around.

ROCKY: When I dance, I dance. (*Even now he goes into contortions as music is heard from gym.*)

CROSBY: Hm-m-m. Seems to me there should be a little rearranging of partners around here. Here, Rocky, let me see that. (*He takes shoe and heel, goes to desk and picks up heavy bookend and goes to work*) So you don't like the new dances, Marilyn?

MARILYN: Heavens, no . . . especially at a prom.

ROCKY (*Dancing and chewing gum with equal gusto*): What's the diff? Dancing is dancing, isn't it, at a prom or at the Snazzy Pigeon?

CROSBY (*Looking up from his work*): The which?

ROCKY: The Snazzy Pigeon . . . down on the corner of Eighth and Lincoln. Haven't you ever been there, Mr. Crosby? Terrific discothèque—great bands.

MARILYN: Really, Rocky! Mr. Crosby at the Snazzy Pigeon! What do you think he is?

CROSBY: Sounds interesting.

ROCKY: It's respectable . . .

CROSBY: I'm sure of that . . . perhaps some night I'll look in at the . . . uh . . . Snazzy Pigeon. (*Looking at repaired shoe*) Well, Marilyn, I think that will hold, provided, of course, Rocky tempers his dancing a bit.

MARILYN: Oh, thank you, Mr. Crosby.

ROCKY (*Taking shoe and putting it on* MARILYN'S *foot*): Let's go, babe. There . . . O.K.?

MARILYN (*Standing*): Fine . . . you're a good shoemaker, Mr. Crosby.

CROSBY: In my business you have to be a bit of everything. Now you two run along . . . and take it easy!

ROCKY: Easy's the word. Come on. Let's get going. Time's a-wastin'. (MARILYN *reaches for her bag, picks* SUSAN'S *up by mistake, looks at it, then puts it down and takes her own.* MARILYN *and* ROCKY *exit.* MR. CROSBY *smiles, takes his magazine and once more is about to return to his corner when* SUSAN, *very excited, dashes in, followed by* MRS. CROSBY. SUSAN *goes directly to settee, picks up bag and goes through it hurriedly.* CROSBY *comes down stage.*)

CROSBY: What's the trouble?

SUSAN (*Still pawing through bag; hysterically*): It's not here . . . it's gone!

MRS. CROSBY: My dear . . . let me . . . (*She takes bag and empties contents on settee.* SUSAN *searches frantically.*)

CROSBY: What is this . . . what's the matter?

SUSAN (*Almost in tears*): My ring . . . my mother's ring . . . it's gone . . . it's gone!

CROSBY: Ring?

SUSAN: An emerald ring. It was in my bag . . . in a coin purse.

MRS. CROSBY (*Replacing articles in bag*): You're sure you put it in here?

SUSAN: Yes . . . when I washed my hands. I meant to put it on, but I forgot . . . and now it's gone!

CROSBY: Is it a valuable ring, Susan?

SUSAN: It's my mother's . . . and I didn't tell her I was wearing it. It's a real emerald, an heirloom. Mr. Crosby, (*Crying*) what'll I do?

CROSBY (*Leading her to settee. They both sit down*): Control yourself, Susan. If the ring is in the building, we'll find it, don't you worry. Tell me . . . when did you first miss it?

SUSAN: Just now when Mrs. Crosby was cleaning my dress. I suddenly remembered I'd left it in my bag, and I came back.

CROSBY: You're positive it was here when you came in with Eddie?

SUSAN: I know it was.

MRS. CROSBY: Were you here all the time Susan and I were away, Howard?

CROSBY: Yes . . . I was . . . and four others were, too.

SUSAN (*Excited*): Who were they? It must have been . . .

CROSBY: Now, Susan, we must be careful. After all, we can't accuse anybody wrongfully. There is always the possibility that you might have lost the ring somewhere else.

SUSAN: But I didn't, I tell you. I had it when I came in here. I know I did.

MRS. CROSBY: We can have those four people you mention in and question them.

SUSAN: Can't we call the police? They'd soon find the thief.

CROSBY: We may have to, eventually, but remember, Susan, it will be better for the school, and for you, too—since you took the ring without your mother's permission—if we can recover it without undue publicity. If we call the police, the whole matter may get into the papers . . . Do you see, Susan? (*She nods*) Good. But I will call in those four students.

SUSAN: Who were they?

CROSBY: First, Robert French and Myrna Hayes . . .

SUSAN: Myrna Hayes . . .

MRS. CROSBY: And the others, Howard?

CROSBY: Rocky Blake and Marilyn Stone. I'll get them. (*Exits*)

SUSAN: Do you think they took it . . . I mean . . . maybe one of them?

MRS. CROSBY: Let's hope not. I'd hate to think one of our students would do such a thing . . . and Susan . . . (*She sits down.*)

SUSAN: Yes, Mrs. Crosby?

MRS. CROSBY: Let Mr. Crosby handle this. If the ring can be found, he'll find it, I'm sure.

SUSAN: Yes, Mrs. Crosby.

MRS. CROSBY: And control yourself, Susan. Don't make any accusations. We'll hear what these people have to say.

SUSAN: Yes, Mrs. Crosby. (CROSBY *enters, ushering in* ROBERT, MYRNA, ROCKY *and* MARILYN, *who look bewildered.*)

CROSBY: Come in, please. (*They all come downstage*) Sit down, girls. (MYRNA *sits in easy chair at right,* MARILYN *next to* MRS. CROSBY. BOYS *stand right, just back of* MYRNA'S *chair.* MR. CROSBY *occupies center of stage*) Something unfortunate has happened. (*The four look at each other in surprise.*)

ROBERT: Unfortunate?

CROSBY: Yes . . . and we thought perhaps we could settle it here right now . . . without the necessity of calling in the police. (*He looks closely at all four for any reactions. For once* ROCKY *stops his gum chewing.*)

ROCKY: The police!

CROSBY: Yes, Rocky, the police.

ROCKY: What's up?

CROSBY: Well, this is the story. Susan came in here a short time ago, just before you people, and left her evening bag on the settee for a few minutes while she left the room with Mrs. Crosby. In the bag was a very valuable ring.

MYRNA: You mean that emerald ring, Susan?

SUSAN: Why, yes.

CROSBY: Yes, Myrna . . . an emerald ring. How did you know?

MYRNA: Why, I saw it on Susan's finger . . . in the washroom.

CROSBY: I see. Well, anyway, in Susan's absence the ring disappeared.

ROCKY: You mean somebody stole it?

CROSBY: "Stole" is a word I dislike using, Rocky. Anyway, it's gone, and it disappeared from this room within the last fifteen minutes.

ROBERT: Maybe somebody came in while Susan was gone. There are a lot of strangers here tonight.

CROSBY: No, Robert, I was here the whole time, and during that time the only ones to enter this room were you four.

MYRNA: Well, you're not accusing us, are you?

CROSBY: I'm not accusing anyone, Myrna. I just thought that if . . . uh . . . by accident the coin purse might have been picked up . . . it could be returned, and that would end the matter. If not, well, it means a lot of unfortunate publicity for the school.

MYRNA: Well, I don't have it.

ROCKY: You can search me.

CROSBY: You wouldn't object?

ROCKY: Why should I? Look! (*Reaches into one hip pocket, pulls out white handkerchief. Reaches into other pocket, pulls out red bandanna. Hides it hurriedly*) Jeepers! How did that get in there?

CROSBY: Hold it, Rocky. I'll call the coach. You boys can go into his office.

ROCKY: Sure. (CROSBY *and boys start for door.*)

MRS. CROSBY: May I see your bag, Myrna? (*She rises.*)

MYRNA: Why not? (*Rises and empties contents of her bag on chair*) There!

MRS. CROSBY: Marilyn . . . yours?

MARILYN (*Pausing, then with sudden determination*): No! (CROSBY *and the boys stop and come back, surprised at* MARILYN's *refusal.* MYRNA, *replacing articles in her bag, stops and stares at* MARILYN.)

SUSAN: But, Marilyn . . .

MARILYN (*On verge of tears*): I'm not showing what's in my bag, and nobody's going to search me.

MRS. CROSBY: But Marilyn, if you're not afraid . . .

MARILYN: I'm not afraid.

MRS. CROSBY: Then why . . .

MARILYN: I don't have the ring. If my word isn't good enough . . .

SUSAN: Of course it is, Marilyn, but don't you see . . .

MARILYN: No, I don't.

MRS. CROSBY: It will look funny if everyone else submits to a search . . .

MARILYN: Let it look funny, I don't care. I don't have it. (*The* CROSBYS *look at each other, uncertain of the next move.*)

MYRNA: Well, I showed my bag, and I don't see any reason why you can't show yours, unless (*with a toss of her head*) . . . of course, the sweet little Marilyn is a thief.

MRS. CROSBY: Myrna!

MARILYN (*Rising*): I'm not a thief. (*Bursting into tears*) I'm not! I'm not!

MRS. CROSBY (*Comforting her*): There, now.

MYRNA: Then why don't you show what's in your bag?

MARILYN: That's my business.

MYRNA: And an emerald ring is pretty good business, I'd say. Here . . . (*She reaches out suddenly and snatches the bag from* MARILYN *and gives it to* MR. CROSBY) There, Mr. Crosby, I think you'll find the ring.

CROSBY: I'm sorry, Marilyn. I'd much rather you opened it. (*He starts to open the bag.* MARILYN *sinks sobbing to settee. As* CROSBY *reaches into the bag,* EDDIE *enters, now in rare good humor.*)

EDDIE: Hi, Susan. (*He stops and looks around*) Oh, excuse me, I just came in to get Susan. (*Downstage*) Why . . . what's wrong? What's going on. Marilyn, you're crying!

MRS. CROSBY: Eddie, Susan has lost a very valuable ring.

EDDIE: Ring? Valuable? She's crazy. Susan never owned anything valuable in her life . . . unless you'd call me valuable, and Susan sure thinks she owns me . . . Ha! Ha!

SUSAN: No, Eddie, it's true . . . my mother's ring.

EDDIE: Oh, your mother's ring . . . that's different.

SUSAN: I had it in my evening bag . . . in a coin purse . . . and now it's gone.

MARILYN: And they think I stole it.

SUSAN: No, Marilyn.

EDDIE: Huh? Coin purse? (*Reaching into his pocket*) You mean this? (*Holds up coin purse*)

SUSAN (*Grabbing it*): Eddie! Yes, this is it. (*Opening it and withdrawing ring*) Oh, Eddie, you darling. (*In tears*) Where did you get it?

EDDIE: Where did I get it? Why, it fell out of your evening bag when you hit the floor a little while ago.

SUSAN: Why didn't you tell me?

EDDIE: How did I know it had anything valuable in it? The only thing you ever carry in it is carfare, and not that when you're certain I'll be around. Besides, you were in no state to be told anything, if you will remember, Miss Susan Woodford.

MYRNA (*With a toss of her head*): All that fuss for nothing. We could do with a little intelligence around here. Come on, Robert. (*They leave.*)

MR. CROSBY: And all's well that ends well. (*Handing bag to* MARILYN) Here you are, my dear.

MARILYN: Thank you.

SUSAN: But, Marilyn, if you didn't have the ring . . .

MARILYN: I know I acted stupidly but, well . . . (*She looks appealingly at* MRS. CROSBY, *who motions* MR. CROSBY *out. He signals to the boys. They all leave, the boys shaking their heads.*)

MARILYN (*As door closes*): I suppose it's silly, but I just couldn't show what was in my bag . . . not with that Myrna Hayes around.

MRS. CROSBY: I don't understand, Marilyn.

MARILYN: Promise you won't tell?

MRS. CROSBY: Of course.

MARILYN: Look! (*Opens bag and takes out small piece of pasteboard*) See . . . I didn't have the money for a new evening gown, and I had to rent one. This is the ticket. I just couldn't let Myrna see it. She'd have blabbed it all over school.

MRS. CROSBY (*Taking ticket, reading*): "The Hi-Class Shop . . . gowns for sale and rent . . . one evening gown . . . rental fee three dollars." (*Sympathetic, yet hiding a smile*) Why, you poor dear!

SUSAN: Marilyn, I'm sorry, and I don't blame you a bit. I wouldn't want Myrna to know about this.

MARILYN: You're sure you won't tell?

MRS. CROSBY: Not in a million years. Now, come on, dear, we'll get rid of those tears. Coming, Susan?

SUSAN: I'll wait here for Eddie. See you later, Marilyn.

(MRS. CROSBY *and* MARILYN *go out.* SUSAN *pulls out compact and makes herself up.* EDDIE *appears at door.*)

EDDIE: Can I come in?

SUSAN: Sure . . . everything is all right.

EDDIE (*Consulting his dance program*): I guess it's our dance.

SUSAN: Is it?

EDDIE: Yes . . . and listen, you've caused enough trouble with all that wild dancing.

SUSAN: All right, Eddie, anything you say.

EDDIE: I fixed it with the band so we'll get a nice, slow waltz.

SUSAN: All right—I'm ready.

EDDIE: Then come on. The music's starting. (*They go to door,* EDDIE *opens it, and noisy, loud rock music is heard.* EDDIE *shrugs shoulders helplessly, takes* SUSAN'S *hand, and they go out, as the curtain falls.*)

THE END

Background for Nancy

by Susan Manning

Characters

NANCY BARTLETT, *15*
MRS. BARTLETT } *her parents*
MR. BARTLETT }
AUNT NORMA
WILLIE, *15, a neighbor*
MRS. LEROY
CRANE, *17, her son*

SCENE 1

SETTING: *The living room of the Bartlett home.*

AT RISE: NANCY *is sprawled in a chair, deep in thought. Her shoes are on the floor beside her, and her coat is on the floor, nearby, partly under a table.*

NANCY (*Swinging feet down from arm of chair and hitting back of chair with both fists*): I could *die!* I could *just die!* (*She goes to telephone and dials.*) Hello, Aunt Norma, this is Nancy. . . . Oh, all right, I guess. That is, physically all right. Every other way I feel terrible. . . . Listen, Aunt Norma, you simply have to help me! I can't let things go on like this. I'm in the most awful trouble. I could *just die!* What? . . . Of course, I'll tell you what's wrong. It's Mother who's causing all the trouble. . . . What? . . . Of course I'm not crazy. Listen, Aunt Norma, it's just that this wonderful man, this dreamboat, is visiting the Harpers next door. His name is Crane Leroy and he came over today to ask Mother where the nearest service station was so he could get a tire changed. . . . Of course, he knows how to change one himself, but he's the type that has service stations do it for him. Anyhow, he's a stranger in town, and when he came, Mother was scrubbing the front steps! . . . Of course I talked to him, too, but how can a girl impress a sophisticated man as being beautiful and glamorous when he sees her mother scrubbing steps in an old sweater and galoshes! Why couldn't Mother wear those great clothes that they show in *Vogue* and *Harper's Bazaar*? . . . You'll come over? . . . Thanks a lot. (MRS. BARTLETT *comes in left, carrying a pile of school books and ironed laundry. She is wearing a housedress and apron, and low-heeled shoes.*)

MRS. BARTLETT: Here are your books, Nancy dear. You left them in the kitchen. Take them to your room. And as you go, would you mind hanging up your coat?

NANCY (*Absentmindedly*): Yes, Mother. (*Intensely*) Mother, have you ever thought of buying some of those new lounging pajamas all the fashion magazines are showing this year?

MRS. BARTLETT: Lounging pajamas? (*Laughing*) What on earth do you mean? When do I have time to lounge, with you and Dad to pick up after?

NANCY: They're the latest thing, Mother, and think how sophisticated you'd look if Crane—I mean, if anyone came in when you were arranging flowers, or reading, in lounging pajamas and false eyelashes. *That* would be a glamorous background for a glamorous girl who wanted to impress someone.

MRS. BARTLETT: Stick out your tongue, Nancy Bartlett! (*She looks at the tongue, feels her daughter's forehead, and laughs.*) Pajamas! Glamorous! Eyelashes! My goodness! Tidy your room, child, and stop talking nonsense. And hang up your coat.

NANCY (*Sighing*): You just don't understand, Mother. How can a girl impress a sophisticated man—

MRS. BARTLETT: Nancy, pick up your coat and take it with you upstairs!

NANCY: Yes, Mother. (MRS. BARTLETT *exits right.* NANCY *picks up coat, sees magazine on table, opens it, drops coat on the floor, and begins to read. The window at left rear opens, and* WILLIE *appears.*)

WILLIE: Hi, Nance! What smells so good?

NANCY (*Not looking up from magazine; bitterly*): It wouldn't be *Tabu* or *My Sin* or any really glamorous smell in *this* house! (*In her normal tone*) What do you think it smells like, beagle nose?

WILLIE: Your mother's cinnamon rolls.

NANCY: Natch. (*She curls up in a chair, still reading magazine.*)

WILLIE: Yipes! (*Falls over the sill into the room*) May I come in?

MRS. BARTLETT (*Appearing at door right with a plate of rolls*): Hello, Willie. Have a sweet roll. How did you do today with your broadcasting? (WILLIE *takes a roll.* NANCY *reaches for one.*)

WILLIE (*Munching on roll*): Gee, these are good, Mrs. Bartlett! (*Enthusiastically*) I talked to another ham in Ontario and another in Quebec today. Yesterday I got a letter from a guy who heard me in Juneau!

MRS. BARTLETT: How wonderful, Willie! Come into the kitchen and tell me all about it. (*With his eyes on the rolls, he follows her right.*)

WILLIE: Thanks a lot, Mrs. Bartlett, may I? I've fixed up a

new hookup that's a honey. (*He turns toward* NANCY *as he reaches the door at right*) I suppose you want to go to the big game Saturday, Nancy. Well, you can relax because I'll take you.

NANCY (*Looking up from magazine*): If a certain party who is visiting next door isn't too disgusted with the squalor of my surroundings, perhaps he will ask me to go with him—

MRS. BARTLETT: Nancy! You deserve a spanking! (*Sees coat lying on the floor*) *Will you pick up your coat!*

WILLIE (*As he and* MRS. BARTLETT *exit*): It's like this, Mrs. Bartlett—I tried the new hookup—(NANCY, *jumping up, closes the door at right, picks up coat but lets it slide off her arm when the door at rear opens and* AUNT NORMA, *carrying a dress box, enters. She is fashionably dressed.*)

NANCY (*Rushing up to her and kissing her*): Aunt Norma, you have saved my life! I know you will help me do something with Mother—make her use eye shadow—lipstick—fake eyelashes—or something! She really must look like you—smart and sophisticated! (AUNT NORMA *puts the box on the table.*)

AUNT NORMA: Nonsense, Nancy! Your mother is a very nice-looking woman! She married very young, and she has always had your father and you to look after. (MRS. BARTLETT, *unseen by* NANCY *and* AUNT NORMA, *has opened the door at right. She listens with her hand over her mouth to keep from laughing.*) Your mother really hasn't the time to spend on herself that I do. I don't have anyone to worry about except me!

NANCY: But it isn't fair! I want Mother to be chic and glamorous, the way all those jet set women are—as I expect to be when I have a daughter. (*Doorbell rings.* MRS. BARTLETT *closes door at right as* NANCY *goes to door at rear and opens it for* MRS. LEROY, *who is smartly dressed.*)

MRS. LEROY (*Coming part-way into room*): I'm Evelyn Leroy, visiting the Harpers—

NANCY: Oh! How do you do, Mrs. Leroy? I'm Nancy Bartlett, and this is my aunt, Miss Bartlett. (AUNT NORMA *nods.*) Won't you sit down?

MRS. LEROY: No, thank you, Nancy. I'd like to post a letter, and Mrs. Harper has gone out and her new maid doesn't know where there's a mailbox in the neighborhood.

NANCY: May I mail it for you? There's a mailbox just a block or so down the street.

MRS. LEROY: No, thank you. I need the exercise. (*She stops.*) Nancy Bartlett. . . . Of course! (*She turns to* NANCY) We Leroys seem to need a lot of attention from neighbors. This morning your maid gave Crane—that's my son—explicit directions for finding a service station, but he actually forgot them—he was so enchanted by your sprightly conversation.

NANCY (*Embarrassed, trying to smile*): Thank you.

MRS. LEROY (*Smiling pleasantly*): I wonder if you'd mind if Crane drops in for a little while this evening. (NANCY *smiles easily.*) The Harpers—well, Crane would enjoy talking to someone nearer his own age.

NANCY: Oh, I'd love to have him come!

MRS. LEROY: Seven, then. Goodbye, Nancy. Very nice to have met you, Miss Bartlett. (*She exits.*)

NANCY: Goodbye, Mrs. Leroy. (*She closes the front door, as* MRS. BARTLETT *appears at door at right. Neither* NANCY *nor* AUNT NORMA *sees her.*)

AUNT NORMA: What a stunning outfit she was wearing!

NANCY (*Resentfully*): She said Crane thought Mother was a maid! How can I have the right background with Mother always wearing housedresses! (*She kicks at the table leg.*) I fed Crane Leroy my best line—but what's the use?

AUNT NORMA: Forget it, Nancy! Your mother dresses for her job, which is to her credit. (MRS. BARTLETT *closes the door, softly.* NANCY *swallows and wipes her eyes*) I'd like to see her a minute.

NANCY (*Raising her voice*): Mother! Aunt Norma wants to see you! (MRS. BARTLETT *enters right.*)

MRS. BARTLETT: Hello, Norma. How are you? Take off your hat, and stay for lunch.

AUNT NORMA: Can't—sorry. (*She takes the box off the table and hands it to* MRS. BARTLETT) Here's a dress—an evening dress I'm passing on. I think you may be able to make something out of it for Nancy when she's grown up—a little more. (MRS. BARTLETT *opens the box.*)

MRS. BARTLETT (*Lifting up dress and looking at it*): It's lovely! Thank you so much, Norma! (NANCY *hugs* AUNT NORMA *behind her mother's back.* MRS. BARTLETT *puts dress back into box and replaces cover.*)

NANCY (*Trying to be casual*): Where did Willie go, Mother?

MRS. BARTLETT: He went to the basement to rummage among the old magazines. (WILLIE *enters at right. His arms are piled with magazines.*)

WILLIE: Gee, thanks for these, Mrs. Bartlett! One of them has a great article on a ham radio operator who made his radio just out of nothing. Oh, hello, Miss Bartlett!

AUNT NORMA (*Smiling*): Hello, Marconi. (*To* MRS. BARTLETT) Honey, I've always envied you your pretty feet. Dress 'em up again in high-heeled shoes sometime soon —just to give me a treat. (MRS. BARTLETT *looks at her low-heeled oxfords.* WILLIE *goes toward the window.*)

WILLIE (*Climbing out the window*): S'long, everybody. Thanks for listening, Mrs. Bartlett! (*He disappears.*)

AUNT NORMA (*Laughing*): He's a nice, attractive boy, but why does he always have to go through the window?

MRS. BARTLETT (*Smiling*): It's a way Willie has.

NANCY: And lots of times the door is locked. (MR. BARTLETT *enters at rear.*) Hi, Dad!

MR. BARTLETT (*Pinching his wife's cheek and grinning at her*): Hello, beautiful! (*To* AUNT NORMA) Glad to see you, sis! And how's my girl, Nancy? (*To* MRS. BARTLETT) May I have some lunch? I am on my way to the warehouse, and being in the neighborhood—

AUNT NORMA (*Laughing*): Neighborhood! Have you forgotten a straight line is, after all, the shortest distance between two points?

MR. BARTLETT (*Grinning*): Who wouldn't drive around Robin Hood's barn to come home to this? (*He takes* MRS. BARTLETT *and* NANCY *by the hands.*)

MRS. BARTLETT: Stay for lunch—do, Norma.

AUNT NORMA: Don't tempt me. (*Laughing*) You have such heavenly food, I'd gain at least a pound. (*Seriously*) I really haven't time. Bye, everybody.

NANCY: Goodbye, Aunt Norma. I'll call you—later.

MR. BARTLETT: Bye, sis. (NANCY *follows* AUNT NORMA *to the door.* MRS. BARTLETT *draws her husband downstage.*)

MRS. BARTLETT (*In a low voice*): Do I look frumpy—awfully plain to you, Clarence?

MR. BARTLETT: Frumpy—plain! Look in your mirror! You're absolutely the best-looking woman in the world!

MRS. BARTLETT (*Hurrying, exiting right*): How hungry you must be! I'll have lunch ready in two shakes!

MR. BARTLETT (*Leaving by door at left*): I'll wash up. (NANCY *saunters from the door at rear to the table, takes up magazine. Reads dramatically*)

NANCY: "The First Lady wore a glamorous hair-do which consisted of tiny dark-green velvet bows, and yellow roses perched atop her shining curls. . . ." (*Looking *up*) Glamorous! And she's older than Mother! (*She slams the magazine shut, drops it onto the floor, and runs out left.* MRS. BARTLETT *enters through door at right, takes the dress from the box, and holds it up to her. She looks in the mirror, smiles at herself, then puts the dress in the box, takes up the telephone and dials.*) The Lido Club? This is Mrs. Clarence Bartlett. . . . I want to reserve a table for tonight for two. Mr. Bartlett and I will arrive about eight. (*Quick curtain.*)

* * *

SCENE 2

TIME: *Evening of the same day.*

SETTING: *The same as Scene 1. The lamps are lighted.*

AT RISE: NANCY *enters left. The sound of pounding beyond door at right is heard.* NANCY *exits right.*

NANCY (*Offstage*): Why, Crane Leroy! (NANCY *and* CRANE *enter right. He is carrying coat and gloves. He tosses them onto a chair.*) Why didn't you come to the front door, Crane?

CRANE: The back door was closer. At least I don't climb in the window like that character I see over here ten times a day. What's he trying to do—practice being a burglar, or is he playing In-and-Out-the-Window?

NANCY (*Stiffly*): That's Willie. He's used the window ever since we were in kindergarten. I guess he comes in that way now so he won't have to drag Mother or me to the door every time he wants a book, or something. Mother gives him a lot of attention. He likes to be fed, and listened to.

CRANE: He'd better not get attention from you, beautiful. He may have come in on the ground floor, but I'm taking over, here and now. Old General Leroy has landed, and means to take the situation in hand. (NANCY *moves about the room. She is not pleased.*) I see what I like and—

NANCY (*Ill-at-ease, leafing through a magazine lying on the table*): I have some groovy new records. Don't you want to go into the den and play them?

CRANE: Let's go for a ride, and we'd better get started. I have to get the car out of the drive before the Harpers leave the dining room.

NANCY (*Looking up from magazine*): Why? (CRANE *picks her coat up off the floor.*)

CRANE: Hurry up, baby. (*He holds the coat out toward her*) Come on. (NANCY *steps back.*)

NANCY: Why do you want to move the car before the Harpers leave the dining room?

CRANE (*Still holding the coat*): Tsk, tsk! You're beautiful, but so-o-o dense. When Mr. Harper goes into the living room he might look out and see that the car's right fender has a permanent wave in it. (NANCY *drops onto a chair.*)

NANCY: But Mr. Harper is nice. He wouldn't say anything about something that happened to a guest's car, even if he thought the crumpled fender were your own fault. (*She smiles.*) And I guess someone ran into you!

CRANE (*Shaking the coat, impatiently*): It isn't my car. It's his. Come on.

NANCY (*Frowning*): You're going out in Mr. Harper's car?

CRANE (*Grinning*): *We're* going out in Mr. Harper's car. And just to make it more exciting, I was the one who put the wave in the fender today.

NANCY (*Jumping to her feet*): And you didn't tell him?

CRANE: Of course not! I ran into the fireplug *after* he told me I absolutely could *not* borrow his car. (NANCY *presses her lips together, and frowns*) But a little thing like that won't stop us!

NANCY: You have the nerve to tell me this, and to think—(*She chokes.*)

CRANE (*Shrugging*): It's all Mother's fault. She thought she had to explain that we didn't come in our own car because my license was suspended. But she'll have the fender fixed. So come along. (*He grins, foolishly.* NANCY *snatches the coat from him and throws it onto the floor.*)

NANCY (*Angry*): What kind of a girl do you think I am—you—you—

CRANE (*Brazenly*): I think you're the kind of a girl who would like me if you knew me better! Give yourself a chance—come along! You can't be as small-townish as you pretend to be! (*He stoops to pick up her coat. She kicks it out of his reach.*)

NANCY (*Furious*): I wouldn't go out with you if you were the last boy on earth—you—you elderly delinquent! (CRANE, *chagrined, picks up his gloves and coat.*)

CRANE (*With a superior air*): Willie appears to be your type, after all!

NANCY (*Running to rear door, jerking it open*): You—you worm! You crawl right back under the board you came out from! (CRANE, *scowling, hurries toward door. As he passes her, she stamps her foot*) Scat! (*She slams the door behind him, runs to phone and dials. She begins to sniffle; to herself impatiently*) Answer the phone, Aunt Norma! (*She hangs up*) Aunt Norma's not at home. I could *just die!* To think I wanted Mother to be like somebody else just to impress that jellyfish—that clod! (*She runs off left, sobbing.*)

WILLIE (*Opening the window*): Nancy! Mrs. Bartlett! (*He slides into the room*) May I come in?

MRS. BARTLETT (*Offstage*): Certainly! I'll be there in a minute.

WILLIE (*Picking up the magazine*): O.K., Mrs. Bartlett. (MRS. BARTLETT *enters right. She is dressed in* AUNT

NORMA'S *evening dress, wears long gloves and high-heeled shoes. Her hair is smartly done*) Gee, Mrs. Bartlett, you look like a million dollars!

MRS. BARTLETT: Thank you, Willie. (*She takes compact and lipstick from her purse, and puts on lipstick.*)

WILLIE (*Dubiously*): I thought you didn't like such a lot of make-up. (NANCY *enters at left, unseen by* WILLIE *or* MRS. BARTLETT.)

MRS. BARTLETT: All the fashion magazines are featuring this kind of make-up. It's the very latest thing. (NANCY *registers shock.*)

WILLIE: Oh-oh! (*Grinning*) I came over to tell you I—

MRS. BARTLETT: I shall have to hear about that another time. I have to hurry my husband along. We've decided to dine out and then go dancing. (*She turns.* NANCY *is staring at her.*)

NANCY: Mother! You look—oh, my goodness!

MRS. BARTLETT (*Stepping daintily over the coat lying on the floor*): Don't you like the way I look, Nancy? Willie does.

NANCY: Yes—but—I haven't had any dinner! I'm hungry! I thought you were helping get Dad ready for a banquet—or something. (MRS. BARTLETT *goes to the mirror, and pats her hair.*)

MRS. BARTLETT: Oh, you're old enough now to rustle yourself enough calories to keep from starving. There are some TV dinners in the refrigerator.

NANCY (*Amazed*): TV dinners!

MRS. BARTLETT: You can make excellent cocoa. Maybe Willie would like to stay for dinner.

WILLIE: That'll be swell, Nance—unless you want to come over to my house, and listen to my radio. (MRS. BARTLETT *exits left.* WILLIE *takes a magazine off the table, and begins leafing through it.*)

NANCY (*Bitterly*): Calories! TV dinners! And dumb short-wave radio stuff! (*Curtain*)

* * *

SCENE 3

TIME: *The following Saturday.*

SETTING: *The same. Nancy's coat is hanging on the back of a chair untidily. There are magazines, books and opened mail lying on floor and chairs. The table is littered with candy bar wrappings.*

AT RISE: NANCY *is on her knees, picking up newspapers.*

NANCY (*Sitting back on her heels*): I can't seem to get this room straight. (*The door at rear opens.* AUNT NORMA *enters.* NANCY, *throwing newspapers right and left, jumps up and runs to embrace her*) Oh, Aunt Norma! I'm so glad to see you I could *just die!*

AUNT NORMA: What's happened now? (NANCY *seats her in a chair, sits on the floor and kicks off her shoes. In doing so, she drags her coat off the chair onto the floor.*)

NANCY: I think Mother's lost her mind—or is losing it, Aunt Norma.

AUNT NORMA: What's she done? Tell me about it.

NANCY: She's gone *glamorous* on us. She won't cook because it will spoil her manicure! (AUNT NORMA *appears to be shocked.*)

AUNT NORMA: Do we eat out?

NANCY: *We do not!* We live on cold cuts and potato chips! (*She stands.*) See how thin I've grown for want of real food! And Dad's positively gaunt! Mother always kept her figure, you know. But now she's—oh—er—*svelte,* she calls it.

AUNT NORMA (*Apparently incredulous*): No cinnamon

rolls—no chocolate cake, no fried chicken—no chef's salad, or strawberry shortcake?

NANCY (*Wagging her head from side to side*): No cooked food of any kind. Just warmed-over stuff out of cans and frozen dinners. Dad's given her a new evening dress, and lately she's been lying around all day reading fashion magazines. Every evening she and Dad go out to dance at the Boat Club, or some place like that.

AUNT NORMA (*Taking off her gloves*): Anything else?

NANCY: I'm really worried because she doesn't seem to be interested in saving magazines and things—for Willie. And I heard her refuse—once—to listen to him when he wanted to tell her about a foreign ham operator he'd talked to.

AUNT NORMA: That *is* strange. Is that all?

NANCY (*Whimpering*): The worst thing—the *very* worst thing is—she never tells me to hang up my coat! (*She buries her face in her hands and sobs.*)

AUNT NORMA: Poor child! Where is your mother now?

NANCY: I think she's in the kitchen. I stayed awake till she and Dad came in last night, and when I woke up this morning I thought I'd try to straighten up this room. I haven't seen her. When I do, if she's wearing her new lounging pajamas, I'll *just die!* (*Tragically*) And, Aunt Norma, *I've lost Willie!*

AUNT NORMA (*Impressed*): No!

NANCY (*With resignation*): It's true! He never comes here any more! (*The window sash goes up.* WILLIE *leaps onto the sill.*)

WILLIE (*Sliding into the room*): May I come in, Nance? Hello, Miss Bartlett!

NANCY (*Coldly*): If you want to. (*Crossing the room, he goes to her.*)

WILLIE: Of course I do. I want to tell your mother something. Say, look who's here! (MR. BARTLETT *stands at the rear door.*) Hi, Mr. Bartlett!

NANCY (*Jumping to her feet*): What's the matter, Dad? Why did you come home this early? (AUNT NORMA *rises.*) Are *you* starved? I am!

MR. BARTLETT: Me, too. Glad to see you, sis. Don't go. I smell—(*Sniffs*)

WILLIE (*Sniffing*): Cinnamon rolls! (MRS. BARTLETT *appears at door at right. She is wearing a housedress, apron and low-heeled oxfords.*)

MRS. BARTLETT: They sent me a grand roast of beef, Clarence! Thank you! Come back for dinner, Norma. (NANCY *opens her mouth but no sound comes*) We're having your favorite pie! (*She makes the table tidy.*)

WILLIE: And cinnamon rolls! (NANCY *rushes to her mother and throws her arms around her*) And can I bring my radio over this afternoon?

MRS. BARTLETT: Certainly, Willie.

NANCY: Mother! I love you in your housedress! You're beautiful in it!

MRS. BARTLETT: Have you had enough of lounging pajamas, dear? (*She kisses* NANCY *on the cheek, then picks up newspapers, places books in the bookcase.*)

NANCY (*Hanging her head*): Yes, Mother. I never want to see a pair again!

MR. BARTLETT: How about the glamorous background, Nancy?

NANCY (*Looking at him, grinning*): I've had enough for a lifetime! And could Willie and I have—*just anything*—to eat?

WILLIE (*Licking his lips*): Cinnamon rolls!

AUNT NORMA (*Pretending to be sensible*): It'll spoil their lunches!

MRS. BARTLETT: Just this once won't matter. And while I'm

putting a cheese souffle together—(*In placing magazines on table, she steps over* NANCY's *coat.*)

NANCY: Is it lunch time?

WILLIE: It's almost twelve o'clock! And the game's at one.

MRS. BARTLETT: Willie can be bringing me up to date on his short-wave stuff while I cook. (MR. BARTLETT *goes to* NANCY, *and lifts up her chin.*)

MR. BARTLETT: Everything all right? Huh?

NANCY: I won't feel all right until you two do *just one thing.*

MRS. BARTLETT (*Smiling*): What is it, dear? (*She picks up the wastebasket.*)

NANCY: Tell me to hang up my coat. (*Her parents look at each other.* AUNT NORMA *nods at them.*)

WILLIE: Gee! Girls are funny!

MR. *and* MRS. BARTLETT: *Nancy! Hang up your coat!*

WILLIE (*Running toward door at right*): The cinnamon rolls are burning! (*All follow him. Quick curtain.*)

THE END

Election Day in Spooksville

by Rose Kacherian Rybak

Characters

DR. JACK L. HYDE, *President of the Spooksville Civic Association*
ZACH, *Vice-President of the Spooksville Civic Association*
IGOR, *Sergeant-at-Arms*
MAYOR LUCIFER, *Deadbeat Party candidate*
MUMMY FYDE, *Repulsive Party candidate*
FRANK N. STEIN, JR., *Reform Party candidate*
VAMPIRA LUCIFER, *Mayor's daughter*
CHARLIE, *campaign manager for Frank N. Stein, Jr.*
FRANK N. STEIN, SR., *monster*
TWO WITCHES
HAIRY MANE
THREE CHAIN RATTLERS
MA COBBER
LORELEI
TWO GHOSTS
(Two Witches through Two Ghosts: *Spooksville residents*)
EXTRAS, *ghosts, goblins, skeletons, vampires*

SCENE 1

TIME: *Evening.*
SETTING: *Meeting room in Spooksville Town Hall.*
AT RISE: DR. JACK L. HYDE *and* ZACH *enter.*

ZACH: Nobody's here yet. I was afraid we were late.

HYDE: This'll give us a chance to set up more chairs.

ZACH: Do you really expect a big turnout? We seldom get more than three or four members at these Civic Association meetings.

HYDE: That's because the Spooksville Civic Association hasn't had many vital issues lately. But things are different now. This coming election has the whole town in an uproar.

ZACH: That was pretty clever of you to line up some of the candidates for a debate tonight.

HYDE (*Incensed*): Don't be silly, you fool. Nobody dares refuse a request by Dr. Jack L. Hyde! (*Threateningly*) Don't you remember what happened to the last idiot who crossed my path?—which reminds me—why isn't Igor here to help us move this table? (*Calling loudly*) Igor . . . Igor . . . . (*Pause*) He's probably hiding in the belfry. (IGOR *runs down the aisle from the rear of the auditorium. Swinging his arms in apelike fashion, he lopes up onto stage, places table center, puts three chairs behind it, then runs over to* DR. JACK L. HYDE, *and stands at attention in front of him.*)

IGOR: You rang?

HYDE: It's about time you showed up. We're expecting a big crowd tonight, so I'll be needing you. Just stay right here until the guests arrive. This should be quite a meeting. (IGOR *walks left and stands quietly at attention.*)

ZACH (*Rubbing his hands*): I can feel the excitement creeping into my bones already. (*Loud, shrill screams are heard from offstage.*)

HYDE: There's the doorbell, Igor. Let the citizens in. (IGOR *exits left and re-enters quickly with* TWO WITCHES.) If it isn't the Spooksville Space Twins! Good evening, ladies.

1ST WITCH: How long is this meeting going to take?

2ND WITCH: We have serious business to attend to. We dropped out of our fifth orbit around the moon to be here tonight.

1ST WITCH: If people don't see a black witch silhouetted against the moon, they'll get to thinking we're falling down on the job.

2ND WITCH: What's so urgent about hearing campaign speeches, all of a sudden? We're going to vote for Mayor Lucifer anyway, just as we've done for three hundred years.

1ST WITCH: That is right. I'm a registered Deadbeat from way back.

HYDE: Hold your horses—excuse me, I mean your *brooms.* Haven't you heard this year's election is going to be the most controversial in the history of Spooksville? Mayor Lucifer is running for the Deadbeat Party, but the Repulsive Party is putting Mummy Fyde in the race against him.

1ST WITCH: So what? We've had a two-party system in this town for years, but that doesn't mean a thing. Nobody can beat Mayor Lucifer.

ZACH: Now don't be too quick to judge. You haven't heard Mummy Fyde's platform yet.

2ND WITCH: I know Mummy Fyde pretty well, and let me tell you something. There's just no platform that can carry him very far. I tell you the two-party system is like everything else in this town—it's dead.

HYDE: Aha! Maybe the two old parties are, but the new third party—

2ND WITCH: Third party? What third party?

HYDE: That's what I said—the *third party!* Now that should provide plenty of fireworks this election. (*Shrill shrieks are heard from offstage.*) There goes the doorbell again. Someone's at the door, Igor. Answer it, and while you're at it, leave the door unlocked. Everyone should be arriving soon. (IGOR *exits briefly and re-enters with* HAIRY MANE.)

HAIRY MANE: Greetings and felicitations, fellow spooks! I hope I'm not too late for the great debate!

HYDE: Not at all, Hairy. We'd never think of starting a Civic Association meeting without Spooksville's favorite barber.

ZACH: A meeting without Hairy Mane? (*Grabbing at* HAIRY'*s hair*) Why, he's our "main" citizen! By the way, Hairy, how's business lately?

HAIRY: A lot sharper than your sense of humor, Zachie, old boy. (*Menacingly*) Why don't you come in for a close shave tomorrow? (*Runs the back of his hand against* ZACH'*s cheek*)

ZACH (*Pulling away*): I wouldn't count on it, Hairy. You're not exactly a walking advertisement, you know.

HAIRY: Are you kidding? I guarantee you twenty more shaves with my new Wolfman blades than you'd get with your old "beep-boop."

1ST WITCH: Will you please cut out this ghastly kid stuff and get back to the business of the meeting! Now what's this third party you mentioned?

ZACH: You'll have to see it to believe it! I never figured in my wildest dreams that we'd see a reform movement in Spooksville.

2ND WITCH: Reform movement?

HYDE: That's right. Young Frank Stein is running on a Reform Party ticket.

2ND WITCH: Did you say Frank Stein?

HYDE: That's right.

2ND WITCH: Frank *N*. Stein? (HYDE *nods gravely.*)

1ST WITCH: But he's the most powerful, the most grotesque monster in the history of Spooksville.

HYDE: Correction: You're thinking of Frank N. Stein, Sr.!

You'd never catch *him* trying to reform Spooksville. This is his son, Frank N. Stein, *Jr.*, who's causing all the controversy. (*Noise of rattling chains is heard from offstage.* THREE CHAIN RATTLERS *enter.*)

ZACH: Oh, it's the Rank and File of the Chain Rattlers Union.

1ST CHAIN RATTLER: I'm Rank.

2ND CHAIN RATTLER: And I'm File.

3RD CHAIN RATTLER: And I'm not committing the labor vote until I hear this debate tonight. What are we waiting for?

HYDE: The candidates should have been here ten minutes ago.

3RD CHAIN RATTLER: Is Mayor Lucifer going to be here?

HYDE: No, Mayor Lucifer doesn't think it's dignified for the incumbent to engage in debate.

ZACH: He'll be at a Deadbeat Party rally tomorrow morning. . . . We're having the Repulsive Party and the Reform Party candidates tonight.

HYDE (*Looking off*): I think I see Mummy Fyde coming in the door now. (MUMMY FYDE *enters with* TWO GHOSTS.)

HYDE: Welcome to the Spooksville Civic Association, Mr. Fyde. I see you brought your followers with you.

MUMMY: Don't be silly. These are my writers, my "ghost" writers.

HYDE: Of course. Won't you take your place at the table? (HYDE *escorts* MUMMY *to seat at table.* VAMPIRA *and* LORELEI *enter. Everyone stares at them in amazement.*)

1ST WITCH: Are my eyes playing tricks on me or is that Vampira Lucifer?

2ND WITCH: It sure is. Now why do you suppose Mayor Lucifer's daughter came here tonight?

1ST WITCH: I don't know, but you can bet she's up to

something. She's the most treacherous descendant of the vampire line.

LORELEI: Vampira, are you sure you did the right thing coming to this meeting?

VAMPIRA: Now, Lorelei, put those eerie thoughts out of your mind. Of course, I had to come. How else could I evaluate my father's opposition?

LORELEI: But you could use your wiles on any Repulsive Party member and find out that information.

VAMPIRA: It's not the Repulsive Party I'm thinking about. It's that new Reform Party candidate that has me worried. I hear he's got a lot of heart.

LORELEI: Why, there's nobody you couldn't snare.

VAMPIRA: I'm not worried about stealing any man's soul, darling, it's just that it's a little harder to infiltrate the heart.

LORELEI: *I* have complete confidence in you! Now can't we get out of here?

VAMPIRA: Keep cool, darling. Besides, we're just exercising our rights as citizens. (*Sarcastically*) Don't you want to become an informed voter?

LORELEI: Why? I have to vote for your father, anyway. It's better that I vote in ignorance. (HYDE *approaches them.*)

HYDE: Well, this is indeed an honor, having you two bewitching beauties with us!

VAMPIRA (*To* LORELEI): You see, we're perfectly welcome. (*To* HYDE.) We really should attend more of your meetings, Dr. Hyde, but we're so busy every evening. The hall looks positively weird. Have you recently redecorated it? (*She walks across stage, looking around room carefully.* FRANK N. STEIN, JR. *enters with* CHARLIE.)

FRANK N. STEIN: Sorry I'm late, folks, but I had a devil of a time finding this place. Why do you keep the Spooksville Town Hall so hidden with vines and trees and overgrown shrubbery?

HYDE: It's part of the local color.

ZACH: Is there a better way to create atmosphere?

FRANK: Well, we'll see about that. (*Suddenly sees* VAMPIRA *across stage*) Hello! What have we here?

CHARLIE (*Grabbing* FRANK'*s arm*): Wait, Frank. Don't go near that vixen. Do you know who she is?

FRANK (*Disregarding* CHARLIE): I'll say I do! That is the most beautiful creature I have ever laid my eyes on.

LORELEI: You've done it again, Vampira! He's a dead lame duck! You've got him under your spell. (VAMPIRA *stares, as if in a trance.*)

CHARLIE: Frank, get away before it's too late. That's Mayor Lucifer's daughter, and she's bad for your blood. (FRANK *and* VAMPIRA *continue looking at each other, spellbound.*) Somebody do something! Mr. President, start the meeting!

HYDE: Excellent idea! (*Runs behind table, raps gavel*) Order, order! This meeting will now come to order! Will our two guest speakers take their places, please? (*Everyone is seated.*) Boys and ghouls, tonight we are privileged to have—(MA COBBER *enters, holding her crystal ball in both hands.*)

MA COBBER (*Out of breath*): You'd think they'd send me some notices about these meetings. If it weren't for my crystal ball, I wouldn't even have known about this one.

HYDE: Now just a minute, Ma Cobber. We did send out notices. We left one for you on your dungeon steps.

MA: Well, I didn't get it, but don't let me hold you up now. I'll just sit here while you go on with the meeting. (*Sits down*)

HYDE: As I started to say, we have with us tonight, two of the three distinguished candidates who are running for the office of mayor. First I'd like you to meet a citizen who's been an upstanding Spooksville resident for 2,000 years. May I present the Repulsive Party candidate, Mummy Fyde! (*Applause*) As most of you know, Mummy Fyde is awake to all civic issues. He takes nothing lying down. His volunteer and charity work are known to all of us, especially in hospital clinics where he rolls bandages. In fact, you might say he's all wrapped up in this town. So without further ado, I give you Mummy Fyde. (*Applause.* MUMMY FYDE *stands up.*)

MUMMY: My friends, it is indeed an honor and privilege to be standing before you tonight.

CHARLIE: It's also a miracle.

MUMMY: I would have been here sooner, but as you might guess, a person in my position occasionally gets tied up. Nevertheless, I am just dying to tell you about the Repulsive Party platform on which I'm running.

CHARLIE (*Heckling*): Your running days are over, Mummy!

MUMMY (*Ignoring him*): Specifically, I am disturbed about many things in Spooksville, and as soon as my political opponent is formally introduced, I shall start the debate. President Hyde?

HYDE: Thank you, sir. And on my other side sits a young man whose name is a household word in Spooksville. In fact, Frank N. Stein, Sr., was one of the Founding Fathers of this great town. Of course young Frank, Jr., hasn't been too active in Spooksville activities, but perhaps that's because as a young man he moved to the outlying suburbs. Now he's back to tell you all about his plans to change Spooksville. Let's have a big hand for Frank N. Stein, Jr. (*Boos and catcalls*)

FRANK: Good evening. I had hoped to find you in better spirits, but no matter. Shall we get on with the debate?

HYDE: Fine. Mummy Fyde, will you kick off?

CHARLIE: He already has, seems to me!

MUMMY: Thank you, Mr. President. As I stand here looking into this audience, I see many reasons why Spooksville needs the Repulsive Party. Take Ma Cobber, for example.

CHARLIE (*Heckling*): You take her!

MUMMY: Poor Ma Cobber.

MA: That's right! What about me and my crystal ball? Ever since automation hit this town, nobody hires me. Now they just call in one of those Uniwacky machines to forecast everything, even elections!

FRANK: But those machines need live programmers. Why not take a course or two at Yell University? With your foresight, you'd be a natural!

MUMMY: Don't be taken in by his smooth talk, folks. What will the rest of you do? For instance, you Chain Rattlers, now you know how hard it is for you workers to get steady jobs!

1ST CHAIN RATTLER: You said it! The way they've eased the building code around here, the buildings rattle themselves nowadays.

MUMMY: That's right. So I say to you, Workers of Spooksville, unite; you have nothing to lose but your chains! Join the Repulsive Party's movement for progress!

FRANK: Look at you all, just look at you! You keep hearing about progress, but your appearances reflect just the opposite!

VAMPIRA (*Admiringly*): Oh, Lorelei, have you ever heard such a dynamic speaker? And he's so handsome, too!

LORELEI: If he doesn't stop talking this way, he'll be jailed for sedition.

FRANK: Just look at yourselves, dressed in those ridiculous get-ups that went out with the Dark Ages!

HYDE: But it's expected of us. Who ever heard of spooks in plain clothes?

ZACH: What would become of the world at Halloween? People look to us for inspiration.

FRANK: Spooksville needs reform, I tell you. Already the suburbs are bulging with discontented young people who refuse to conform to the old ridiculous way of life.

CHARLIE: You tell 'em, Frankie!

FRANK: You witches, can't you just picture yourselves in the latest creations from the House of Dior?

1ST WITCH (*Turning to* 2ND WITCH): House of Dior? Have we haunted that place lately, Gertrude?

2ND WITCH (*Reflectively*): House of Dior, House of Dior . . . Nope, that's not one of our regular haunts.

FRANK: You see, you have no sense of fashion. Beautiful colors—all the hues of the spectrum—can be yours.

1ST WITCH: "The Spectrum for the Spectres." That sounds pretty good, Mr. Stein, but say, what does your father, Frank N. Stein, Sr., think about this reform idea?

CHARLIE: I'll answer that one. You see, the Monster is getting on in years, so we don't want to burden him with politics. Frankie has him in an Old Ogres' Home out in the country where he can spend his declining years.

HYDE: I think I'll have to interrupt; it's getting late, and we all have to go to work, but before we adjourn the meeting, may I remind you to stack your chairs against the wall on your way out.

HAIRY: I move that the meeting be adjourned.

IGOR: I second that.

HYDE: We stand adjourned. Good night, everyone. (*Everyone but* FRANK, CHARLIE, LORELEI *and* VAMPIRA *exits, stacking a chair near door on way out.*)

LORELEI: Come on, Vampira, we'd better be going.

VAMPIRA: You go ahead, I'd like to hear Mr. Stein's ideas on a few other topics. I have a few questions to ask him.

LORELEI: From the looks of things, I'd say he might be inclined to pop a question or two himself!

VAMPIRA: Don't be absurd, darling. You heard him say how ridiculous he thinks we Spooksville residents are. Why, I don't stand a chance.

LORELEI: Well, I must say, if you don't get your fangs into him, your reputation will be ruined in this town!

VAMPIRA: I'd trade my reputation for a future with Frankie Stein any time!

LORELEI: Oh, Vampira! (*Shakes her head in disbelief and runs out*)

CHARLIE: Come on, Frankie, let's go. This place gives me the creeps!

FRANK: You go ahead, Charlie. I'll meet you in the car.

CHARLIE: Oh, no, you don't. I'm not leaving you alone with that vampire. She's just waiting to get her claws into you!

FRANK: I'm a big boy, Charlie. Now run along. I can take care of myself.

CHARLIE (*Singing*): A pretty ghoul . . . is like a melody . . . she haunts you night and day . . . (*He exits. For a moment* FRANK *and* VAMPIRA *stare silently across the room at each other; then* FRANK *approaches* VAMPIRA.)

VAMPIRA: I—I thought that was a wonderful speech you gave tonight.

FRANK: Did you?

VAMPIRA: Oh, yes, it was so—so down-to-earth!

FRANK: Did you really think so?

VAMPIRA: Oh, yes.

FRANK: I didn't know there was such a beautiful creature left in this town. Why, you're out of this world!

VAMPIRA (*Bashfully*): I'll bet you say that to all the ghouls. (*Pause*) You probably prefer the wholesome suburban outdoor woman. . . . You don't have to answer; I can see the answer in your eyes.

FRANK: Vampira . . .

VAMPIRA: Don't say it—I couldn't bear to know the truth. I do have a confession to make, Frankie. When I came here tonight, I was determined to ruin your chances of winning against my father, but—

FRANK: Please, you don't have to explain. The minute I laid eyes on you, I knew that deep down you were really good.

VAMPIRA: Oh, Frankie, do you suppose I could be good enough for you? I mean—if I were to reform—as you said—and change my ways—

FRANK (*Excitedly*): But of course! And if you would wash your face and comb your hair, why, you'd be a perfect suburban type!

VAMPIRA: Then I can see you again?

FRANK: I'll be counting the hours. How about tomorrow morning?

VAMPIRA: I have to attend my father's election rally.

FRANK: I could meet you there. Please say yes.

VAMPIRA: I—I guess so. I just hope I'm doing the right thing, Frankie. I just hope I'm doing the right thing.

CURTAIN

* * *

SCENE 2

TIME: *The next morning.*

SETTING: *Election headquarters, in the meeting room at Town Hall. Large board simulating computer, wired with blinking Christmas tree lights, is at upstage center.*

AT RISE: MAYOR LUCIFER *is pacing back and forth at front of stage.* DR. HYDE *enters.*

MAYOR (*Indignantly*): What is the meaning of this, Hyde? Where are all my constituents? This rally was supposed to start at ten o'clock sharp, and not a soul has shown up! Why the polls will be opening in a little while and—

HYDE: Take it easy, Mayor Lucifer; you know you have to watch your blood pressure.

MAYOR: Don't talk to me about my blood pressure!

HYDE: But, Mayor, I'm only the President of the Spooksville Civic Association. What can I do if the citizens don't want to hear your final campaign speech?

MAYOR: Just what went on at that meeting of yours last night? I want to know who's responsible for this. Never in all my three hundred years as Mayor has my public failed to attend my election morning rally! Just what is going on?

HYDE: To be perfectly honest with you, it looks as if this year's election may be won by the Reform Party. Their candidate has fantastic voter appeal! (VAMPIRA *enters, wearing blue jeans. She has a pony-tail hairdo. At first,* MAYOR *doesn't recognize his daughter.*)

MAYOR: That's ridiculous, Hyde. Why, here comes one of my constituents now. (*He approaches* VAMPIRA *to shake hands, then draws back with a start, as he recognizes her.*)

VAMPIRA: Hello, Father.

MAYOR: Good grief, Vampira, is it really you? What are you doing in that costume?

VAMPIRA (*Dramatically*): I may as well tell you the truth, Father; I'm in love with your opponent Frank N. Stein. (FRANK N. STEIN, JR. *enters.*)

FRANK: That's right, sir, and I want to marry your daughter as soon as possible.

MAYOR: Is this some kind of joke, Vampira?

VAMPIRA: I was never more serious in my life, Father.

MAYOR: How could such misfortune befall me? First my constituents desert me, then my daughter falls in love with my arch enemy. (*Wringing his hands.*) This is absurd, Vampira! Do you think you could really be happy with this renegade? How long do you think you'd be content parading in that costume? Your beautiful hair tied back like a horse's mane, your gorgeous fangs clipped down to nothing—

FRANK: It's her decision, sir.

MAYOR: You bet it's her decision, and she'd better decide wisely. But if you think a beautiful vampire could give up the exciting night life of Spooksville for your peaceful suburbs, then you're pretty naive!

FRANK: What do you say, Vampira?

VAMPIRA (*Upset*): I don't know. I just don't know!

FRANK: In that case I had better leave. Vampira, it's obvious the Spooksville tradition is deep in your blood, and I want no part of that tradition . . . I guess this is goodbye. (*He exits.* VAMPIRA *starts to follow, then stops*)

MAYOR: There, there, daughter, don't fret, everything works out for the best. Now why don't you go and get dressed properly for our victory celebration. The election is just about to get started downstairs. (*He escorts* VAMPIRA *left. She goes out, and* MAYOR *returns to center stage.*)

HYDE: I wish I could share your confidence, Mayor, but the voters are showing their independence this year!

MAYOR (*Angrily*): Bah! What do the voters know? Do you know what this town was like before I was elected Mayor three hundred years ago? Why it wasn't safe for haunting! Wide streets, bright lights, absolutely no place for a spook to hide!

HYDE: They've probably forgotten all you've done for them.

MAYOR: Why, I turned this town into a model Hades. Take a look down there at Inferno Street. Every house was remodeled so there'd be a creak in every joint, a squeak in every hinge, and a rattle in every window.

HYDE: Perfect for the most discriminating ghost. . . .

MAYOR: And as for the witches—why they've never had it so good! I installed broom closets galore—and threw in free brooms.

HYDE: But you see, things are changing; even the witches frown on broom travel.

MAYOR: Ungrateful wretches, all of them! Get out, get out. . . .

HYDE (*Apologetically*): I'm sorry, Mayor. . . .

MAYOR: Not half as sorry as you will be! (MUMMY *enters.*) Now if this isn't adding insult to injury! (*To* MUMMY) Did you come here to gloat too?

MUMMY: Now just relax, Lucifer, and hear me out.

HYDE: I'm sure you two have a lot to talk about, so I'll leave you. (*Exits hurriedly.*)

MAYOR (*Glancing after* HYDE): Traitor!

MUMMY: Don't be unfair, Lucifer. Hyde has been most impartial!

MAYOR: Humph! A fine reference you are! I wouldn't be surprised if you were behind this whole conspiracy! But of course! Why didn't I see it before? Who else but Mummy Fyde could head this underground movement?

MUMMY: Just a minute, Lucifer. Simmer down. I know it's asking too much of you, but you have to keep cool! My party had nothing to do with this. In fact, I came here to help you and my beloved Spooksville. We must join forces!

MAYOR: Why should you be trying to help me, your opponent, Mummy?

MUMMY: Because suddenly we're not opponents any more. Analyze it, Lucifer. What do you stand for? A bleak, desolate city, too eerie for humans—ghouls and ghosts all pledged to one Bill of Frights! Well, I'm for the same things, the spookiest Spooksville possible, but what's the biggest threat to that dream?

MAYOR (*Reflectively*): Frankie Stein!

MUMMY: Frank N. Stein, Jr., and that's why we must form a coalition to stop this infernal menace. Can you envision this town if he gets into power?

MAYOR: But what can we do to stop him?

MUMMY: We have to re-create the old Spooksville image.

MAYOR: There's only one person who's feared enough to do that, and he's away in an Old Ogres' Home.

MUMMY (*Laughing diabolically*): That's where you're wrong! Frank N. Stein, Sr., is right down here (*Pointing offstage*) in the voting dungeons now, waiting to register all Spooksville residents who may have been planning to step out of line and vote for the Reform Party candidate. One look into his eyes, and they'll see things our way.

MAYOR: An ingenious plan! Who would dare cross the old monster? But how did you . . . ?

MUMMY: As I told you, Mayor, in times of crisis, we ghouls have to stick together. (*Looks at watch*) We won't have long to wait. The polls have opened. (*Both laugh gleefully.* VAMPIRA *enters, dressed again as a vampire.*)

VAMPIRA: Father, you've reached a new low, and I think it's beastly of you! Just what will this monster, Frankie's father, do when the voters come to register?

MAYOR: Nothing, daughter, that's the beautiful part of it. They innocently go down to the dungeon, prepared to vote the Reform Party ticket. They then give their names to the registrar, Frank N. Stein, Sr. They look into his eyes and then—(*Shrill shriek is heard from offstage.*) and then they cast their ballot for the old Deadbeat Party. (LORELEI *enters, screaming. She runs to center.*) Have you cast your ballot, my dear? (LORELEI, *obviously petrified, nods her head and runs out.*)

MUMMY: When Monster Frank N. Stein heard what his son was up to, he deemed it his patriotic duty to scare Spooksville back to its senses.

MAYOR: But I wonder what'll happen when young Frankie Stein finds out what's going on?

VAMPIRA (*Bitterly*): I can tell you. He's probably fifty miles from here telling all the suburbanites how provincial the Spooksville people really are. And when he learns of this latest trick, he'll really be furious!

MAYOR: Well, we'll soon see about that. Here he comes now. (FRANK N. STEIN, JR., *enters dejectedly.*) Here to cast your ballot, young man? (*Another scream is heard from offstage. Everyone stares at computer, which has started to blink on and off.*)

MUMMY: Another vote for Lucifer! Frankie, you must be concerned about the election. Have you seen the returns so far?

FRANK: I'm not the least bit interested. (*Gazing lovingly at* VAMPIRA) What is losing a political office compared to losing the one you love?

MAYOR: Then you're not angry about our using your father to help us win? Answer me, boy! Has the devil got your tongue?

FRANK (*To* VAMPIRA): I've been wrong, I've been terribly wrong, Vampira. Will you have me back?

VAMPIRA: You mean you'll come back to the dungeons? Oh, Father, did you hear that? Frankie is coming back to the fold!

MAYOR: I knew he'd see the dark! This calls for a celebration! (*Calling offstage*) Stein, Frank N. Stein! Come up here at once! Your son has conceded the election. I've won the election, and I'm winning him for a son-in-law as well!

MUMMY (*Still watching the computer with the lights blinking*): Extraordinary! Extraordinary! Just look at those votes rolling in. What manner of monster is this grotesque creature whom everyone fears? What beast can this possibly be? (FRANK N. STEIN, SR. *enters, wearing a horrible mask.*)

VAMPIRA (*Gasping in terror*): Oh, horror of horrors! No wonder it is so feared! Frankie, who *is* this monster? (FRANK N. STEIN, SR. *removes mask and faces audience, revealing a popular teacher or student. He hands mask ceremoniously to* FRANK N. STEIN, JR.)

FRANK N. STEIN, JR. (*Accepting mask, and waving it with a flourish*): *This* is my heritage! (*Curtain falls slowly, as all "freeze" in horror.*)

THE END

A Case for Two Detectives

by John Murray

Characters

ANNOUNCER, *male*
SUSAN, *about twenty*
MRS. BARTON, *her mother*
MRS. ASHBY, *a weekend guest*
TWO SERVANTS, *male*
MISS MARLOWE, *a secretary*
ANNIE, *a maid*
MR. ALLEN, *a tycoon*
MRS. ALLEN, *his talkative wife*
QUENTIN VAN QUENTIN, *an armchair detective*
RIVETS O'NEILL, *a private eye*

SCENE 1

TIME: *Morning.*

SETTING: *The drawing room in the Bartons' Long Island home.*

BEFORE RISE: ANNOUNCER, *a refined young man, steps before curtain and nods to audience.*

ANNOUNCER: Ladies and gentlemen, we are going to witness a murder. Rather, we are concerned with the solution of the murder because, when our play begins, the victim has already been "done in." We will not meet him and it is small loss because I understand he was a bit of a rotter. We are going to present two solutions to the crime. One solution is offered by Quentin Van Quentin, the typical armchair detective. The other solution will be delivered by Rivets O'Neill, the rough-and-ready private eye. (*He steps to apron of stage and addresses a particular member of the audience.*) If this prologue tires you, imagine how I felt when I had to memorize it! (*Addresses general audience.*) The setting of our play is the palatial Long Island estate of Cyrus Barton. Has anyone ever realized that murder mysteries are invariably set on Long Island estates? It seems as though murder is a privilege enjoyed by the extremely wealthy. Won't you join me in the drawing room? (*He steps back as curtain rises upon the drawing room. He glances at room.*) Not bad. We wanted something more lavish, but this was the best furniture that the prop man could swindle from the members of the cast. (*Points to floor at center*) Cyrus Barton was found on this spot. The body has been removed. The body created a serious traffic hazard for our actors as they entered right and exited left. (*Gestures right and left*) The body was found by Annie, the Irish maid. Annie has an exceptionally strong pair of lungs and she awakened the household when confronted with the body of Cyrus Barton. No mystery play is complete without a terrified Irish maid. (*Calling*) Oh, Annie! (ANNIE, *the bright maid, enters left. She curtsies and smiles.*) Won't you scream for us? (ANNIE *screams hysterically, a soul-chilling, bloodcurdling screech. She smiles, nods and exits left.*) Thank you, Annie. But now to get on with the play. I'll be in the left wings should you need me. (*Exits left. Immediately,* MRS. BARTON, *a dowager, and* SUSAN, *her attractive daughter, enter right. Both are nervous.*)

SUSAN: Oh, Mother, what are we going to do?

MRS. BARTON: It'll be all right, Susan. Cyrus was a dreadful man.

SUSAN: But they'll think that I—

MRS. BARTON: Don't say it.

SUSAN: Quentin Van Quentin has started asking questions. He'll soon find out that I wasn't Cyrus' daughter—that I am your child by another marriage.

MRS. BARTON: I shouldn't have invited a famous detective here as a house guest. (*Sighs*) Oh, well—he's a remarkable fourth at bridge. (MRS. ASHBY, *an elderly woman, enters right. She is quite agitated as she joins others.*)

MRS. ASHBY: This is terrible! Terrible! Mrs. Barton, I will not stand for this outrage.

MRS. BARTON: I am sorry, Mrs. Ashby. I wouldn't have invited you had I known that someone was planning to kill Cyrus.

MRS. ASHBY: Murder! And before breakfast, too! Oh, I feel like a character in an Agatha Christie novel!

MRS. BARTON: Quentin Van Quentin will come downstairs soon. He'll solve our mystery. (*Commotion is heard offstage.* TWO SERVANTS, *carrying* VAN QUENTIN *in an armchair, enter left. They place the armchair rather ceremoniously in the center of set.* SERVANTS *then assume a stiff pose at either side of the chair.*)

MRS. ASHBY: Quentin Van Quentin!

SUSAN: The armchair detective!

MRS. BARTON (*Quickly*): My husband has been murdered and—

MRS. ASHBY: And I haven't had breakfast yet! (*Women stare icily at one another and begin talking simultaneously.*)

MRS. BARTON: My husband—

MRS. ASHBY: My breakfast—(QUENTIN *leaps from chair and waves women to silence.*)

QUENTIN: Quiet! (*He focuses his attention upon the floor and drops to the carpet, taking a magnifying glass from his pocket. He searches carpet intently with the glass. Members of cast follow his path.* QUENTIN *pauses, pounces upon an object and waves it triumphantly.*) Aha! I found it! I found it!

SUSAN: Do you know the murderer?

MRS. BARTON (*Excitedly*): What have you found?

QUENTIN (*Rising*): My cuff link. I lost it yesterday. (*All sigh with disappointment as* QUENTIN *returns to his armchair. He waves hands impatiently, dismissing* SERVANTS. *They bow reverently and exit right. Finally* QUENTIN *stares pointedly at* MRS. BARTON.) Why did you kill your husband?

MRS. BARTON (*Flustered*): Why—I—I—

QUENTIN: Don't deny it. I know everything. You hated Cyrus Barton. You quarreled with him yesterday. He threatened to cut you out of his will.

MRS. BARTON: That's not true.

QUENTIN: He threatened to cut you out many times. You met him in this room last night. When he insisted that he was calling his lawyer this morning, you took a gun and shot him.

MRS. BARTON: But the coroner said that my husband had been poisoned.

QUENTIN: Don't confuse the issue. I have no time for petty details. (ANNOUNCER *enters left and addresses audience.*)

ANNOUNCER: This part of the play is known as the "Red Herring" or the false clue. All writers use this gimmick. They wish the audience to focus suspicion upon an innocent person. I might as well tell you that Mrs. Barton did not murder her husband. The Red Herring is a successful device because it usually helps an author to prolong his play, making it a full-length, three-act drama.

Who knows? He may have another *Dial M for Murder* on his hands. (ANNOUNCER *exits left.*)

MRS. BARTON: But I couldn't have killed my husband. This was his private room. He had a key and so did Annie, our maid. No one else was ever allowed into this room. When Annie found Cyrus this morning, the door had been locked.

QUENTIN: What about the French doors?

MRS. BARTON: They were locked and bolted on the *inside!*

QUENTIN (*Jumping from armchair*): Why doesn't somebody tell me these things? (*Points at* MRS. ASHBY) Why did you kill Cyrus Barton?

MRS. ASHBY (*Indignantly*): This is ridiculous!

QUENTIN: Madam, I can recognize the criminal type! (MRS. ASHBY *stands aghast.* QUENTIN *turns quickly to* MRS. BARTON) Why did Annie have a key to this room?

MRS. BARTON: She cleans the place. Cyrus wouldn't let anyone else touch the room.

QUENTIN: And he had a key, too?

MRS. BARTON (*Nodding*): Until a week ago. He lost it.

QUENTIN: His key was lost?

MRS. BARTON: Yes, it was misplaced. We never found it. Fortunately, the door was unlocked at the time. (QUENTIN *thrusts his hands into his pockets.*)

QUENTIN: We're getting nowhere. Locked windows and doors. Men who were poisoned and shot. No clues, no motives—Erle Stanley Gardner wouldn't leave Perry Mason in such a situation. (*He pauses as he studies desk rear left.* MRS. BARTON *notices his observation.*)

MRS. BARTON: That was my husband's writing desk. (QUENTIN *walks to desk and begins reading papers. He drops them as he reads. Finally, he clutches one excitedly.*)

QUENTIN: Aha! Cyrus Barton wrote this letter shortly before his death. It bears yesterday's date. (*Everyone gathers about him.*)

MRS. BARTON: What does it say?

QUENTIN (*Reading*): "Dear Sir: I have heard of your intention to marry into my family." (*Raises his eyes and stares at* SUSAN. *He resumes reading.*) "It is my contention that you are a fortune hunter, and there is something you must know. This girl is not my daughter and—" (*He looks at* SUSAN *again.*) The letter ends at this point. He was murdered before he finished. (*To* SUSAN) You'd better tell us everything.

SUSAN (*Hysterically*): I didn't kill him!

QUENTIN: He was unmasking you to your fiancé. Who is this man, anyway?

SUSAN: His name is Waldemere. I—I met him at a mahjong tournament.

QUENTIN: Interesting. And this young man planned to marry you for your money?

SUSAN: No! Waldemere doesn't care about money. He could support me. He's a Good Humor salesman!

QUENTIN (*Nodding*): Where is he now?

SUSAN: I won't tell you. I won't let you drag him into this. (ANNOUNCER *steps onto stage from left.*)

ANNOUNCER: We had intended to introduce Waldemere into our play, but we couldn't find anyone suitable for the role. Furthermore, the dramatic coach felt he didn't want anyone else cluttering up the stage. Consequently, no Waldemere. (ANNOUNCER *exits left.*)

MRS. BARTON: But my husband knew all about Waldemere. He said in his letter that he heard of his intention to marry my daughter. Why, Cyrus knew about Waldemere for ages.

QUENTIN: That's odd. (*To* SUSAN) Why don't you admit that you killed Cyrus Barton?

SUSAN: Oh, I didn't kill him. If I did, would I leave an incriminating letter on the desk?

QUENTIN: I wish you'd stop asking embarrassing questions.

(*To* MRS. BARTON) What did your husband eat for dinner last night? (MRS. BARTON *pauses meditatively.*)

MRS. BARTON: We had a simple meal. Annie, the maid, had been away for two weeks and got back late yesterday afternoon. She fixed something in a hurry—canned vichysoisse, stuffed pheasant's tongue and à la mode, à la mode.

QUENTIN (*Nodding*): The usual thing. You say Annie had been away.

MRS. BARTON: Yes. Two weeks' vacation.

QUENTIN: Very interesting. I'm beginning to see the light. (*He walks left and pulls call bell.*) I must question that young lady.

MRS. BARTON: Surely, you don't think—

QUENTIN: Madam, I wish you'd finish your sentences. It's most distressing. (ANNIE *enters right.*)

ANNIE (*To* MRS. BARTON): You rang, ma'am?

QUENTIN: Ah, Annie! I would like a word with you. I understand that you returned from your vacation yesterday.

ANNIE: Yes, sir. I spent it at Coney Island.

QUENTIN: Most exclusive. Is it true that you have a key to this room?

ANNIE (*Nodding*): I unlocked the door this morning and found Mr. Barton. (*She prepares to scream, but* QUENTIN *clamps his hand across her mouth.*)

QUENTIN: No dramatics, if you please. (*Sternly*) You're a very clever girl.

ANNIE: Oh, thank you, sir.

QUENTIN: Won't you tell us about the young man you met on your vacation?

ANNIE (*Smiling*): He was awfully nice. He told me that—how did you know about him?

QUENTIN: Elementary. Annie, I accuse you of the murder of Cyrus Barton!

MRS. BARTON: Ridiculous!

SUSAN: Not Annie.

ANNIE: I didn't do it!

MRS. BARTON: Why would this girl kill Mr. Barton?

QUENTIN: Mr. Barton found out about Annie's young man at the beach. You see, she posed as Mr. Barton's daughter while on vacation!

MRS. BARTON: Oh, no!

SUSAN: Then he wasn't referring to me in that letter. He was writing to Annie's young man, telling him that she wasn't his daughter.

QUENTIN (*Nodding*): Annie enjoyed the name of a rich man's daughter for two weeks. The young man probably called this house and Cyrus found out about the deception. He threatened to expose Annie. She decided to kill him while preparing that simple meal last night.

ANNIE: I'm innocent!

QUENTIN (*To* ANNIE): You served the food. You were the only one who had the opportunity to poison the vichysoisse.

MRS. ASHBY: Poisoned the vichysoisse—how distressing!

QUENTIN: Mr. Barton thought so. A little later he came to this room to write that letter to Annie's young man. Annie was impatient. She came here, too. She found him writing the letter.

SUSAN: And she shot him!

MRS. BARTON: But the doors were locked!

QUENTIN: Precisely! It was that clue that told me she had killed Cyrus Barton. She wanted to confuse the police. She thought that Mr. Barton had the second key to *this* room. She didn't know that the key was lost *while she was on vacation!* After killing him, she left the room and locked the doors behind her.

SUSAN: I get it. When you realized that the door had been

locked by someone who had the *only* key, you knew that Annie was the murderess.

MRS. BARTON: Ingenious!

QUENTIN (*Nodding*): The locked room was Annie's Waterloo. (*Walks left and pulls bell cord.* 1ST SERVANT *enters left.* QUENTIN *points to* ANNIE.) Take her away.

1ST SERVANT: Yes, sir. (*Takes* ANNIE *by the arm and starts left with her*)

ANNIE (*Desperately, as they exit*): I didn't do it, I tell you! I didn't do it!

SUSAN (*To* MRS. BARTON): You're free! Cyrus won't dominate you anymore.

MRS. BARTON: And you can marry *your* young man.

MRS. ASHBY: And I can have my breakfast. (*To* QUENTIN) I'm a little puzzled, though. Couldn't someone have found Cyrus' missing key and murdered him?

QUENTIN: Of course not! While I was searching for my cuff link this morning, I made another discovery. (*Takes key from pocket*) It was lying on the floor where Cyrus Barton had evidently dropped it.

MRS. BARTON: Incredible! But how did you know about Annie's young man? How did you know that she had told him that she was Cyrus' daughter? (ANNOUNCER *enters left.*)

ANNOUNCER: Now, isn't that a silly question? (*Reaches into pocket and takes out script*) He merely read the last page of the script of this play! (QUENTIN *returns to armchair as* ANNOUNCER *exits left. Curtain falls.*)

* * *

SCENE 2

TIME: *A short time later.*

SETTING: *The same as Scene 1.*

BEFORE RISE: ANNOUNCER *steps before curtain and addresses audience.*

ANNOUNCER: Thus, we have seen the armchair detective at work. He wasn't a bad chap, if you don't mind the stuffy type. He will continue to solve mysteries until the author's contract runs out or until he falls out of his armchair at the age of ninety-two. And now we will meet Rivets O'Neill, American Detective. The Private Eye. The-Cloak-And-Dagger-Blood-And-Guts-Bottle-And Fist-Women-And-Trouble Detective. His methods are incredibly different and it will be interesting to see his solution. We have one consolation. It won't be any worse than the Quentin Van Quentin ordeal. (ANNOUNCER *exits left as curtain rises upon the drawing room.*)

* * *

AT RISE: SUSAN *stands near French doors, looking into garden. Suddenly, six, quick, successive shots are heard.* SUSAN *screams.* RIVETS O'NEILL *enters center, brandishing a smoking revolver. He is dressed in a dark suit, black hat and trench coat with turned-up collar. He stares furtively around the room, removes a handkerchief from his pocket and polishes revolver. He places the handkerchief and the revolver in his pocket. He winks at* SUSAN.

SUSAN: Oh, Rivets! What have you done? You shot the chauffeur, the gardener, the gateman, the servant, the stable boy, and the upstairs maid.

RIVETS (*Nodding*): A fellow can't be too careful these days. (*He takes* SUSAN *in his arms and kisses her.*)

SUSAN (*Surprised*): Oh! (*He kisses her again.*) Oh! Oh! (*He kisses her again.*) Oh! Oh! Oh! (*He pushes her aside.*)

RIVETS (*Disgruntledly*): You talk too much. (SUSAN *regains composure.*)

SUSAN: I sent for you because someone killed my father.

RIVETS: So somebody did Old Baldy out of his social security.

SUSAN (*Nodding*): He had been working on an important government project. He was a scientist, you know.

RIVETS: Everybody knew your old man. Didn't he invent a mink-lined mousetrap for wealthy rodents?

SUSAN (*Nodding*): His present work was far more important. He was interested in atomic research.

RIVETS: And you think that someone bumped him off because of that work?

SUSAN: Yes. Daddy had secret experiments in his lab upstairs. He was prepared to announce his findings to the government today.

RIVETS: Who knew about his work?

SUSAN: His secretary, Miss Marlowe. You'll meet her later.

RIVETS: Anybody else in the house?

SUSAN: Mother and I. There are servants, of course. Then there are Mr. and Mrs. Allen. Mr. Allen's a big businessman—a friend of Dad's.

RIVETS: What happened to your dad?

SUSAN: We found him in this room this morning. He had been stabbed, shot and poisoned. There was a heavy rope around his neck, too.

RIVETS (*Seriously*): Yeah, it sounds like foul play. (*Brighter*) I never met the case I couldn't handle. I'd like to speak to this Marlowe dame.

SUSAN: I told her we'd be down here.

RIVETS: Good! I'll clean up this case and then you and I can be on our way.

SUSAN: Oh, Rivets!

RIVETS: I'll take you to the Big City and show you the sights.

SUSAN: Oh, Rivets!

RIVETS: We'll stay at the best places. I'll show you how to really live.

SUSAN: Oh, Rivets!

RIVETS: Take it easy, honey. Your needle's stuck. (*Glancing left*) Where's that pencil pusher? (MISS MARLOWE, *a lovely-looking girl, enters left. She smiles coyly as she sees* RIVETS.)

MISS MARLOWE: Mr. O'Neill, I presume.

RIVETS (*Gruffly*): What did you do last night? (*He studies* MISS MARLOWE *for a moment.*) Better still, what are you doing tonight?

MISS MARLOWE: Oh, are you going to find the murderer?

RIVETS: With you around, I should look for somebody else, already?

SUSAN: Keep your mind on business.

RIVETS: Oh, I am! (*To* MISS MARLOWE) I understand that Barton finished his work for the government.

MISS MARLOWE: Yes, a government man was due to pick up the papers today.

RIVETS: Where are the papers now?

MISS MARLOWE: In the lab.

RIVETS: Can you check on them?

MISS MARLOWE: Yes, I have the key.

RIVETS: Good! We'll go together. (*He starts left with* MISS MARLOWE. SUSAN *pushes him aside and glares at him frostily.*)

SUSAN (*Coldly*): I'll go with Miss Marlowe. (SUSAN *and* MISS MARLOWE *exit left.*)

RIVETS (*Shrugging*): So, kill a guy for trying! (*He walks around the room. He steps in front of wall mirror and cockily adjusts his tie.* 2ND SERVANT, *wearing a mask and carrying a gun, enters right.* RIVETS *is unaware of his presence.* SERVANT *crosses stage until he is a few feet from* RIVETS. *He raises the gun and takes careful aim.* RIVETS *spins and grasps* SERVANT'S *gun arm. A scuffle ensues and the gun falls to the floor.* RIVETS *and* SERVANT *roll across stage, upsetting furniture. The fight is accom-*

panied by loud groans and grunts. RIVETS *is victorious. He drags the defeated* SERVANT *to his feet and tears the mask off his face.*) Who are you?

SERVANT: I'm not talking. (RIVETS *twists* SERVANT'*s arm.*)

RIVETS: I'll snap it off.

SERVANT: No—

RIVETS: Yes.

SERVANT: I'll talk.

RIVETS: Let's hear it. (*He loosens grip on* SERVANT'*s arm.*)

SERVANT: My arm!

RIVETS (*Loudly*): Who are you?

SERVANT: John.

RIVETS: John *who?*

SERVANT: Smith.

RIVETS: Unusual. Who paid you?

SERVANT: I can't tell. (RIVETS *begins to twist* SERVANT'*s arm again.*) Nobody paid me.

RIVETS: You're lying.

SERVANT: No.

RIVETS: Somebody wanted to get me.

SERVANT: No.

RIVETS: Yes.

SERVANT: Oh!

RIVETS: Who's your boss?

SERVANT: Cyrus Barton.

RIVETS (*Loudly*): You're lying.

SERVANT: He was my only boss.

RIVETS: He's dead. You're lying.

SERVANT: No—

RIVETS: Yes!

SERVANT: I don't know who killed him.

RIVETS: Where did you get the gun?

SERVANT: A birthday present from my mother.

RIVETS: Where's your boss's hideout?

SERVANT: I don't know.

RIVETS: Who bumped off Barton?

SERVANT: I don't know.

RIVETS: You're lying!

SERVANT: No—

RIVETS: Yes.

SERVANT (*Strongly*): No.

RIVETS: Yes.

SERVANT: No!

RIVETS (*Quickly*): No.

SERVANT: Yes!

RIVETS (*Triumphantly*): I fooled you that time! (ANNOUNCER *quickly steps onto stage from left.*)

ANNOUNCER: I would like the audience to take notice of the short, crisp dialogue. This dialogue flourished during the Ernest Hemingway school of literature. It has traveled a long way since that time. (*Sadly*) I won't say in *which* direction! (*Exits left*)

RIVETS: I'll give you one more chance. Start talking!

SERVANT (*Helplessly*): All right, I'll talk. I saw you coming into the house. I—I had to kill you.

RIVETS: But why? (SERVANT *apparently suffers inwardly, as he decides to reveal the attempt on* RIVETS' *life. He sighs weakly.*)

SERVANT (*Pointing*): I hate that tie! (*He dusts off hands and exits jauntily left.* MR. *and* MRS. ALLEN *enter right.* ALLEN *is the typical, successful businessman.* MRS. ALLEN *is a thin, nervous, talkative woman.*)

MRS. ALLEN (*Clucking*): Poor Cyrus!

ALLEN: Martha, be quiet! They'll find the killer. (*To* RIVETS) Who are you?

RIVETS: Skip that, bud! Who are *you?*

ALLEN (*Pompously*): I am *the* Edgar Allen. Financier, Tycoon, Wall Street Wizard and Suburban Commuter. (*Points to* MRS. ALLEN) And this—(*Swallowing hard*) is my wife!

MRS. ALLEN (*Gushing*): Poor Cyrus! (*To* RIVETS) Young man, do you know who killed him? Of course, he was an important man. And he had enemies. His work—all top-secret, you know. He never had any time to spend with his poor wife. It wasn't easy for her. She never left the house. And she always loved the arts. (*Proudly*) I enjoy the arts, too. Have you read any of Molière's plays? (RIVETS *opens his mouth to speak, but* MRS. ALLEN *rattles on.*) I loved *Les Precieuses Ridicules,* but there are some people who prefer *Le Misanthrope.* Of course, there are others who don't like Molière at all. He's too—too *French,* if you know what I mean. (RIVETS *scratches his chin in bewilderment.*) Ah, the arts! And English literature! Oscar Wilde! Shaw! I don't suppose there are too many people who mention them in the same breath. (*Sadly*) The poor American novel! Do you think it will ever find itself? Ah, the days of Sinclair Lewis and Faith Baldwin! Well, I suppose one mustn't live in the past, must one? (*To* ALLEN) Oh, Edgar, you're so quiet! Haven't you anything to say?

ALLEN (*Sweetly*): Oh, yes, my dear. (*Loudly*) Shut up! (MRS. ALLEN *is taken aback.*)

RIVETS (*To* ALLEN): You're a big businessman?

ALLEN: I dabble. In the past few months, I haven't been too busy. Meetings at Du Pont. A merger with General Motors. Small stuff like that.

RIVETS (*Nodding*): Things are tough all over. Were you here last night?

ALLEN: Yes, Barton wanted to confer with me on his atomic project.

RIVETS: You knew about his work?

ALLEN: He trusted me, all right. (MISS MARLOWE *and* SUSAN *enter left.*)

MISS MARLOWE (*Excitedly*): The papers—they're gone!

SUSAN: The lab was ransacked!

RIVETS: Well, we have a motive for Barton's death.

SUSAN: What can we do?

RIVETS: When we find the papers, we'll have the murderer.

SUSAN: But the killer might have taken the papers and escaped.

RIVETS (*Shaking head*): There weren't any strangers in this house. Barton was robbed and killed by someone he trusted.

MISS MARLOWE: Do you mean that one of us killed him?

RIVETS (*Dramatically*): I'm not just shooting off my cotton-picking mouth. The murderer is in this room! (*He pulls revolver from pocket and tugs at* ALLEN'*s wig. When the wig comes off, the secret papers fall from* ALLEN'*s head onto the floor.*) Allen, you're the killer! You hid the papers under your wig!

MRS. ALLEN (*Tearfully*): Oh, Edgar! (*Points to wig*) And I thought *that* was your own curly hair.

RIVETS (*To* ALLEN): I knew that you killed Barton when I heard that he had been stabbed, strangled, shot and poisoned. You're a successful businessman. You wouldn't leave anything to chance. He caught you stealing the government papers and you killed him.

SUSAN: How did you know he had hidden the papers under his wig? (ANNOUNCER *enters left.*)

ANNOUNCER (*Pointing to* RIVETS): He read the script, too! (ANNOUNCER *exits.*)

RIVETS (*To* ALLEN): Now, you're going to die! (*He fires revolver and* ALLEN *falls to floor.*)

MISS MARLOWE: You killed him! You fiend! (*She lunges at* RIVETS *but he sidesteps and levels revolver at her.*)

RIVETS: You were Allen's confederate. He couldn't get into the lab without *your* key.

MISS MARLOWE: Yes, I helped him!

RIVETS: Why did he want the plans?

MISS MARLOWE: Allen was going to invest in a new bubble

gum company. The Atomic Bubble! It would have been worth a fortune. And you killed him! (*She laughs shrilly*) But you haven't won. Allen and I wired the atomic bomb to explode in exactly *one minute!* (*She glances at wristwatch.*) You can't escape!

SUSAN: What can we do?

MISS MARLOWE: You have thirty seconds!

RIVETS: Where is the bomb?

MISS MARLOWE: You'll never find it. (*Glances at watch*) Twenty seconds!

MRS. ALLEN (*Indignantly*): This isn't good for my nerves. Loud noises frighten me. And my vellum-covered edition of Bernard Shaw will be ruined! (*To* RIVETS) Do you like Shaw? Some people think that he is rather—

RIVETS (*Sharply*): Shut up!

MISS MARLOWE: Ten seconds!

SUSAN: Goodbye, Rivets.

RIVETS: Goodbye—

MISS MARLOWE (*Studying watch*): Five seconds—four—three—two—one! (MRS. ALLEN, RIVETS *and* SUSAN *steel themselves for the explosion. A faint "pop" is heard off-stage.* ANNOUNCER *enters left. He bows rather apologetically.*)

ANNOUNCER: We had planned to introduce a deafening explosion at this point, but our plans went wrong. (*Shakes head sadly*) Our sound-effects man is strictly for the birds! (*He exits.*)

RIVETS (*To* MISS MARLOWE): And this is for you, sister! (*Points gun at her and fires. She falls to floor. He turns to* SUSAN.) Well, I cleared up this case.

MRS. ALLEN (*Sighing*): Thank heavens that's over. It reminded me of one of those thrilling mystery stories. Do you like mysteries? (RIVETS *levels gun at her.*) Really, I think that mystery writers are quite ingenious. Of course, their stories are always filled with doddering old ladies and retired colonels, but one can't have everything. And another thing—(RIVETS *fires gun.* MRS. ALLEN *falls to floor.*)

RIVETS (*To* SUSAN): Let's get out of here. (*Points to "bodies."*) This place is getting crowded. (*He and* SUSAN *step across bodies and exit center. Curtain falls.* ANNOUNCER *enters left and addresses audience.*)

ANNOUNCER: I hope that you have enjoyed *A Case for Two Detectives.* Their methods were different, but each gentleman came up with a surprising solution. There's one thing, though. Each detective was WRONG! (*Pause*) Who killed Cyrus Barton? (*Shakes head sadly at audience*) Why, the *butler,* of course! Didn't you know that the *butler* is always the murderer? And who is the butler? Well, I'll tell you—

MRS. BARTON (*Calling from offstage*): Jarvis! Jarvis! (ANNOUNCER *straightens and faces left.*)

ANNOUNCER (*Pompously*): Coming, madam! (*He strikes a stiff, aristocratic pose, throws back his shoulders. He exits left with a solemn step.*)

THE END

The Shop Girl's Revenge

by Robert Downing

Characters

MIKE, *a stock boy*
PATTY, *a cash girl*
MR. BEADLE, *a store detective*
HORACE FALMOUTH, *a floorwalker*
GLADYS WORTHING, *a poor but honest shop girl*
MRS. ELLA GANT, *a society matron*
JACK, *Mrs. Gant's foster son*

TIME: *At the turn of the century.*
SETTING: *The notions counter at Gant's Department Store.*
AT RISE: *The stage is empty. Offstage, eight mournful bongs of a store clock indicate the hour.* MIKE, *a stock boy, enters from right, lackadaisically pushing a broom.*

MIKE: Here it is, eight o'clock in the mornin' at Gant's Department Store, an' eight o'clock *this* mornin' is just like eight o'clock *every* mornin', an' I'm the first person in the store. (*Leans on broom*) I work harder around here than anybody else. I'm the last person to go home at night. Work, work, work! (*Yawns*) I can tell you, for Mike the stock boy, life's no bed of roses! (PATTY, *a cash girl, enters from left, hurrying past* MIKE)

PATTY: Oh! I'm late! I'm late! I'm late! (PATTY *knocks*

MIKE's *broom out from under him.* MIKE *falls with a thud.* PATTY *turns.*) I'm real sorry, Mike. (PATTY *picks up the broom, sets it carefully against the counter, and hurries out right, leaving* MIKE *still on the floor.*)

MIKE (*Lifting himself to one elbow*): That's Patty, the cash girl. Lots of vim an' vigor, but not much upstairs, (*Taps forehead*) if you know what I mean. (*Rises, starts to sweep*) Oh, Patty's all right, you understand. Heart of gold, an' all that—(MR. BEADLE, *a stout store detective, charges in from left, huffing and puffing*)

MR. BEADLE: Oh! I'm late! I'm late! I'm late! (MR. BEADLE *knocks* MIKE's *broom out from under him.* MIKE *falls again.* MR. BEADLE *turns.*) Oh, Mike, I'm very sorry—sorry, indeed. (*He leans the broom against the counter, rushes out right, muttering, in worried tones.*) Late! Late! Late!

MIKE (*Propping himself on the other elbow*): That's Mr. Beadle, the store detective. He can't tell a pickpocket from a shoplifter, an' he wouldn't know how to arrest a crook if he saw one. (*Rises*) Heart of gold, though. But not much up here. (*Taps forehead*) Come to think of it, I'm about the only brainy one around this joint! (*Leans on broom, yawns.* HORACE FALMOUTH, *a floorwalker, faultlessly attired, stalks in from left. He pauses, strokes his heavy black mustache, and glares at* MIKE.)

FALMOUTH: Good morning, Michael!

MIKE (*Jumping*): Eek! Mr. Falmouth! (*Starts sweeping, vigorously*)

FALMOUTH: I'm glad to see that you know how to apply yourself, Michael, I shouldn't like to give a bad report of you to Mrs. Gant. (*As he walks by counter, he runs his finger along over it, looking for dust. He peers at stock, and looks around suspiciously.*)

MIKE (*Aside*): That's Horace Falmouth. He's the floor-walker here at Gant's. *Mister* Horace Falmouth to all of us *common* people. But I have a better name for the likes of him!

FALMOUTH: Get busy, Mike!

MIKE (*Hustling the broom*): Yes, sir! Yes, sir!

FALMOUTH (*Consulting a large gold watch*): Late again!

MIKE: No, sir! No, sir! I've been here for hours!

FALMOUTH: Not you, you idiot!

MIKE: Not me? (*Looks around, perplexed*) Then who?

FALMOUTH: You know very well that I refer to the shop girl who presides at this notions counter.

MIKE: Yup. I had a notion—

FALMOUTH: Quiet!

MIKE (*Finger on lips*): Sh-h!

FALMOUTH: Gladys Worthing has been late every morning this week!

MIKE: I guess you're right, Mr. Falmouth.

FALMOUTH: I am *always* right!

MIKE: Yes, sir! Yes, sir!

FALMOUTH: I shall report that young lady to Mrs. Gant.

MIKE: Aw, gee, Horace, don't do that!

FALMOUTH: What did you say?

MIKE: I mean—please don't do that, *Mister* Falmouth.

FALMOUTH: That's better. I shall have respect from my inferiors!

MIKE: Oh, yes, yes, indeed, sir! (*Aside*) *His* inferiors! If you want my opinion, the very lowest bum on the Bowery stands head an' shoulders above Horace *Falmouth!* (*To* FALMOUTH) Oh, Mr. Falmouth, please don't report Gladys for bein' late. That girl has a mighty hard time in life as it is.

FALMOUTH: Tardiness is inexcusable.

MIKE: But Mr. Falmouth, Gladys lives a long way from the store, an' her wages are very small, an' she has to walk every step of the way to work, an' mostly it's all uphill.

Mr. Falmouth, sometimes that poor girl just can't help bein' late!

FALMOUTH: Enough of your lip! Get on with your work, Mike! *I'll* tend to Miss Worthing.

MIKE: Yes, sir! Yes, sir! (*Goes out right, sweeping*) Oh, it's a black day at Gant's, an' that's for sure! (FALMOUTH *stares after* MIKE *for a moment, then he looks off left. He consults his watch again.*)

FALMOUTH (*Aside*): It's a lucky thing for me that Gladys Worthing is late! And every time I can discover that wretched girl in a defection of any sort in this department store, I mean to make the most of it! (*Looks around, sneering*) Gant's Department Store, indeed! The day will soon come when all of this will belong to me! (*He laughs, rubbing his hands together.*) I already have old lady Gant wrapped around my little finger! She believes in me—the silly old fool! And before she knows it, I'll get this store away from her. By hook or by crook, I'll get this store for my very own! (*Laughs wickedly*) Nothing can stand in my way! Mrs. Gant is already in my power, and as for her foster son Jack—he's a wastrel and a spendthrift! I think I have poisoned Mrs. Gant's mind against *him!* Jack will soon find himself in the stock room, where he belongs! No one can stop me! (*Recoils*) Except—alas—one person! (*Clenches fists*) *Gladys Worthing!* (*Looks off left*) And here she comes! (GLADYS *hurries on.* FALMOUTH *consults his watch, glares at her.* GLADYS *stops, facing* FALMOUTH, *trembling.*) Well, Miss Worthing!

GLADYS: Oh, Mr. Falmouth!

FALMOUTH: Late again!

GLADYS: Oh, sir, I am afraid you're right.

FALMOUTH: I am *always* right!

GLADYS: Please forgive me.

FALMOUTH: It seems to me, young lady, that you are forever asking me to forgive you. Late every day this week! What's your excuse this time?

GLADYS: I have no excuse, sir.

FALMOUTH: I thought as much! (*Aside*) She's one of those fools who thinks that honesty is the best policy! (*Laughs wickedly, turns to* GLADYS) No excuse, eh?

GLADYS: No, sir, it's just that my poor little room is so far from the store, and I have to walk—nay, *run!*—to get here on time even though I arise at crack of dawn. It's uphill all the way, Mr. Falmouth, and the streets are crowded with trams and wagons and—

FALMOUTH: Hush! This begins to sound like an excuse!

GLADYS: Oh, no, sir!

FALMOUTH: Remove your hat, girl, and get to work!

GLADYS: Yes, sir! (*She hurries out.*)

FALMOUTH (*Aside*): Little does Gladys Worthing know what *I* know! She is the rightful heir to the Gant millions and to this emporium, for Gladys is the long-lost daughter of Mrs. Ella Gant! (*He looks around, darkly*) But Mrs. Gant must never know the truth—for if she did, I'd be ruined! (*Clutches his brow*) Ruined! (*Staggers a bit*) Ruined! *Ruined!* (PATTY *dashes in from right, wearing a cash apron which contains pockets full of coins and bills. She observes* FALMOUTH *reeling.*)

PATTY: What's the matter with you? Got the bends?

FALMOUTH (*Quickly recovering*): Mind your manners, miss!

PATTY: I'm no miss! I'm Patty the cash girl! (*Darts out, left, calling*) Cash! Cash! Cash!

FALMOUTH: Insolent creature! When I take over this store, I'll get rid of her! (GLADYS *returns from right, moves behind counter*)

FALMOUTH: Aha! Finally in your place, Miss Worthing?

GLADYS: Yes, sir.

FALMOUTH: There'll be no lunch hour for you today, Miss Worthing.

GLADYS: Oh, Mr. Falmouth—

FALMOUTH (*Silences her with a gesture*): My word is law!

GLADYS: But, Mr. Falmouth—

FALMOUTH: Get to work, girl! Arrange your notions!

GLADYS (*As her hands fly helplessly over the stock*): Oh, Mr. Falmouth, I fear that if you allow me no time for lunch today, I shall collapse at this very counter!

FALMOUTH (*Sneering*): Nothing as dramatic as that, I trust.

GLADYS: I ate no breakfast, sir, for fear of being late.

FALMOUTH: Your problems are not my problems, Miss Worthing.

GLADYS: If I am not able to have at least one tiny bun, and perhaps a sip of fresh milk at noon, I am so afraid that I —(*Grips counter*) that I—(*Weaving from side to side*) Oh, dear! Oh—*dear!* (*She falls behind the counter with a thud.*)

FALMOUTH: Hm-m. Very interesting. Methinks that this young lady ate no dinner last night, and perhaps no lunch yesterday. That's my guess.

GLADYS (*Rising, suddenly*): You are *right,* Mr. Falmouth.

FALMOUTH: I am *always* right!

GLADYS: Yes, sir. (*She drops from sight with another thud.*)

FALMOUTH: This will never do—fainting on company time! (*Starts behind counter, but pauses to look off left*) Egad! Who comes thither? Why—'tis Mrs. Gant herself! (*Snarls*) And that no-good foster son of hers! (MRS. GANT *enters from left, followed by* JACK, *a bored dandy.*)

MRS. GANT: Good morning, Mr. Falmouth.

FALMOUTH (*Bowing, almost to the floor*): Your servant, Mrs. Gant. (*Bows to* JACK) Top of the morning to you, sir. (*Aside*) The young *puppy.* (*Grits his teeth*)

JACK (*Stifling a yawn*): Mornin', Horace. Mater, I do wish

you'd give me a farthing or two. I must visit my tailor, y'know. I simply haven't a decent rag to my back.

MRS. GANT: Now, Jack, you promised you'd come to the store with me today, and begin to learn the ropes.

FALMOUTH (*Aside*): If *he* ever learns the ropes, I am *undone!*

JACK: Dear mater, I do wish you wouldn't use such vulgar expressions! "Learn the ropes!" No one of quality speaks like that.

MRS. GANT: Then more's the pity! Besides, I am plain Ella Gant. I'm a shopkeeper's widow, Jack—and you are a shopkeeper's foster son. Rid yourself of false pride, Jack. True quality is in the honest heart!

JACK (*Bored*): Yes, mater. Now, how about some cash?

PATTY (*Leaping in from left*): Cash! Cash! Cash! Did I hear somebody call for cash? I'm Patty the cash girl, and I'm here with cash!

JACK: Splendid! (JACK *helps himself to considerable cash from the pockets in* PATTY'S *apron.*)

PATTY (*Objecting*): *Hey!* (FALMOUTH *silences her with a gesture.*)

JACK (*Pocketing the cash*): What a very thoughtful service. Your idea, Horace? (*Smiles at* PATTY) Thank you, miss. (*Starts out, left*) Ta, ta, mater. See you at tea time! (*Goes*)

PATTY: Why that bum took almost all my cash! (*Looks around*) Say, where's Gladys? I saw her hangin' up her hat, but I don't see her now. Where's Gladys, Mr. Foul—er—Mr. *Fal*mouth?

FALMOUTH: Get on with your business, girl!

PATTY: Can't get on with my business till I get more cash. (*Hurrying out, right*) Need cash! Need cash! Need cash!

MRS. GANT (*Turning to the counter*): Ah, yes! The notions counter. I must have a notion or two. (*She puts her purse on the counter, examines the stock.*)

FALMOUTH (*Aside*): The old lady must not see Gladys!

What if she recognized the girl as her long-lost daughter who was stolen by gypsies years ago! (*Goes to* MRS. GANT) Dear lady, do come into my office. There you can sit in a comfortable chair, and we shall bring the stock for your approval.

MRS. GANT: Nonsense, Mr. Falmouth. I enjoy poking around the store. (*She moves along the counter.*)

FALMOUTH (*Aside, biting his nails*): *Drat!* (*He turns, sees* MRS. GANT's *purse on the counter*) *Aha!*

MRS. GANT: Did you say something, Mr. Falmouth?

FALMOUTH: No, dear lady. A slight cough. (*Taps his chest*) An old complaint, alas.

MRS. GANT: You must take care of yourself, sir. I am eager for all my employees to be in the best of health. Their welfare is my constant concern, Mr. Falmouth. Tell me, is there no salesgirl at this counter?

FALMOUTH (*Stepping behind counter*): *I* shall serve you, ma'am!

MRS. GANT (*Picks up an article, studying it*): Well, I had thought . . .

FALMOUTH: Yes, ma'am?

MRS. GANT (*Puts the article down*): On the other hand, I think I see something over here. (*She goes out, right.* FALMOUTH *seizes the purse* MRS. GANT *has left on the counter. He stuffs the purse under the counter, and follows* MRS. GANT *off right.* GLADYS *commences to moan behind the counter.* MIKE *and* PATTY *hurry in from opposite sides of the stage, looking back over their respective shoulders. They collide, center, and fall flat.* MIKE *helps* PATTY *to her feet.*)

PATTY: Where's Gladys?

MIKE: I don't know.

PATTY: I don't like the looks of this!

MIKE: Why not?

PATTY: I think that old Foulmouth is up to something!

(GLADYS *groans.* MIKE *and* PATTY *rush behind the counter, from opposite ends.*) Gladys!

MIKE: Golly! (*They help* GLADYS *to her feet.*)

GLADYS (*Weakly*): Where—am—I?

PATTY: Gee, the poor kid must have fainted.

MIKE: She's weak as a cat.

GLADYS (*Wavering*): Food—food.

PATTY: She's hungry!

MIKE: That's funny—it's not even noon!

PATTY: Do you have something to eat?

MIKE: Maybe. Let's see. (*Rummages in his pockets, and brings out a plug of tobacco.*)

PATTY (*Seizing the tobacco*): Give me that!

MIKE: Hey, wait! That's chawing tobacco!

PATTY: Mike! You don't—*chaw?*

MIKE: Heck, no. I just keep that in my pocket to discourage moths! (*Takes back the tobacco*)

PATTY: Well, I'd *never* marry a man who *chawed!*

MIKE: Best reason I ever heard for takin' up chawin'! (*Pretends he is going to bite into the tobacco*)

PATTY: Stop your foolin'! Gladys needs food!

GLADYS (*Weakly*): Food—food.

MIKE (*Finding a square of chocolate in his pocket*): Here's some chocolate. Mighty good for energy!

PATTY (*Takes the chocolate from* MIKE, *gives it to* GLADYS): Eat this, dearie.

GLADYS (*Weakly*): Just a nibble. (*She gulps the whole square, chewing vigorously.*)

MIKE: Just a nibble? She nibbles like a *beaver!*

PATTY (*To* GLADYS): Feel better?

GLADYS: Yes—yes, I do.

PATTY: What happened?

GLADYS: I fear I fainted.

MIKE: No breakfast? (GLADYS *shakes her head.*)

PATTY: No supper last night? (GLADYS *shakes her head.*) I thought so! Why not?

GLADYS: I gave my supper money to a poor old lady who had lost her way in the city streets.

MIKE (*Aside*): I don't know what other folks may think, but for my money, this here Gladys is *true blue!*

PATTY: Oh, stop your horsin', Mike, and let's help Gladys to the lounge. You've got to rest a little, dearie.

GLADYS (*As they lead her out, left*): But what will Mr. Falmouth say?

PATTY: Don't you worry about him.

MIKE: He'd better not say a word! If he says a single word, I'll—I'll—

PATTY: You'll *what?*

MIKE: I won't listen to him! (*They exit, left.* MR. BEADLE *clumps in from right. He picks his teeth with a toothpick. He looks right, then left.*)

MR. BEADLE: Not much crime around here today. None at all, I'm glad to say. (*Stretches*) Well, guess I'll mosey down to the boiler room an' have me a little ol' nap. Beadle, my boy, you got yourself a cushy job at last! (*Goes out left.* FALMOUTH *enters from right with* MRS. GANT.)

MRS. GANT (*Distressed*): Oh, how stupid of me! What a foolish thing to do!

FALMOUTH: Be calm, dear lady.

MRS. GANT: But I know I had my purse in my hand just a moment ago.

FALMOUTH: I shall find it, ma'am, never fear!

MRS. GANT: But where? Where? Oh, dear! It isn't the loss of the seven thousand dollars in cash that I always carry in my purse that worries me—

FALMOUTH (*Aside, gulping*): A Croesus! A female Midas! (*To* MRS. GANT) Now then, it seems to me that you had the purse when you paused here at the notion counter.

MRS. GANT: I did! I did! Oh, Mr. Falmouth, I beg of you to help me find it! You don't understand its value to me.

FALMOUTH (*Aside*): Seven thousand dollars! I can understand *that!*

MRS. GANT: It's the keepsake, the treasure, the heirloom, the darling little golden locket in my purse that I must not—*dare* not lose! (*Begins to weep*) Oh, Mr. Falmouth! (PATTY *and* MIKE *enter left, as* FALMOUTH *is about to put his arm around* MRS. GANT.)

FALMOUTH: What are you two doing here?

MIKE: Just passin' through.

FALMOUTH: Get on about your business! No loafing on company time!

MRS. GANT (*Overcome*): My purse! my purse! (*She reels.* PATTY *and* MIKE *rush to support her, one at each elbow.*)

PATTY: Gee, ma'am, did somebody cop your purse?

MRS. GANT: It's gone! Gone!

FALMOUTH: Mrs. Gant, if we do not find your purse within two minutes, I shall order the front doors locked and have Mr. Beadle search every person in this store!

PATTY: Ol' Beadle better not lay his hands on me!

MIKE: Don't you worry, Patty, I'll protect you!

MRS. GANT: Find the purse!

FALMOUTH: Now, let me see. You paused first at this counter to examine the notions.

MRS. GANT: Yes, yes.

FALMOUTH: You moved along the counter—so! (*He demonstrates.*)

MRS. GANT: Yes, yes.

FALMOUTH: Then we went into the next department.

MRS. GANT: Yes, yes.

MIKE (*Aside*): Aw, come on, ma'am, give the bum a diff'rent answer for a change!

FALMOUTH: Now, I don't recall that you had your purse—over there. (*Points off right*)

MRS. GANT: No, no—

MIKE (*Aside*): That's the ticket!

FALMOUTH: Therefore, my deductions lead me to believe that you left the purse—right about *here!* (*Slaps counter*) Now, where could it be? (*Rummages in the stock*)

MRS. GANT (*Faintly, as* PATTY *and* MIKE *support her*): Oh, the locket! The dear little locket! (PATTY *and* MIKE *exchange glances.*)

PATTY (*To* MIKE): Maybe she's gone off her rocker! (MIKE *nods.* FALMOUTH *moves behind the counter. He spies the purse. He reacts violently.*)

FALMOUTH: *Aha!!*

PATTY (*Ducking*): He's been hit by lightnin'!

MIKE: No such luck!

FALMOUTH: *Eureka!!*

MIKE: Nobody here by that name.

FALMOUTH (*Seizing the purse*): Here it is! (*He holds it high.*)

MRS. GANT (*Jubilant*): My purse! You found it! (*She reaches for it.*)

FALMOUTH (*Coming forward*): One moment, please. We must investigate this matter. I have found the purse behind the counter of Gladys Worthing. All of you are witnesses to that fact. This can mean only *one* thing! Gladys Worthing stole your purse when your back was turned, Mrs. Gant!

MRS. GANT: Who is Gladys Worthing?

FALMOUTH: She is a wretched shop girl, soon to cool her heels in *jail!*

PATTY: Gladys is no wretch! She's the dearest—

MIKE: The sweetest—

PATTY: The nicest—

FALMOUTH: Silence! Mike, go get Mr. Beadle. Tell him to arrest Gladys Worthing for stealing Mrs. Gant's purse.

MRS. GANT: But are we sure that she—

FALMOUTH (*Bowing to* MRS. GANT): Madam, permit me. (*To* MIKE) Tell Beadle to take Gladys to the nearest precinct house. I shall lodge formal charges within the hour. (*Roars*) Well, do as I say!

MIKE (*Reluctantly*): Yes, sir. (*Goes out, left*)

FALMOUTH: Patty, go find Gladys. Make sure that she does not escape before she is arrested. (PATTY *starts out, her head bowed, sorrowfully.*) Remember! I shall hold you personally responsible for Gladys until she is arrested!

PATTY (*Aside, as she goes*): Not only a Foul*mouth,* but a black heart! Oh, woe, woe, woe! (*Exits left*)

FALMOUTH (*Returning the purse to* MRS. GANT): And here, dear lady, is your property.

MRS. GANT (*Looking inside the purse*): Ah, 'tis safe! The little golden locket is safe!

FALMOUTH (*Peering eagerly over* MRS. GANT'S *shoulder*): And the seven thousand dollars?

MRS. GANT: Oh, I guess that's all here.

FALMOUTH: You *guess!* (*Aside*) Her indifference to large sums of money *astounds* me!

MRS. GANT: Now that my purse is safely returned, I don't think that charges should be pressed against that poor girl. Have her released, Falmouth. This instant! Do you hear?

FALMOUTH (*Aside*): Released? That will ruin all my plans! This is my one opportunity to dispose of Gladys Worthing forever! And now the old lady seeks to spoil my chances. What to do? (*Bites his nails*) What to do? (JACK *re-enters from left*)

JACK: Mater, dear, I need a few quid more. I found some very nice boots to go with the suit I ordered. I say, has there been some excitement hereabouts?

FALMOUTH (*Laughing to cover a sneer*): Not much, Mr. Jack. I apprehended a miserable shop girl who attempted to steal your mother's purse. No excitement. Just Horace Falmouth, on the job—as usual!

JACK: I ran into Beadle at the front door, escorting the poor girl to jail, Mater. I told him to release her.

FALMOUTH: You *what!!*

JACK: She doesn't look like a criminal.

FALMOUTH (*Rushing at* JACK *furiously*): You fool! You crazy idiot!

JACK: I say, you're mighty redundant today, old man.

FALMOUTH (*Recovering*): Sorry, sir. (*Aside*) What now? What move will save the day? (*Bites his nails.* GLADYS *rushes in from left, followed by* BEADLE, PATTY, MIKE. GLADYS *flings herself at* MRS. GANT'S *feet.*)

GLADYS: Oh, ma'am, it is not true!

FALMOUTH (*Aside*): Curses! The jig is up! (FALMOUTH *starts out, but* JACK *puts an arm around his shoulder, affectionately, pretending to restrain him.*)

MRS. GANT (*To* GLADYS): Now what's all this? Get up, girl!

GLADYS (*Sobbing*): I did not steal your purse! It is true that I fainted on company time, and for that infraction I beg of Mr. Falmouth to deduct a suitable amount from my wages. But to steal a purse—that I could *never* do! (*Sobs*)

MRS. GANT: Get up, dear child. Let me dry your tears. (PATTY *helps* GLADYS *to her feet.* MRS. GANT *looks in her purse for a handkerchief.*)

BEADLE: If nobody wants nobody arrested, can I go back to the boiler room and—er—look for prowlers?

JACK (*Sarcastically*): Just be patient, Beadle. We may yet find work for you. (*To* FALMOUTH) Eh, Falmouth? Don't you agree? (FALMOUTH *glares at* JACK. MRS. GANT *removes a handkerchief from her purse. A small golden locket falls to the floor.* GLADYS *stoops to retrieve it.*)

MRS. GANT: How clumsy of me!

GLADYS (*Staring at the locket*): Why—why—this little locket is exactly like my own!

FALMOUTH (*Aside*): Curse those careless gypsies!

MRS. GANT (*To* GLADYS): What did you say, my dear?

GLADYS: The locket that fell from your purse, ma'am—it matches the one I wear around my neck. See—(*She shows* MRS. GANT *the locket she wears.* MRS. GANT *reels.* MIKE *catches her.*)

MRS. GANT: Sweet angels of mercy!

FALMOUTH (*Breaking away from* JACK, *rushes at* GLADYS): Away with you! Thief! Miscreant! Beadle, do your duty! Arrest this girl! She has stolen Mrs. Gant's purse! I found the evidence! I have witnesses! I demand that she be punished for the evil creature that she is!

GLADYS: You would not dare insult me, sir, if Jack were only here!

JACK (*Striding forward*): I know not what Jack you may mean, fair lady, but *this* Jack is here!

FALMOUTH (*Brushing* JACK *aside*): Keep out of this, you fool! (*He grabs* GLADYS *by the arm. The women scream.*)

GLADYS (*Trying to pull away*): Unhand me, villain!

JACK: Time for action! Horace Falmouth—on your guard! (JACK *spins* FALMOUTH *around, and punches him on the chin.* FALMOUTH *collapses into* BEADLE*'s arms.*) Beadle, hold the quarry fast! (*To* MRS. GANT) Mater, let me pull together the loose ends of this puzzle.

MRS. GANT: Pray do, dear boy.

JACK: For some time I have been suspicious of yonder gent. (*Points to* FALMOUTH) I discovered a nefarious plan of his, Mater, to take over this store, lock, stock, and barrel.

MIKE: I'm the stock boy around here! He'll answer to me! (*He assumes a fighting stance.*)

JACK: I also perceived that Falmouth was engaged in a

campaign to persecute poor Miss Worthing. I wondered how any man could harass one so fair! (*Bows low to* GLADYS)

GLADYS (*Averting her eyes*): Why, thank you, sir.

JACK: 'Tis nothing. I noted the locket 'round Miss Worthing's neck, Mater, and saw that it was identical with the locket you have always carried. A small amount of research in the gypsy encampment by the Old Bridge revealed all. Mater, this girl is your long-lost daughter!

MRS. GANT (*Extending her arms to* GLADYS): My darling!

GLADYS (*Rushing into* MRS. GANT'S *arms*): My own dear mother!

PATTY (*Stifling a tear*): What a picture!

JACK: As for yonder article— (*Points at* FALMOUTH) It was he, dear Mater, who placed your purse behind Miss Worthing's counter.

FALMOUTH: You'll have to prove that!

JACK: I saw you with my own eyes!

FALMOUTH: You weren't anywhere around!

JACK: What a simpleton you are! Do you suppose I *went* to my tailor's? Nay, Falmouth. I hid myself behind that marble pillar. I saw it all! Now, Beadle, do your duty!

FALMOUTH: You'll pay for this!

JACK: I doubt it.

FALMOUTH: I'll show you! (*He breaks free from* BEADLE *and rushes at* GLADYS. *The women scream.* JACK *simply extends his foot and trips* FALMOUTH, *who falls flat on his face.* JACK *places his foot on* FALMOUTH'S *back, and folds his arms across his chest.*)

PATTY: Hooray!

MIKE: That's our Jackie! That's our champ!

BEADLE: Couldn't have done better myself. (*Picks his teeth*)

MRS. GANT: My son! My precious son!

JACK: Your *foster* son, Mater. And fortunately so. (*Taps his chest*) For here beats a heart that yearns for the love of dear Gladys!

FALMOUTH (*A last gasp*): *Curses!*

MRS. GANT (*Beaming*): Well, what do you say, Gladys?

GLADYS: I am overcome, yet somehow I knew that things would come right in the end! (*Goes to* JACK) Now I see that the ways of Providence are merciful, that the long road has a turning, that darkness pales when comes the dawn, that—

JACK (*Impatiently*): Gladys—

GLADYS: Yes, dear Jack?

JACK: What about us?

GLADYS: Jack! My hero! (*She embraces him. Curtain.*)

THE END

Jump for Joy

by Albert Schaaf

Characters

AMBROSE BAINBRIDGE, *a theatrical agent*
SALLY CARTWRIGHT, *his secretary*
DORA MARTINDALE, *a rival agent*
JOY DARLING, *a movie glamour queen*
VIOLA SHARPE, *her companion*
HOBART SANBORN, HARRY JOEY, LAURA CLYDE, PHIL, THE BIG NOISE, THREE OTHER NOISES — *Bainbridge's clients*
TELEGRAPH BOY
DELIVERY BOY

SETTING: *The office of Ambrose Bainbridge in New York City.*

AT RISE: SALLY, *a pretty young girl, is at the desk at right. The telephone rings, and she answers it.*

SALLY (*Into phone*): Good afternoon, Bainbridge and Bainbridge. . . . No, Mr. Bainbridge isn't in. . . . I'm sorry, he will not be available all day. He's having an important conference. . . . I'm sorry, Miss Martindale, I cannot divulge the nature of the conference. . . . No.

. . . (*Holds phone away from her ear, then, firmly*) Goodbye, Miss Martindale. (*Hangs up quickly*) That woman is the most persistent person in the world. Well, I guess that's natural. She's a theatrical agent. Ambrose Bainbridge is a theatrical agent, and *he's* persistent! (*She starts to type some letters.* HOBART SANBORN *enters. He is gray-haired and distinguished looking.*)

HOBART: Good afternoon, my dear Miss Cartwright. Hobart Sanborn is here, and punctual, too, you will note. (*He draws out pocket watch and looks at it.*) It is precisely two o'clock.

SALLY: And Bainbridge and Bainbridge appreciates your promptness. Have a seat.

HOBART (*Sitting*): Ah! Thank you.

SALLY: Do you know why Ambrose asked you to come in?

HOBART: Don't you know?

SALLY: All I know is that Amby has sent for several of his clients——

HOBART: Several of his clients? Oh. I rather thought he just wanted me . . . perhaps for a television play or something.

SALLY: I'm sorry, Mr. Sanborn. I didn't mean to mislead you. He doesn't have a play for you, though.

HOBART: No, I suppose not. Really, Miss Cartwright, if you could only have known the great star I once was in the legitimate theatre.

SALLY: I know. I've read all about you.

HOBART: You can't possibly know.

SALLY: Anyway, you *are* on television. You do those men's wear commercials where you sit on a white horse or a pile of oranges or something, looking distinguished.

HOBART (*Brightening a little*): No one looks quite as distinguished as I do, you must admit.

SALLY: Of course. So, as I was saying, the meeting this

afternoon includes several of Amby's clients. He wants them here to make an impression on Joy Darling.

HOBART: Who on earth is she?

SALLY (*Sarcastically*): She's only the biggest glamour queen in Hollywood, that's all.

HOBART: If she's that big, I'm quite sure *Ambrose* doesn't have her for a client.

SALLY: Mr. Sanborn! That isn't very kind.

HOBART: Oh, I mean no slur on Ambrose's ability as an agent. You and I know he's one of the best. But he doesn't push himself enough.

SALLY: I know what you mean. He's always so busy doing things for his clients, he never does anything for himself.

HOBART: How did he meet this Joy Darling?

SALLY: A friend introduced them at a party, and Ambrose remembered reading that Miss Darling had recently fired her agent.

HOBART: I wish him luck. He'll probably get Miss Darling the best pictures and personal appearances in the world, and get *himself* the lowest agency fee in the world.

SALLY: Let's hope he manages to get himself Joy Darling, *and* a good agency fee!

HOBART: *That* would be something!

SALLY: By the way, do you have the afternoon paper?

HOBART: No, why?

SALLY: Oh, nothing. I'm just interested in the theatrical reviews.

HOBART (*Smiling*): Why, is there one about you?

SALLY: I don't think so. I'd just like to see the paper to . . . (*At this point,* HARRY JOEY *comes bounding in. He runs to* SALLY.)

HARRY: Darling, we just have time to make the second show at the Paramount. Come, fly with me to the popcorn stand, and I'll buy you anything you want.

SALLY: As long as it's popcorn, I know, Harry.

HARRY: My intentions are good, though, Sally, my sweet. Say, you said Amby wanted me. What can I do to help the greatest agent in New York?

HOBART: Ambrose sent for *you,* too? Do I understand, Miss Cartwright, that I am to share in this bit of nonsense with Harry Joey, the world's worst comedian?

HARRY: Just a minute, there, Hobart. At least I don't do men's wear commercials for a living.

HOBART (*With sarcasm*): No, you certainly don't. You're the man who created Crackpot the Clown!

HARRY: So what's wrong with that? The kids love it.

HOBART: Yes, that's true. It must be nice to know you have a public that's a match for your mentality.

HARRY: Now, just a minute, Hobart. I'll bet you couldn't play the part of a clown if you wanted to.

HOBART: No? I'll have you know when I was younger, I played the *fool* in *King Lear*.

HARRY: That's the difference between the two of us. *I* know when to stop.

HOBART: Harry, one more crack like that, and, so help me, I'll . . .

SALLY: For heaven's sake, you two. You're supposed to be here to help Amby.

HARRY: I'm sorry, Sally. You know Sanborn and I would do anything to help Amby. Do you remember the time Amby booked me into a Brooklyn theatre by offering the manager a discount on my salary?

HOBART: You never knew the difference because the discount was Ambrose's agency fee!

SALLY: He gave up his entire fee to get you a job?

HARRY: Of course.

HOBART: You should have seen one turkey I was in—one of the few, of course. Almost nobody came to see it, and I found out later that the little audience we *did* have was provided by Ambrose. Amby used his part of the money to buy people tickets, just to keep the show going longer!

HARRY: Speaking of shows, how did yours go last night, Sally?

SALLY: Pretty well, I thought. But then, how can I judge?

HARRY: Was there a review in this morning's paper?

SALLY: I bought every edition of every paper this morning. There wasn't a word.

HOBART: Wait a minute, you two. What *is* all this? What are you talking about?

HARRY: Hobart, where have you been? Sally starred in a musical comedy that opened last night.

HOBART: Oh, come on, now. How could that be possible? She's still working for Ambrose as a secretary, isn't she?

SALLY: Oh, it wasn't as big as all that. It was a little off-Broadway theatre downtown. Chances are the papers are going to ignore it.

HARRY: Never mind. Don't underrate off-Broadway productions. Sometimes people who are successful off-Broadway become stars overnight.

HOBART: That's true. Well, now I know why you wanted to see the afternoon paper, Sally.

SALLY: It was silly. I just thought . . . oh, forget it for now. We have a job to do. Did either of you see Laura Clyde on the way here?

HARRY: I saw her at the TV studios this morning. She said she'd be a little late.

HOBART: I shall be overjoyed to see Laura again. It's been quite a while since we've exchanged pleasantries.

HARRY: You know something? Laura and I both do comedy, yet our acts are entirely different.

HOBART: Of course. *Hers* is funny!

SALLY: Please, Mr. Sanborn. Let's not start that again.

HOBART: But the *nerve* of this buffoon, comparing himself to one of England's greatest comediennes . . . the incomparable Laura Clyde! (LAURA *breezes in at this precise moment.*)

LAURA: Thank you, duckie. Good evening, ladies and gentlemen. For my opening number, I shall perform an old English folk song, called "I'm a Silly Goose, but I'll Take a Gander at You." Professor, please.

HOBART (*Advancing*): Laura, my dear, you are as charming as ever. (*Kisses her hand*)

LAURA: Hobart Sanborn! What a delightful surprise! What are you doing here?

HOBART: The same thing you are, I'm afraid.

SALLY (*Interrupting*): Please sit down, everybody, and let me brief you. Amby will be here in a minute.

LAURA: All right, Sally. (*All sit.*)

SALLY: Now Amby is trying to get Joy Darling as a client. She's coming up here in a little while to discuss the whole thing with him.

LAURA: Joy Darling! I heard she fired her agent.

HARRY: Yeah. So did I. It would mean a lot of money for Amby!

LAURA: I'll say. She's the highest-paid actress in Hollywood!

HARRY: I hope Amby handles the deal right. You know, if Amby were more hard-boiled, he'd be the most successful agent in New York. He's terrific with producers, he has an uncanny knack for discovering talent—but he gives the stars he represents the shirt off his back!

LAURA: He can't get a bad deal from Joy Darling. Even if he gets only *two* per cent of *her* salary, he'll be a wealthy man.

HARRY: That's true enough. But he should get ten per cent and other benefits besides. He needs to look out for his own welfare once in a while.

SALLY: We can worry about that later. Right now, we have to get Joy Darling to sign with Amby. It would certainly be a wonderful thing to have a big, successful star in this agency.

HARRY: Never mind, Sally. I'm not exactly unsuccessful. Do you know how many viewers see Crackpot the Clown?

HOBART: I know one who *doesn't.*

LAURA: Oh, that's right. You *are* on that kiddie show, aren't you, Harry? Do you think they can work in an English character sometime?

HOBART: He's lucky they work in the clown.

HARRY: Now, that's not true.

SALLY: Look, Harry. Nobody's criticizing your abilities. Just remember, when . . . Amby! (AMBROSE BAINBRIDGE *enters with* DORA MARTINDALE.)

AMBROSE: Good afternoon, all. Now, Miss Martindale, I've told you a million times. This afternoon's conference is very important.

DORA: How important can it be? Is this the group? (*Indicates various actors*) The conference can't be much at that rate. Is this the group that's so important?

AMBROSE: Now, just a minute, Miss Martindale. I won't have you . . .

DORA: All right. All right. Don't be touchy. Look. What I have to say won't take a minute. You are not exactly the most successful agent in New York, right?

AMBROSE: Well, I admit that . . .

DORA: Right or wrong?

AMBROSE: Right. Right.

DORA: My agency is moderately successful, right?

AMBROSE: Moderately, yes, moderately.

DORA: What do you say to a partnership?

AMBROSE: What? A partnership? You and me? Partners? Are you crazy?

DORA: No. Not at all. (*Removes envelope from purse*) In

this envelope is a legal contract that would make us partners under a set-up I think you would like.

AMBROSE: But why would you want to be my partner in the agency business?

DORA: Look. You're not as successful financially as I am. You can use me. What's the difference between us?

AMBROSE: I'm in a hurry.

DORA: Be serious. Think for a minute. You and I differ in one important way. You're a terrific agent. You get good jobs for your people, even though your clients aren't much. You know how to develop talent, but you're too soft. You don't make any money because you worry about everybody else and never consider yourself.

AMBROSE: But that's not a great crime.

DORA: No, but with me as a partner, you could go on being your charming self and let me handle the things you're not good at. I'm pretty hard-boiled when I want to be.

AMBROSE: Yes, I know.

DORA: I'll be your buffer, your shield. I'll be the nasty one. You be the clever agent. (*Pushing contract at him*) Read the contract. (*He removes contract from envelope and looks at it quickly.*) Well?

AMBROSE: It looks pretty good, of course, but . . .

DORA: But what?

AMBROSE: I can't tell you. I can't even discuss it or consider it right now. What we're doing here is extremely important to me. I'll call you tomorrow.

DORA: Really, Mr. Bainbridge. You are very vexing. It is important that I have your answer right away.

AMBROSE: I'm sorry. I can't give it. That's final. See me later. 'Bye now, Miss Martindale.

DORA: You might be sorry. Tomorrow may be too late.

AMBROSE: Tomorrow may be very different, too.

DORA: What do you mean by that?

AMBROSE: 'Bye now, Miss Martindale.

DORA: Very well. But I shall return. (*She storms out.*)

HARRY: And you can be sure she will, Amby.

AMBROSE: I don't care. I won't need her or anyone else if I can get Joy Darling to hire me.

SALLY: You could use Miss Martindale's offer, though, Amby. Don't you think so?

AMBROSE: Not if I get Joy Darling.

SALLY: But suppose Joy Darling doesn't sign? Then what?

AMBROSE: It is true that we can't go on like this much longer. We're hardly making enough to pay the electric bill.

SALLY: Do you think Dora Martindale will wait? Maybe she'll take her offer to somebody else.

AMBROSE: I'll just have to take that chance. If Joy Darling signs with me, I don't want Dora Martindale taking half of all the fees.

LAURA: Will Joy Darling really come here, Ambrose?

AMBROSE: Of course. This is the story. She was interested in some ideas I had for her, and she said she might hire me. But she wanted to see what kind of agency I have, and what other clients I handle.

HOBART: In that case, you were smart to have *me* come. But why did you ask Crackpot the Clown? Do you want to ruin the whole thing?

LAURA: Oh, have a heart, Hobart. Harry isn't so bad. Tell us a joke, Harry.

HARRY: All right. Let's see. Yeah. It was so hot today . . . I saw a *tongue* walking down the street with a *dog* hanging out!

HOBART: Laura, my dear, what were you trying to prove?

LAURA: Tell him another one, Harry.

HARRY: All right. Uh . . . a funny thing happened to me on my way here today.

HOBART: Oh, ye gods!

HARRY: A tramp asked me for a dime for a cup of coffee.

So I gave him a dime, and he gave me a cup of coffee!

HOBART: Ambrose, is it really true that you turned down Bob Hope to represent this individual instead?

AMBROSE: It's just as Miss Martindale said . . . I'm too soft! Come on, now, let's get down to business. Where are the Four Noises? Did you call them, Sally?

SALLY: I called the Big Noise himself, and he said they'd be here.

AMBROSE: Well, they're not, and it's past time.

HARRY: By the way, Amby, have you seen the afternoon paper?

AMBROSE: No, I haven't. Why?

SALLY: Never mind, Harry.

HARRY: Sally was in a play last night, Amby.

AMBROSE: I know. Oh! You wanted to look for reviews.

SALLY: Never mind, Amby. There aren't any reviews.

AMBROSE: Sh-h-h! I think somebody's coming down the hall. (VIOLA SHARPE *opens office door.*)

VIOLA: Mr. Bainbridge?

AMBROSE: I'm Mr. Bainbridge.

VIOLA: How do you do. I am Viola Sharpe, personal secretary to Miss Joy Darling. Is everything ready for Miss Darling's arrival?

AMBROSE: Well, I guess so.

VIOLA (*Looking around*): Can *he* (*Indicates* HARRY) move his feet in a little? I don't want Miss Darling to trip.

AMBROSE: Certainly. Harry, do you mind?

HARRY: Not at all. I could sit backwards on the chair, if you want, Amby. (*He tries it.*)

AMBROSE: Please, Harry. (HARRY *resumes normal position.*)

VIOLA: Ask your secretary not to type while Miss Darling is here, Mr. Bainbridge. It gives Miss Darling a headache.

AMBROSE: Of course. You heard that, didn't you, Sally?

SALLY (*Faking a salute*): Yes, sir. I'll just sit here and loaf.

AMBROSE: Fine.

VIOLA (*Dubiously*): Well, I suppose everything is as orderly as can be expected. All right, everyone. (*Announcing*) Miss Joy Darling is now down the hall and approaching this office. Please be ready.

LAURA: What, no trumpet?

AMBROSE: You may tell Miss Darling to come right in.

VIOLA: Thank you. (*Exits*)

AMBROSE: This is it, everybody. Now look. Try to make a good impression. Let her think you're each big in your field. She's probably never heard of any of you, but we might get away with it.

HARRY: We're with you, Amby.

LAURA: Good show.

HOBART: I'll try.

AMBROSE: Good. (*Gets some scripts from desk and gives them out*) Here. Be studying scripts, as though you have a part in something.

SALLY: I hear them coming.

AMBROSE: Put it on thick, now. (VIOLA *re-enters, followed by* JOY DARLING.)

VIOLA: Miss Joy Darling.

AMBROSE: Miss Darling! This is a pleasure!

JOY: Ambrose, sweetie. You may call me Joy.

AMBROSE: It will be a Joy, Miss Pleasure. I . . . I mean it will be a pleasure, Miss . . . I mean, Joy.

JOY: I am so anxious to meet your clients. Anyone with ideas as bright as yours must have a wonderful collection of stars.

AMBROSE: Oh, we do, we do.

JOY: Name a few for me.

AMBROSE: Well, let's see . . . I . . . well . . . I'll introduce you around the office. This is my secretary, Sally Cartwright.

JOY: How do you do.

SALLY: Pleased to meet you, Joy.

JOY: You may call me Miss Darling.

SALLY (*Deflated*): Oh.

JOY (*Turning, speaking to* AMBROSE): She's pretty. I don't allow that.

AMBROSE: What?

JOY: Pretty secretaries. We must keep all attention on the star. (*Indicates herself*)

AMBROSE: Oh. Well, Sally isn't really *that* pretty, Joy. And she could muss up her hair.

JOY: We'll see. Now, *this* woman will do nicely.

LAURA: I don't think that's a compliment.

AMBROSE: Joy Darling, this is Laura Clyde, the famous English star.

JOY: Really? I've never heard of you, Miss Clod.

LAURA: Clyde, Miss Darling. Clyde.

JOY: I'm sorry. What do you do?

LAURA: I'm a comedienne. And I sing.

JOY: Really? No, I've never heard of you.

LAURA: That's a shame. I've heard lots of things about you.

JOY: That's wonderful. That's all publicity. Isn't it, Ambrose, sweetie?

AMBROSE: Certainly, Joy. Certainly. Publicity is everything. And at Bainbridge and Bainbridge, you get the most unusual, most effective . . .

JOY: Yes, of course. By the way, Ambrose, why do you call the agency "Bainbridge and Bainbridge"? Who's the other Bainbridge?

AMBROSE: There really isn't any. I'm the only Bainbridge.

JOY: That's funny. Why repeat it?

AMBROSE: It makes the agency sound bigger and more important to have two names in the title.

JOY: Oh, I see. That's clever. You are a clever man. Isn't he, Viola?

VIOLA: Oh, yes, Miss Darling.

AMBROSE: Thank you.

JOY (*Indicating* HARRY): Who's this?

AMBROSE: This is Harry Joey, the comedian.

JOY: Harry Joey? What kind of name is that?

HARRY: Maybe you would recognize me by the name I use when I perform.

JOY: Who are you when you perform, Mr. Joey?

HARRY: Well, you've certainly heard of Crackpot the Clown?

JOY: Who the what?

HARRY (*Deflated*): Crackpot the Clown. I appear on that kiddie show.

JOY: Kiddie show! What do you take me for? Do you think I watch that sort of thing on television?

HARRY: I just thought you might have heard of me.

JOY: You thought I might recognize Crazy the Horse or Clancy the Cop, or whatever it is you are? Really!

HOBART: Nice going, Crackpot.

HARRY: Shut up.

JOY: Who is this other gentleman, Ambrose?

AMBROSE: This is Hobart Sanborn . . . Joy Darling. I know you've heard of *him*.

JOY: Oh, yes, I have. How do you do, Mr. Sanborn. I read about you in a history of the drama in America. (*Turning*) My goodness, Ambrose, I thought he was dead.

HOBART: Really, young lady. The only difference in our little conversation is that until a few minutes ago, *I* had never heard of *you*.

JOY: What? Ambrose, did you hear what he said? Viola, did you hear?

VIOLA: It certainly can't be true, Miss Darling!

AMBROSE: Oh, I'm quite sure he's joking, Joy. You're really kidding, aren't you, Hobart?

HOBART: Is this a crime? Sally explained who Miss Darling was when I arrived.

AMBROSE: Really, Sally?

SALLY: Really and truly. But you have to excuse Hobart. (*Innocently*) After all, Miss Darling isn't exactly his type.

JOY: My dear Miss Cartwheel . . .

SALLY: Cartwright.

JOY: Well, whatever it is. You should realize that I am *everybody's* type.

SALLY: I guess I can't argue with that. You make enough money to prove it!

JOY: Exactly. Now the question is whether or not sweet little Ambrose is going to make any of it with me. (PHIL, *the Big Noise, runs in. He frightens* JOY, *who jumps back.*)

PHIL (*Announcing*): Ladies and gentlemen—introducing the Four Noises. (*He runs to the door just as another man and two girls enter. They are snapping their fingers and beating out a typical modern rhythm.*)

JOY (*Loudly*): Ambrose, what is this?

AMBROSE: Hey, stop it! (*They do.*) I'm sorry, Joy. This is the famous singing group, the Four Noises.

JOY: Yes, they certainly are.

AMBROSE: They're quite good, really.

JOY: I can't say that I want to find out. What did you say they were called?

AMBROSE: The Four Noises.

JOY: I've never heard of them.

VIOLA: Neither have I.

BIG NOISE: We can do our latest number for you, Miss. I made the arrangement myself.

JOY: Ambrose, call him off, will you?

AMBROSE: Please, Phil. Not now. Just stand over there. (*They go right, snapping their fingers and walking in rhythm. They remain there, somewhat jittery, throughout the following dialogue.*)

JOY: Now, I think we'd better talk business, Ambrose.

AMBROSE: By all means.

JOY: Is this a town meeting, or what is it?

AMBROSE: What do you mean?

JOY: All these people sitting around like an audience. After all, business matters *are* private.

AMBROSE: But these people don't really care, Joy. I mean, they're all in on each other's business arrangements and everything.

VIOLA: I'm sure they're not in on Miss Darling's arrangements.

AMBROSE: I hate to ask them to leave.

JOY: Why shouldn't they? You won't be representing them any more.

AMBROSE: What did you say?

JOY: I've decided I want you to represent me. I'm hiring you as my agent.

AMBROSE: Why, that's wonderful! Did you hear that, Sally?

SALLY: Congratulations, Amby. This is a great step forward for you.

AMBROSE: Thank you, Joy. Thank you very much. I'm very honored.

VIOLA: You certainly are!

JOY: So, of course, that's why you won't be representing these assorted characters any more.

AMBROSE: Won't be representing them? But why not?

JOY: You don't think I'd have an agent representing me who was also representing a crew of people like this, do you?

AMBROSE: But you don't understand. This is an agency. These are my clients . . . my stars!

JOY: Really? You mean this five-and-ten Beatrice Lillie here, and Joey the Crackpot, over there? And *this* one

. . . the mummy's ghost? Not to mention the jittery little troupe over there. They all have to go. Or *I* go.

AMBROSE: Surely you don't mean that.

JOY: You must choose between us.

HARRY: Amby, look. I see you're in a tough position, so I won't make it hard on you. Don't worry about me. I'll just go. Take your big chance while you have it.

LAURA: Yes, of course, Ambrose. Harry is right. Don't even consider any of us. There are other agents who will represent us. This is your golden opportunity.

HOBART: True, Laura, my dear. Miss Darling is obviously a gold mine, Ambrose. Don't think twice about it.

SALLY: Amby, I'm willing to do anything that's best for your future. But isn't it a little unfair to your clients to let them walk off . . . I mean . . . well, who does she think she is?

AMBROSE: Sally, please. I know how you feel. Miss Darling, maybe you don't know it, but I'm the only agent in New York who will take these people. I'm really not very successful, I guess. These people are my friends. They have no other place to go. The fact that they'd leave and let me represent you, without interfering, proves their friendship. I can't let them walk out. I won't let them go.

JOY: Very touching, I'm sure. Well, you may wish to hang on to this moth-eaten rogues' gallery of yours, but I have my publicity to think about. I've had at least three other offers from agents. I won't go begging.

HARRY: No, but Amby might. Really, Amby. This is your chance. Don't be silly.

AMBROSE: My mind is made up, Harry. I'm sorry, Miss Darling.

JOY (*In amazement*): You're either a hero or crazy. In either case you're not going to be my agent. Viola, we're going.

VIOLA: Very well, Miss Darling. (*They exit.*)

SALLY (*Jumping up from her desk and throwing her arms around* AMBROSE): Amby, I love you!

AMBROSE: Good. Marry me, and there really will be two Bainbridges in the agency. Both starving.

SALLY: Never mind. You stood up for your principles. That's what's important.

HOBART: Really, Ambrose, it was wonderful of you to stand by us.

HARRY: Come on, everybody. Amby has enough trouble. Let's go our merry way and try to make some money for him and for us.

HOBART: Excellent.

LAURA: Right with you. (*Telephone rings.* HOBART, *closest to phone, answers it.*)

HOBART (*Into phone*) Hello, Bainbridge and Bainbridge. No, young lady, this is *not* Sally Cartwright. Do I sound like a Sally Cartwright to you? (*Pause*) Just a moment, please. (*Covers phone with his hand and addresses* SALLY) Sally, this is a long-distance call from Hollywood. They claim someone is interested in talking to you about a movie contract.

SALLY: To me? Movie contract? But who would. . . . Oh! I know. That must be Jack Schwartz! He calls up every so often from wherever he is and plays some crazy joke on me. Tell him to call me later.

HOBART: Really! (*Uncovers phone*) Please inform Mr. Jack Schwartz that he may call Miss Cartwright later. (*Hangs up immediately*)

PHIL: Hey, Amby. Before we leave, I want to tell you the latest. We're comin' into the chips. We have a recording date.

AMBROSE: You do?

PHIL: Absolutely. And we are sure this one will be a big hit.

SALLY: What makes you so sure?

PHIL: Well, it's not a professional recording. We do it in a booth in the shooting gallery near Broadway and Forty-third Street. I do solo, the rest back me up, and the gunfire in the background is really *wild,* man.

HARRY: You know, I think that might sell.

LAURA: Let's go. (*They exit, leaving* AMBROSE *and* SALLY *alone.* AMBROSE *sits down, head in hands.*)

SALLY: I know how you feel, Amby. But you have the satisfaction of knowing you didn't desert your friends.

AMBROSE: Yes, I know. Why do I have to be such a hero? Anybody else would have jumped at the chance to represent Joy Darling at any cost. But not old Ambrose. "Old Faithful." Stand back, Sally. I'm about to erupt.

SALLY: It's a shame. Say, what about Dora Martindale? She wants to form a partnership with you. Was that agreement any good?

AMBROSE: Not bad. She still would have the biggest share, really, but it wasn't bad.

SALLY: Will you sign it?

AMBROSE: I'll have to. We're going downhill here. But since I practically threw Dora out before, she probably doesn't want me any more.

SALLY: Why don't you call her?

AMBROSE: No. I couldn't. Not only am I a hero, but I have too much pride. Why don't you try to get a job with another agency?

SALLY: Because no other clients are as wacky as yours.

AMBROSE: You can say that again. (TELEGRAPH BOY *enters.*)

BOY: Telegram for Miss Sally Cartwright. (*Looks at what is in his hand*) Wait. *Two* telegrams for Miss Sally Cartwright.

SALLY: Two telegrams?

AMBROSE: What do they say, Sally?

BOY: Would you sign first, please? I'm very busy.

SALLY: Oh, certainly. (*She does, and takes the telegrams.*)

AMBROSE (*Tipping the boy*): Here you are.

BOY: Thank you. (*Exits*)

AMBROSE: Open them, Sally. What do you suppose they say?

SALLY (*Tearing at the telegrams*): I have no idea. (DORA MARTINDALE *strides into the room, carrying a newspaper under her arm.*)

DORA: Now see here, Ambrose Bainbridge. I am not a fool. I know what's going on here.

AMBROSE: You do? What is it?

DORA: Don't be funny. So you threw over Joy Darling, huh?

AMBROSE: Well, not exactly.

DORA: Don't not exactly me. I know why you threw her over.

AMBROSE: Well, what could I do?

DORA: I still don't see how you figured it out. But you did. I didn't know you had it in you to see a good thing, even when it was right under your nose! But you were smart enough to let even Joy Darling go to sign Sally Cartwright!

AMBROSE: Who's Sally Cartwright?

SALLY: I'm Sally Cartwright, Amby.

AMBROSE: Oh, of course. I mean, what did I sign her for?

DORA: Ambrose Bainbridge! Are you being deliberately coy, or aren't we talking about the same thing?

AMBROSE: If you came over to shout at me, I'm not interested. If you came over to talk partnership, please start talking.

DORA (*Confused*): Oh! Partnership! Yes. Of course. Well, you saw the contract. Are you interested? (*Phone rings again.*) I'll get that for you. You sit there and think. (*She answers the phone.*) Hello, Mr. Bainbridge's office, Dora Martindale speaking. (*To* SALLY *and* AMBROSE)

It's a long-distance call from Hollywood, and the man says, "Who's Jack Schwartz?"

SALLY (*Laughing*): Oh, I'll take that. (*She does.*) Hello, Jack. You certainly picked a fine time to . . . what? . . . This *isn't* Jack Schwartz? . . . Oh, I'm terribly sorry. M-G-M wants me to what? . . . Would you say that once more, slowly? . . . Look, can I call you back in about an hour? . . . Thank you very much. (*Hangs up*)

AMBROSE: What was that?

SALLY: Well, it wasn't Jack Schwartz. It was a representative from M-G-M. They want me for a screen test!

AMBROSE: But why . . . *wait* a minute! You opened in that *musical* last night! You were in that *show!*

SALLY: Do you think they know about it?

AMBROSE: Certainly. They have scouts everywhere. See what those telegrams say.

SALLY: All right. (*Opens them and reads*) "Congratulations on the most brilliant musical comedy performance of the entire season. Signed—(*Insert name of critic.* SALLY *reads other telegram.*) "A brilliant performance! Most promising star I've seen in five years. Signed—(*Another insert*) Amby! (*She throws her arms around his neck.*)

DORA: Well, Mr. Bainbridge. Let's sign her up. She might be better than Joy Darling.

AMBROSE: She *is* better than . . . say, wait a minute. Did you know all about this, Miss Martindale?

DORA: About what?

AMBROSE: About Sally's success.

DORA: Of course. I keep my eyes and ears open. I'm really going to be an asset to you. Roscoe Smart tipped me off this morning that he was going to write a *rave* review of Sally for this afternoon's paper. His review alone can make a star!

AMBROSE: So you wanted to cash in on Sally. That's the only reason you offered me a partnership!

DORA: Certainly. I knew she'd never sign with anybody but you. But I knew you wouldn't go into partnership with me if you knew about Sally. There would be no reason for it.

SALLY: Miss Martindale is right about this much, Amby. She *is* shrewd.

DORA: Well, it's no secret any more. It's all over New York by now.

SALLY: And I didn't even know it!

AMBROSE: Do you have that review?

DORA: What do you think *this* is? (*Produces newspaper she has been holding.* AMBROSE *takes it.*)

AMBROSE: There it is, all right. (*Looks at it very quickly*) Listen to this part: "Undoubtedly the brightest element in the show is its star, Sally Cartwright. She is not just pretty; she is thoroughly charming. She is not just a singer; she has a fine voice and is a talented actress as well. Her every word, every inflection, every gesture is perfect. Rarely have I seen an audience so captivated; rarely have I been so captivated myself by a performer in the theatre. There is no doubt about it. Sally Cartwright is the next big star of the Broadway stage. Here is another Julie Andrews, another Mary Martin."

SALLY: I can't believe it!

DORA: Now, Mr. Bainbridge. About the legal arrangements . . . I think we should . . .

AMBROSE: I don't think we need any legal arrangements now, Miss Martindale.

DORA: But, of course we do. You're still the same person. You can still use me. Remember? Your buffer? Your shield?

AMBROSE: I don't need the buffer or shield any more, Miss Martindale.

DORA: Then you mean you're not interested in a partnership?

AMBROSE: Oh, yes. I'm interested in a partnership. (*Puts arm around* SALLY) But not a business partnership. Let's say, a private one.

SALLY: Amby! We can be Bainbridge and Bainbridge . . . and not be starving! (DELIVERY BOY *enters with huge bouquet of flowers.*)

BOY: Flowers for Miss Sally Cartwright.

DORA: I'll take them. (*She does and hands them to* SALLY *as* DELIVERY BOY *leaves.*) Here, Sally. Here's an engagement present for you. You've had much better luck with him than I've had.

SALLY: Thank you. (*Puts flowers on desk. Telephone rings. She answers.*) Hello? Yes, this is Miss Cartwright. (*Pause*) What kind of contract?

DORA: Mr. Bainbridge, I'm leaving. Your success is beginning to bother me. (SALLY *continues on the phone.* DORA *attempts to leave, but almost walks into the* TELEGRAPH BOY, *who enters left.*)

TELEGRAPH BOY: Three more telegrams for Miss Cartwright.

AMBROSE: She's on the phone. Wait a minute.

SALLY (*Hanging up the phone*): I'll take them. (*Phone rings again.*) Oh! Wait a minute. (*Answers phone*) Hello? (*Talks under following dialogue*)

DORA: This time I'm really leaving, if I can get out your door.

AMBROSE: Goodbye, Miss Martindale. Oh, by the way. If you're interested in making a lot of money, I understand Joy Darling is looking for an agent. If you can stand her!

DORA: I can't and I won't. I'm leaving before I lose any more ground. With *your* luck, the next teen-age sensation will probably be Crackpot the Clown! (*Curtain*)

THE END

The Mystery at Tumble Inn

by Elizabeth Lello

Characters

LOVELLA WICKWIRE, *owner of Tumble Inn*
DUKE, *handyman at Tumble Inn*
OPAL, *a maid*
MRS. TUSHINGHAM, *a traveler*
TERRY, LORI, GARTH, TOM — *teen-agers*
RADIO ANNOUNCER'S VOICE

TIME: *A stormy evening in September.*

SETTING: *The living room of the Tumble Inn, a few miles outside of Des Moines. The furniture is covered with sheets.*

AT RISE: DUKE *sits on the arm of a chair, down right, reading a newspaper. The sounds of a storm are heard off, and continue throughout the play.* DUKE *starts suddenly, as though hearing someone's approach from off left. He folds the paper quickly, looks around for a place to hide it, then drops it on the seat of the chair. He is arranging the sheet over the chair back as* OPAL *enters left and drops wearily onto couch down left.*

OPAL: What a storm! (*Pause*) Want to know something?

DUKE (*Pulling cover into place*): What?

OPAL: All my muscles are saying "Ouch!" (*She rubs her legs.*)

DUKE (*Sitting on chair arm*): Same here. My charley horses think they're racing at Lincoln Park.

OPAL (*Smiling*): Which one'll win?

DUKE: Neither. (*Rises*) I'm just going to lead 'em to their stalls. I'm bushed. (*Starts left*)

OPAL: Don't go, Duke. Come over here and take a load off your feet.

DUKE (*Crossing to couch and sitting beside* OPAL): O.K. (*He stretches.*) When's Miss Wickwire locking up the Inn?

OPAL: It's closed now. I've stripped all the beds, and the linens and blankets are put away.

DUKE: I hate to have the season end. Seems as though I just came.

OPAL: You did! A week isn't very long. (*Flirts*) Not long enough, Duke.

DUKE (*Smiling at her*): You're a good kid, Opal.

OPAL: Thanks! What're you going to do now the Inn is closed?

DUKE: Move on, I guess. A handyman can always get a job. How about you?

OPAL: I have to go back to Missouri Valley and the farm! (*Thunder crashes*) Oh! (*She cringes and moves closer to* DUKE.) I hate thunder! (DUKE *starts to put his arm around her shoulders, then changes his mind and rests it on the back of the couch.*)

DUKE: It won't hurt you. Lightning's worse.

OPAL: I hate that, too. Listen, it's pouring cats and dogs.

DUKE: Yeah.

OPAL: What'd you do before you came here?

DUKE: Worked at a couple of hotels in Des Moines and

Chicago. (*As an afterthought*) I hopped cars in Los Angeles.

OPAL (*Wide-eyed*): Did you ever see any movie stars?

DUKE: No. Los Angeles is a big place, you know.

OPAL: Uh-huh. (*Sighs*) I've never been any place, except Des Moines, once.

DUKE: How'd you happen to go there?

OPAL: We went to the fair. You ever been on a ferris wheel? (*He nods.*) Weren't you scared? (*He smiles in a superior manner.*) It gave me knots in my stomach! (*Thunder crashes off.*) There it goes again! (*She moves closer to* DUKE. LOVELLA WICKWIRE *enters right, stops when she sees* DUKE *and* OPAL, *and watches them with an indulgent look on her face.* DUKE *and* OPAL *are unaware of her presence.*)

DUKE: Thunder never hurt anyone. If you want to know the truth, I ordered it specially. (*His arm drops to her shoulders.*)

OPAL (*Pleased but embarrassed*): Oh, Duke.

LOVELLA: Well! (*They spring up, startled.*) Have you seen the Des Moines *Register,* Duke? (*She crosses to them.*)

DUKE: No, ma'am, not today.

LOVELLA (*Seeing it on the chair*): Here it is! (*She picks it up and examines it.*) What does it say about the storm? (*Reads*) "Rain to continue." (*Her glance moves over the paper. She looks up startled, looks at* DUKE, *then back to the paper.*) That's strange!

OPAL: What?

LOVELLA: This picture.

OPAL (*Crossing to* LOVELLA): Let me see. (*She examines picture, then looks at* DUKE *in amazement.*) It looks like you, Duke! (*She takes the paper.*)

DUKE (*Crossing quickly*): Me? (*Looks at picture*) Well, sort of, if you stretch your imagination.

OPAL (*Reading aloud*): "Jasper Collins, parolee, sought

for the theft of the Vanderlip diamonds." (*Gives* DUKE *a troubled look*) Oh, Duke!

DUKE: Don't look at me like that! (Laughs) That's not my picture.

LOVELLA (*Suspiciously*): There's a strong resemblance.

DUKE (*Being very charming*): Miss Wickwire, don't you trust me?

LOVELLA (*Disarmed; answering his smile*): I guess so. (*She taps him playfully on the shoulder.*) Shame on you for looking like a criminal! (*All laugh. There is a knock on door up center.*) Oh dear, we can't receive any guests tonight! Duke, just say that the Inn is closed for the season. (*She exits left.*)

DUKE (*Crossing to door*): Yes, ma'am. (*He speaks through door.*) Sorry, the Inn is closed. (OPAL *takes another look at the picture, then tosses the paper on the couch.*)

MRS. TUSHINGHAM (*From offstage*: Open the door! Please, please open it!

DUKE (*Opening the door a crack*): I'm sorry, the Inn is . . . (MRS. TUSHINGHAM *pushes the door wide and enters, carrying a small suitcase.*) . . . closed for the season.

MRS. TUSHINGHAM (*With great excitement*): They're after me! A car has been following me!

OPAL *and* DUKE: What?

MRS. TUSHINGHAM (*Breathlessly*): When I stopped, they stopped, too! A car with several people in it! (*She takes a small jewel case from her purse.*) Here. (*Holds it out to* DUKE) Put this in the safe! (OPAL *stares at her, open-mouthed.*)

DUKE (*Not taking it*): Pardon me?

MRS. TUSHINGHAM: Quick, put it in the safe!

OPAL: We don't have a safe.

MRS. TUSHINGHAM: No safe? Oh, dear! (*She returns case*

to her purse.) Take a look outside, will you? (DUKE *opens the door and looks out.*) Are they still there?

DUKE: I don't see anyone.

MRS. TUSHINGHAM: Lock the door! (DUKE *starts to close the door, but it is pushed open from outside by* TERRY. *She enters, followed by* LORI, TOM *and* GARTH.)

TERRY (*Removing her wet scarf*): Am I soaked!

GARTH: Sorry to barge in like this!

LORI: Our car barely made it to the bottom of your hill!

TOM: The engine conked out.

TERRY: We were sure glad to see your lights!

MRS. TUSHINGHAM (*Indignantly*): Why were you following me?

GARTH: We weren't.

MRS. TUSHINGHAM: A car behind me stopped every time I stopped.

TOM: It wasn't us!

MRS. TUSHINGHAM: That's very queer!

LORI (*Looking around*): What is this place? A hotel?

OPAL: This is Tumble Inn, but we're closed for the season.

LORI: Tumble Inn? That's a pretty good name for it.

TERRY: Lori!

LORI: I think it's groovy! It would be great for a Halloween party!

TOM (*To* DUKE): Don't mind her! Say, could we use your phone?

DUKE: I'm not in charge. Better call Miss Wickwire, Opal.

OPAL (*Moving left*): O.K. (*She meets* LOVELLA *entering left.*) Oh, Miss Wickwire, these people just came . . . (*She indicates the teen-agers standing in a group up center, and* MRS. TUSHINGHAM *down right.*)

MRS. TUSHINGHAM: I am Mrs. Cornelius Tushingham. (*She crosses to* LOVELLA.)

LOVELLA: Yes?

MRS. TUSHINGHAM: Your man said that your inn is closed,

but I would appreciate it if you would let me stay to-night.

TERRY: The roads are flooded.

LORI: Water's up to here! (*Holds her hand up to her waist*)

TERRY: Not that high!

LORI: Almost! Anyway, it's like driving through a lake.

TOM: You can say that again!

LOVELLA: I'm sorry, but we aren't prepared to take guests.

MRS. TUSHINGHAM (*Indignantly*): Surely you'll let me stay until the rain stops! (LOVELLA *shakes her head.*) But you must! I insist.

LOVELLA: Our rooms are not made up. We've spent the whole day dismantling them.

OPAL: It's O.K., Miss Wickwire. We can fix up a room for her.

DUKE (*Protesting*): What?

OPAL: Have a heart, Duke. We can't send her out in the storm.

DUKE (*Disgusted*): Oh, boy!

LOVELLA (*Shrugging*): All right, if you want to do the work.

MRS. TUSHINGHAM: Thank you, very much.

LOVELLA (*To teen-agers*): Are you all together?

GARTH: Yes, we were on our way to a dance.

TOM: Could we use your phone? Our car stalled.

LOVELLA: Yes. (*Nods toward phone on desk up center*) Duke, fix up No. 5 for Mrs. Tushingham, please.

DUKE: Yes, ma'am. (*To* MRS. TUSHINGHAM) This way, ma'am. (*He moves left.*)

LOVELLA (*To* MRS. TUSHINGHAM): You can register later. The room will be ten dollars.

MRS. TUSHINGHAM: Thank you. (DUKE *starts to exit left, followed by* MRS. TUSHINGHAM. *He carries her suitcase.*)

OPAL (*Following them*): I'll help you.

DUKE: O.K. (*They exit.*)

TOM (*At desk*): Could you tell me the name of a garage near here?

LOVELLA: Lou's Service Station—but he doesn't stay open this late.

TOM (*Jiggling the phone*): There's no dial tone.

GARTH: Lines must be down.

LORI (*Wailing*): We'll never get to the dance!

TERRY: We'll never get home! That's worse.

GARTH: I'm supposed to have the car in the garage by one o'clock. If I don't (*He draws his finger across his throat.*) —curtains!

LORI: What are we going to do?

GARTH: Stay here until the telephone lines are fixed. (*Looks at* LOVELLA) That is, if you don't mind, ma'am.

LORI: At least we're inside a house, even if it is moldy.

TERRY: Lori!

LORI (*Realizing her mistake*): Oh! I didn't mean your inn was moldy, I meant—well (*Gives an embarrassed laugh*) —it's a lovely place.

LOVELLA (*Patiently*): Tumble Inn is noted for its age, not its beauty. It was here before the Civil War. Runaway slaves were hidden in the passages below.

TERRY: They were?

LOVELLA (*Proudly*): It was part of the Underground Railroad. Tourists come from all over to see it.

TOM (*Impressed*): Could we take a look at the tunnels?

LOVELLA: No, the season's over. No one is allowed down there without a guide. (*Studying the group*) What am I going to do with you? Your car's stalled, and the phone doesn't work. (*The teen-agers look at each other and shrug.*)

GARTH: The car'll probably start when it dries out.

TOM: Fat chance it has in this weather!

TERRY: Looks as if we're stuck!

LOVELLA: I suppose I'd better have rooms prepared for you, too (*Steps to left exit and calls*) Duke!

DUKE (*From offstage*): Yes?

LOVELLA: Fix up No. 7 for the boys and put the girls in No. 3. (*To teen-agers*) Go along down the hall and Duke will take care of you.

TERRY: Shouldn't we register, or something?

LOVELLA: Later. My register's put away.

TERRY (*Moving left*): How much will the rooms be?

LOVELLA: We'll discuss that later.

GARTH (*Moving left*): We're sort of—well, broke, you know, but our folks'll send you a check. (LOVELLA *nods.*) Thanks a lot. (*Teen-agers exit.* LOVELLA *shakes her head, watching them exit, then crosses to outside door, opens it, looks out and closes it. She comes down center.* OPAL *enters left, carrying an armload of bedding.*)

OPAL: First you strip 'em, then you make 'em up again! At least the beds have been aired!

LOVELLA: I'm sorry, Opal.

OPAL: Can't be helped. Duke said you were putting the kids up for the night.

LOVELLA: What else could I do?

OPAL: Nothing. Seven and three, huh? (LOVELLA *nods.*) O.K. (*She exits left.* LOVELLA *picks up the newspaper and looks at the picture, shrugs and drops it on the couch. She exits right. The room is empty for a moment, then* DUKE *pokes his head in left, looks around, and crosses to window up left. He looks over his shoulder again, then raises the blind and lowers it, raises and lowers it. He moves right, looks out the doorway, then crosses to couch, picks up paper and begins to read.* OPAL *re-enters left and speaks to him with mock indignation.*) Well, Duke!

DUKE: I'm taking a breather.

OPAL: I could use one, too. (*Crosses to couch and sits near* DUKE) Where's the picture that looks like you?

DUKE: I don't know.

OPAL (*Taking paper*): Let me see. (*Turns the page*) Here it is.

DUKE (*Without interest*): Uh-huh.

OPAL: Duke, it looks just like you! (*She looks at him closely.*)

DUKE (*Leaning toward her menacingly*): I'm a desperate criminal, and you'd better not tell the police, if you know what's good for you! (OPAL *looks frightened.* DUKE *laughs.*) I'm only joking, Opal.

OPAL (*Laughing, relieved*): Stop it, Duke! Let me read what it says. (*He sits back, hands behind his head. She reads.*) "Reward of $1,000 offered for information leading to the arrest of Jasper Collins." Golly! (*Reading*) "Until his disappearance, he was employed by the Vanderlip family as a chauffeur."

DUKE (*Playfully*): Are you going to turn me in?

OPAL: Silly! Is your name really "Duke"?

DUKE: No.

OPAL: What is it?

DUKE (*Looking around*): Sh-h! I never say it out loud. Will you promise to keep it a secret?

OPAL (*Giggling*): Yes.

DUKE: Marmaduke!

OPAL: No! Marmaduke Wainright! Your mother sure had fancy ideas!

DUKE: How would you like to be stuck for life with that name?

OPAL (*Flirting*): Why, Duke, I didn't know you cared! (DUKE *starts to put his arm around her shoulders as* MRS. TUSHINGHAM *rushes in left. They jump up from couch.*)

MRS. TUSHINGHAM (*Agitated*): My jewel case is gone!

OPAL: What?

MRS. TUSHINGHAM: My small jewel case! You saw me put it in my purse!

DUKE: And it isn't there now?

MRS. TUSHINGHAM: I told you, it's gone! I was afraid someone would take it from my purse, so I hid it under the mattress in my room.

DUKE: Who could have taken it?

MRS. TUSHINGHAM: Probably one of those young people! You can't trust any teen-ager these days. I want them all searched! (LOVELLA *enters right.* MRS. TUSHINGHAM *rushes to her.*) Miss Wickwire, there is a thief, or thieves, among us! I had a very valuable piece of jewelry in my purse when I entered this inn, and now it's gone!

LOVELLA (*Calmly*): I'm sure you have just misplaced it. Opal, are you and Duke finished?

OPAL: Just about. We were just catching our breath.

LOVELLA: Better get those young people taken care of.

OPAL: Yes, ma'am. (*Moves left*) Come on, Duke.

DUKE: O.K. (*He follows her off, taking newspaper with him.*)

MRS. TUSHINGHAM: This is no small matter, Miss Wickwire. The missing medallion is part of a collection of ancient Egyptian jewelry. You must search everyone in the Inn. (*Pauses*) If you don't, I shall call the police.

LOVELLA: That will be difficult with the phone out of order. (*Crosses to couch*) Come now, sit down. I'm sure it will turn up. (MRS. TUSHINGHAM *joins her on the couch reluctantly.*) Are you from around here?

MRS. TUSHINGHAM: No, San Francisco. But my husband's business keeps us traveling all the time. He buys and sells rare *objets d'art.* I should never have let it out of my hands!

LOVELLA: The medallion will turn up. (*Pause*) A dealer in rare *objets d'art!* What a fascinating occupation!

MRS. TUSHINGHAM: After a while the glamour wears off.

Traveling becomes very tiresome. My husband is waiting for me in Chicago now. This medallion completes the collection which he is offering for sale. I simply cannot face him without it! (GARTH *enters left, followed by* TOM.)

GARTH: May we try the phone again, ma'am?

LOVELLA: Surely.

MRS. TUSHINGHAM (*Whispering*): Aren't you going to search them? (LOVELLA *shakes her head.*)

GARTH (*At phone*): If I could only get through to my dad! (*Listens*) It's still dead. (*Hangs up*)

MRS. TUSHINGHAM: Please tell me when it's fixed. I'm going to phone the police! (*She gives the boys a suspicious look and exits left.*)

TOM (*Looking at* MRS. TUSHINGHAM *as she goes out*): What's with her? (GARTH *shrugs.*) Try the phone again.

GARTH: It's no use. (TERRY *and* LORI *enter left.*)

TERRY: Any luck?

TOM: Nope.

LORI: I wanted to go to the dance! Tommy, why don't you stand down on the road and flag someone going by?

TOM: That's bright! Who's going to be driving by in this flood?

LORI: We did! So did that lady—Mrs. Tushingham.

GARTH: The water wasn't so high then. Nobody's on the road now, Lori.

TERRY: Why don't *you* go down to the road, Lori?

LORI: And ruin my hair? You're out of your mind!

TOM: No one's going down, so don't argue. (*To* LOVELLA) Are there any homes near here, Miss Wickwire?

LOVELLA: The Bartletts live down the road.

TOM: Their phone might be working.

LOVELLA: We're on the same line.

TOM: Oh.

LOVELLA (*Rising*): You're safe and dry, so be thankful and

make the best of it. (*Crosses to left exit and goes out*)

TERRY (*Running after her; calling*): Miss Wickwire, do you have a record player?

LOVELLA (*From offstage*): No.

TERRY (*Turning back to group*): No record player!

LORI (*Suddenly remembering*): I have my transistor radio! (*She takes radio from purse and turns it on.*)

RADIO ANNOUNCER'S VOICE: You are asked to report to the Des Moines police if a dark-haired man in his twenties should apply at your home for a job as chauffeur, gardener, or handyman. Such a man is being sought by the police . . .

TERRY (*Breaking in*): Can't you find any music? (LORI *turns dial.*)

LORI: I'm trying. (*She tunes in dance music.*) There! (*Hands radio to* GARTH, *as* TOM *takes her hand and they start to dance.*)

TERRY: I'll teach you a new step, Garth. (*As she walks toward* GARTH, *the lights go out. The girls scream.*) What happened?

GARTH: The lights went out! (*He switches off radio.*)

TERRY: I know that! (*Loud knocking is heard, which seems to come from beneath the floor.*) What was that?

LORI: Listen! (*Knocking is repeated.*) It seems to be coming from underneath the floor. Oh, Tommy!

TOM: Relax. The lights will come on in a minute. (*Knocking is repeated.*)

TERRY: Lori, where are you?

LORI: Here. (*The girls move toward each other and meet at center.*) Oh, Terry! Someone's down in those passages she told us about! (*Footsteps are heard outside door at right. Girls gasp.*)

GARTH: Sh-h! Someone's coming!

TOM (*Bravely*): Who—who's there? (DUKE *enters right,*

carrying a flashlight, which he shines on the girls. They scream.)

DUKE: Don't be afraid. It's just me, Duke. (*He wears a wet slicker.*) Why are you in the dark?

GARTH: The lights went out.

DUKE: Darned storm! It wrecks everything! (*He flashes his light around the room. The lights come on suddenly.*)

GIRLS: Oh-h-h! (*They fall onto the couch, relieved.*)

LORI: We thought you were a prowler!

DUKE: I've been outside, taking a look at your car, and I came up through the basement.

TERRY: Were you knocking?

DUKE: Knocking? No. Oh, yes, I was pounding a door shut. (OPAL *enters left.*)

OPAL (*Exasperated*): Duke! Where have you been?

DUKE: Checking on the kids' car.

OPAL: I looked everywhere for you. The lights went out.

DUKE: I know.

OPAL: Mrs. Tushingham's hysterical. She thinks someone's after her, personally.

DUKE: I'll see if I can calm the old girl. (*He crosses to left. To* TERRY) Here, take my flashlight in case the lights go out again.

TERRY: O.K. Thanks. (DUKE *exits.*)

OPAL (*Shaking her head*): What a night! (*She follows* DUKE *out.*)

TERRY: What a night is right! Try the phone again, Tom.

TOM: O.K. (*Lifts receiver and listens, then replaces it*) Still dead.

LORI: This is weird! What are we going to do?

TERRY (*Gleefully*): I know what I'm going to do!

LORI: What?

TERRY: Investigate the tunnels!

LORI: You wouldn't dare!

TERRY: Sure I would! I have a flashlight. What is there to be afraid of? Let's go down.

GARTH: Great! Lead the way.

LORI: No, sir! I'm not going down into an old dark tunnel.

TOM (*Taking* LORI *by the arm*): Come on, let's go!

LORI: No! (*Pulling away*) Stop it, Tommy! No!

TOM: O.K., stay then! (TERRY *and* GARTH *exit right, and* TOM *starts to follow.*)

LORI: Don't leave me!

TOM: Come on, then!

LORI: No.

TOM: Have it your way! (*He follows* TERRY *and* GARTH *out.*)

LORI (*Running to right exit and calling*): Tommy! I'm afraid! Come back! Please. (*There is no answer.*)

DUKE (*Running in left*): What's the matter?

LORI: Well—er—nothing.

DUKE: Why are you yelling?

LORI: The kids went off and left me.

DUKE: Where did they go?

LORI: To the kitchen, I guess. No place. It doesn't matter. I just don't like to be left alone.

DUKE (*Sitting on the arm of the couch*): I'll bet you're not left alone very much, a pretty girl like you.

LORI (*Crossing to couch; smiling*): Oh, I'm not so popular. (*Sits*)

DUKE: Don't tell me that! (*He slides down from arm and sits beside her.*) Any time you're afraid, you just call on me. (LORI *moves away.*) What's the matter, Lori? You aren't afraid of me, are you? (*She gets up quickly and runs to right exit.*)

LORI: I—I think I'll go find the others. (*She runs off right.* DUKE *shrugs, gets up and starts to exit left as* MRS. TUSHINGHAM *appears in the doorway.*)

MRS. TUSHINGHAM: You're just the one I want to see. If I

don't find my jewel case and its contents, I want you and the maid to be my witnesses that I had it when I came to this inn.

DUKE (*Leaning on back of chair*): I can swear you had the case, but it may have been empty for all I know.

MRS. TUSHINGHAM (*Exasperated*): Oh!

DUKE: You didn't open it and show us, did you?

MRS. TUSHINGHAM: No. Why won't that Wickwire woman have everyone searched?

DUKE: You have to be careful when you accuse people, you know. They could turn around and sue for defamation of character.

MRS. TUSHINGHAM: I suppose they could. I'll search my room once more. (*Exits left*)

DUKE (*Watching her exit; then to himself*): Yes, do that. (*He crosses to right exit, looks out, then comes back to center, reaches into his inside pocket and takes out* MRS. TUSHINGHAM'*s jewel case. He opens it and takes out a medallion on a chain and holds it up. He admires it, slips it into case and puts case into his pocket. He moves quickly to the window and pulls the shade back cautiously, and peeks out. Voices are heard off right, and he turns quickly as* TERRY, *holding flashlight, enters, followed by* LORI, TOM, *and* GARTH, *who is carrying a package wrapped in newspaper.*) Where have you been?

TERRY (*Snapping off flashlight*): Down in the dungeons!

DUKE: That's dangerous. The tunnels might have been flooded. Miss Wickwire will be angry if I tell her.

GARTH: We didn't hurt anything.

TOM: Let's see what you found, Garth.

DUKE (*Quickly*): Where did you find that package? (*He starts to take the package from* GARTH, *but* GARTH *pulls it away.*)

GARTH: Just a minute! Don't get grabby! (*He begins to*

unwrap package.) This little item was way back on a shelf in a cubbyhole.

LORI: Maybe it's been there for more than a hundred years, since before the Civil War!

GARTH (*Looking at newspaper*): The paper's only three months old!

LORI (*Disappointed*): Oh!

DUKE: Anything you found down there belongs to Miss Wickwire, you know.

TOM: Don't worry, we'll give it to her (GARTH *drops the newspaper and holds up a jewel case, larger than* MRS. TUSHINGHAM's.)

GARTH: What do you know!

TERRY: Open it! (GARTH *opens the case and holds up a diamond necklace.*)

TOM: Wow!

TERRY: Oh, Garth! It's gorgeous!

GARTH: Man! These stones didn't come from a dime store!

LORI: Whose is it?

DUKE (*With authority*): I'll take the necklace. (*He puts out his hand.*)

GARTH (*Pulling back*): I don't know.

TERRY: Better give it to Miss Wickwire.

DUKE: I'll see that she gets the necklace. Give it to me, please.

GARTH: Well, O.K. (*He puts the necklace in the box and hands it to* DUKE.) There's something funny about this.

DUKE: Thanks. I'll see that it gets to the right party. In the meantime— (MRS. TUSHINGHAM *strides in left, interrupting him.*)

MRS. TUSHINGHAM: It's definitely disappeared, vanished! (*Sees case in* DUKE*'s hand*) Where did you find that?

TERRY: We found it in the basement. Is it yours?

MRS. TUSHINGHAM: No. (*Crosses to* DUKE) My jewel case is much smaller.

LORI: Maybe it grew! (*Teen-agers laugh.* DUKE *gives them a stern look, and they become quiet.*)

TERRY: Did you lose your jewel case?

MRS. TUSHINGHAM (*Giving her a suspicious look*): Yes.

TERRY: This is the only one we found.

MRS. TUSHINGHAM: What's inside?

TOM: A diamond necklace. At least they look like diamonds.

MRS. TUSHINGHAM: May I see? (*As* DUKE *opens case,* LOVELLA *enters left, unnoticed by others, and stands in the doorway, watching.* MRS. TUSHINGHAM *holds up necklace.*) Oh! Beautiful! These diamonds are worth a fortune.

LOVELLA: Indeed they are. (*All turn to her, surprised.* MRS. TUSHINGHAM *drops necklace back into case.*) If you please, Duke. (*She takes a step toward him, holding out her hand.*)

DUKE: I don't think so, Miss Wickwire. (*As he speaks, he reaches inside his coat and draws out a gun. All gasp and draw back.*)

OPAL (*Entering left*): Is it O.K. if I go to bed now, Miss Wick— (*She breaks off, amazed.*) What's going on?

LOVELLA (*Over her shoulder*): Shut up! (*To* DUKE) You rat!

DUKE (*Calmly*): Hands up, Lovella Wickwire. (*She raises her hands halfway.*) All the way! (*Her hands go up higher.*) That's better, Lovella. One of the best fences in the business, aren't you? (LOVELLA *glares at him.*) Garth, reach in my coat pocket, will you? (GARTH *looks surprised.*) Go ahead, I just want you to pull out my credentials.

GARTH (*Taking out card holder; reading*): "James Kendrick, Des Moines Police Department." (*He looks at* DUKE, *then back to card.*) This is his picture all right. (*He returns card to* DUKE'*s pocket.*)

LORI: Is he a policeman?

TERRY: Sh-h!

DUKE: Now if you'll reach in my other pocket, you'll find a pair of handcuffs. (GARTH *pulls them out.*) Put them on her, please.

GARTH (*Hesitating*): Do I have to?

DUKE: Please.

GARTH (*Approaching* LOVELLA): Sorry, ma'am. (*She backs away.*)

DUKE: Don't give us any trouble, Lovella. Go on, boy.

LOVELLA (*As* GARTH *clamps the handcuffs on her wrists*): You rat! You dirty, rotten rat!

DUKE: Now we can relax. At last we've got the fence.

LORI: What's a "fence"?

TOM: Someone who gets rid of stolen goods for thieves.

MRS. TUSHINGHAM: And I walked in here and asked her to hide my medallion! (*To* LOVELLA) What have you done with it? (*Crosses to her.*)

DUKE (*Reaching into his pocket and taking out her jewel case*): Here it is. (*He hands it to* MRS. TUSHINGHAM.)

MRS. TUSHINGHAM: Well! And you called *her* a thief! (*Opens the case and takes out the medallion.*) Thank heavens it's safe!

DUKE: I had to check it out. You might have been her accomplice, you know.

MRS. TUSHINGHAM: Well, thank you very much! (*Exits left, clutching case.*)

OPAL: What is all this about? (DUKE *opens jewel box and holds up the necklace.*) The Vanderlip diamonds?

DUKE: There aren't any Vanderlip diamonds. This necklace is part of the famous Roth jewel collection which was stolen several months ago.

OPAL (*Puzzled*): But the newspaper said—

DUKE: That story about the Vanderlip robbery was a fake. It was put in the paper as part of the plan to catch

Lovella. I wanted her to think that I was a jewel thief so she would confide in me. (LOVELLA *glares at him.*)

OPAL (*Still puzzled*): I guess I see.

DUKE (*To* TOM): There's a police car behind some bushes at the end of the road. Will you go down and tell the officers in the car that I've caught Lovella with the goods? Tell them to get up here right away.

TOM: Sure! (*He opens door up center, turns back*) Sir, could we use the police car radio to get help for our car?

DUKE: Certainly.

TOM: Thanks. (*Looks outside*) It's stopped raining!

LORI: Good! We'll all go with you. Come on, Terry, Garth!

TERRY (*To* DUKE, *as teen-agers start to exit*): Was it the police car that was following Mrs. Tushingham?

DUKE: Yes! This place has been covered for weeks. (*To* LOVELLA) I'll bet you never suspected that.

LOVELLA: You double-crosser! (*Teen-agers exit.*)

DUKE: Now, Opal, take Miss Wickwire to her room and help her pack a bag. As soon as the officers get here, she's going on a little trip.

OPAL (*Frightened*): You want *me* to take her? (DUKE *laughs.*)

DUKE: O.K., Opal. I'll come with you to protect you. Let's go, Lovella. (*They exit left as the curtains close.*)

THE END

The Gold Mine at Jeremiah Flats

by Robert A. Anderson

Characters

MRS. ALLSPENT, *the duty-bound mother*
PATIENCE ALLSPENT, *her daughter, the heroine*
DO-WELL GOODWORTHY, *Patience's fiancé, the hero*
JACK TURMOIL, *the villain*
MR. QUICKBUCK, *a not-too-honest banker*
MISS TRUEBEAUTY, *a secretary from the bank*
SOURDOUGH, *an itinerant miner*
1ST MINER
2ND MINER
SHERIFF

SCENE 1

TIME: *1890. Afternoon.*

SETTING: *The modest Allspent living room. A door off right leads outside; a door at left leads to the rest of the house. A cabinet is against one wall.*

AT RISE: MRS. ALLSPENT *is seated right center.* PATIENCE *is arranging flowers in a vase at upstage left. The stage is dark except for the light of a small candle on table downstage left. The lights come on gradually.*

MRS. ALLSPENT (*Pulling shawl around her*): Patience, my dear, will you add more wood to the fire? My bones feel chilled clear through.

PATIENCE: But, Mama, we have no more wood. I used the last of it this very morning.

MRS. ALLSPENT: Oh, dear, I don't know what we are to do now. I don't see how we can go on. Your poor papa left us without a cent when he passed on to his permanent resting place.

PATIENCE: But, Mama, he left us the Lucky Strike Mine.

MRS. ALLSPENT: The mine, yes. But what can we do with a worthless gold mine? The gold is beneath the water that is flooding the mine. Even your papa couldn't get the water out. How can *we* expect to? No, the mine is of no value to us.

PATIENCE: But, Mama, Do-Well thinks he can make the mine pay. And he said that after we are married, he'll take care of both of us. He will ward off the cold and ward off our creditors and ward off pestilence and . . .

MRS. ALLSPENT (*Interrupting*): Do-Well Goodworthy couldn't ward off a crippled housefly.

PATIENCE (*Shocked*): Mama, how can you say such a thing about the man I'm going to wed? Do-Well is kind and gentle and . . .

MRS. ALLSPENT (*Interrupting*): Yes, yes, I know. I'm sorry, my dear, but you must admit that he is a bit dense. If you love him, however, and no other man is available, you will have my blessings when the time comes. (*Sound of kicking offstage right*) Who's kicking my door?

PATIENCE: I'll see, Mama. (*She exits right.* MRS. ALLSPENT *rises, crosses to candle and warms her hands by it.* DO-WELL *and* PATIENCE *enter right.* DO-WELL *is carrying firewood.*) Mama, see what Do-Well has brought us.

MRS. ALLSPENT: Where did you get that wood, Do-Well?

DO-WELL (*As always, trying especially hard to please.*

He sets wood down upstage): I cut it with my own hands up by the mine, and I have more outside.

MRS. ALLSPENT: Thank you, Do-Well. You really have been a help to us in these trying times. Patience tells me that you have a plan for our mine.

DO-WELL: Yes, ma'am. I figure with a few tools I can divert that water out through another tunnel. My father did the same thing once in a mine that he was working. (*Taking out map*) Look, I have a map here of your mine. (*Crossing to* MRS. ALLSPENT) You see, the water is here, and down here below the water is another shaft with no water in it. All I have to do is dig through the floor here, and the water will empty itself out. I say dig, but what I mean is blast it out. I know I can do it, ma'am.

MRS. ALLSPENT: Do-Well, you are our last hope. (*Going to cabinet and taking out a few bills from a sugar bowl*) Take this, Do-Well, and buy your tools. This is all we have left. Our icebox is bare, and our taxes are overdue. I hope your plan works.

DO-WELL: I'll do my best. I'd better go to the store now so I can get started on the mine. You won't regret putting your faith in me, Mrs. Allspent. (*Taking* PATIENCE'*s hand*) It won't be long now before we are married.

PATIENCE: Oh, Do-Well, I'm so happy.

DO-WELL: But now I must go. Off to get the tools. Good-bye.

PATIENCE: Please do good, Do-Well. (DO-WELL *exits right.*) Mama, now we have a chance. (*There is a knock offstage right.*)

MRS. ALLSPENT: If it's a creditor, tell him to go away. (PATIENCE *exits right and enters with* MR. QUICKBUCK, *the banker.*)

MR. QUICKBUCK (*Very businesslike*): Good afternoon, Mrs. Allspent. (PATIENCE *exits left.*)

MRS. ALLSPENT: What is it this time? You know that I don't have any money to pay you.

MR. QUICKBUCK: That's just it. Your taxes are so far in arrears that my bank can no longer wait. I'm sorry to say that unless you give us the money in two days you'll have to move.

MRS. ALLSPENT: Impossible. Where would I get money in two days?

MR. QUICKBUCK: If I may make a suggestion, you could probably make enough out of your mine if you sold it.

MRS. ALLSPENT (*Indignantly*): Mr. Quickbuck, I promised my husband on his deathbed that I would never let the mine go, and a promise is a promise.

MR. QUICKBUCK: But the mine is worthless to you.

MRS. ALLSPENT: I would rather lose the house and move to the mine before I'd sell it.

MR. QUICKBUCK: Have it your own way. As your banker, I must advise you that you are being very foolish. Outside in my buggy right now is a gentleman who wants to buy your mine.

MRS. ALLSPENT: I'll talk to him, but I won't sell the mine.

MR. QUICKBUCK: I'll call him. (*Goes off right and calls*) Oh, Mr. Turmoil, will you come in here, please? (*Steps back into room.* MR. TURMOIL *enters with a flourish. He grimaces continually and speaks with obvious insincerity.*) Mrs. Allspent, may I present Mr. Turmoil of Denver.

MR. TURMOIL: But, Mr. Quickbuck, you misinformed me. You said that we were dealing with an older woman. (*Looking at* MRS. ALLSPENT) I had no idea that she was such a wonder of preserved beauty, an ageless madonna, a fresh breath of springtime. Madam, it is my pleasure to meet you.

MRS. ALLSPENT (*With a giggle*): Well, aren't you a polite man! What is your interest in my mine, may I ask?

MR. TURMOIL: I work for the Society for the Preservation of Historic Mines. We are located in Denver.

MRS. ALLSPENT: The Society for the Preservation of Historic Mines? My, that sounds interesting.

MR. TURMOIL (*To audience*): This old bag will be a pushover. (*He laughs. To* MRS. ALLSPENT) It's a nonprofit organization, ma'am. We preserve old mines and make them national monuments. Your mine is of particular interest to us because of its long history of gold production. (*To audience*) Little does she know that this purchase will make me fabulously wealthy.

MRS. ALLSPENT: Why, Mr. Quickbuck, why didn't you tell me more about this gentleman and the nice society he works for?

MR. QUICKBUCK (*Confused*): Well—I didn't know.

MRS. ALLSPENT: Didn't know what?

MR. QUICKBUCK: What I meant is, you didn't give me time to tell you.

MR. TURMOIL (*Putting hand into inside coat pocket*): Madam, may I present my credentials?

MRS. ALLSPENT: Oh, that isn't necessary. I can tell that you're a gentleman and a man of honor.

MR. TURMOIL (*Rubs his hands and grins at audience*): Mrs. Allspent, I'm authorized by my society to offer you five hundred dollars in cash for your worthless mine.

MRS. ALLSPENT: Five hundred dollars?

MR. QUICKBUCK: That's a lot of money. (PATIENCE *enters left.*)

PATIENCE: Am I intruding?

MRS. ALLSPENT: No, come in, my dear, I want you to hear this.

MR. TURMOIL (*Crossing to* PATIENCE): This house is filled with the beautiful flowers of springtime. This fresh bloom can only be one of *your* progeny, Mrs. Allspent.

MRS. ALLSPENT (*Giggling a bit*): Why, yes, this is my

daughter, Patience. (*To* PATIENCE) This gentleman is Mr. Turmoil of the Society for the—the—the—

MR. TURMOIL (*Interrupting*): For the Preservation of Historic Mines.

MRS. ALLSPENT: Yes.

MR. TURMOIL (*Kissing* PATIENCE*'s hand*): Miss Allspent, never before have I seen such freshness of summer. What radiant and charming femininity (*Looking her over*), such pulchritudinous proportions. You will have to forgive me, miss, but whenever I see such devastating beauty, I lose all control of myself. (*To audience*) Perhaps I can win this fair blossom along with the gold mine. (*He laughs.*)

MR. QUICKBUCK: I think you should accept his five-hundred-dollar offer, Mrs. Allspent.

PATIENCE: Five-hundred-dollar offer?

MR. QUICKBUCK: Yes. Mr. Turmoil has offered your mother five hundred dollars for her worthless mine.

PATIENCE (*To* MRS. ALLSPENT): But what about your vow to Papa?

MRS. ALLSPENT: Mr. Turmoil is going to make the mine an historic landmark. It wouldn't be like selling it for someone to work.

PATIENCE: But what about Do-Well?

MR. QUICKBUCK: What does Do-Well have to do with this?

PATIENCE: He is going to work the mine and make money at it.

MR. QUICKBUCK: What? *He* will work the mine? It's the most ridiculous thing I've ever heard of. What will he do with the water in the mine, drink it?

MRS. ALLSPENT: Do-Well *does* have a theory.

MR. QUICKBUCK: A theory? He doesn't even know the meaning of the word.

PATIENCE: I think we should at least give Do-Well a chance, Mama.

MRS. ALLSPENT: Perhaps you are right. We do have a small investment in him now.

MR. QUICKBUCK: An investment?

PATIENCE: Yes, he's out right now buying the necessary tools.

MR. QUICKBUCK: But you'll never get a better offer. Why . . .

MR. TURMOIL (*Interrupting*): May I interrupt? (*To* MRS. ALLSPENT) Madam, I will be in Jeremiah Flats for two days only. I shall return after you have thought my offer over. We don't want to rush you.

MR. QUICKBUCK: And let me remind you that my bank will be forced to take your house away and maybe even your mine. Now, before I leave, may I ask how Do-Well plans to rework the mine?

PATIENCE: Well, he has a map of the mine and . . .

MR. QUICKBUCK (*Interrupting, and with surprise*): A map? (*Angrily to* TURMOIL) You told me you had the only map.

MR. TURMOIL (*Quickly*): Shut up—that is, he can't have a map. There aren't any maps of the mine. The fool can't have one.

PATIENCE: Please, sir, do not refer to my affianced as a fool.

MR. TURMOIL: Your affianced?

PATIENCE: Yes. We are to be married soon.

MR. TURMOIL (*To audience*): Curses. I must work fast if I am to salvage this proud beauty for myself.

MR. QUICKBUCK: We must leave now, but we shall return. (*He exits right.*)

MRS. ALLSPENT (*Going right*): We'll think it over. (MR. TURMOIL *follows* MRS. ALLSPENT *off but then comes back in.*)

MR. TURMOIL (*To* PATIENCE): My dear, I'd like to make you a proposition. If you come back with me to the big city of Denver, I'll make you a rich woman. I can take you away from all this. You shall live like a queen.

PATIENCE: No. I am in love with Do-Well.

MR. TURMOIL: Please, my little flower, let me take you along.

PATIENCE: No, never. Don't talk like that, sir.

MR. TURMOIL (*To audience*): Now watch me make this little wretch squirm. (*To* PATIENCE) If you don't come with me, I'll see to it that your mother will be turned out into the cold. Mr. Quickbuck will get this house, and I'll get the mine. Now, will you come with me and save your mother from the fate of being turned out into the cruel world?

PATIENCE: No! No! I would prefer the cru-el, cru-el, cru-el world to a life with you. I do not trust you, sir.

MR. TURMOIL (*Grabbing her wrist*): All right, my proud beauty, all I ask for now is one kiss. I must have and *will* have one kiss before I leave.

PATIENCE: No! No! I would rather die first. Please unhand me, sir. You are hurting my wrist, sir.

MR. TURMOIL (*Struggling with* PATIENCE): Kiss me, you flower of Babylon.

PATIENCE (*Struggling*): Please, sir, let me go, let me go.

(DO-WELL *runs in right, carrying a pick and shovel.*)

DO-WELL (*Dropping tools and running to* MR. TURMOIL, *whom he grabs by the shoulder*): Unhand her, you snake in the grass. (*He strikes* MR. TURMOIL *and knocks him to the floor.*)

MR. TURMOIL (*Recovering himself, he starts to exit right, Shaking his fist at* DO-WELL): I shall return tomorrow and get even with you—you—you fool. (DO-WELL *raises his arm to hit him again, but* TURMOIL *quickly exits right.*)

PATIENCE: Oh, Do-Well, you saved me from that horrid man. He wants to buy our mine—and he tried to kiss me.

DO-WELL: Have no fear when Do-Well is here. If I see that skunk around again, I'll . . . I'll . . .

PATIENCE (*Interrupting*): Do-Well, you are the epitome of virtue, the Samson of Jeremiah Flats, the—the champion of womanhood.

DO-WELL (*Shyly*): Shucks, you don't have to say all that.

PATIENCE: But I mean it. You tell me when you want to be married, and I'll be ready.

DO-WELL: First I have to work the mine. (*Picking up tools*) I bought some tools and dynamite, and now I must go. (DO-WELL *exits right.*)

PATIENCE (*Calling*): Hurry back. (MRS. ALLSPENT *enters right.*)

MRS. ALLSPENT: I see Do-Well bought some equipment.

PATIENCE: Oh, Mama, what are we to do if Do-Well doesn't do well?

MRS. ALLSPENT: We can always sell out to the gentleman from Denver.

PATIENCE: Gentleman? That cad tried to kiss me.

MRS. ALLSPENT: Mr. Turmoil tried to kiss you?

PATIENCE: Yes.

MRS. ALLSPENT: That cad. Oh, my poor daughter, I shouldn't have left you alone. I figured that maybe as the last resort we could sell to Mr. Turmoil. Now I'm not sure. I don't know if he can be trusted. I think that maybe we should do a little checking on Mr. Turmoil.

PATIENCE: Checking? But how?

MRS. ALLSPENT: The sheriff will know more about these things than we do. It might be a good idea if you went into town to speak to him before we decide anything.

PATIENCE: I will go if you say so, but what will I ask him?

MRS. ALLSPENT: Just ask him if he has any information on a John Turmoil of Denver. If he is a dishonest man, the sheriff will find it out. Give him a description of Mr. Turmoil, too. But go directly to his office, pay no heed to others along the way, and above all, don't talk to any strange men.

PATIENCE: No, Mama. I will go, then. I will do my best. (*As she exits right*) I'm off. (*Curtain*)

* * *

SCENE 2

TIME: *A short while later. Dusk.*

SETTING: *Near the entrance of the Allspent mine. A wooden box is downstage left. Attached to the back wall is a sign reading* LUCKY STRIKE MINE, *which points offstage right.*

AT RISE: *Pounding sounds are heard offstage right. The sounds stop as* DO-WELL *enters right, mopping his brow. The lights are dim.*

DO-WELL (*Crossing to downstage left to pick up wooden box*): In two more hours I'll prove to the world that my theory is right. With this dynamite I'll empty every drop of water in the mine, and the mother lode will be exposed once more. (*Exits right.* MR. TURMOIL *and* MR. QUICKBUCK *enter left.*)

MR. TURMOIL: Sh-h-h. Sh-h-h. Quiet now. Listen. (*Pounding sounds are heard once again.*) He's still in there. Good.

MR. QUICKBUCK: You can't go through with this. I may agree to a slightly dishonest business transaction, but this is too much.

MR. TURMOIL: You're in it too deeply already. You can't back out now. Quickly, get the box out of the buggy.

MR. QUICKBUCK: This is murder, and I refuse to help you.

MR. TURMOIL (*Taking out his gun*): Now, let's get one thing straight around here. I'm running this pageant, and you'll do what I say. There's a million dollars left in this mine, and I'll get it if it means killing you, too. (*Pushing* MR. QUICKBUCK *left*) Now get that box out of the buggy. (MR. QUICKBUCK *exits left, as* TURMOIL *strides across stage to look things over.*) It won't be long now before I own this whole mine, and that fool Do-Well will be blown to bits. (*He laughs.* MR. QUICKBUCK *enters carrying a heavy box filled with "dynamite sticks," spool of wire, and plunger generator.*) Set it down over here. (*Indicating right center. He takes a few sticks of "dynamite" from box and wraps them with wire.*) This will look like an accident.

MR. QUICKBUCK: If I'm forced to go through with this, remember that half of the profits will be mine.

MR. TURMOIL: Yes, yes, of course. (*To audience*) This old fool. As soon as he has made the transaction for me, I'll polish him off, too. (*He laughs.*)

MR. QUICKBUCK (*Putting hand to ear*): Hush. Someone is coming. (*Both back up and crouch down.* SOURDOUGH *enters left, dressed in old mining clothes. He stops and looks the situation over.*)

SOURDOUGH (*Reading sign*): The Lucky Strike Mine. At last I'm here.

MR. TURMOIL (*Rushing forward with his gun drawn*): Hands up.

SOURDOUGH (*Raising arms*): Don't shoot! Don't shoot! I have no money.

MR. TURMOIL: You old fool—who wants your money?

SOURDOUGH: Well, what do you want?

MR. TURMOIL: I want to know what you meant by saying: "At last I'm here."

SOURDOUGH: I've been searching for this mine for a week now.

MR. TURMOIL: The Lucky Strike Mine?

SOURDOUGH: Yes, the one in Gunnarson County. This is Gunnarson County, isn't it?

MR. QUICKBUCK: Yes, it is. What is your business here?

SOURDOUGH: I own part of this mine.

MR. TURMOIL: You lie.

SOURDOUGH: No, I don't. Three years ago I bought twenty-five per cent of it from a Mr. John Allspent. He was short on funds, and so I staked him to some equipment, and he gave me a share of the mine.

MR. TURMOIL (*To* QUICKBUCK): You told me this mine was clear.

MR. QUICKBUCK: I thought it was. (*To* SOURDOUGH) Have you recorded this in the courthouse?

SOURDOUGH: Not yet. This is my first time in this territory. I received the share in Silverton where I met Mr. Allspent. I do plan to go to the courthouse while I'm here, though.

MR. TURMOIL: What proof do you have of owning part of the mine?

SOURDOUGH (*Lowering arms and taking out deed*): Here is the deed.

MR. TURMOIL (*Snatching paper*): Give me that, you old fool.

SOURDOUGH (*Pleadingly*): But I need that for proof. I'll be on my way to the courthouse soon.

MR. TURMOIL: You're on your way some place else.

SOURDOUGH: The mine is all I have in the world. I'm broke. I need money to support my wife and five children. Please give it back to me.

MR. TURMOIL (*Pushing him roughly*): Shut up, you old fool. Your whining bores me. (*Pointing off left*) Do you see that tree over there?

SOURDOUGH: Yes—but my deed . . .

MR. TURMOIL: Forget your deed, and start walking.

SOURDOUGH: What are you going to do?

MR. TURMOIL: Never mind. Just start walking.

SOURDOUGH: But . . . but . . . (TURMOIL *pushes him*

off left and follows him. Offstage) What are you doing with that gun?

MR. TURMOIL (*Offstage*): Shut up.

SOURDOUGH (*Offstage*): Please. Think of my wife and children.

MR. TURMOIL (*Offstage*): The devil with your family, you old fool. (*Three shots ring out.* MR. TURMOIL'S *laughter is heard offstage. He enters blowing smoke from his gun*) Now let's get down to business.

MR. QUICKBUCK: Mr. Turmoil . . . that is . . . I don't think . . .

MR. TURMOIL (*Crossing to* QUICKBUCK *and sticking gun in his ribs*): You don't think what?

MR. QUICKBUCK (*Frightened*): Ah . . . ah . . . nothing. Nothing at all.

MR. TURMOIL: Well, let's get busy then.

MR. QUICKBUCK: Yes, of course.

MR. TURMOIL: All right. (*Puts gun away. Taking wire from box*) Unwind this wire and take the kinks out of it. (MR. QUICKBUCK *takes wire and unwinds it by walking around stage with the spool.* TURMOIL *holds one end that is attached to "dynamite."*) That should be enough. (TURMOIL *goes to box and takes out a plunger-type generator used for setting off explosives and goes to downstage left with it.*) All right, I think we are about ready to give that Do-Well fellow the surprise of his life. (*Hands sticks of "dynamite" to* MR. QUICKBUCK) Now take this dynamite and get as close to that young fool as you can without being seen. Set the sticks on the floor, and come right back here. Is that clear?

MR. QUICKBUCK: Yes, but . . .

MR. TURMOIL (*Interrupting*): But what?

MR. QUICKBUCK: Well, I just don't like this.

PATIENCE (*Offstage left*): Yoo-hoo, yoo-hoo, Do-Well?

MR. TURMOIL: Curses, that sounds like the girl. What is

she doing here? Quick, get these things up there. (*Indicates upstage left, where they move the box and generator.* TURMOIL *and* QUICKBUCK *back up to wall to allow* PATIENCE *to enter without seeing them.* PATIENCE *enters, one hand to mouth as though calling. She is carrying paper bag.* QUICKBUCK *and* TURMOIL *tiptoe out left.*)

PATIENCE: Yoo-hoo, yoo-hoo, Do-Well? Are you there? (*Crosses to right and shouts offstage right*) Do-Well? Do-Well? Are you in there?

DO-WELL (*Faintly, from offstage*): Coming. (DO-WELL *enters right carrying a pick. To* PATIENCE, *sharply*) Patience! What are you doing here? Is there anything wrong?

PATIENCE: No, nothing is wrong. I was just coming from Jeremiah Flats, and I thought I'd stop by. I brought you something to eat. (*Hands him paper bag*)

DO-WELL: Thank you. What were you doing in town?

PATIENCE: Mama sent me to ask the sheriff about Mr. Turmoil.

DO-WELL: Mr. Turmoil?

PATIENCE: Yes. Mama thinks he might be a dishonest man.

DO-WELL: I *know* he is. What did the sheriff have to say?

PATIENCE: He didn't know Mr. Turmoil, so he will have to do some checking on him and let us know.

DO-WELL: Well, I wouldn't worry about him any more. He's probably on his way to Denver right now.

PATIENCE: I hope so. How is the mine coming?

DO-WELL: I should be finished by tomorrow noon. It's going to be easier than I expected. I'm putting a fire in the hole today and will clean up the mess tomorrow.

PATIENCE: A fire in the hole?

DO-WELL: Yes, to blast it with dynamite.

PATIENCE: Please be careful with all that dynamite.

DO-WELL: Don't you worry one bit. Run along now before your mama worries about you. I'll be along later.

PATIENCE: Can't I wait for you?

DO-WELL: No. I'll be here for a while yet. Go along home, and I'll stop by after I finish blasting.

PATIENCE: All right, Do-Well. But please be careful with all that dynamite. (*Blowing him a kiss*) Bye-bye.

DO-WELL: Bye, now. (PATIENCE *exits left.* DO-WELL *exits right.* TURMOIL *and* QUICKBUCK *enter left.*)

MR. TURMOIL: Quickly now, let's finish this job. We've wasted too much time already. (*He picks up "dynamite sticks" with wire attached.*)

MR. QUICKBUCK: I refuse to be a further part of your scheming machinations. You are a true cad, sir, and I would challenge you to a duel if I had a weapon. I will no longer break the law.

MR. TURMOIL (*Taking out gun*): You old fool. I have the upper hand here. You'll do what I say, or I'll shoot you full of holes. Now take this dynamite and get into the shaft with it. (*He throws the bundle of "dynamite" at him carelessly.* QUICKBUCK *barely catches it.* TURMOIL *points gun at* QUICKBUCK) Now get in there and get as close to Do-Well as you can. (*Forces* QUICKBUCK *to right.*)

MR. QUICKBUCK: This is against my better judgment.

MR. TURMOIL: The devil with your better judgment. Get moving. (QUICKBUCK *exits right with "dynamite."* TURMOIL *lets out wire.*) We don't want to get this wire all tangled. (*Looking about*) Where is the end of this? (*Finds end of wire and attaches it to generator. He lets out more wire*) He should be far enough into the mine by now for this blast to take care of both of them. (*Raising handle of generator*) That old fool. If he'd played along with me he'd be a rich man instead of a dead banker. (*Yells*) Two birds with one stone. Forgive me, Mother. (*With great exertion he pushes the plunger. A blast is heard offstage right. Smoke drifts in from right.* TURMOIL *laughs loudly as curtain falls.*)

* * *

SCENE 3

TIME: *Two days later.*

SETTING: *Same as Scene 1.*

AT RISE: MRS. ALLSPENT *is seated right center.* PATIENCE *is arranging flowers in a vase at upstage left.*

MRS. ALLSPENT: Oh, woe is us, woe is upon us. Oh, woe, woe. Lackaday, daughter, lackaday. What are we to do?

PATIENCE (*Crossing and putting her hand on her mother's shoulder*): Courage, Mama. We must have courage. Someone (*Pause*), somewhere will help us. Have courage, Mama.

MRS. ALLSPENT: But with Do-Well gone, I see no one left to help us.

PATIENCE: They haven't found Do-Well's body yet. He may still be alive.

MRS. ALLSPENT: Patience, my dear, it will take time, many days before they clear the main tunnel. It has been two days now that they've been working at it. Everyone says that no one could live through such a blast. (*Patting* PATIENCE'*s hand*) Let us not build up false hopes, my dear.

PATIENCE (*Sighing*): Perhaps you are right. Mama, do you know what my last words were to Do-Well?

MRS. ALLSPENT: No, what were they?

PATIENCE: I told him—I told him, please be careful with all that dynamite. (*Bursting into tears as knock offstage right is heard.*)

MRS. ALLSPENT (*Patting* PATIENCE): There, there, now, daughter. Control yourself. I shall see who is at the door.

(MRS. ALLSPENT *exits right.* PATIENCE *dries her tears and composes herself.* MRS. ALLSPENT *re-enters with* TWO MINERS, *who are each carrying a cloth-covered gallon jug.*)

PATIENCE: Who is it, Mama?

MRS. ALLSPENT: These men are from the mine. They came to fill their water jugs.

PATIENCE: I'll fill them. (*She exits left, taking jugs.*)

MRS. ALLSPENT: How are things at the mine?

1ST MINER: The boys are still working, but some had to give up to go back to their regular jobs. It'll take a week to get all that rock out.

2ND MINER: No one could live through that mess.

1ST MINER: They'll find the body, though. (PATIENCE *enters left with the jugs.*)

2ND MINER (*Taking jugs*): Thank you, miss. (MINERS *exit right.*)

PATIENCE (*Starting off left*): Come, Mama, we must begin to pack.

MRS. ALLSPENT: But we have no place to go.

PATIENCE: The good Lord will be with us, Mama. (*Knock on door right is heard.*)

PATIENCE: I'll get it. (*Exits right and enters with* MISS TRUEBEAUTY, *secretary to* MR. QUICKBUCK. *She is a frail girl, and acts uneasy. She carries a briefcase.*) You say you work at the bank?

MISS TRUEBEAUTY: Yes, I'm Mr. Quickbuck's secretary.

PATIENCE: This is my mother. Mother, this is Miss Truebeauty.

MRS. ALLSPENT: How do you do? Won't you be seated? (*All sit.*)

MISS TRUEBEAUTY: Mr. Quickbuck was supposed to be here, but we think he must be ill. He hasn't been at work these past two days. Since I'm his secretary, the bank sent me over on this unpleasant task. I'm really uncertain as to the procedure, though I guess we'll be able to work it out.

MRS. ALLSPENT: It seems strange to have a woman working in a bank. We were expecting someone, however. I guess there is no way to save our property now?

MISS TRUEBEAUTY: No, I'm afraid not. My instructions are to have you sign these papers. (*Takes papers from her briefcase*) This will turn your property over to the bank.

PATIENCE (*Crossing to left*): I'll fix some tea. I think we have a little left. (*She exits.*)

MISS TRUEBEAUTY: Now if you will just look these papers over . . . (*Knock offstage right*)

MRS. ALLSPENT: Excuse me. (*Exits.*)

MISS TRUEBEAUTY: Certainly. (MRS. ALLSPENT *re-enters, followed by* MR. TURMOIL, *who is carrying a bag of groceries.*)

MRS. ALLSPENT: Come in, Mr. Turmoil. Miss Truebeauty, this is Mr. Turmoil of Denver.

MR. TURMOIL: Good heavens, is there going to be a beauty contest here?

MRS. ALLSPENT: Why, no. Why do you ask?

MR. TURMOIL: Every time I enter this abode I am surrounded by ravishing beauties. (*Kissing* MISS TRUEBEAUTY'*s hand*) It is my pleasure, to be sure.

MISS TRUEBEAUTY (*Pulling hand back quickly and wiping kissed spot on side of her dress*): Sir, how dare you?

MR. TURMOIL: How dare I what?

MISS TRUEBEAUTY (*Aghast*): You . . . you . . . (*Struggling for a word*) kissed my hand! Oh, I feel faint. (*She puts hand to her head and looks for chair.* MRS. ALLSPENT *leads her to chair.*) He . . . he . . . kissed me. (*Puts head on back of chair as if in a faint.* MRS. ALLSPENT *goes quickly to cabinet for smelling salts and revives her.*) Is he gone?

MRS. ALLSPENT: No, Mr. Turmoil is here on business, too, I think.

MR. TURMOIL: I'm so sorry, miss.

MRS. ALLSPENT: You're all right now, Miss Truebeauty.

MISS TRUEBEAUTY: But he . . . he . . .

MRS. ALLSPENT (*Interrupting*): There, now, it's all right.

MR. TURMOIL (*Crossing to* MISS TRUEBEAUTY): A thousand apologies. Never would I think of taking liberties, but the kissing of a lady's hand is a Continental custom.

MISS TRUEBEAUTY: A gentleman here in the West wouldn't think of kissing a lady until he was engaged to her.

MR. TURMOIL: Of course. I'm sorry.

MRS. ALLSPENT: Miss Truebeauty works at the bank.

MR. TURMOIL: Yes, I have seen her down there. (*Handing groceries to* MRS. ALLSPENT) Here are some groceries, madam. I thought that under the circumstances you might need some.

MRS. ALLSPENT: Why, thank you, Mr. Turmoil. (PATIENCE *enters left with tea service and sets it down on a table.*)

MR. TURMOIL (*Bowing to* PATIENCE): Miss Allspent. (*To* PATIENCE *and* MRS. ALLSPENT) I want to express my deep and sincere condolences on the loss of Do-Well. He was a fine boy . . . even though we did have a slight misunderstanding. In fact, I've been down at the mine all morning helping to remove the rubble.

MRS. ALLSPENT: How nice of you!

MR. TURMOIL: I believe they have now given up the search.

MISS TRUEBEAUTY (*Fully recovered*): That was such a catastrophe.

MR. TURMOIL (*To* PATIENCE): And I wish to apologize most profoundly for my actions the other day. I was so completely enthralled by your charm that I could not control myself. I am truly sorry for my actions.

MRS. ALLSPENT: I'm sure Patience will accept your apologies. (*To* PATIENCE) Won't you, dear?

PATIENCE: Now, Mama.

MRS. ALLSPENT: I think that Mr. Turmoil has proved himself by working so hard at the mine and by bringing us food.

MR. TURMOIL: I would like to make one more gesture of my good intentions before I return to Denver. My offer to buy the mine still holds good. I offer you four hundred dollars.

PATIENCE: But you offered us five hundred dollars before.

MR. TURMOIL: Yes, I did, but it will cost me at least one hundred dollars to clean up the rubble from Do-Well's unfortunate accident.

MISS TRUEBEAUTY: Four hundred dollars will save your house, Mrs. Allspent.

MRS. ALLSPENT (*To* PATIENCE): My dear, I'm going to accept Mr. Turmoil's offer. I no longer see any other way out.

MR. TURMOIL (*Quickly taking out papers*): I have the papers all drawn up and ready to sign. Do you have the deed to the mine?

MRS. ALLSPENT (*To* PATIENCE): Get the deed for him. (PATIENCE *takes deed from drawer in cabinet.*)

MR. TURMOIL: And I also have the three hundred dollars in cash with me.

PATIENCE (*Correcting him*): Four hundred dollars.

MR. TURMOIL: Yes, four hundred. That's what I meant to say. (*To* MISS TRUEBEAUTY *as he takes money out*) And will you accept this money as a payment on the house?

MISS TRUEBEAUTY: I certainly wish Mr. Quickbuck were here. This sounds a bit complicated.

MR. TURMOIL: Mr. Quickbuck?

MISS TRUEBEAUTY: Yes, I believe he is sick in bed.

MR. TURMOIL: Come to think of it, he did have a slight cold the last time I saw him. I'm sure he's some place keeping warm. (*Sneers and laughs at audience. Speaks to*

MISS TRUEBEAUTY) There is nothing complicated about this transaction. All I do is give Mrs. Allspent three . . . ah, four hundred dollars; then she signs the mine over to me; next she gives you your money, and you take it back to the bank as payment for the taxes. Very simple.

MISS TRUEBEAUTY: Let's see. You give Mrs. Allspent four hundred dollars. Then she signs the mine over to you. She gives me the money, and I take it back to the bank. But what about the taxes that are due on the house?

MR. TURMOIL: That money is for the taxes. Get it?

MISS TRUEBEAUTY: Oh, I see. That money which you pay Mrs. Allspent will really be the bank's money.

MRS. ALLSPENT: That's right.

MISS TRUEBEAUTY: I understand. It isn't too complicated, is it?

MR. TURMOIL: No, it's very simple, and I'll tell you what I'll do. I'll drive you back to the bank in my carriage and explain a few other business transactions to you. (*To audience*) Perhaps I can add another proud beauty to my collection. (*He laughs. To* MRS. ALLSPENT) Now then, if you will just sign this paper and then sign your deed over to me, everything will be in order.

MRS. ALLSPENT: I'll get a pen.

MR. TURMOIL (*Quickly taking pen from his pocket*): Allow me, madam.

MRS. ALLSPENT (*Taking pen*): You are always so prepared. (*Takes deed from* PATIENCE, *who is sobbing audibly.* MISS TRUEBEAUTY *is busying herself with papers in her briefcase.*) Where do I sign?

MR. TURMOIL (*Pointing*): Right on this line. (*He packs up and rubs his hands together greedily.* PATIENCE *sobs loudly. A crash is heard offstage right, and* DO-WELL *runs on stage from right with a flying leap. His clothes are tattered, and his face is blackened. He stops, stretches out his right arm bent at the elbow and points up—the classic hero's stance.*)

DO-WELL (*Dramatically*): Stop!

MR. TURMOIL: Curses—foiled again! (*At this moment all except* DO-WELL *register looks of great surprise.*)

PATIENCE (*Dramatically*): Do-Well! (*She runs to* DO-WELL, *drops to her knees and hugs his legs.*) Do-Well, my hero!

DO-WELL (*Helping her to her feet*): Everything will be all right now.

LADIES (*Ad lib*): But we thought you were dead! How did you escape? Are you all right? (*Etc.*) QUICKBUCK, *also tattered from the explosion, enters right with the* SHERIFF.)

MISS TRUEBEAUTY: Mr. Quickbuck, what happened? What happened? How is your cold? You're hurt, Mr. Quickbuck. (*Putting arm to head*) Oh, dear, oh, dear, I feel faint. Oh, dear, oh, dear. (MRS. ALLSPENT *leads* MISS TRUEBEAUTY *to chair.* MISS TRUEBEAUTY *sits and rests her head on back of chair as if in a faint.*)

MR. QUICKBUCK: Allow me to explain. This no-good cad (*Pointing to* TURMOIL, *who is cringing*) inveigled me into a scheming plot to kill Do-Well. I refused to have any part in it, so he tried to kill me, too. It was he who blew up the Lucky Strike Mine hoping to kill both Do-Well and me. Then he figured he could buy the mine cheaply from you. You see, he knows that there is plenty of gold left in the mine.

MRS. ALLSPENT: But how did you get out of the mine?

DO-WELL: Mr. Quickbuck came and told me what Turmoil was up to. We quickly hid in a cranny just in time to avoid the blast.

MR. QUICKBUCK: Then we dug through to a lower shaft.

DO-WELL: And the blast had just the effect I thought it

would. The water is all drained out, and the mine is workable.

MR. QUICKBUCK: You will be a rich woman, Mrs. Allspent.

PATIENCE: And we can get married, Do-Well.

DO-WELL: Yes, but first, Sheriff, arrest that man. (SHERIFF *takes a step towards* TURMOIL.)

MR. TURMOIL (*Drawing a gun*): Not so fast. I have a gun. (MRS. ALLSPENT *and* PATIENCE *cower upstage.*)

DO-WELL (*Pushing* SHERIFF *aside*): Step aside, Sheriff. I shall take care of this cad.

PATIENCE: No, Do-Well, no! (SHERIFF *retreats, and* DO-WELL *stands to the left of him.* TURMOIL *comes towards* DO-WELL *menacingly pointing his gun.* MISS TRUE-BEAUTY, *recovering from her faint, steps forward and hits* TURMOIL'*s gun hand with her briefcase.* TURMOIL *drops his gun as* DO-WELL *lunges at him. An exaggerated fist fight ensues in which* TURMOIL *is knocked down three times.*)

MR. TURMOIL (*On his knees, pleading with folded hands*): Please don't hit me again. Please. Not again. I beg you not to hit me again. (DO-WELL *raises his arm as if to strike him again, but* PATIENCE *rushes forth and grabs his upraised arm.*)

PATIENCE: No, Do-Well, no! He has had enough.

DO-WELL (*Pointing to* TURMOIL): There is your man, Sheriff. (SHERIFF *crosses and grabs* TURMOIL. MISS TRUEBEAUTY *goes to* MR. QUICKBUCK *and locks her arm in his.* PATIENCE *locks her arm in* DO-WELL'*s left arm, as he bends his right arm and holds fist upward.* And thus to any man who dares do injustice to humanity. (*Curtain*)

THE END

Mud Pack Madness

by Dawn and Marshall French

Characters

GINNY
MARGE
BARB
KAREN
LAURABELLE

TIME: *The present; one evening.*
SETTING: *The living room of Ginny's house.*
AT RISE: GINNY, BARB, MARGE *and* KAREN *are seated about the room, setting their hair and talking.*

GINNY: I can't imagine why we didn't think of this before! A whole evening to do each other's hair, and nails and —Barb, would you give me a facial, later?

BARB: Sure! (*Filing nails*) I'd sure like to give that pest, Danny, a facial. (*Makes slapping motions viciously in the air with her hands*) Boy, *would* I give him a facial! He'd glow for weeks.

KAREN: All of this (*Waves her hand at all of the nail polish, curlers, etc.*) is all right, but I still say that to get her man, a girl has to keep an eye on her figure.

MARGE (*Gets up to dig for a piece of cotton in her overnight bag that is sitting on a tray*): If *she* doesn't, nobody else will.

KAREN: There's not one of us here that couldn't stand to trim down! (*Stands and begins bending exercises, touching the floor with her hands. This continues through next several speeches.*)

MARGE (*Huffily*): Speak for yourself!

GINNY: No, I think Karen's right. After we get our hair done up, let's exercise to records!

MARGE: Speaking of hair, I'm not positive that I want to have one of you characters experimenting on *mine*.

BARB: Danny Martin had better get his head shaved, like Yul Brynner, before *I* see him again.

MARGE: Um-m-m. I think Yul Brynner is just the most! (*Dreamily*) You know, Danny would look just wonderful with his head shaved. If he doesn't appeal to you—just send him along to me!

BARB (*Angrily*): Just because I feel like yanking his hair out is no sign I want to throw him to *you,* Vampira!

GINNY: Hey, now! We promised not even to *talk* about boys tonight. Remember, if we're going to teach them a lesson, we'll just have to pretend they don't even exist—for tonight, at least.

KAREN: What I don't understand is how this is all going to do me any good. (*Stops exercises and flops down on the floor*) Ron doesn't know I exist, so how can I ignore him? He never even notices me!

GINNY: Now don't you worry! When Ron gets around to noticing anything but a football, I'll bet it will be you.

KAREN: The only time he thinks about me now is when he wants a report typed.

BARB (*Jumping up and waving her comb*): Typing! That was my big mistake! When I think of all the reports I've typed for that rockhead—and did I ever get one word of thanks? Did I?

MARGE (*Innocently*): Did you?

BARB: That so-and-so just took me for granted! Tonight he

can just wonder where I am. He can just eat his heart out waiting for me to get home. (*She starts sniffling.*) Mother has strict instructions not to tell him where I am!

MARGE: Oh, bro-ther! (*Mocking her*) He might die of a broken heart. I'll bet *I* could revive him, though.

BARB (*Getting up and starting for her*): Oh, you— (*Just then* LAURABELLE *appears in the doorway, holding a large jar of something green.*)

GINNY: Oh, Laurabelle! Are you all settled in your room?

LAURA (*Speaking in strong Southern drawl*): Sure am, honey. Everything's in apple-pie order.

GINNY: Kids, this is my cousin Laurabelle. I told you about her. Her school's on vacation right now, so we invited her here to stay for a while. Bet you can't *guess* where she's from!

MARGE: Well, corn my pones, I couldn't imagine.

LAURA (*Laughing*): Oh, you, go on now. I haven't that much of an accent, have ah?

GINNY: You do have just a—ah—trace, Laurabelle.

LAURA: You know, girls, I couldn't help but overhear what you were saying about teaching your boy friends a lesson.

BARB: I'll just bet!

LAURA: It's none of my business, but I sure would think mighty carefully before I went overboard on this sort of thing. Men are sure funny critters!

BARB: Critters is right! More like beasts! Believe me, mine needs taming!

KAREN: I'm trying to get one to tame.

MARGE: I'm still not so sure about this whole thing, but it stands to reason that it'll sure be noticed if I'm out of circulation for even one evening. (*Stands up, primping*)

LAURA: If you all are sure of what you're doing, I reckon it's all right. Anyway, I brought something with me that you might like to see—and you all can use it if you would like to. (*Holds up the jar*)

GINNY: What is it? (*Takes bottle*) Listen! "Granny Garthman's Good Old-Fashioned Gumbo Grease for Graying Gooey Complexions."

BARB: Sounds like embalming fluid.

LAURA: I know it sounds just dreadful—but you'd be amazed at the results!

GINNY: Come to think of it, I've been needing something to get some color in my cheeks. Does this really work?

LAURA: It sure does! Would you like to try it?

KAREN: Seems to me that deep knee bends and standing on your head for half an hour would do the same thing. (*Doubtful*) I don't think I want that stuff on my face.

MARGE: Personally, I don't have a very flat head, like some people I know. I'll try it—(*Quickly*) but somebody else can go first!

GINNY: I guess, if you're sure it works, Laurabelle . . . (*She pulls her hair back and ties a towel around it.*) I'm ready. (*She sits down at a table, closes her eyes and screws up her face.*)

LAURA: Relax, honey. I'm not going to hurt you! This is just nice and cool. Sort of soothing, in fact. (*Starts smoothing the paste from the jar onto* GINNY'*s face*)

MARGE: Ugh! What's it like, Ginny?

GINNY: Well-l—

BARB: Couldn't feel any worse than it looks!

GINNY: Why, it's not bad, not bad at all!

KAREN: Here, I'll try some. (*Dips her fingers into the jar, starts dabbing the stuff on*)

MARGE (*Dabbing on her hand*): Hm-m-m. Well, here goes! (*Puts it on her face*)

BARB: Here's mud in your eye, Danny old boy! (*Slaps it on her face. All apply thick layers of paste from jar to their faces.*)

MARGE: I wonder if this stuff can actually make me better looking than I already am?

BARB (*Sarcastically*): It *would* be hard to improve on such rare and flawless beauty!

MARGE: I didn't mean that, crazy!

GINNY: If you girls want to look at a couple of living dolls, take a peek in the mirror. (*Hands them the mirror.*)

MARGE (*Screaming loudly*): What have I done to myself? Who is this Granny Garthman, anyway? A witch doctor?

KAREN: Here, let me see— (*Wails*) Oh-h-h-h no-oo!

BARB: Karen, you have to admit, Ron would notice you now! (*Suddenly gets an idea*) Quick, a camera! Boy, what a picture! Couldn't I blackmail you, Marge, you old mudhen? (*She rummages in overnight bag for a camera, then gets the flash attachment.*) Boy, oh boy! Here I come, ready or not!

GINNY: You don't look any better than they do!

LAURA: Sure enough, honey. That's right!

BARB: Yes, but I'm *trying* to make Danny suffer. (*She tries to focus on* KAREN, *who hides her face, then on* MARGE, *who throws a towel over her head. She tries* KAREN *again and* KAREN *starts running around the room, hiding her face.*)

KAREN (*Running*): Oh, no, Barb, don't! Please! Don't! I'll shoot myself if a picture of this gets out. Oh, no, don't —wait now— (*She runs out of the room with* BARB *right behind her.*)

LAURA: Oh, my, they shouldn't go outside with that stuff on. They might cause an accident. (*Door opens and both* KAREN *and* BARB *back rigidly into the room, looking frightened. Suddenly they turn and start talking at once.*)

BARB: Hide, everybody! Hide, quickly!

GINNY: What's wrong?

LAURA: Goodness gracious, what's the flurry?

KAREN: It's—it's—oh, hide me! (*Runs behind the sofa.*)

GINNY: What on earth is wrong?

LAURA: Who's there?

KAREN (*Sticking her head up from behind the couch*): The boys!

GINNY: Let's get this junk off!

MARGE: I'm ruined—just ruined! Where's a towel? Why did I ever agree to this?

BARB (*Undecided*): I ought to leave mine on, just to give Danny a shock, but somehow, I just can't. (*Grabs a towel*)

LAURA (*Quickly excusing herself*): Since you girls are all busy, I'll go tell the boys to wait till you come out.

BARB: Halt! Don't do me any favors. (*Grabs* LAURA'*s arm and spins her around*) I'm not coming out! I'm going to teach that jerk a lesson, if it kills me!

LAURA (*Center stage*): You girls shouldn't feel that way. In South Carolina, we treat our men like real gentlemen.

MARGE: So? Maybe they *are* real gentlemen!

LAURA: No, now, you all know what I mean. We just treat them like kings. We surely do. Why, do you know that when my old boy friend, Jefferson Lee Davis, came calling on me, *I* used to give *him* candy!

KAREN: You did? Do you still go with him?

LAURA: Now, that's a touchy little old subject, honey. I do declare, I don't want to talk about it, much.

GINNY: Come on, Laura. Do you still date him? (*The girls have temporarily stopped removing the make-up.*)

LAURA: You all aren't interested in me! Now tell me true —are you really going through with this plan to punish your sweet little old boy friends?

BARB: You bet your sweet little old life!

MARGE: I'm not exactly *punishing* them, just sort of playing on their emotions!

KAREN (*Sighing*): I'm just trying to get someone to punish.

LAURA: If you all are sure—guess I'll just keep them entertained. We southern girls don't leave a herd of handsome boys running around loose. Besides that, you girls may be kind of busy. (*She smiles knowingly and exits waving her hanky at them.*)

GINNY: I wonder what she meant. (*Rubs face with towel*)

MARGE: You know, something about that little magnolia blossom rubs me wrong. She's up to something! (*Rubs face with towel*) Wonder why she *really* came here in the first place. Hey— (*She rubs harder.*) Hey! This isn't coming off!

BARB: Try sandpaper, dearie. (*Smiles sweetly*)

GINNY: Kids, do your faces feel funny? Mine's beginning to feel so stiff and hard—

KAREN: Mine, too—it's all crackly around my eyes—and it's hard for me to smile. Oh, it feels awful—

BARB: Mine's getting hard, too. It's just like cement. It's hard even to talk.

MARGE: That's a blessing. You're right—it *is* hard to talk! Almost impossible! (*The girls' speech becomes stiff and comes slowly.*)

GINNY: I can just barely move my mouth. This is terrible!

MARGE: If I ever get my hands on that charming little cousin of yours, I'll shove Granny Garthman down her throat!

BARB: Try to scrape it off. (*She takes out a fingernail file and scrapes at the goo.*) Ginny, get her. Make her tell us how to get it off. (*The girls are clawing frantically at their faces and are bent into all sorts of odd positions.*)

GINNY: I can't—she just left, with Danny!

MARGE: We can't just stay around with this on us! Do something!

KAREN: But what?

BARB: Did you say—Laurabelle left with Danny? (GINNY *nods.*)

MARGE (*Spitefully*): He's sure learning his lesson!

BARB: Oh—

GINNY: Come on, girls, let's put our heads together and think of a way out of this. There must be something to take it off. (*The girls sit in a circle on the floor.*)

KAREN: What about spot remover?

MARGE: You leave my freckles alone. Jack thinks they're cute!

BARB: That would probably do it, but I'd rather keep my skin.

GINNY: What about vinegar? (*They nod.*) I'll go get some. (GINNY *exits.*)

KAREN: I knew we should have stuck to exercises.

MARGE (*Looking in mirror*): My face, my beautiful face—what have I done to you?

KAREN: I'll take a good old-fashioned charley horse any day, compared to this!

BARB: Danny left with Laurabelle! Danny? (GINNY *rushes in, carrying bottle of vinegar.*)

GINNY (*Sitting on floor*): Here, I'll try it first. (*She applies vinegar to her face.*) Oh, kids, it doesn't work! (*All wail.*)

BARB: She's trying to steal Danny!

MARGE: *Trying?*

KAREN: Quick, call the drug store. They'll have something.

GINNY: Here, I'll do it. (*Goes to phone, and dials*) Hello? Prescription department, please. Hello? Sir, could you tell me how to remove Granny Garthman's Gumbo Grease? No, no, it isn't a disease! What? No, I'm not joking. It's all over my face! Of course I haven't seen a doctor. . . . Why would I need a . . . I'm not sick . . . It's for the complexion! Oh. Then, give me the cosmetic department! Hello? Cosmetic counter? Can you *please* tell me how to remove Granny Garthman's Gumbo Grease for . . . what? What? But I just talked to the prescription department. No, don't bother. Forget it. I don't want a doctor . . . I don't think I do anyway. (*Hangs up*)

BARB: No luck, huh?

MARGE: I have some nail polish remover. That takes anything off!

BARB: As I said before, I value my skin!

KAREN (*Engrossed in something outside*): Girls, look out there! (*Points out of window.*)

MARGE: Laurabelle is returning to the scene of the crime!

BARB: Let's get her in here and get this stuff off. Ginny, you call her in.

GINNY: *Me?* I'm not going to show my face out that door! You call her!

BARB: And let Danny see me? Marge, how about you?

MARGE: Listen, doll, I have my public to think about! Not this kid! (*All turn toward* KAREN *who starts backing off.*)

KAREN: Why me? Oh, all right. But if Ron laughs, I'll die —just die, and it'll be your fault!

GINNY: Here, put this over your head, then he won't know who it is. (*Hands her a towel*)

BARB: Disguise your voice, too. (*She helps arrange the towel on* KAREN*'s head.*) Go on now!

KAREN (*Sticking her head cautiously out of door*): Laurabelle? (*She uses a high squeaky voice, but pulls her head right back in.*) I can't! He's out there!

MARGE: Come on, call her again. My face is beginning to itch! I have to get this stuff off—hurry! (*Pushes* KAREN *almost completely out the door*)

KAREN: Oh, stop! Laurabelle—Laurabelle, will you please come in here for a minute—*please?* (*Pulls her head back in*)

GINNY: Oh, my face itches, too. Oh, golly—

BARB: Stop talking about it or mine will, too. (*Scratches her face*) You don't suppose this stuff is pulverized poison ivy, do you? (*The girls are scratching away, when* LAURABELLE *appears, smiling sweetly.*)

LAURA: Did you girls want to see me? Why, gracious, what's the matter?

MARGE (*Starts toward her threateningly*): You monster! You planned this all the time!

LAURA: Why, whatever are you talking about?

BARB: Did you enjoy your walk with Danny? Did he try to hold your hand—or—

LAURA: Oh, my, yes. We had a lovely walk—and (*She giggles a little*), to tell the truth, he did sort of keep my hands warm. I forgot my gloves you see, and he—oh, dear! He isn't your beau is he? (*Innocently*)

GINNY: Talk about that later. Right now for heaven's sake, tell us how to get this stuff off!

LAURA: You all mean I forgot to give you the antidote for Granny Garthman's Good Old-Fashioned Gumbo Grease for Graying—

GINNY: Antidote! Maybe we do need a doctor!

MARGE: Yes, that's what we mean! Now, for heaven's sake. Come on, give!

LAURA (*Laughs*): You know, girls, if I give you the antidote, then I won't have all those good-looking boys flocking around me like blackbirds!

BARB: Danny will look like a plucked chicken when I'm through with him! Kept your hands warm, did he?

MARGE: Yes, and the rest of those blackbirds are going to hear from me. We may fight the Civil War all over again!

LAURA: Now, you girls just have the wrong idea. Why, those boys are the sweetest little old things. It really upsets me when I think about you all mistreating them.

KAREN: Are you going to get this stuff off us?

LAURA: As I was saying, I can't be around all the time, to keep those boys feeling proud and pert. Why, when I go home to South Carolina, I'd know you were back here, undoing all the good I've done. Menfolk just *ought* to be treated like kings. That's what I've always been brought up to believe, and I truly think it's the only way.

GINNY: Please, Laurabelle, give us the antidote.

BARB: I hate to do this, but I promise not to say anything to Danny, if only you'll get this junk off.

MARGE: Please, Laurabelle. This is like medieval torture!

LAURA: If you all will truly agree not to say one mean ole word to those boys, and treat them the way we southern girls treat our beaus, from now on—(*All the girls nod and agree, answering "yes," etc.*) all right then, the antidote is— (*Phone rings.*) Oh, my, that just may be for me. I'd better get it.

MARGE (*Jumps in front of her*): Oh, no, you don't. You fix up the stuff to take this goo off. *I'll* get the phone!

LAURA: If it's for me, call me. (*Exits to kitchen*)

MARGE: Hello—what? South Carolina! (*Covers the phone and talks to the girls*) Hey, kids, it's South Carolina. (*Back to the phone*) Who? Who's calling? Jefferson Lee Davis! For Miss Laurabelle Prescott? Why, yes—yes, I'll call her! Hold on a second! (*To the girls*) Quick, see if she has the antidote ready yet. Now we'll get a real sickening dose of that southern sweet talk. Who knows? Maybe we'll learn something. No boy ever called me long distance from that far away!

BARB: Much as you hate to admit it!

GINNY: She's coming with it. Will I be glad to get rid of this awful goo!

KAREN: I feel as if somebody put itching powder in my make-up.

LAURA (*Entering with cosmetic jar*): Here it is, girls. Is it for me? (*Goes to the phone*)

MARGE: It sure is. Here. Now let me at that antidote, quick! (*The girls start smearing it on their faces as* LAURABELLE *speaks on phone.*)

LAURA (*On phone*): Hello . . . Why, Jefferson Lee Davis! Why are you calling me? How sweet, Jefferson! Our little old misunderstanding? Why, ah haven't thought a thing about it. . . . Why, bless your little old heart. . . . No, no, it wasn't your fault at all, Jeffie. . . . What? . . . Well now, Jeffie, I wouldn't exactly say it was my fault either. Not really. Now would you?

MARGE (*Wiping face*): Oh, so that's why she's here—had a little old misunderstanding with Jeffie. (*Sighs*) It's good to have my face back.

KAREN: It sure is.

BARB: I thought southern girls didn't *have* arguments with their beaus. Treat them like kings and all that jazz.

LAURA (*On phone*): Jefferson Lee, I don't think that it was all my fault. Matter of fact, seems to me that it was more like all *your* fault. *What?* Now, you listen to me, Jefferson Lee Davis, I don't want to hear any more back talk from the likes of you. When I come home, do you know what you're going to mean to me? About as much as a nasty little old boll weevil! That's what! And furthermore . . . (*She looks at the girls, who are staring, then turns her back and takes the phone upstage and continues to talk. She can still be heard.*)

KAREN: She's not treating him much like a king!

MARGE: Sure, she is . . . King of the Boll Weevils! (*The girls stifle laughs and strain to hear* LAURA.)

LAURA (*On phone*): Besides that, you, sir, are a cad! You are a worm, a lowdown cad, and nothing would please me more than never setting these big southern eyes on you again! Mr. Davis, sir, you had better be long gone when I step off that train or I'll . . . (*Curtain starts closing*) sure fix you . . . the very idea! Letting that Melinda Matson stand there at the cotillion and bat her goo-goo eyes at you, all evening long! You just take me for granted, Jefferson Lee Davis. (*Curtain closes.*)

THE END

Surprise Party

by John Dorand

Characters

JAMES ELIOT
FRAN ELIOT
ROSEMARY, *their teen-age daughter*
TED, *their younger son*
MRS. TAVELTITE
ERSKINE DOBSON, *10*
DAISY ELIOT, *James Eliot's sister-in-law*
MARY ROSE ELIOT, *11, her daughter*

TIME: *A Saturday afternoon.*
SETTING: *The Eliot living room.*
AT RISE: JAMES ELIOT *is seated on the sofa at center. He is reading the newspaper.* FRAN ELIOT *enters right, wearing a coat and carrying a purse.*

FRAN: Now remember, James, you simply must be ready by six-thirty.
JAMES (*Affirmatively*): Mm-m—m-m-m!
FRAN: And don't forget to fold your newspaper and put it in the magazine rack when you're finished.
JAMES (*Vaguely*): Uh-huh.
FRAN (*Stooping to pick up an object from the floor*): Honestly! Another of Rosemary's bobby pins! I've been pick-

ing them up all morning. I think she's blazed a trail from the front door to the backyard incinerator with them. (*Puts it into her purse*) James, did you move the furniture into the spare room?

JAMES (*Resignedly*): Yes, dear.

FRAN: And if Mimi Nickson calls, you're not to let on that you know anything about anything. Do you understand? (*Not waiting for a reply.*) I can't think what possessed Erma and the others. . . . Goodness knows, we've had other anniversaries and they've not thought it necessary to give us a surprise party! It's not as though this were china or crystal or linen. Heavens! It's not even tin or pottery . . . and, really, they know that we're expecting Daisy and the house is a sight! (*She looks about.*) Now where did I put those keys?

JAMES (*Setting his paper aside*): Have you looked in your purse? That's usually where you carry them. (*He looks at her quizzically.*) Weren't you going out, dear?

FRAN: Goodness, yes! I have to get some things at the market. I just threw my coat on over this old housedress. I hope I don't see anyone I know . . . but I suppose I will. (*Starting toward door left*) Dear me! There is so much to do when friends decide to give you a surprise party. Tell Ted that if he wants a snack, he's to eat it in the kitchen. (*She exits.*)

JAMES: All right. (*Shaking his head*) Deliver me from surprise parties! (*Folds newspaper and puts it in rack*) I wonder where Rosemary and Ted are? (*He stands up and walks toward door, right, calls*) Rosemary! Ted! Rosemary, are you outside?

FRAN (*Entering left*): Dear!

JAMES (*Whirling around*): Well! That was a fast trip. Say, I'll bet you got a lift from that fellow Ted's always talking about . . . that Captain Comet!

FRAN (*Icily*): There is no need for sarcasm, James. I forgot to tell you something.

JAMES (*Wryly*): I can't imagine what.

FRAN: Just that Mrs. Taveltite is coming by this afternoon.

JAMES: All right, Fran! Now you'd better get started if you . . . Mrs. Who?

FRAN: Mrs. Taveltite . . . you know . . . Harriet Grebhorn's sister. The one who lost her husband last month. That is, he didn't die or anything, but one night he went to the store for a can of cat food and that's the last anyone saw of him. Mrs. Taveltite always tells everyone that she lost her husband, which, when you think about it, isn't far from wrong.

JAMES: I guess so. I'll just have to think about it a little more. But why is she coming here? Was Mr. Taveltite seen feeding cats in the vicinity?

FRAN: Really, James! She's a dressmaker, and she's going to help me with the hem of my black velvet. Now I *really* must get to the market! If Mrs. Taveltite comes while I'm gone, you *will* tell her to wait for me?

JAMES: Yes, Fran. (*Taking her by the elbow.*) And this time I'll put you into the car myself. (*They exit left.*)

TED (*Entering from right*): Where is everyone? I'll bet they all just piled into a neat spaceship and took off for Mars or someplace! (*He takes a magazine from the rack, piles several pillows at one end of the sofa, and plops down full length.*) Yes, sir! I'll bet that's what happened . . . never even thought about me. (JAMES *enters from left.*) Hi, Dad! Back so soon?

JAMES: I just went out to the car with your mother. Where did you think I'd been . . . Mars?

TED (*Sarcastically*): Oh, sure.

JAMES: Oh! (*Looking for something*) Ted, did you see the book I was reading last night?

TED: Nope! (*Sitting up*) Hey, Dad! Listen to this . . .

Space Magazine says that Captain Comet is going on a personal appearance tour!

JAMES (*Preoccupied*): That's great.

TED: Do you suppose he'll come to Midborough? One thing is certain; he'll need super-spatial radar to find this town!

JAMES (*Looking up*): What do you suggest? That we move in closer to Mars?

TED: Could we?

JAMES: I'll think about it. If you hear about any Martian interest in electric pencil sharpeners, let me know. I'll try to get the outer space agency for them. (*He sits.*)

TED (*In disgust*): Pencil sharpeners! (*Eagerly*) Say, maybe your plant could convert to secret weapons or something . . . maybe one of those new solar energy radios I saw in last month's *How-To Magazine.*

JAMES: It's an idea. I'll think about that, too. In the meantime (*Getting up*), if you find that book of mine, I'll be out in the garage. (*He exits right.*)

TED: O.K. (*Returning to magazine*) Boy! Captain Comet in Midborough. (ROSEMARY *enters right, wearing robe and slippers. Her hair is in rollers.*)

ROSEMARY (*Examining her newly polished nails*): Someone I know coming to Midborough?

TED (*Grimacing*): I don't know . . . you might know him. You certainly look out of this world!

ROSEMARY: Don't be so smart! And you'd better get your feet off the sofa before Mother gets back . . . and put those pillows back where you found them. You know Mother spent all morning cleaning for the surprise party tonight.

TED (*Swinging his feet off the sofa*): Really! Who ever heard of anyone knowing about a surprise party in advance?

ROSEMARY: Well, it's a good thing Mother did hear about

it. Imagine! Here we had everything topsy-turvy, trying to make room for Aunt Daisy . . . I don't know what we would have done if Mrs. Vaughn hadn't let something slip out about the party. Now Mom's had at least one day to clean house.

TED: But wouldn't a surprise party be more fun if it were really a surprise?

ROSEMARY: Goodness, no! That's the whole point of it. If it were really a surprise, it might be . . . be . . . catastrophic. The living room all every which way . . . Dad in his old clothes . . . Mother in a housedress . . . you stretched out on the sofa . . .

TED: And you with your hair in rollers, as usual.

ROSEMARY (*Defensively*): I'm going to Vera Smith's party tonight. I suppose you'd be happy to see me looking like one of those goony space monsters you're always reading about! (*She sits, tightens roller.*)

TED (*Squinting at her closely*): They aren't so bad.

ROSEMARY (*Ignoring him*): And anyway, it wouldn't hurt *you* to comb *your* hair once in awhile. You know what Grace Carlson's sister asked me the other day?

TED (*Feigning boredom*): I couldn't guess.

ROSEMARY (*Triumphantly*): She asked me if you wore a wig!

TED (*Groaning*): You'd think *she'd* recognize a wig when she saw one! Everybody is still laughing about the time she stooped over the water fountain and her bangs fell into the basin.

ROSEMARY: Honestly! There's no point wasting my time talking to you. I'm going to lie down for awhile in a darkened room. I want my eyes to sparkle tonight.

TED (*Amazed*): You must be kidding! Say, not that it matters too much, but what character are you going out with tonight?

ROSEMARY (*Rising suddenly*): Ah . . . er . . .

TED: Not Hot Rod Harry! Boy, you'd better take along a few nuts and bolts and some good strong cord! Those wheels of his will never get out of the driveway in one piece!

ROSEMARY: You're *so* funny! And his name is not Harry. It's Jerome . . . and I haven't even seen him for three days!

TED (*Incredulous*): You're not going out with Tidy Tommy again? The one who asked Mom if she had an apron he could wear when he helped you with the dishes? What a creep!

ROSEMARY: He is not! Be quiet!

TED (*Curiously*): But if you're not going with one of them, who are you going with?

ROSEMARY (*Still evasive*): Well, ah . . . er . . . you don't know him.

TED: Say! I'll bet you're going to that party alone!

ROSEMARY (*Furious*): Theodore Eliot! How could you! I'll have you know that I've never gone to a party alone in my entire life. Why, the very idea fills me with . . . with *revulsion!*

TED: Well, then, come on . . . tell your old brother who this character is.

ROSEMARY: Well, if you must know, he's Vera Smith's cousin. I've never seen him . . . and Vera forgot to tell me his name.

TED: Rosemary, do you know what you're doing? You're going on a *blind date.*

ROSEMARY: If you dare to breathe one word . . . one *syllable* to Mother or Dad, I'll . . . (*Thinking*) I'll hide your space helmet!

TED: I'll bet he's even better than Hot Rod Harry or Tidy Tommy. I'll bet this one is *really* something! I wonder what he'll look like.

ROSEMARY: You can save yourself the effort. Vera told me

what he looks like. (*Dreamily*) He's about five-feet-eleven, has a real dreamy tan, and black curly hair. (*Sighs in anticipation*) Sort of a Tony Curtis.

TED: Wow! You sure do take the fur-lined trophy cup, you do! Here are poor Mom and Dad, minding their own business, dusting a chair here, shaking a doily there, getting ready for a surprise party (*Dramatically*) not to mention getting all excited about seeing Dad's only brother's widow . . . our old Aunt Daisy, whom no one in the family has *ever* seen. And all this time, Rosemary, their only daughter, is painting herself up in order to go to a party with some . . . some *slicker,* some Tony Curtis-type slicker she's never even laid eyes on before. (*Exhausted, he collapses on sofa.*)

ROSEMARY (*Annoyed*): Don't be so silly! You sound just like an announcer on one of those soap operas! After all, we'll only be going three blocks to Vera's house. And her parents are going to be there. Goodness, I'm not going to elope with the man.

TED: Boy, one never knows with you.

ROSEMARY: Ted, what do you think she'll look like?

TED: Who? Vera Smith? Goony, as usual, I guess!

ROSEMARY: No, you idiot child! Not Vera Smith . . . Aunt Daisy.

TED: How would I know? Like Dad I suppose.

ROSEMARY: Really, how stupid can a boy be? Why should Dad's sister-in-law look like him? Honestly! I'll bet she's rather tall with all kinds of style . . . and she'll probably have lots of mysterious-looking luggage. She might even wear a dark veil. Mourning, you know.

TED: Huh! You and your imagination!

ROSEMARY: Well, anyway, I can't sit here all day listening to your feeble chatter. (*Standing*) I have to get some rest, so I can sparkle tonight (*Sighs*) for him. (*She exits right.*)

TED: Boy! There's one that really got away! (*Rises*) Guess

I'll go next door and see if Burpy's home. Maybe I can talk him into letting me use his new atomic mixture set. (*Starting toward door left*) Yes, sir! I can be mighty convincing when I use the old charm! (*He exits. After a moment* JAMES *enters right.*)

JAMES: I wonder if there's anything in here that Fran wanted moved into the spare room? (*Looks at small chair*) Now no one ever uses that. (*Phone rings.*) Who the dickens can that be? Not Mimi Nickson, I hope. (*Lifts receiver*) Hello! Yes . . . What was that again? (*Pause*) Daisy? Daisy Eliot! But . . . but we didn't expect you until the day after tomorrow. (*Pause*) Oh, our anniversary. Think of your remembering that! (*Pause*) No . . . not at all. (*Pause*) Of course it's no imposition. But listen, Fran has the car! Can you find your way out here all right? (*Pause*) Yes, you do that. All right. See you soon. Goodbye! (*Sits for a minute*) Ye gods! And that party tonight! Say, I'd better get busy. (*Starts moving chairs around*)

TED (*Entering left*): You and Mom are really making sure the old homestead will be clean tonight.

JAMES: Haven't time to talk.

TED (*Flopping on a chair*): Burpy wasn't home. He'd probably want rent for his atom set anyway. (*Watches his father*) Anything around here for me to do?

JAMES (*Grimly*): No, son . . . no! Nothing at all! I'm just picking up a few things, moving a piece of furniture here and there. Your mother is doing some last-minute shopping. Twenty or twenty-five guests will be rolling in before too long, and your Aunt Daisy phoned a few minutes ago, saying she decided to get here in time for our anniversary. But no, don't you disturb yourself. You've probably had a busy morning.

TED: Well, say, Dad . . . I have a little time on my hands. (*Rises*)

JAMES: If you think you'd be able to spare a few minutes "for your old Dad," you might move the lamp over there next to that chair. Then you can straighten the carpet behind the bookcase. I have a couple of things to do outside. (*He exits right.*)

TED: A lamp here . . . a lamp there! I don't see any difference. Now if we had one of those ultra-radial beamed jobs that Captain Comet uses . . . (*Doorbell rings.*) Boy, I hope that's not the surprise party. (*He exits left. Speaks from offstage*) Yes, this is the Eliot house. (TED *re-enters followed by* MRS. TAVELTITE. *She carries an old-fashioned valise and an oversized handbag and wears shabby clothes.*) Say, you can't be—I mean, you must be— Well, gosh, come on in.

MRS. TAVELTITE: I was expected, wasn't I?

TED: Oh, of course. We've all been looking forward to your visit.

MRS. TAVELTITE (*Dubiously*): Well, that's very cordial of you, I'm sure.

TED: Mother's at the market. Dad will be in in a minute. He just went outside. Say, let me call Rosemary. Excuse me! Please sit down, won't you.

MRS. TAVELTITE: Thanks. I am a mite weary after the ride out here.

TED: I'll bet you are. (*Goes to door right and calls*) Rosemary! Come here. We have company.

ROSEMARY (*Offstage*): Who is it?

TED (*Happily*): Oh, that heavily veiled lady we've been expecting. (MRS. TAVELTITE *looks at him oddly.*) You know, the one with all that mysterious luggage. (*He looks at the old valise.*)

ROSEMARY (*Offstage*): Oh, goodness! (*Enters right*) How wonderful! (*She sees* MRS. TAVELTITE, *and stops and stares.*)

MRS. TAVELTITE: Well! Well! You're Rosemary! My, I've heard a lot of nice things about you.

TED: Hah!

ROSEMARY (*Recovering*): Ah! Er . . . did you have a comfortable trip?

MRS. TAVELTITE: Well, I wouldn't exactly call it a trip, but I guess it was comfortable enough. You have a lovely home here. (*Uneasily*) When do you expect your mother back?

TED: Oh, any minute. I'd better see what Dad's doing. (JAMES *enters.*)

JAMES (*To himself*): One thing more to store in that garage and we'll have to move the car into the living room. (*Sees* MRS. TAVELTITE) Oh!

ROSEMARY (*In stage whisper*): Daddy! It's *Aunt Daisy!* What are we going to do?

JAMES: *Daisy?* (*Gulps audibly, then goes up to* MRS. TAVELTITE) Well, this is . . . is an occasion. We've all been looking forward to your arrival.

MRS. TAVELTITE: That's just what your son said a few minutes ago. My! You *are* the friendliest group of people.

JAMES: Here. Let Ted take your suitcase into the bedroom for you.

MRS. TAVELTITE: Oh, my! That won't be necessary.

ROSEMARY: Wouldn't you like to freshen up a bit?

MRS. TAVELTITE: I think I'll wait until your mother gets back.

ROSEMARY: I could be unpacking for you.

MRS. TAVELTITE: Heavens! Don't go worrying about that. I don't need to unpack. I have everything I'll need right here in my purse. (*The Eliots stare at each other.* FRAN *enters from left, carrying groceries.*)

FRAN (*To no one in particular*): Oh! If there's one thing I detest, it's last-minute shopping. (*Removes coat and puts it and bag of groceries on a chair*)

JAMES: Fran, look who's here. Daisy phoned just after you left. She decided to get here in time for our anniversary and . . . well, here she is!

FRAN (*Puzzled*): Daisy? Daisy? James, are you out of your mind? Daisy Eliot, indeed! This is Mrs. Taveltite!

JAMES: What!

TED *and* ROSEMARY (*In unison*): Mrs. *who?*

FRAN: The lady who is going to help me with the hem of my dress. I'm so sorry I've kept you waiting, Mrs. Taveltite. (JAMES *and* ROSEMARY *glare at* TED *who looks sheepish.*)

MRS. TAVELTITE: Oh, that doesn't matter. Gracious, you do have a courteous family, though. They made me feel right at home.

JAMES: May I inquire, Mrs. Taveltite, why you are carrying a suitcase?

MRS. TAVELTITE: It does seem a bit strange, I know. But a letter came from home this morning. Seems the police finally found my poor husband, Wilfred. He's been lost, you know, and they want me to come back and identify him. So I thought I'd stop off here and help your wife, and then catch the 6:40 bus.

FRAN: They found your husband! Why, how wonderful!

MRS. TAVELTITE: Yes, it is, isn't it? Funny thing, too, he still had that can of cat food. He's had ammonia all this time.

TED: *Ammonia?*

MRS. TAVELTITE: That's right! That disease you have when you can't remember who you are, or where you are, or what you're doing there.

ROSEMARY: Oh! Amnesia.

MRS. TAVELTITE: Yes. That's what's been the matter with Wilfred.

FRAN: Now you come along with me, Mrs. Taveltite. It won't take us any time at all to fix that dress. And then you can be on your way. (*She picks up coat, and they start toward door right.*) Ted, you take the groceries into the kitchen. (FRAN, MRS. TAVELTITE *and* TED, *carrying groceries, exit right.*)

ROSEMARY: I have trillions of things to do. *He'll* be here soon! (*She exits.*)

JAMES (*To himself*): Daisy! (*Shakes head*) Cat food! What next? (*Doorbell rings.*) Now who in thunder can that be? (*He exits, then re-enters with* ERSKINE DOBSON, *who carries a bouquet.*) You want Mary Rose? You must mean *Rosemary.* (*Looking at him, puzzled.*) Hm-m. Won't you sit down? (ERSKINE *sits.*)

ERSKINE: I presume I'm a bit early.

JAMES: Oh, don't let that bother you! Rosemary's never on time. (*Looking at him closely*) Are you sure it's *Rosemary* Eliot you want?

ERSKINE (*Firmly*): Yes, sir! My aunt said that she would be expecting me this evening.

JAMES: Hm-m-m! Not that it's any of my business, but . . . well, isn't Rosemary a bit (*Pause*) *old* for you?

ERSKINE: There may be a slight difference in our ages. (*Loftily*) But age doesn't really matter so much.

JAMES (*Softly*): Sometimes I wonder if Ted isn't right about Rosemary. Well, let me call her for you. (*Calling at door right*) Rosemary! Rosemary! (*Looks at* ERSKINE *again*) Your escort is here.

ROSEMARY (*Offstage*): Oh! Oh, goodness! I'll be right there.

JAMES: He'll wait.

TED (*Entering right*): Did I hear someone say (*Stops*) something about . . . (*He stares open-mouthed at* ERSKINE, *as* ROSEMARY *enters right, dressed for the party, but with a few rollers still in her hair.*)

ROSEMARY (*Smiling*): How terribly nice. (*Sees* ERSKINE) Oh! Oh, dear! There must be some mistake.

ERSKINE (*Handing bouquet to* ROSEMARY): My aunt told me where you lived.

ROSEMARY (*Taking bouquet, then putting it down quickly*): Your aunt? Vera Smith's mother? It's not a mistake? (FRAN *and* MRS. TAVELTITE *enter*.)

ERSKINE (*Puzzled*): Smith? But—

FRAN: What is all the commotion about out here?

TED: It's her date, Mom. (*To himself*) Oh, boy, Rosemary's really done it this time!

FRAN: Rosemary, what in the world is going on?

ROSEMARY: Mother . . . well, I didn't say anything to you or Dad because I wanted you to meet him first . . . but Vera Smith asked her cousin to take me to her party tonight and . . .

ERSKINE (*Desperately*): But . . . but . . .

ROSEMARY (*Glaring at him*): And she said that he was five-feet-eleven, had a—dreamy tan and looked like . . . Oh!

TED: Oh boy!

FRAN: That will be enough, Ted! Yes, dear. I know all about it.

ROSEMARY: You do?

FRAN: Mrs. Smith phoned me yesterday to ask if it was all right with your father and me. (*Looks at* ERSKINE) Although, I admit, I did think the boy was a bit older.

ERSKINE: You're right. You see . . .

ROSEMARY: I do see. And I'm *not* going to any party! And Vera Smith will certainly hear from me. Why, I'd be the laughingstock of Midborough. (*Points to* ERSKINE) He's young enough to be my *son!*

JAMES: Rosemary! There's no reason to be rude. It's not the boy's fault.

ROSEMARY (*Sobbing*): I don't care, Daddy. (*Doorbell rings.*) I was so happy about the party tonight. (FRAN *exits left and returns with* DAISY ELIOT *and* MARY ROSE ELIOT, *who carry suitcases.*)

FRAN: Look, everyone . . . look who's here! The *real* Daisy Eliot! She's arrived here at last. (*All greet one another.* ROSEMARY *and* ERSKINE *hang back.*) And she's brought a surprise with her! Rosemary and Ted, this is your cousin, Mary Rose Eliot!

JAMES: Oh, no!

FRAN: Whatever is the matter, James?

DAISY: You are all just as we pictured you. Aren't they, Mary Rose?

MARY ROSE: Yes. Daddy looked like Uncle James . . . a little bit.

DAISY: So he did. (*Sees* ERSKINE) And who is this young man? Someone we should know?

ERSKINE: Yes! I think so. I'm Erskine Dobson.

DAISY: No! Why how very sweet of you . . . and of your aunt. My, you're very punctual!

ROSEMARY: You know each other?

DAISY: Not really, but I do know his aunt. When I wrote that Mary Rose and I were coming to Midborough for a visit, she wrote back that her nephew, Erskine, was about Mary Rose's age, and he could introduce her to some of the young people here.

ROSEMARY: I don't feel too well.

ERSKINE (*To* ROSEMARY): I tried to tell you that I don't have any aunt named Mrs. Smith, but you wouldn't listen. (*Phone rings.*)

TED: Boy!

JAMES (*Answering phone*): Hello! Yes, yes, she's here. Hold on a minute. Rosemary, it's for you—it's Vera Smith.

ROSEMARY (*Crossing and taking phone*): Yes, Vera. (*Pause*) No, your cousin hasn't arrived yet. (*Pause*) What? He did? It did? You did? (*Pause*) Thanks. . . . See you. 'Bye. (*To others*) Vera said her cousin just phoned that he'd be a little late in picking me up. His car had a flat. But she told him I wouldn't mind.

TED: I knew it! Another Hot Rod Harry! (ROSEMARY *glares at him.*)

MRS. TAVELTITE: Goodness! I'll have to hurry if I'm going to catch that 6:40 bus. (*Picks up her suitcase and starts for door left*)

FRAN: Why, it can't be as late as that! (*Doorbell rings.*) Heavens! Who can that be? (*Looking out window left.*) James! They're here! The surprise party! James, we're not ready . . .

ROSEMARY: Mother! It really is a surprise party! Look at the living room! And Daddy's in his shirt sleeves. . . . You have on a housedress. (TED *goes to window.*)

TED: And you'd better get those rollers out of your hair, Rosemary. I think one of the people at the door looks like your date. (ROSEMARY *shrieks, and frantically takes rollers from hair, as doorbell rings again. Others rush about straightening room. Then all stop, look at one another, and laugh as the curtain falls.*)

THE END

Miss Cast

by Barbara Brem Heinzen

Characters

JUDY JOHNSON
LARRY JOHNSON } *her parents*
HELEN JOHNSON }
BILL JOHNSON, *her younger brother*
MARGARET JOHNSON, *her cousin*
RAY MEAD, *Margaret's boyfriend*
JOHN ANDERSON RANDELL
DAVID RANDELL, *his son*

SCENE 1

TIME: *Saturday morning.*
SETTING: *The Johnson living room.*
AT RISE: MRS. JOHNSON *is running a carpet sweeper over the rug.* BILL *sits at a card table working on a model plane.* JUDY *is off left; when she speaks her voice is affected and stagey.*

JUDY (*Off left*): Romeo, where art thou, Romeo, my handsome, elusive Romeo?

BILL: Mom, can't you do something about Judy? She's driving me out of my mind!

MRS. JOHNSON: Now, Bill, be patient. You know how

worked up your sister is about trying out for the play this afternoon.

JUDY (*Off left*): Romeo, Romeo, 'tis your fair Judith beckoning to thee.

BILL: But, Mom, she's been going on like this for weeks. (MR. JOHNSON *enters left.*) Hi, Dad.

MR. JOHNSON: Morning, Bill. Be sure to get the front yard mowed this morning, will you? (DAVID RANDELL *puts his head in at window.*) Hello, David. Anything we can do for you?

DAVID: My father wanted . . . (JUDY *is heard again off left reciting.* DAVID *grimaces.*) Never mind. I'll be back later. (*He leaves window.*)

BILL: Can't say that I blame him.

JUDY (*Off left*): Romeo, I call to thee, I beg thee. . . .

MR. JOHNSON: Helen, please speak to Judy about those sunglasses. She's going to ruin her eyes wearing dark glasses twenty-four hours a day. (*As he exits right*) I'm late. See you this afternoon. (JUDY *enters left, wearing sunglasses.*)

JUDY (*Dramatically*): Hark! Hark! 'Tis Lady Judith entering the drawing room.

BILL: Judy, you have about as much chance of getting the lead in that play as I have of winning the Kentucky Derby with one leg in a cast and the other in a bucket of bread dough.

JUDY: My dear, dear brother, how many times must I tell you . . . my name is Judith!

BILL (*Mocking her*): Of course, fair maiden! But thou must remember to call me Sir William!

JUDY: You just don't understand the theater, do you, little brother? I'm simply trying to sustain a mood!

BILL: Ha!

JUDY: Just wait until I'm discovered! I'll have the last

laugh then. (*Dancing a brief ballet*) I shall be the darling of tinsel-town!

MRS. JOHNSON (*Perturbed*): Judy!

JUDY: But, Mother, let's face it! Someday I'll be the hottest property in Hollywood! (*She sprawls on the sofa, feet in the air.*)

MRS. JOHNSON: Judy, you know perfectly well how your father and I feel about Hollywood.

JUDY: But, Mother, my innate creativity is like a powerful magnet pulling me to stardom . . . pulling . . . pulling!

BILL: Ick!

JUDY (*Ignoring* BILL): Where was I? Ah! Yes! (*Reciting*) Romeo, why dost thou ignore me? Art thou blind to my beauty?

MRS. JOHNSON: Judy, dear, will you please clean up that room of yours? I've never seen such a mess in my life. (*She takes magazine off the floor.*) I'm tired of finding movie magazines all over the house. (*Pauses*) Judy, are you listening?

JUDY (*Still reciting*): Why art thou so obstinate? Canst thou not see I am the essence of charm and grace? (*Suddenly turning to* MRS. JOHNSON) Mother! Please! It's *Judith.* Try to remember, or I shall perish, simply perish.

BILL: Is that a promise?

MRS. JOHNSON: Bill.

BILL: But, Mom! (*Mocks* JUDY) She is *rahlly* getting to be more than I can take.

JUDY (*Reciting*): If thou wouldst only speak to me! (*She abruptly drops the pose, sits up and looks out the window. For the first time, she speaks naturally*) Gosh, what's wrong with David Randell, anyway? It's been exactly one month today since the Randells moved in next door, and David hasn't said two words to me!

BILL: Yes, he has—hello, and *goodbye!*

MRS. JOHNSON: Mr. Randell tells me that David is quite shy.

JUDY (*Excitedly*): David's father? You mean you talked to David's father? What's he like, Mother? Is he nice? What did he say?

MRS. JOHNSON: Well, they're having a terrible time getting rid of the crabgrass on their front lawn, but I told him about the weed spray that Dad put on our lawn last year; it really did the trick. (*Pauses*) But I couldn't remember the name of it.

JUDY: You mean that's *all* you talked about? Crabgrass?

MRS. JOHNSON: It is a problem, dear, and it's so unsightly! That reminds me, Judy, you still haven't straightened up your room. I want it done . . . (JUDY *sighs.* MRS. JOHNSON *goes over to her and speaks loudly.*) *now!*

JUDY: Mother! Must you be violent? (*She slinks left.*) It's simply imperative that my emotional equilibrium is not disturbed! Tryouts start in less than an hour and I must be at my zenith! (*She exits and is heard off left.*) My absolute zenith!

MRS. JOHNSON (*Sinking onto the sofa*): Oh, dear, I hope she gets a part in the play; maybe it will cure her once and for all!

BILL: Well, she'd better make a quick recovery. Everyone at school thinks she's popped her gourd! (BILL *gets up and does an imitation of* JUDY.) Hello-o, Margaret, darling! Marvelous to see you again! Simply, simply marvelous! I haven't seen you since gym class this morning . . . that baggy blue gym suit looked divine on you, dear . . . and those tennis shoes! They are so marvelously cruddy! We must get together soon, darling . . . we simply must! Ta, ta, Margaret! (MARGARET *and* RAY *enter right.* MARGARET *carries a script.*)

MARGARET: Did I hear someone mention my name?

MRS. JOHNSON: Hello, Margaret. Hello, Ray. (RAY *and* BILL *ad lib greetings.* MARGARET *sits by* MRS. JOHNSON.) Where have you been keeping yourself, Margaret?

MARGARET: Oh, I've been extra busy this semester, Aunt Helen. I've had loads of homework.

BILL: What she means, Mom, is that she hasn't been around because she can't stand Judy anymore!

MARGARET: Oh, Bill, that's not so. Judy is still the same old wonderful Judy as far as I'm concerned. She's just . . . (*Groping for words*) well, she's just going through a phase, that's all.

BILL: Well, I'm beginning to wish she'd phase out altogether!

MRS. JOHNSON (*Warningly*): Bill, you had better get out the lawn mower before your father comes home. (BILL *exits right.*)

MARGARET: Is Judy . . . I mean, is Judith about ready, Aunt Helen? Tryouts start at one o'clock.

MRS. JOHNSON: I'll tell her you're here, dear. (*Exits left.*)

RAY: About tonight, Margaret, I think that. . . .

MARGARET: What about tonight, Ray? I thought it was all set.

RAY (*Squirming*): Well, I think we'd better call off Judy's blind date with David Randell.

MARGARET: What do you mean, Ray?

RAY: Well, I would have told you before, but. . . .

MARGARET: But what?

RAY: David's father is famous, Margaret. He's a famous playwright.

MARGARET: Oh, Ray! If he's such a famous playwright, how come I've never heard of him before?

RAY: You've never heard of John Anderson Randell?

MARGARET: Well, of course, silly, I've heard of John—(*She stops short and spins around to* RAY.) You don't mean David's father is *the* John Anderson Randell? The playwright?

RAY (*Triumphantly*): That's exactly what I mean!

MARGARET: Well, what's he doing in Harrisville, of all places?

RAY: Writing a novel. David said his dad needed a new atmosphere, away from Broadway. Peace and quiet, you know?

MARGARET: I see. Oh, Ray, if Judy finds out about this, she'll be absolutely impossible.

RAY: She *is* absolutely impossible. But think of poor Mr. Randell. It would be the end of his peace and quiet. He'd be better off trying to write his novel in the middle of Grand Central Station.

MARGARET: And Judy would never leave David alone. (*Dismayed*) What are we going to do?

RAY: First of all, I'm going to tell David the blind date is off.

MARGARET: Oh, no, Ray. We just won't tell Judy about David's father, that's all.

RAY: She'd find out. It's just not fair to David—he's too nice a guy. You haven't said anything to Judy about the blind date, so she'll never know the difference, right?

MARGARET: But I know the difference and I'm disappointed. Oh, Ray, Judy doesn't always act like this; it's just been lately. (*Coaxing*) David would like her, once he got to know her.

RAY: Know her? I don't even know her anymore! Even Judy doesn't know who she is anymore!

MARGARET: Please, Ray, for me?

RAY: Well, O.K., Margaret. I'll get David here tonight if I have to blindfold and gag him. (*He has a second thought.*) And I'll have to, if I tell him who his blind date is!

MARGARET: Oh, Ray, don't worry. I know the four of us will have a wonderful time. (JUDY *enters left.*)

JUDY: Hello-o, darlings! How marvelous to see you again! It seems like aeons since I've seen you . . . simply aeons!

MARGARET (*Laughing*): It was yesterday, silly.

RAY: Hi, Judy.

JUDY: Judith, remember?

RAY (*Snapping his fingers*): Right! I'm going out to give Bill a hand with the lawn. I'll be out in front when you're ready to go. (*He starts to exit right.* MRS. JOHNSON *pokes her head in from left.*)

MRS. JOHNSON: There's a platter of sandwiches in the kitchen, kids. Come on in and help yourselves. (*She exits.* RAY *does an about-face and follows her off left.*)

JUDY: Food! How on earth could anyone think about food at a moment like this? I'm consumed with tension! My innate creativity is like a powerful magnet pulling me to stardom . . . pulling . . . pulling. . . .

MARGARET: Oh, come on, Judy, I've heard all about your magnet a hundred times. Forget about it and relax. You'll do a lot better at tryouts if you aren't so keyed up!

JUDY: Oh, if only I could relax, if only I could, Margaret, but, for a creative person like me it is nigh impossible to relax, to really let go.

MARGARET: Tryouts aren't the end of the world, Judy.

JUDY: Maybe not for you, Margaret . . . but for me . . . (*Melodramatically*) but for me it will be the end of the world if I don't get the leading role. I'll die! Simply wither and die.

MARGARET: I doubt that. Besides, Judy, there are loads of good character parts.

JUDY: I—take a character part? Margaret, darling, you must be joking, simply joking!

MARGARET: Ray is trying out for one of the character parts, and so is David Randell, I hear.

JUDY: David Randell? He is? But, Margaret! He should be trying out for the male lead! He'd be perfect. Simply perfect! He is so good-looking, so magnetic . . . yet shy and boyish.

MARGARET: While we're on the subject of good-looking boys, Judy, would you like a blind date for the drama club party tonight?

JUDY: Blind date? Darling, you must be joking.

MARGARET: Say yes, Judy. I know you won't be disappointed. Your date is a dreamboat! I promise.

JUDY: A dreamboat, huh? (*Considering*) Well, I suppose it would be good for my image. All right, Margaret, darling, I'll go!

MARGARET (*Glancing at her watch*): Good. Look at the time! We'd better get going if we don't want to be late. (*Calling*) Ray, let's go.

JUDY: By the way, Margaret, darling, what part are you reading for? Have you decided?

MARGARET: Oh, Judy . . . I mean Judith, I thought you knew! I'm trying out for the female lead, too! (JUDY *looks stunned. Fast curtain*)

* * *

SCENE 2

TIME: *Afternoon.*

SETTING: *The same as Scene 1.*

AT RISE: MRS. JOHNSON *sits knitting as* BILL *enters right.*

MRS. JOHNSON: Oh, there you are, dear. I can't knit another stitch until I measure you across the shoulders. (*Holds sweater up to him, measuring*)

BILL: Will you have it done by tonight, Mom? I thought I'd wear it to the drama club party.

MRS. JOHNSON: Isn't the party just for the students who tried out for the play?

BILL: That's right.

MRS. JOHNSON: Why, Bill, don't tell me you tried out for the play, too?

BILL: I cannot tell a lie. I did.

MRS. JOHNSON: Why, that's wonderful! What part did you try out for?

BILL: Just about everything, except the female lead.

MRS. JOHNSON (*Laughing*): Oh, Bill, between you and Judy there's never a dull moment here. Tell me, how did Judy do?

BILL: Just between you and me, Mom, she was awful!

MRS. JOHNSON: Really?

BILL: Yes! She was a one-woman disaster area! (*Shaking his head*) Old Sarah Heartburn really did herself in this afternoon. One thing for sure, she didn't get the female lead; Margaret walked off with that role, no question about it.

MRS. JOHNSON: Are you sure, dear? I understood Judy to say that Mr. Wilson, the director, was going to call everyone tonight to announce the parts.

BILL: Well, you asked me, Mom! I doubt if the director will let her pull the curtain, let alone assign her a part.

MRS. JOHNSON: Oh, dear! If only she'd realize . . . (*She shakes her head despairingly.*)

BILL: It's too late, now, Mom. She really blew it this afternoon. (*Doorbell rings*) I'll get it, Mom. (*He opens the door and* MR. RANDELL *enters.*) Oh, hi there, Mr. Randell.

MR. RANDELL: Hello, Bill, is your dad home?

BILL: I think so. Dad's home, isn't he, Mom?

MRS. JOHNSON: Oh, hello, Mr. Randell. (*To* BILL) Yes,

he's in the study. Would you call him, dear? (BILL *exits left.*) Sit down, Mr. Randell. My, isn't the weather nice for this time of the year? (*He sits.*)

MR. RANDELL: Especially nice for working in the yard! (*They laugh.*) I hope your husband remembers the name of the weed killer you mentioned; the weeds are taking over our lawn. (MR. JOHNSON *and* BILL *enter left.*)

MR. JOHNSON: Hello there, John. (JUDY *bursts in front door.*)

JUDY: Hello, my darlings! I'm home!

BILL: Big deal!

MRS. JOHNSON: Bill! (*To* JUDY) How were tryouts, dear?

JUDY (*Sweeping around the room*): Sensational! Simply sensational! I am the toast of the town! (*She twirls around giddily and bumps into a piece of furniture.*) I am simply the toast of the town!

BILL: If you don't mind my asking . . . where did you get that crummy idea?

MRS. JOHNSON: Children, that's enough.

JUDY: Can you sit there and deny that I held everyone spellbound this afternoon? Mr. Wilson was awed by my brilliant performance. Simply awed!

BILL: He was stunned!

JUDY (*Ignoring him*): And Margaret! Dear, sweet Margaret. When I read that last scene, it actually brought tears to her eyes.

BILL: You can say that again! She felt so sorry for you, she was crying.

JUDY (*Wounded*): How can you say such a thing, Bill Johnson?

BILL: Because it's the truth.

JUDY: The truth is, you're jealous! Well, at least my friends appreciate me.

BILL: The truth is you don't have any friends left! Half

the kids in school think you're a big phony and the rest can't stand the sight of you. You make all of us sick!

JUDY (*Visibly upset*): Mother!

MR. JOHNSON: Bill, that's enough. Why don't you run out to the garage and look for that weed killer.

BILL: Gladly! (*He exits.*)

MRS. JOHNSON: Judy, I'd like you to meet . . .

JUDY (*Interrupting*): Mother, you are simply going to have to speak to Bill about his boorish behavior! (*Almost in tears*) He is positively rude! (*She starts left.*)

MRS. JOHNSON: Judy, you haven't met. . . .

JUDY (*Over her shoulder*): Mother, I simply haven't time for trivia. (*She sniffs.*) I must get ready for the party. I can't disappoint my fans, you know. (*Exits*)

MRS. JOHNSON: Forgive us, Mr. Randell. I think we all have a touch of the jitters since the tryouts this afternoon.

MR. RANDELL: Yes, David told me about the play. I understand perfectly. Tryouts can bring out the best or the worst in almost anybody.

MR. JOHNSON: And he should know, Helen. John was just telling me about his own theatrical background.

MRS. JOHNSON: Wonderful! The little theater needs more members. (*Men smile.*)

MR. JOHNSON: Helen, don't you realize who John is?

MRS. JOHNSON (*Baffled*): Well, of course, Larry. He's our new neighbor.

MR. JOHNSON: Remember the show we saw in New York—*Avocado Blues?* This is that John Anderson Randell, the playwright.

MRS. JOHNSON: I had no idea! My goodness. (*Telephone rings*) Oh, dear. Excuse me. (*On phone*) Hello. . . . Yes, Margaret, I'll call her. (*Calling*) Judy.

JUDY (*Off left*): Coming. (*She enters and takes phone.*) Hello. . . . Margaret, darling! I'm exhilarated, of course, simply exhilarated. . . . That's too bad. . . . Poor Ray, tryouts must have been too much for him. . . . O.K., if you two aren't here by eight, I'll go on to the party by myself. Thanks for calling, Margaret. (*Hangs up phone; bleakly*) I won't have to go on a blind date tonight, after all.

MRS. JOHNSON: What happened, dear?

JUDY: Ray feels simply awful. (*She shrugs her shoulders.*) If he doesn't get better by tonight, they won't be going to the party, that's all.

MRS. JOHNSON: That's a shame.

JUDY (*With a brave front*): Frankly, I'm relieved, simply relieved. (*Starts to exit*)

MRS. JOHNSON: Judy . . . Judith, come here, dear. (JUDY *turns slowly and listlessly*) Judith, we've just learned that our new neighbor, Mr. Randell, is John Anderson Randell, the playwright.

MR. RANDELL: Hello, Judith, I'm glad to meet you. (*For a moment* JUDY *is stunned; then she assumes her theatrical style.*)

JUDY (*Gushing*): Oh! I can't believe this is happening. Imagine, the divine John Anderson Randell, right here in our humble little home! (BILL *runs in.*)

BILL: Dad, I can't find that weed spray anywhere. Can you help me look?

MR. JOHNSON: Sure, Bill. Be right back, John. (*He exits with* BILL.)

MRS. JOHNSON: I'll just make some coffee. Judy, would you entertain Mr. Randell for a few minutes? (*She exits left.*)

JUDY (*Affectedly*): I suppose Harrisville must seem deadly dull to you, Mr. Randell.

MR. RANDELL: Well, no it doesn't, Judith. We like it here in Harrisville . . . crabgrass and all!

JUDY (*With a forced laugh*): You are so terribly witty, Mr.

Randell. Simply terrible! What I mean is, you are so terribly simple! Oh, you must forgive me, Mr. Randell, you really must! I've had an exhausting day. Tryouts for the school play were this afternoon, you know.

MR. RANDELL: Yes, I know.

JUDY: Then you know what enormous pressure I've been under. Simply enormous!

MR. RANDELL: You must take acting very seriously.

JUDY: Oh, I do! I do! My innate creativity is like a powerful magnet pulling me to stardom . . . pulling . . . pulling! Frankly, I can't resist it. I'm desperate, simply desperate!

MR. RANDELL (*Going along with* JUDY): Like a compulsion, is that it?

JUDY: Compulsion? Yes! Yes, a compulsion! That's it, exactly. A compulsive force, throbbing, taunting, whispering in my ear . . . you must go to Hollywood! You must be on Broadway . . . you must! You must!

MR. RANDELL: I think I get the idea.

JUDY: I'm leaving the second I graduate.

MR. RANDELL: Hollywood is a long way from Harrisville, in more ways than one, you know.

JUDY: I'm not worried, Mr. Randell. My wagon is hitched to a star and I'm going wherever it takes me. (MR. *and* MRS. JOHNSON *enter. He carries a box of weed killer.*)

MR. JOHNSON (*Holding up box*): I thought I'd never find it! (*He hands box to* MR. RANDELL.)

MRS. JOHNSON: Judy, would you serve the coffee, please?

JUDY: Of course, Mother, darling! (*As she slinks toward the kitchen she turns and smiles*) Ta, ta, my darlings. I'll be back in a moment. (*Exits left*)

MRS. JOHNSON: Judy is normally a sweet, sensible, girl, but lately! (*She shakes her head in dismay.*)

MR. RANDELL: Judith is a little stagestruck, but it's not too unusual at her age. Why, every year there are hundreds of young girls just like Judith who flock to Hollywood. Inexperienced and immature, most of them, with more hope than talent.

MR. JOHNSON: Sounds like Judy, all right. Say, John, maybe you could give Judy a little talking to.

MRS. JOHNSON: Oh, that's a wonderful idea! She'd listen to Mr. Randell.

MR. RANDELL (*Reluctantly*): Well, I, ah . . . (JUDY *enters with tray holding coffeepot and cups.*)

JUDY: Here I am, darlings! (MR. *and* MRS. JOHNSON *look at* MR. RANDELL *beseechingly; he nods.*)

MR. JOHNSON: Hm-m-m, that coffee smells delicious, Judy. (JUDY *puts the tray on the coffee table and serves coffee.*)

JUDY: Now, Pa-pa (*French accent*), remember, I'm Judith. (*To* MR. RANDELL) After aeons of calling me Judy, my entire family is having great difficulty adjusting to my stage name.

MR. RANDELL: Judy, I think you will have to change more than your name if you sincerely want to become an actress.

JUDY (*Enthusiastically*): Well, you're the expert. Where do I start?

MR. RANDELL: You could start by being yourself.

JUDY (*Taken aback*): But . . . but I am myself!

MR. RANDELL (*Calmly*): Are you?

JUDY (*Wailing*): Of course! I simply have a dramatic flair, that's all. My innate magnet is forcing me . . . I mean my creative magnet is . . . I mean I'm pulling my magnet . . . (*She throws up her hands in frustration.*) Oh, I don't know what I mean! (*Pauses*) Except that I'm going to become an actress, and a good one.

MR. RANDELL: Well, Judy, right now, I'd say you lack the background and especially the maturity that a professional actress needs. In fact, the best thing you could do for your career is plan to go on to college after you graduate.

JUDY: College? You must be joking!

MR. RANDELL: Actually, I've never been more serious in my life.

MRS. JOHNSON: You know he's right, dear.

MR. RANDELL: Believe me, Judy, I've been in show business long enough to know that being an actress takes more than a pair of dark glasses. It takes discipline and hard work. (*He rises.*) Think about what I've said, won't you, Judy?

MR. JOHNSON: Sounds like good advice to me, John. Want some help with your lawn?

MR. RANDELL: Sure. (*To* MRS. JOHNSON) Thanks for the coffee. Goodbye, Judy. (*He exits with* MR. JOHNSON. JUDY *has been standing by the window, sniffing; now she wipes away tears under her sunglasses.*)

MRS. JOHNSON: Judy, dear, do you have something in your eye?

JUDY (*Almost sobbing*): Just a little stardust, Mom. (*She turns and removes sunglasses*) I've been such a fool! (*She runs off, left.*)

MRS. JOHNSON: Judy— (BILL *enters right.*)

BILL: Mom, it's almost time for the party.

MRS. JOHNSON: Oh, dear, is it that late already? Poor Judy. I guess Margaret isn't coming by for her.

BILL: No blind date? (*Shrugs*) Well, I can't blame them for backing out. Who could stand Judy for a whole evening?

MRS. JOHNSON: That isn't the reason. Ray just wasn't feeling well. (*Doorbell rings*) Bill, that might be Margaret now.

BILL: I doubt it. (*He opens door and* MARGARET, RAY, *and* DAVID *enter. Greetings are exchanged.*)

MARGARET: Bill, you were marvelous this afternoon. I had no idea I had such a talented cousin!

BILL: Neither did I. I think we should be billed as the Johnson Family Thespi-hams. (*He puts his arm around* MARGARET'*s shoulder and they strike a pose. Everyone laughs.*)

MRS. JOHNSON (*To* RAY): I'm so glad you're feeling better, Ray. It would have been a shame to miss the party tonight. (RAY *looks at* DAVID.)

RAY (*Glumly*): Yeah, it would have been a shame.

MARGARET: I hope Judy hasn't given up on us, Aunt Helen.

MRS. JOHNSON: Of course not. I'll go tell her you're here. (*Exits left*)

RAY: I wish I had stayed home! And so does David.

MARGARET: Will you stop fuming, Ray? Everything is going to work out. At least I hope so!

RAY: Well, for David's sake, I hope so, too. You almost died this afternoon when I told you who your blind date was, didn't you, David?

DAVID (*Embarrassed*): I was just surprised, that's all. I'm sure we'll have a good time tonight.

MARGARET (*Relieved*): Oh, David, we will. Once you get to know Judy, you'll really like her. And I'm not saying that just because she's my cousin. Judy really is a wonderful person, friendly and full of fun.

RAY (*Dryly*): Simply ho-ho-ho. (MARGARET *glares at him.* MR. JOHNSON *enters.*)

MR. JOHNSON: Margaret, I hear you brought down the house at tryouts today.

BILL: In fact, if I were Mr. Wilson, you'd get the lead. (*Unnoticed,* JUDY *enters with* MRS. JOHNSON. *She is without her sunglasses, and wears a simple dress.*)

MARGARET (*Modestly*): Thanks, Bill, but I doubt it.

JUDY: Well, I don't doubt it, Margaret. You were wonderful this afternoon. (*Everyone looks at* JUDY, *amazed.*)

MARGARET: Gosh, Judy, I thought you were . . . well, you were . . .

BILL: Terrifically bad.

MRS. JOHNSON: Bill!

JUDY: Mom, Bill's right. It's about time I faced up to the truth.

MRS. JOHNSON: Oh, I'm sure you'll get a role of some kind.

JUDY: It's O.K., Mom, really it is. It doesn't matter if I get a role in the play or not. You see, I learned something today. I discovered that the most important role I'll ever have in my life is being myself. Right now, all I want to be is plain old Judy Johnson of Harrisville High.

BILL (*Parodying a soap opera narrator*): Friends, be sure to tune in next week, at the same time, for another thrilling chapter in the life of plain old Judy Johnson and her search for happiness! (*Everyone laughs.*)

JUDY: And, David, well, now that I have my feet on the ground, maybe I . . . maybe we . . .

BILL: What she means is, now that she's back down to earth, she'll be glad to help you pick the crabgrass out of your front lawn! (*All laugh.*)

DAVID: Gosh, Judith, I can't believe . . .

JUDY: Call me Judy, O.K.?

DAVID: Why, Judy, this is the first time I've ever seen you . . . I mean really seen you, without your dark glasses, and . . . (*Phone rings.* MRS. JOHNSON *answers it.*)

MRS. JOHNSON (*On phone*): Hello . . . Oh, hello, Mr. Wilson. . . . Yes, the whole gang is here. I'll let Judy take the message. (*To* JUDY) Judy, it's Mr. Wilson. (JUDY *takes the phone.*)

JUDY (*On phone*): Hello, Mr. Wilson. . . . Yes, of course I'd be glad to tell them. . . . Oh, that's wonderful! That's perfect! . . . Oh! Why, thank you, Mr. Wilson!

. . . Yes, I'm sure we'll have a wonderful time tonight! . . . Yes, see you on Monday. 'Bye. (*Spins around, obviously delighted*) Guess what? Margaret got the female lead, and Ray got the male lead! (*Everyone congratulates them.*) And Bill and David both play stage-door Johnnies. (*They receive congratulations.*) Oh, and I got a part, too!

MRS. JOHNSON: Oh, that's wonderful, dear. I'm so happy!

BILL: What part did you get, sis?

JUDY (*Laughing*): Well, he said the part was perfect (*Mimicking herself*), simply perfect for me.

MR. JOHNSON: Don't keep us in suspense!

JUDY: I play the part of a kooky teen-age actress! (*All laugh and groan. Curtain.*)

THE END

Virtue Is Her Own Reward

by Michael Hervey

Characters

CLARISSA CANDLEWICK
DUNCAN CANDLEWICK, *her father*
AMELIA CANDLEWICK, *her mother*
ISABELLA, HERMIONE, GERTRUDE — *her sisters*
RODERICK, *her brother*
ERNEST ENDEAVOR, *the hero*
BASIL BLACKHEART, *the villain*
ABANDONED WIFE
CHILD
POLICEMAN

SCENE 1

TIME: *Early 19th century.*

SETTING: *The kitchen of the Candlewicks' home. Up center there is a Dutch door with the top half open. A table set for dinner is at center.*

AT RISE: CLARISSA, DUNCAN, AMELIA, ISABELLA, HERMIONE, *and* GERTRUDE *are seated at the table.*

CLARISSA (*Crying*): But I don't want to marry Basil Blackheart!

DUNCAN: You will do as you're told, Clarissa!

CLARISSA: But I don't love him! My heart belongs to Ernest Endeavor!

AMELIA (*As she goes to stove*): Ernest Endeavor hasn't a name to his penny! We cannot allow you to throw yourself away on a pauper.

ISABELLA (*Aside*): He may be a pauper, but, oh, those biceps!

CLARISSA: I don't care if he is a pauper! Money isn't everything! I love him! I love him!

AMELIA (*Bringing food to table*): You will have to forget him, dear. It's for your own good. Basil Blackheart will make you a fine husband. He has everything a wish could girl for—money, position, prestige, property—

HERMIONE (*Aside*): And pigeon-toes. Give me Ernest any time! Oh, that torso!

DUNCAN: He's also promised to pay all our debts.

AMELIA (*Serving food*): Yes, he has a whale as big as a heart!

GERTRUDE (*Aside*): Yes, and a nose to match. Clarissa is welcome to him. Once she is out of the way, I'll get Ernest to marry me, even if it means tossing my Girl Scout oath to the winds!

AMELIA: He's even promised to have my spinning wheel retreaded, and buy your sisters some new hockey sticks.

DUNCAN (*Aside*): What they need is a face lift, but that would be asking too much!

CLARISSA: You're selling me into bondage! I shall die of a broken heart!

DUNCAN: Where's your sense of duty, child? We've slaved and sacrificed to give you a good education and everything, and now, when we're on the verge of being thrown into the street, you turn your back on us!

AMELIA: Yes, to hear you talk, anyone would think you were about to suffer a death worse than fate! Basil Blackheart is considered to be the best catch in town! Why, if I were twenty years younger, I'd marry him myself! (*She sits.*)

ISABELLA: You really are being ungrateful, sister dear.

HERMIONE: Yes, it's the least you can do under the circumstances.

GERTRUDE: You know better than anyone else how badly we need those new hockey sticks!

CLARISSA: I don't care about your silly hockey sticks! All I care about is Ernest! I can't live without him! He's all the world to me! I shall die if you make me marry Basil Blackheart! I know I shall!

AMELIA: You're just being childish, Clarissa. After all, what does Ernest have that Basil doesn't have?

ISABELLA (*Aside*): Is she kidding?

AMELIA: As a matter of fact, I think Basil is far more manly than Ernest. He's taller, for a start, and far better built.

HERMIONE (*Aside*): Especially around the midriff. (RODERICK *enters up center.*)

DUNCAN: Where have you been, Roderick? Dinner's almost over!

RODERICK: I'm sorry, Papa, but I've only just finished delivering the morning papers!

DUNCAN: You've only just finished! They are supposed to be delivered before seven o'clock in the morning—not seven o'clock at night!

RODERICK: Yes, I know, Papa, but my bicycle broke down. I had to deliver all the newspapers on foot. And you know how difficult it is for me to walk on my two left feet.

AMELIA (*Rising, and helping him to a seat*): You poor child, you must be exhausted!

RODERICK: Yes, I must have carried that bicycle at least fifty miles.

AMELIA (*Handing him some food*): You carried it?

RODERICK: I couldn't very well leave it there by the roadside. Somebody might have stolen it.

GERTRUDE (*Aside*): That'll be the day! We tried giving it away last week but the junkman refused it!

AMELIA: Yes, of course.

RODERICK: I really could do with some new tires, Papa, and a new bicycle seat. The one I have now is worn to a point.

ISABELLA (*Aside*): So's his head.

DUNCAN: New tires! I've never heard of such nonsense! You must think I'm made of money! Why can't you make things last the way we do?

RODERICK: But I've already had them fifteen years!

DUNCAN: Exactly! They're practically new!

RODERICK: But I've been riding on the axles for months now! My feet keep dragging on the ground most of the time!

AMELIA (*Patting him on the head*): Never mind, dear. After all, you don't have so far to fall now, have you? Anyhow, every lining has its silver cloud. Perhaps we can persuade Basil to buy you a new bicycle when he becomes one of the family.

RODERICK: Do you really mean it, Mama?

AMELIA: Yes, of course.

RODERICK: Do you think I could have one with pedals this time? It gets a bit tiring at times pushing it with my feet —especially up hills.

AMELIA: We'll see what we can do. You'd better hurry and finish your supper. We're expecting Basil any minute. Isabella, Hermione, and Gertrude, you'd better start clearing the table.

ISABELLA, HERMIONE, *and* GERTRUDE (*Together*): Yes, Mama. (*They rise and begin to clear table.*)

DUNCAN (*Rising*): I think I'll take a little stroll round the park. I need the exercise. . . . (*Exits left*)

GERTRUDE (*Aside*): He also needs a hole in the head! Who does he think he's kidding? Stroll round the park, indeed! He hasn't made it all the way around yet—and he's been at it for thirty years. (BASIL *enters up center.*)

BASIL (*Twirling his mustache*): And how are the lovely Mrs. Candlewick and her four charming daughters this evening?

AMELIA (*Coyly*): Well, if it isn't Mr. Blackheart! What a pleasant surprise!

BASIL (*Aside*): Four charming daughters, indeed! She could hold a witches' convention here any time without any help from Macbeth! (*To* AMELIA) Call me Basil. All my enemies do.

AMELIA: Very well . . . Basil. It's not unlikely you'll be one of the family soon, so I suppose I'd better get used to the idea of calling you by your Christian name.

BASIL (*Aside*): Yes, it's a heavy price to pay, but it's worth it. Little does the silly old goat know that Clarissa isn't her daughter at all! She is, in fact, the daughter of Lord and Lady Scuttle-Bottom. A wicked nurse deliberately switched babies when Clarissa was only a few days old, as a means of avenging herself on Lord and Lady Scuttle-Bottom. When I divulge the secret, Clarissa will inherit their entire estate, which will fall into my lap like a ripe plum as soon as I marry her! (*Rubbing his hands*) Nothing must stand in my way. (*To* AMELIA) I can hardly wait to call you Mother!

AMELIA (*Coyly*): Neither can I! Clarissa, aren't you going to say hello to Mr. Blackheart—I mean, Basil? (CLARISSA *turns her back on* BASIL.) The dear child is shy. All right, Isabella, Hermione, and Gertrude, you can tidy up later on.

ISABELLA (*To* HERMIONE *and* GERTRUDE, *as they all exit*

right): I'll play them some romantic music on my trombone, just to set the mood, so to speak. And if that doesn't work, I'll blow down the gas pipes and put the lights out.

BASIL (*To* AMELIA): You really shouldn't send the girls out on my account. (*Aside*) If she hadn't gotten rid of the three hags, I'd have stuffed them into a crate and shipped them off to the Foreign Legion. Who knows, they might even be welcome there!

AMELIA (*Coyly*): Two's a crowd and three's company, I always say! (*To* RODERICK) You'd better join your sisters in the living room.

RODERICK: But I haven't finished my supper yet!

AMELIA (*Handing him his plate*): You can finish it in the living room. (*Bundles him toward door at right*)

RODERICK: But there isn't any furniture in the living room!

AMELIA (*Aside*): No, and there isn't any living room, either, for that matter! (*To* RODERICK) Try sitting on the floor. It's very good for your posture, I'm told.

RODERICK: Yes, but the mice keep sneaking bites off my plate while I'm not looking. (*Exits*)

AMELIA: I'm afraid he's not very bright, but he has a heart of gold. Do anybody for anything.

BASIL: I'm sure he would. (*Pointedly*) Don't let me keep you, if you have something better to do.

AMELIA: It's odd you should say that, because I've been meaning to cheep the swimney in the living room for weeks, and this is the first opportunity I've had to make a start on it. Perhaps you can persuade Clarissa to brew you a cup of tea while I am otherwise occupied. (*Exits*)

BASIL (*Aside*): If there's any persuading needed, it won't be because I fancy a cup of tea! (*To* CLARISSA) Have you nothing to say to me, Clarissa?

CLARISSA: No, I do not, and I'm not making you any tea either! So you might as well leave!

BASIL: Not until you give me your answer.

CLARISSA: I've already given you my answer! I'd sooner die than marry a cad like you!

BASIL (*Trying to embrace her*): You will be mine! I refuse to take no for an answer! (CLARISSA *ducks, and* BASIL *ends up embracing the coatrack.*)

CLARISSA (*Defiantly*): I shall never be yours! (BASIL *begins to chase* CLARISSA *about the room, but he trips over chairs, etc., and cannot catch her. He finally collapses onto a chair, and* CLARISSA *runs off left.*)

BASIL (*Calling after her*): You'll be mine, my proud beauty, never you fear! It's only a question of time!

RODERICK (*Entering*): Are you alone, Mr. Blackheart?

BASIL: No, I'm having tea with the entire cast of *Don Giovanni*!

RODERICK: Oh. . . . Well, in that case I'll come back when you're free. . . .

BASIL: Never mind. What did you wish to see me about?

RODERICK: It's about my bicycle . . . It's broken down. . . .

BASIL: I'm sorry, but repairing bicycles is a little out of my line.

RODERICK: I didn't mean you should repair it. . . . I was kind of hoping that you might buy me a new one.

BASIL: Oh, you were, were you? Well, it so happens I don't go around making gifts to people. It's against the union rules.

RODERICK: I wasn't exactly expecting you to make me a gift of one. . . .

BASIL: What did you have in mind then?

RODERICK: I propose to earn it.

BASIL: How—by acting as a part-time scarecrow?

RODERICK: No, as a matter of fact I've already tried doing that, but all the crows did was to laugh themselves silly. What I had in mind was a sort of a deal . . .

BASIL (*Leaning back in his chair*): Like what, for instance?

RODERICK (*Lowering his voice*): I think I know how you can get Clarissa to accept your proposal of marriage.

BASIL (*Sitting up quickly*): Really? How? (RODERICK *whispers in* BASIL'*s ear.*) Are you sure?

RODERICK: I saw it with my own two eyes!

BASIL (*Shaking his head*): No, it's out of the question, Roderick. I may be low, but I draw the line at anything like that. Besides, we'd never get away with it. But don't worry, you'll get your bicycle.

RODERICK: Really?

BASIL: Yes, but I shall expect a little favor in return.

RODERICK: Just name it, and I'll do it!

BASIL: I will, but first I'd like you to slip out and get me a container of mustache wax. (*Hands him some money*)

RODERICK: All right. I'll be back in a flash. (*Exits*)

BASIL (*Aside*): I may have to use the little tidbit that idiot just let drop, but in either case the wench *shall* be mine! I can see it all now. . . . The organ will be playing softly as she comes down the aisle. . . . (*If possible, the lights dim, and* BASIL *quickly exits left. A spotlight shines on wedding procession, as the Wedding March is heard and* DUNCAN *and* CLARISSA *enter right, followed by* ISABELLA *and* HERMIONE. AMELIA *and* GERTRUDE *are next in line.* AMELIA *is crying, and* GERTRUDE *keeps bumping into* ISABELLA *and* HERMIONE, *who keeps slipping and falling.* BASIL *and* RODERICK *enter left and face procession. Others are wearing appropriate formal dress;* BASIL *and* RODERICK *have added carnations and top hats to their costumes.* RODERICK'*s hat is too big for him and keeps slipping down over his eyes.*)

CLARISSA (*Coming to a sudden halt*): No, I won't do it! (*Throws bouquet to the ground, and exits.*)

BASIL: Curse it! Foiled again! (*Stamps his foot in rage.*)

RODERICK: Don't worry, Mr. Blackheart. I'll fetch her back! (*Spotlight follows* RODERICK *as he goes left and exits.*

Spotlight dims as BASIL *removes his hat and others exit.*)

BASIL (*Back in his chair, as lights come up*): She'll go through with it even if it means chaining her to my side! (*If desired, members of the audience, selected beforehand, may boo and hiss.* BASIL *rises; to audience.*) If you don't watch out, I'll do in the lot of you! (ERNEST ENDEAVOR *appears at door up center. The audience may cheer.* BASIL *wheels around.*) What are you doing here?

ERNEST: I might ask you the same thing!

BASIL: It's none of your business, Ernest Endeavor!

ERNEST: Oh, yes, it is! I know what you're up to, you beastly cad, and I'm here to tell you that you won't get away with it!

BASIL: That's what you think!

ERNEST: I'm warning you, Basil Blackheart, that if you persist in your nefarious scheming, I shall be forced to take drastic action.

BASIL: And I'm warning you, Ernest Endeavor, better known as Dimples, to keep out of my way, or I'll pour ink all over your stamp collection!

ERNEST: Those are fighting words! Put up your hands! (*He squares off with* BASIL.)

BASIL: You don't mind if I put my gloves on first, do you? I'd hate to spoil my manicure.

ERNEST (*Politely*): Not at all.

BASIL (*Aside, as he puts on pair of large gloves*): Little does the poor fool know that I always carry a pair of knuckle-dusters inside my gloves.

ERNEST (*Starting toward door up center*): Perhaps it would be better if we settle this outside. It would be a shame to ruin all this beautiful furniture.

BASIL (*Aside, as he follows* ERNEST): He's the one that's going to be ruined, not the furniture!

ERNEST (*Squaring off once more*): Are we ready?

BASIL (*Pointing over* ERNEST'*s shoulder*): Look, a flying saucer!

ERNEST (*Turning*): Where?

BASIL (*Pretending to hit* ERNEST, *who turns around in a complete circle*): There! (ERNEST *rallies bravely and returns the blow in slow motion. They continue to clout each other in turn, still in slow motion, as "The Anvil Chorus" is heard. Finally,* BASIL *sinks slowly to the floor.*)

ERNEST: Have you had enough?

BASIL: Yes, but only for the time being . . . (*Aside*) Next time I'll slip a few horseshoes into my gloves.

ERNEST: If you so much as dare to speak to Clarissa again, or show your long nose in these parts, I shall thrash you within an inch of your life!

BASIL (*Still making no attempt to rise*): Aw, go jump in the lake!

ERNEST: I shan't warn you again! (*Exits*)

BASIL: I'll fix him if it's the last thing I do! I'll get that oaf, Roderick, to help me. He'll do anything in order to get a new bicycle. . . . It'll have to be something relatively simple, like getting him to push Mr. Dimples there under a steamroller—otherwise the idiot's sure to make a mess of it. (*Exits*)

CURTAIN

* * *

SCENE 2

TIME: *The following afternoon.*

SETTING: *The same as Scene 1.*

AT RISE: CLARISSA *is sadly mixing the batter for a cake.*

RODERICK (*Entering, carrying a letter*): Here's a letter for you, sister dear.

CLARISSA: A letter! It must be from Ernest! (*Snatches letter from him*) My heart rejoices! I am transported to the heavens above!

RODERICK (*Aside, as he exits*): Did you ever hear such slush? (*Mimicking her*) I am transported! She's lucky not to be deported!

CLARISSA (*Opening envelope and taking out newspaper clipping*): It's not a letter! It's a newspaper clipping! I wonder what it's all about.

BASIL (*Poking his head in, at Dutch door up center; aside*): Well, you silly ninny, suppose you read it and find out! (*He ducks back out of sight.*)

CLARISSA: It's a wedding announcement dated a year ago. (*Reading*) "The marriage of Agnes, older daughter of Mr. and Mrs. B. Thankful of Paddington, to Ernest Endeavor, son of Mr. and Mrs. I. Endeavor of Woop Woop, will be solemnized at St. Mary's Church on Sunday, May 5th, 1804. . . ." (*Clutching at her heart*) Oh, no! It can't be! Oh-h-h-h! (*She swoons.* DUNCAN *and* AMELIA *rush in from right.*)

DUNCAN: What's the matter?

AMELIA: What's happened? (*They kneel beside* CLARISSA *and try to revive her.*)

BASIL (*Poking his head in again, at Dutch door; aside*): I told you I'd fix him! She'll never speak to him again! His name will be mud! That'll teach him to cross swords with Basil Blackheart! (*He ducks out of sight again.*)

AMELIA: What happened, child? Were you struck by lightning or something?

DUNCAN: Don't be foolish, woman! We haven't had a storm in weeks! (*Seeing newspaper clipping and picking it up*) What's this? It's a newspaper clipping! I wonder what it's all about?

BASIL (*Poking his head in again; aside*): Oh, no! Not

again! Are they all morons in this family? (*Ducks out of sight.*)

AMELIA (*Taking clipping from him*): Let me see it. . . . (*Reading*) "The marriage of Agnes, older daughter of Mr. and Mrs. B. Thankful of Paddington, to Ernest Endeavor, son of Mr. and Mrs. I. Endeavor of Woop Woop, will be solemnized at St. Mary's Church on Sunday, May 5th, 1804. . . ." (*She clutches her heart and cries out.*) Oh, no! It can't be! Oh-h-h-h! (*She swoons.*)

DUNCAN (*Shaking her roughly*): What are you swooning for, you silly old goat? This is what we've been waiting for!

AMELIA (*Sitting up*): It is?

DUNCAN: But, of course! We shan't have any difficulty in getting Clarissa to marry Basil now! She'll accept him on the rebound, as the saying goes!

BASIL (*Poking his head in*): Exactly! (*Ducks out of sight*)

AMELIA: Do you really think so?

DUNCAN: What else could she possibly do under the circumstances? (CLARISSA *moans and stirs.*)

AMELIA (*Comforting her*): There, there, sweet. Everything's going to be all right. You should have listened to us in the pirst flace. Then this wouldn't have happened.

DUNCAN: The best thing you can do now is to marry Basil Blackheart.

BASIL (*Appearing in doorway*): You called?

DUNCAN: Speak of the Devil—I mean, you couldn't have timed it better! (*He assists* CLARISSA *to a chair*) We have just had some dreadful news!

BASIL: Don't tell me the government is going to put a tax on do-it-yourself poison kits? They're one of my best lines—!

DUNCAN (*Dragging him off into a corner*): No, it's nothing like that. This is the opportunity you've been waiting for. All you need do now is . . . (*He whispers in* BASIL*'s ear.*)

AMELIA (*Fanning* CLARISSA *with her apron*): Are you feeling better now, dear?

CLARISSA (*Moaning*): I want to die. . . . Where is the nearest precipice?

AMELIA: Well, you catch the bus at Market Streeet and ask the driver to put you down at the corner of Robertson Road. Then it's just a short walk to Lovers' Leap.

CLARISSA (*Struggling to rise*): I'll go right away.

AMELIA (*Holding her back*): But you haven't had any lunch yet. You couldn't possibly jump off a precipice on an empty stomach! Besides, you know how heights always make you dizzy! You'd be better off throwing yourself in the river—except that the water is so terribly cold this time of year! (CLARISSA *starts to sob, as* ABANDONED WIFE, *pushing baby carriage with* CHILD *in it, bursts in.* CHILD *is at least twenty-one years old and has a handlebar mustache.* POLICEMAN *follows them.*)

ABANDONED WIFE: Where is he? Where is the miserable villain who abandoned my poor little mite and me on May 5th, 1804, in a howling snowstorm? We would have died of cold and hunger if one of the keepers at the zoo hadn't sneaked us into the monkey cage. Unfortunately, Junior now calls everybody who looks like an ape "Daddy."

CHILD (*To* POLICEMAN): Daddy!

AMELIA: I'm afraid you must be in the wrong house—

ABANDONED WIFE: Oh, no, I'm not. I was told he was here! He's been courting your daughter, Clarissa—the slimy cad!

DUNCAN (*Coming forward*): What's going on here?

CHILD: Daddy! (BASIL *starts sneaking toward door up center.*)

AMELIA: She's looking for the miserable villain who abandoned her and her poor little mite on May 5th, 1804, in a howling snowstorm! They would have died if one of the monkeys at the zoo hadn't sneaked her into the keeper's cage. The trouble is all the apes now think Junior is their daddy.

DUNCAN: Did you say, May 5th, 1804?

ABANDONED WIFE: Yes. On that date, we'd no sooner finished dinner than he slipped out for a short walk—at least, that's what he told me.

DUNCAN: Now, I get it! You must be Mrs. Ernest Endeavor!

CLARISSA (*Clutching her heart*): Oh, no! She can't be!

ABANDONED WIFE: You must be mixing me up with somebody else. The name's Blackheart. (*Catching sight of* BASIL) There he is! (*To* POLICEMAN) Arrest the villain! (*She runs after him, still pushing the baby carriage, and* POLICEMAN *chases him, too.*)

CHILD (*Calling to* BASIL, *who quickly exits*): Daddy! Daddy! (ABANDONED WIFE, CHILD, *and* POLICEMAN *exit, still chasing* BASIL.)

AMELIA: How can she possibly be Mrs. Blackheart if she's married to Ernest Endeavor?

DUNCAN: I don't know, but somebody's been awfully mixed up, that's for sure! (*Top half of Dutch door opens, as* ERNEST *appears behind it.*)

ERNEST: Dear Clarissa! You mustn't believe the lies contained in that newspaper clipping. Blackheart forced your brother, Roderick, to fake it with his do-it-yourself printing kit! Basil Blackheart was the one who married Agnes B. Thankful and *Basil* is the one who abandoned her and her poor little mite in a raging snowstorm—on May 5th, 1804! I wasn't even in town at the time.

CLARISSA (*Running to him*): I knew you couldn't do anything underhanded! Now we can be married after all!

DUNCAN: I'm sorry, but I still forbid it! It's not that I have anything against you personally, Ernest, but I couldn't let Clarissa marry a penniless nobody—

ERNEST (*Entering, thus revealing that he is wearing tight slacks and carrying a guitar*): But I'm not a penniless nobody! I've been discovered! You are now looking at Twitching Thomas, the Rocker with Rocks in his Head! (*Twitches and strums his guitar briefly as* CLARISSA *runs to his side. Girls in audience may scream, indicating their approval of* ERNEST'*s playing.*)

CLARISSA (*When* ERNEST *has stopped playing*): Then may we be married, Father?

AMELIA (*Stepping forward*): Wait! Before we give away our fairest daughter, I must divulge a secret. (*All look at her, surprised.*) Yes, all this time I have kept it a secret, but now I must tell the truth. Clarissa is really not our daughter at all, but the daughter of Lord and Lady Scuttle-Bottom.

ALL: Oh-h-h!

AMELIA: The nurse switched babies when Clarissa was but a few days old. But now that her true identity is known, Clarissa will soon inherit the whole of Lord and Lady Scuttle-Bottom's estate.

CLARISSA: Oh, Ernest, isn't that wonderful?

ERNEST (*Solemnly*): Indeed, Clarissa, it is. But it is more wonderful to think that soon you will be mine—and there really shall be a Mrs. Ernest Endeavor.

CLARISSA: Oh, Ernest! (*He begins to sing popular song and all dance to it, as the curtain falls.*)

THE END

Roscoe the Robot

by Anne Coulter Martens

Characters

SCOTTY
HANK, *his pal*
CINDY, *his girlfriend*
ARNOLD, *his rival*
JANET } *Cindy's friends*
SUE }
MRS. POMEROY, *a neighbor*
OFFICER RAFFERTY

TIME: *A Saturday afternoon.*
SETTING: *The workshop in Scotty's home.*
AT RISE: SCOTTY *is working at a long table, holding a portable electric mixer to his ear and listening intently. The telephone rings but he is unaware of it. Knocking is heard offstage and* HANK *enters a few seconds later.*

HANK (*Loudly*): Hey, are you deaf? (*Telephone continues to ring*)
SCOTTY (*Shouting*): What?
HANK: Your phone's ringing.
SCOTTY: Speak up!
HANK: Never mind. (*Picks up phone*) Hello. . . . Who? (*Shouting to* SCOTTY) Shut that thing off! (*Into phone*)

Who? (SCOTTY *turns off mixer*) Oh, hi, Cindy. . . . No, this is Hank. . . . Hi, yourself, baby.

SCOTTY (*Grabbing phone from* HANK): Move! (*Into phone*) Hi, beautiful. . . . Yes, this is Scotty. Sorry I took so long getting to the phone, but I'm working on my entry for the Science Fair. . . .

HANK (*Surprised*): No kidding? (*Surveys disarray of wire and metal on table and grins*)

SCOTTY (*Covering receiver*): Wipe that grin off your face! (*Into phone*) Of course I know a lot about science. But I don't talk about it all the time, like that egghead, Arnold Pence. . . . Now, wait a minute, Cindy. I did *not* insult Arnold. Eggheads *like* to be called eggheads. . . . Cindy? (*Shrugs and hangs up*)

HANK: She hung up on you?

SCOTTY (*Nodding*): All of a sudden I don't rate.

HANK: You mean ever since Arnold Pence made the scene.

SCOTTY: He's not so much. (*Goes back to table*)

HANK: Just another Einstein, maybe.

SCOTTY: Cut the static.

HANK: Know what he's entering in the Science Fair? Something about electronics.

SCOTTY: So who's worried? (*Fusses with some parts on table*)

HANK: You are.

SCOTTY (*Pausing*): Maybe. All the girls in school are acting strange lately. It used to be if a fellow was a good athlete, the girls swooned. Or if he was the class clown—

HANK: Like you?

SCOTTY: O.K., like me. I made the girls laugh and they thought I was super. But not any more. Now they're crazy about scientists.

HANK: Especially Cindy.

SCOTTY (*Optimistically*): She'll drop Arnold like a hot

potato when she sees my invention. Just wait. (*Turns on mixer and listens to motor*)

HANK (*Moving behind table*): What's that?

SCOTTY: Just what it looks like. (*Turns off mixer*)

HANK: Do you call an electric mixer a science project?

SCOTTY: Of course not.

HANK: What is this big project, anyway?

SCOTTY (*Enthusiastically*): You'd be surprised. I almost had it working till all the fuses blew.

HANK: *What* did you almost have working? (*Looks around*) I don't see anything.

SCOTTY: You will. (*Pointing to vacuum cleaner near table*) Will you kindly plug in that vacuum cleaner? (HANK *shrugs and plugs it in.* SCOTTY *turns it on, listens a moment, then turns it off.*) This motor is much more powerful than the mixer's.

HANK: You're a real genius. (*Taps his forehead, then points to vacuum*) Where'd you get this relic?

SCOTTY: I took it from Mrs. Pomeroy's front porch.

HANK: You *stole* it from your next-door neighbor?

SCOTTY (*Indignantly*): No! This is Clean-up Week and I figured since Mrs. Pomeroy put it out for the trash collectors, she wouldn't mind if I used it. (*Works on an assortment of wires and plugs*)

HANK: You mean you didn't ask her?

SCOTTY: Well—no.

HANK: Then you really didn't know that it was supposed to be picked up by the trash collectors. Maybe the vacuum was there for the repairman to fix.

SCOTTY (*Nervously*): Gee, I didn't think of that. Maybe I'd better put it back on her porch. (*Puts on red sports jacket which is lying on a chair*) Guess I should have taken time to ask Mrs. Pomeroy before I took it.

HANK: Now you're getting smart.

SCOTTY: Anyway, it's so old that it might blow more fuses. (*Offstage knock is heard;* CINDY *enters.*)

CINDY: Hi, fellows.

SCOTTY (*Pleased*): Cindy!

HANK: Hi, doll!

CINDY: Did Arnold come yet?

SCOTTY: *Here?*

CINDY: He said he's coming to talk to you about the Science Fair.

SCOTTY (*Annoyed*): So that's why you came over.

CINDY: Why, Scotty, you're not jealous, are you?

SCOTTY (*Scoffingly*): Of *Arnold*?

CINDY (*Deliberately taunting*): Arnold's so clever. And good-looking, too.

SCOTTY: His ears stick out.

CINDY: They do not!

SCOTTY: And he can't see without his glasses.

CINDY (*To* HANK): Glasses wouldn't help *some* people see anything.

SCOTTY: You'll find out who's the real brain around here.

CINDY (*Brightly*): Oh, I forgot. You have an entry for the fair, too.

SCOTTY (*Casually*): I'm working on one.

HANK: He sure is.

CINDY (*Sitting down*): Some darling little project that makes bells ring?

SCOTTY: Something that will make your eyes pop!

CINDY (*Laughing*): You're so funny!

SCOTTY (*Scowling*): This time I'm not trying to be.

CINDY: Where's this eye-popping invention of yours? (*Looks around*)

SCOTTY (*Stiffly*): It isn't perfected yet.

CINDY: Show us anyway—unless you're making the whole thing up.

SCOTTY (*Indignantly*): All right, I *will* show you! (*Goes to tall folding screen and moves it to one side, revealing a robot, with body made from boxes painted silver and with oversized boots for feet.*)

HANK (*Awed*): I'll be a bug-eyed baboon!

CINDY (*Gasping*): A robot!

SCOTTY (*Smiling*): A robot named Roscoe. Roscoe, meet Cindy and Hank.

HANK: Does he *do* anything?

CINDY: Besides just stare at people?

SCOTTY: He almost worked, then the fuses blew and I had to take out all his wires and innards. I need a better motor, I guess.

CINDY: You must be kidding!

HANK: I think he's serious.

SCOTTY: I left one thing fastened inside his head. (*Goes to robot*) Just for kicks. (*Reaches inside head and turns on a blinking red flashlight. One of Roscoe's eyes starts blinking.*)

CINDY: Oh, no! (*Takes step backward*)

SCOTTY: It's just a blinking flashlight, Cindy. And to amuse myself I fastened a couple of metal squawkers on each side of him. (*Stands behind Roscoe and pushes squawkers*)

CINDY: It's like a man from outer space.

SCOTTY: Ask him a question and see if he answers. One squawk for "yes" and two for "no."

CINDY: I won't!

HANK: Then I will. (*Turning to Roscoe*) Hey, Roscoe, do you like Cindy? (*Roscoe, with* SCOTTY'*s help, makes one squawk.* CINDY *giggles.*) Do you think she should go to the movies tonight with Scotty? (*Roscoe replies with one squawk.*) Do you consider Arnold Pence a real brain? (*Roscoe makes two squawks.*) Roscoe says "no."

CINDY: Very funny.

SCOTTY: That invitation to the movies is for real, Cindy.

CINDY (*Sarcastically*): Tell your friend Roscoe that I'll probably go somewhere with Arnold.

SCOTTY (*Indicating Roscoe*): See how sad he looks, poor fellow.

CINDY: Stop clowning. Next, you'll have him crying real tears.

SCOTTY: Sorry. (*Reaches in and turns off blinking light, then moves away from robot and pauses beside vacuum cleaner.*) I wonder if Mrs. Pomeroy really wants this old thing.

HANK: You'd better put it back on her porch. (*To* CINDY) This idiot just took it for granted that Mrs. Pomeroy's old vacuum cleaner was meant for the trash collectors.

CINDY: Uh-oh.

HANK (*Looking out window*): There's nobody on her porch now.

SCOTTY: O.K., O.K.

CINDY: You'd better take it back. Poor Mrs. Pomeroy is nervous and upset enough as it is.

HANK: What's she upset about?

CINDY: She and my mother are on the entertainment committee at the Children's Home, and everything has been going wrong. Besides that, she told Mother she thinks there's a prowler in her neighborhood.

SCOTTY: A prowler in *this* neighborhood?

CINDY: She found enormous footprints in her flower garden.

SCOTTY (*Amused*): Is that so? (CINDY *looks at him a moment, then walks to robot and looks down at his feet.* HANK *does the same. Both turn and look at* SCOTTY.)

CINDY: Roscoe has big feet.

HANK: Monster-sized feet.

SCOTTY (*Grinning*): I bought those boots in a second-hand store for Roscoe, and when I walked past Mrs. Pomeroy's garden, I just couldn't resist leaving a footprint.

CINDY: Always the comic, aren't you? (SCOTTY *laughs.*) But that isn't all. Mrs. Pomeroy hears noises at night. (*She and* HANK *look pointedly at* SCOTTY.)

SCOTTY: I hear noises, too. (*Grinning*) I *make* noises.

HANK (*To* CINDY): He's hopeless. (*To* SCOTTY) Get going.

SCOTTY: With my record, I sure don't want any *more* trouble. (*Picks up cleaner*)

CINDY (*Shocked*): A criminal record?

SCOTTY: I mean my record with my dad. After the wreck I made of Mom's dishwasher, one more speck of trouble and he won't let me apply for my driver's license.

HANK: Then you'd better get going.

SCOTTY: I'm on my way. (*Exits*)

HANK: What a guy! (*Moves folding screen back to hide Roscoe*)

CINDY: Hank, is Roscoe just another one of his jokes?

HANK: Scotty doesn't seem to think so.

CINDY: But it *couldn't* work—could it?

HANK: Not a chance. (ARNOLD *enters.*)

ARNOLD: Hi! I knocked but nobody answered.

HANK (*Indifferently*): Oh, hi, Arnold.

CINDY (*Smiling*): Hi! Scotty's not here right now, Arnold.

ARNOLD: I thought I'd talk to him about the Science Fair. (*Sits down*)

CINDY: That was nice of you.

HANK: Is your entry really about electronics?

ARNOLD: Naturally. That's *the* field today.

CINDY: It amazes me that you can understand such complicated things.

ARNOLD: Nothing to it. (*Glancing around*) What is Scotty's entry?

HANK: He says it's not perfected yet.

ARNOLD: Will it ever be? (*Laughs*)

HANK: You'll have to ask him.

CINDY: Or his friend Roscoe. (*Giggles*)

ARNOLD: Who?

HANK: That's top secret. (*To* CINDY) Do you suppose Roscoe's subject to claustrophobia?

CINDY: I hardly think so.

HANK: Or do you think he might suddenly go berserk? (CINDY *laughs.*)

ARNOLD (*Annoyed*): I don't know what you're talking about.

HANK: You're lucky.

ARNOLD (*To* CINDY): Since Scotty's not home, let's go someplace for a Coke.

CINDY: How about Scotty's refrigerator? His mother always tells us to help ourselves.

ARNOLD: Are you sure it's all right?

HANK: Sure! (ARNOLD *exits.*)

CINDY (*Calling to* ARNOLD): I'll be with you in a moment. (*To* HANK) Talk Scotty out of this foolishness, will you?

HANK: I thought you didn't care about him any more.

CINDY: I don't like to have him laughed at in the wrong way. (SCOTTY *hurries in.*)

SCOTTY (*Excitedly*): They almost caught me!

CINDY: Who?

SCOTTY: Mrs. Pomeroy and some policeman she has over there!

HANK: Wow!

SCOTTY: There I was, easing that cleaner up on the porch, when all of a sudden I heard voices and then the hall door opened. Gol-ly! (*Sinks down on chair*)

HANK: Did they see you?

SCOTTY: I don't think so.

CINDY: Maybe they didn't see *you,* but how could they miss that red jacket?

SCOTTY: Well, I sure hopped over our hedge in a big hurry!

CINDY (*Looking out window*): They're both out in Mrs. Pomeroy's yard now.

HANK (*Looking out*): I know that policeman. He's Officer Rafferty.

CINDY (*Nervously*): They're looking over this way!

SCOTTY (*Jumping up; alarmed*): Oh, no! (*Heads toward exit*) I'd better go out the back door.

HANK: Not that way! Arnold's in the kitchen and he might see you leaving.

SCOTTY (*Stopping short*): Arnold?

CINDY: I'm sure you can trust him.

HANK: Want to bet?

SCOTTY: He'd probably *help* put me in the cooler.

CINDY (*Looking out*): Mrs. Pomeroy's pointing at your house!

SCOTTY: Oh, no! How can I get lost? (*Looks around, then dashes behind screen*)

HANK: Are you crazy? That's the first place anyone would look. If they come over, why don't you just explain your mistake about the vacuum cleaner?

SCOTTY (*Peeking around screen*): Nothing doing. They'd never believe me. I'm staying right here. (*Ducks behind screen*)

CINDY: Suppose they *don't* believe him?

HANK: I didn't think of that.

CINDY: I wonder if they saw Scotty.

HANK (*Looking out*): I don't know, but they're still pointing over here.

CINDY (*Joining him*): And they don't look friendly.

HANK: That's for sure. Rafferty's talking and Mrs. Pomeroy's nodding her head.

CINDY: They must know Scotty came this way.

HANK: They're starting over.

CINDY (*Nervously*): Shall I let them in?

HANK: You'll have to.

CINDY: But what shall we say?

HANK: Just play it cool.

CINDY (*Panicked*): I can't!

HANK: Do you want Scotty to go to jail?

CINDY: Oh, no!

SCOTTY (*Loudly, from behind screen*): I might get twenty years!

HANK: Maybe they'd just put you on probation.

CINDY: But he'd still have a *real* police record all his life.

HANK: Don't push the panic button. (*There is a knock off-stage.*)

SCOTTY (*Loudly*): Get rid of them!

HANK: We'll try.

CINDY: They're sure to look behind the screen! (*Knocking is repeated*)

HANK (*To* SCOTTY): Keep quiet back there! (*To* CINDY) Open the door.

CINDY (*Hesitantly*): I'm shaking.

HANK: I'd better handle this. (*Grabs a couple of magazines from table, gives one to* CINDY, *pushes her into a chair and sits down with magazine*) Come in! (MRS. POMEROY *enters, followed by* RAFFERTY, *who carries a brown paper bag.*)

CINDY: Oh, hello, Mrs. Pomeroy.

MRS. POMEROY (*Nervously*): Hello, Cindy. You'll have to excuse me, but I'm quite upset. (*Looking at* HANK) Who is this boy?

HANK (*Rising*): Hank Brown. We're both waiting for Scotty.

RAFFERTY (*To* CINDY): How long has Hank been here?

CINDY: Oh, about ten minutes, I guess. (*As* MRS. POMEROY *and* RAFFERTY *glance around*) This is Scotty's workshop.

MRS. POMEROY: Oh. Did anyone else come in?

RAFFERTY: A prowler in a red jacket?

MRS. POMEROY: We had a glimpse of him as he ran in this direction.

HANK: How big a fellow was he?

MRS. POMEROY: I'm not sure. (*To* RAFFERTY) But those footprints in my garden were *huge*. They look as if a giant made them.

HANK: We'd know if a giant came in.

RAFFERTY: Mrs. Pomeroy called us last night, and we had a plaster cast made of the footprints. (*Takes large plaster cast from brown bag and shows them footprint*)

CINDY (*Shocked*): Oh, good grief!

MRS. POMEROY (*Upset*): The prowler is probably eight feet tall! Maybe ten feet!

RAFFERTY (*Soothingly*): Now, now, ma'am. Let's not allow ourselves to get hysterical. (*Studies plaster cast and then puts it on table*)

MRS. POMEROY (*Hysterically*): I'm *not* hysterical.

RAFFERTY: You're just a little nervous.

CINDY (*Rising*): What's wrong?

MRS. POMEROY: Your mother knows how nervous I've been. We've been working on the entertainment for the Children's Home, and one of our best acts has just canceled out. I don't know how I'll ever replace it.

CINDY: That's too bad, Mrs. Pomeroy.

MRS. POMEROY: No wonder I can't sleep nights. And then noises—and a blinking red light—and those giant footprints.

RAFFERTY: Right now it's the prowler we're after—the one who stole your vacuum cleaner and then sneaked it back onto the porch.

MRS. POMEROY (*To* RAFFERTY): It's your job to find him and lock him up. (SCOTTY *sneezes from behind screen.* HANK *quickly sneezes as* RAFFERTY *turns toward him.*)

HANK (*Taking out handkerchief*): Pardon me!

CINDY (*Innocently*): Don't let us detain you, officer. (SCOTTY *sneezes again;* HANK *sneezes, too.*)

HANK: Excuse me, please. I must be catching a cold. I always seem to get one this time of year.

RAFFERTY (*Suspiciously*): Anyone else in the house?

CINDY: Just a friend of ours having a Coke in the kitchen.

HANK: Why don't you ask him if a prowler went through the kitchen?

CINDY: That's a good idea. We were reading, and it's just possible we didn't notice anyone.

HANK: That's right. Go ask *him,* officer.

CINDY: Maybe he had a getaway car waiting.

HANK: It's not likely you'll ever see him again, officer.

CINDY (*Sadly*): I hope he gives up his life of crime.

RAFFERTY (*With mock agreement*): Sooner or later the law catches up with them. (*Casually*) That's a nice screen over there. (*Moves toward it*)

CINDY (*Nervously*): Yes, isn't it?

HANK (*Starting toward exit*): Shall we go now?

RAFFERTY: Not so fast. (*Reaches for screen just as* JANET *and* SUE *enter.* RAFFERTY *pauses.*)

JANET: Hi!

SUE: We just stopped by to say hello to Arnold, if he's still here.

CINDY: Arnold's in the kitchen. (ARNOLD *enters.*) No, here he is now.

ARNOLD (*To* JANET *and* SUE): Hi, lovelies. Care for a Coke?

JANET: No, thanks. (*Looks around*) This could be a nice room if Scotty didn't mess it up all the time.

SUE (*Looking at* RAFFERTY *and* MRS. POMEROY): Have we interrupted something?

HANK: We were just going to search the house for a prowler.

JANET: Oh, my goodness! (*Nervously*) Maybe we'd better go.

SUE: I'm not afraid with a policeman here. (*Smiles sweetly at* ARNOLD) And Arnold.

ARNOLD: Thanks, sweetheart.

HANK (*Anxiously*): Ready, officer?

MRS. POMEROY: I'll go with you.

CINDY: Good idea!

RAFFERTY: I have a better one. (*Again reaching for screen*) What's behind this screen?

CINDY: No, don't move it!

RAFFERTY: Why not?

CINDY: Scotty's entry for the Science Fair is back there.

HANK: And no one is supposed to see it.

RAFFERTY: Mind if I take a quick look? (CINDY *gasps as* RAFFERTY *moves screen to one side, revealing only Roscoe.* RAFFERTY *takes a step backward.*)

MRS. POMEROY: Good heavens, what is that?

HANK (*Recovering*): Just a robot Scotty's been working on. His name is Roscoe.

ARNOLD: Don't tell me it *works!*

HANK: No comment.

RAFFERTY: Sorry, kids. I thought you were pulling a fast one on me.

CINDY (*Innocently*): Why, officer!

RAFFERTY (*Looking at Roscoe*): It certainly is a weird-looking thing.

CINDY: Would you like to look through the rest of the house now?

RAFFERTY: Might as well.

MRS. POMEROY (*Looking at robot*): My, what big feet he has! (RAFFERTY *pauses, glances at Roscoe's feet, picks up plaster cast, studies it a moment, then looks again at Roscoe's feet.*)

RAFFERTY (*Thoughtfully*): Very big feet. (SCOTTY, *inside Roscoe, slowly lifts his arm to the top of Roscoe's head and turns on flashlight. As one red eye blinks on and off, he takes a few stiff steps forward.* MRS. POMEROY *and girls scream.*)

CINDY: Roscoe, stop!

RAFFERTY: It moves!

MRS. POMEROY: Oh, look at that awful red eye!

SUE: You don't suppose he's dangerous, do you?

HANK (*Puzzled*): I hope not.

CINDY (*Quickly*): But everyone had better go home, just in case. (*Nudges* HANK)

HANK: Right! When Scotty comes back he'll know how to stop Roscoe. (*Moving stiffly,* SCOTTY *takes a step toward one person and then toward another.*)

MRS. POMEROY: It's the most amazing thing I ever saw! (SCOTTY *bows*)

JANET: It can't talk, can it? (SCOTTY *makes a squawker sound once.*) Yipe! (*She goes behind a chair.*)

RAFFERTY: I'd never have believed it!

SUE (*Nervously*): Do you like me? (SCOTTY *answers with one squawk and takes a step toward her. She goes behind a chair.*) Don't do me any favors!

HANK: How about Cindy? (SCOTTY *makes one squawk.*)

ARNOLD: It's evidently fond of girls.

HANK: Do you admire Arnold? (SCOTTY *makes two squawks.*) I think that means no.

ARNOLD: Don't be afraid, Cindy. (*He takes* CINDY's *hand, trying to pull her toward exit. She remains standing where she is, their arms extended across* SCOTTY's *path. He walks into their clasped hands, forcing them to separate.*)

SUE: He won't let Cindy hold hands with anyone!

JANET: What does a girl *do* about a romantic robot?

HANK (*To* SCOTTY): Do you think Arnold should stay away from Cindy? (SCOTTY *makes one squawk.*) This is remarkable!

RAFFERTY (*Watching with interest*): Yes, quite remarkable.

ARNOLD (*Uneasily; to* CINDY): Let's get out of here.

(SCOTTY *raises his arm and points to* ARNOLD. *Then he points toward exit.*)

JANET: He wants you to go, Arnold. (SCOTTY *walks slowly toward* ARNOLD, *who takes a step backward.*)

CINDY (*To* ARNOLD): Surely you're not afraid of a robot?

ARNOLD: Of course not! (*He sidesteps, trying to get out of* SCOTTY*'s way. Everywhere* ARNOLD *goes,* SCOTTY *follows. They circle table, chairs, etc. Finally* SCOTTY, *behind* ARNOLD*'s back, raises one foot.*)

JANET (*Yelling*): Watch out!

SUE: He'll mangle you, Arnold!

HANK: Run, man, run! (ARNOLD *panics and runs out.* SCOTTY *stalks slowly after him.*)

CINDY: I didn't know Arnold was such a coward! (*Before* SCOTTY *reaches exit,* RAFFERTY *bars his way, an amused look on his face.*)

RAFFERTY: All right, Roscoe, the game is over. Stand right where you are. (SCOTTY *stands still, as* RAFFERTY *places plaster cast on floor.*) Here—try this on for size, Roscoe. (SCOTTY *puts a foot on the print.*) O.K., wise guy—take off your head. (*All but* CINDY *and* HANK *gasp as* SCOTTY *removes Roscoe's head.*)

MRS. POMEROY: Scotty!

SCOTTY: I feel like a sardine in a can.

RAFFERTY: And you're wearing a red jacket.

SCOTTY: Yes, sir. (*To* MRS. POMEROY) I can explain everything. Since this is Clean-up Week, I thought you put your vacuum cleaner out to be picked up by the trash collectors.

MRS. POMEROY: But what about the footprints?

SCOTTY: I did that, too—just for a joke.

CINDY: Anything for a laugh, that's Scotty.

MRS. POMEROY: And the noises?

SCOTTY: It must have been me working on Roscoe.

(*Reaches inside Roscoe's head and turns off flashlight.*) And I guess this is the light you've been seeing.

RAFFERTY: Scotty, I'm afraid you'll have to come with me.

CINDY (*Standing in front of* SCOTTY): You can't arrest a scientist!

SCOTTY: Thanks, Cindy, but I'd better stop kidding myself. I can't make a robot. I guess I knew all along I really couldn't make one.

CINDY: Maybe you could if you keep on trying.

SCOTTY: I doubt it. This whole thing is just a joke—on me.

CINDY: I'm sorry, Scotty.

SCOTTY: All I'll ever be good at is making people laugh.

MRS. POMEROY: And what's wrong with that? (*To* RAFFERTY) Officer, I don't want him arrested. I want him in my children's show!

SCOTTY: W-what?

MRS. POMEROY: Could you work up a robot act, with Cindy and your friend to help you?

SCOTTY: *Could* I!

HANK: Scotty would wow the kids!

MRS. POMEROY: Then it's settled. (*To* SCOTTY) Scotty, it's a fine thing to have a scientific mind. But being able to make people laugh is also a great gift. Be proud of it. (*She exits.*)

RAFFERTY (*Grinning*): Next time, keep your big feet out of other people's gardens. And it's a good thing I didn't need a can opener to get you out of that getup! (*He exits.*)

SCOTTY: Mind if I keep my head? I nearly lost it a while ago. (*Puts Roscoe's head on again and turns to* CINDY *with arms stiffly outstretched. She laughs and takes his hands.* JANET *and* SUE *join in laughter, as curtain closes.*)

THE END

Ride the Gooberville Stage!

by Betty Tracy Huff

Characters

GWENDOLYN BEAMISH, *the new schoolmarm from back East*
TUMBLEWEED KID, *alias the* OLD-TIMER
RANCID NASEBY
ED SOMMERS, *Sheriff*
MRS. SOMMERS, *his wife*
PETE
GUS
PRUDENCE MANNERS, *girl shotgun guard*
PROFESSOR DIXON
CORA, DORA, FLORA — *his daughters*
LITTLE BIRD, *his assistant*

TIME: *The 1870's.*

SETTING: *The stagecoach depot in the little western town of Gooberville.*

AT RISE: PETE, *the ticket agent, is sitting with his feet up on the counter, and his chair tipped back, reading a newspaper.* PROFESSOR DIXON *enters, wearing an old-fashioned suit with a high silk hat. Behind him come* CORA, DORA, *and* FLORA. LITTLE BIRD, *in Indian costume, brings up the rear.*

PROFESSOR DIXON (*Sweeping off his hat and waving it*): Dixon's the name! Medicine's my game!

LITTLE BIRD (*Standing with her arms folded*): Medicine made from secret Indian recipe of my tribe, the Messy-Quik-Kooks. (FLORA, DORA, *and* CORA *hold up old-fashioned bottles labeled "Dixon's Elixir," and wave them in the air.*)

CORA, DORA, *and* FLORA (*Together*):
Professor Dixon's Elixir!
No matter what ails yer, it'll fix yer!

PETE: Save it, folks! The Gooberville stagecoach isn't in yet. There's nobody here but me, and I've already got enough of the Professor's tonic to take a bath in it. (*Girls groan, and put away tonic bottles.*)

PROFESSOR: No matter, Pete. We shall look upon this as a rehearsal.

CORA: Gee, Little Bird, you were the one who was so anxious to get down to the depot today. Now we're too early!

LITTLE BIRD (*Going over to counter*): The Gooberville stage, Pete? When will it arrive?

PETE (*Handing her newspaper*): According to what this paper says, Little Bird, they'll be lucky if they get here at all without being stopped by the Tumbleweed Kid.

LITTLE BIRD (*Throwing newspaper down onto counter*): Paleface press prints with forked type! Handsome young Tumbleweed Kid is innocent—innocent, I tell you! (PROFESSOR, CORA, DORA *and* FLORA *pick up newspaper and read it, pushing each other out of the way.*)

PETE: All right, Little Bird, there's no need to go on the warpath about it. I always liked the Tumbleweed Kid, myself. He was a good boss to us up until he lost the stagecoach line to Mr. Rancid Naseby and turned outlaw.

CORA (*Exclaiming over newspaper*): It says here Tumbleweed tries to stop every coach that goes by, so he can steal the strongbox.

FLORA: Of course, he's never succeeded in stopping a single stage!

PROFESSOR: But you have to give the boy credit. He tries! (*From offstage, sounds of hoofbeats, rumbling wheels, etc., are heard.*)

GUS (*Shouting, from offstage*): Whoa! Whoa, critters! Step down, folks. Gooberville! Gooberville! (LITTLE BIRD *kneels and puts her ear to the ground.*)

LITTLE BIRD: Old Indian trick tell me that coach has arrived.

PROFESSOR: Come, Dora, Cora, Flora, let's get the rest of our props, so that we can give the passengers a real show. (PROFESSOR *and his daughters exit.* PETE *hurries to door as* GUS, *heavily laden with several carpetbags and a mail pouch, enters.*)

PETE: Gee, Gus, you took me by surprise! The coach has never been so nearly on time before.

GUS (*Putting down bags*): We set a new record! (*With a contemptuous gesture at poster*) Ninety miles in ninety hours, ha! We made one hundred miles in one hundred hours. How about that, Pete, huh?

PETE (*Admiringly*): Whew! That sure is going some! Yup, that sure is flying!

GUS: Kept thinking I could hear the Tumbleweed Kid riding behind us. It sure speeded us up! That, plus imagining what Mr. Naseby would say if we lost the strongbox. (MRS. SOMMERS *enters, her bonnet crooked, fanning herself with her handkerchief. The* OLD-TIMER *supports her left arm, and* GWENDOLYN BEAMISH *her right.* OLD-TIMER *wears a long, long white beard, obviously false.*)

MRS. SOMMERS: What a trip! The speed!

GWENDOLYN: Dear Mrs. Sommers, pray compose yourself.

OLD-TIMER: Sit down right here, ma'am. (*He dusts off bench with the tip of his beard.*)

MRS. SOMMERS (*Sitting down, still fanning herself*): Ah, Old-Timer, sir, what would I have done without the aid of your steadying hand when we hit the rough spots on that long and rocky road.

GWENDOLYN: And I, Gwendolyn Beamish, modest though I am, must mention that being the new schoolmarm, from back East, of course, I did my best to improve the education of my fellow passengers by conducting an impromptu spelling bee.

MRS. SOMMERS (*With a telling look at* GWENDOLYN): Ooooh! Am I exhausted!

PETE (*Bringing over a carpetbag*): Is this all your baggage, Mrs. Sommers?

MRS. SOMMERS: No, Prudence is bringing in the rest of my packages from the coach. Have you seen my husband yet? He promised to bring the surrey to carry me and my parcels home.

PETE: No, Mrs. Sommers. We haven't seen the sheriff today. Guess he'll be here as soon as he's through chasing the Tumbleweed Kid.

OLD-TIMER: The sheriff! The sheriff is coming here? (*He reels back with his hand to his brow, then looks around furtively to see if anyone has noticed.* PETE, MRS. SOMMERS *and* GWENDOLYN *are talking aside, and do not hear.* GUS *sorts mail, reading a few postcards.*)

LITTLE BIRD (*Cupping her hand to her ear*): That voice! Do my keen Indian ears deceive me? (*She goes over to* OLD-TIMER *and pulls down his beard, peering at his face, and showing audience that beard is false.*) The Tumbleweed Kid! (*She lets beard snap back onto his face and peers nervously at others. No one notices her action.*)

TUMBLEWEED (*His voice muffled by beard*): M-m-m-m-f?

GUS (*Crossing to them*): What'd he say?

LITTLE BIRD: He said m-m-m-m-f!

GUS: That's what I thought he said. (*Goes back to reading postcards*)

TUMBLEWEED (*Drawing* LITTLE BIRD *downstage*): Careful, Little Bird, lest we are observed. If anyone suspects that under this disguise I am really the brave, handsome and misjudged young outlaw, I am undone!

LITTLE BIRD: Tumbleweed can trust Little Bird not to sing. I see your smoke signal in sky. Come fast with Professor and his daughters to meet coach. Now, what's up?

TUMBLEWEED: I heard, via an anonymous letter, that there would be documents in the strongbox which would clear my name and restore to me the ownership of the Gooberville Stage line. Unfortunately the letter did not say which coach had the documents, so I tried to stop them all, without success, until I had the marvelous inspiration for this new disguise.

LITTLE BIRD: You plenty wise. Coach now guarded well by Prudence Manners, girl shotgun rider. Tumbleweed has plan for breaking and entering strongbox?

TUMBLEWEED (*Dramatically*): Time will find out the way!

LITTLE BIRD: Time? Alas, Little Bird must fly now, to make ready for medicine show. The professor and his daughters await me, the star! (LITTLE BIRD *exits, very dramatically, just as* RANCID NASEBY *enters.*)

TUMBLEWEED (*Starting back, his hand to his brow*): Rancid Naseby, the author of all my misfortunes, here in person!

RANCID (*With false sweetness*): Dear employees, did the cookies my dear old mama made for me come in the strongbox tonight? (*Aside to audience, twirling his mustache*) Little do they dream that what the box really contains is the forged document which enabled me to foreclose the mortgage, and thereby gain ownership of Tumbleweed's flourishing stagecoach line!

PETE: Sorry, Mr. Naseby, sir. We haven't had time to unload the strongbox yet. We've got to sort the mail first —union rules! (PETE *hurries over to help* GUS *with the letters.*)

RANCID: Rancid Naseby waits for no mail! Cross me and it will be the worse for you. (*He raises his fist threateningly.* GUS *and* PETE *cower.* GWENDOLYN *screams, and rushes over to* RANCID, *catching his arm.*)

GWENDOLYN: Cease this deplorable violence, sir. Desist, I say!

RANCID (*Dropping his hand; awestruck*): How brave! How beautiful! (*Raises his hat, bowing low to* GWENDOLYN) I am smitten! I lay my stagecoach line, my heart, and the box of Mom's cookies at your feet. (*Clutches* GWENDOLYN'*s hand*)

GWENDOLYN (*Trying to get her hand back*): Sir, I have heard of Western hospitality, but this is ridiculous.

TUMBLEWEED (*Darting forward*): Unhand that lady, you villain, you!

RANCID (*Dropping* GWENDOLYN'*s hand and moving toward* TUMBLEWEED): Don't I know you from somewhere?

TUMBLEWEED (*Hastily*): No, I've never been there!

RANCID: Take warning, stranger. Do not interfere in the budding romance between me and this charming newcomer, or it will be the worse for you.

TUMBLEWEED (*Aside*): Oh, dreadful dilemma! I wish to save Gwendolyn from the clutches of this villain. Yet I must remain incognito if ever I am to get the documents Naseby hid in the strongbox.

RANCID (*Turning to* GWENDOLYN): We were saying, Miss . . . er. . . .

GWENDOLYN (*Dropping a curtsy*): Gwendolyn Beamish, sir.

I am the new schoolmarm, from back East, of course. And you, sir?

RANCID: Call me Rancid, ma'am. Dare I hope you will allow me the privilege of showing you around beautiful downtown Gooberville? (*Banging and thumping sounds are heard from offstage, and* PRUDENCE, *girl shotgun rider, enters. She is staggering under the weight of the strongbox. Parcels hang around her neck, more packages are under her arms, and a hatbox dangles at her back.*)

PRUDENCE (*Putting down strongbox with a thud, sitting on it, mopping her brow with a bright bandanna*): Oh, marvelous privilege! Rancid Naseby is an equal opportunity employer. Therefore, even though I am only a girl, I am allowed to do all the really interesting chores around here—unloading the strongbox, cleaning the stables, and riding shotgun when there are dangerous outlaws around.

RANCID *and* TUMBLEWEED (*Together*): The strongbox!

RANCID: Oh, goody! Mom's cookies have arrived! Come, Pete, let's open the strongbox.

PETE: Sorry, Mr. Rancid. Mail first, remember.

RANCID (*Aside*): Curse the rules! If Tumbleweed shows up here and gets a load of that forged mortgage which I so unwisely put in the box, I am undone! (CORA *and* DORA *enter, carrying signs which read* DIXON'S ELIXIR *and* IF IT'S CHRONIC, TRY OUR TONIC. *As* RANCID *sees these signs, he begins shouting.*) I do so pay my employees their wages—sometimes! (*Looks again at signs*) Dixon's Elixir . . . gee, for a moment there I thought this was a protest meeting. Sorry. (PROFESSOR *and* FLORA *enter, carrying a trunk which they put down at center.* LITTLE BIRD *enters and stands to one side of trunk, arms folded.*)

PETE (*Anxiously*): Is this all right, Mr. Naseby? I told the Professor he could entertain the passengers.

RANCID (*Expansively*): Certainly! Certainly! It will amuse

our fair newcomer from back East. (GWENDOLYN *curtsies. Aside*) While the show is going on, and everyone's attention is elsewhere, I shall seize the opportunity to remove the documents from the strongbox! (*He rubs his hands in glee.* CORA *and* DORA *put their signs aside and take tambourines from trunk.* PROFESSOR *takes out a few bottles of elixir.* GWENDOLYN, TUMBLEWEED, MRS. SOMMERS, PETE, GUS *and* PRUDENCE *gather around to watch medicine show, sitting on bench or chairs.* RANCID *sits on strongbox.* CORA, DORA, FLORA *and* PROFESSOR *line up and sing, to the tune of "Home on the Range."*)

CORA, DORA, FLORA, *and* PROFESSOR:

Oh, it's Dixon's for you,
If you've got the flu,
And it's good for your furniture, too.
It will cure all your aches
And repair all your breaks,
And your moustache will gleam with it, too.

(*Girls hum as* PROFESSOR *stands on trunk.*)

PROFESSOR: Friends, Little Bird told me the secret formula for this marvelous tonic, known only to her tribe. And what do you think of this grand universal specific, Little Bird?

LITTLE BIRD: Ugh!

PROFESSOR: Another satisfied user! Folks, we're not asking two dollars for this marvelous remedy. Not one dollar, folks! We're giving it away! Yes, that's right, giving it away! All you pay is five dollars and fifty cents for the cost of the container and the wrapping paper. Plus tax. Five dollars and fifty cents, folks, for this grand gout cure and paint remover. No home should be without it.

TUMBLEWEED (*Aside*): Though I have known Gwendolyn for only a short while, yet I feel the pangs of my unspoken love for her burning, burning, I tell you! (*To* PROFESSOR) Professor Dixon, a bottle of your elixir! With my last piece of gold I buy it. (*He hands over coin and takes bottle from* PROFESSOR.) Yet I want not this marvelous mixture for myself. Gwendolyn, I give it to you, as a token of my love!

GWENDOLYN (*Taking the bottle*): Sir, your kindness overwhelms me.

LITTLE BIRD (*Aside*): Ugh! Situation turn rotten. Little Bird love Tumbleweed for many moons. Then, pffft! He's off with first schoolmarm from back East who hits town. Paleface has heap fickle heart. Little Bird has heap big problem. But have swell idea for revenge. When time is ripe, shall snitch on Tumbleweed Kid to Rancid Naseby! (*The* PROFESSOR, CORA, DORA *and* FLORA *are busily selling bottles of the elixir to* PRUDENCE, MRS. SOMMERS *and* GUS. LITTLE BIRD *crosses over to* RANCID NASEBY *and touches him on the shoulder as he surreptitiously works on the lock of the strongbox. He gives a startled yell.*)

RANCID (*Guiltily*): Just, er, seeing that the strongbox is securely fastened.

LITTLE BIRD: Is not time for fiddling with locks, Rancid Paleface. Is time for seeking revenge against the erstwhile object of my dreams. Know, then, Mr. Naseby, that Tumbleweed Kid and the Old-Timer are one and the same!

RANCID: Why, you don't say! I shall now scheme . . . I mean, meditate, on how to reveal Tumbleweed's true identity without losing my reputation for sweetness and light, and the good opinion of the fair Gwendolyn. (*He stalks around, muttering and shaking his head.* SHERIFF *enters.*)

SHERIFF (*Going over to* MRS. SOMMERS): Welcome home, Delphine! How was your trip to the city?

MRS. SOMMERS: Exhausting, Ed. It's good to be back in

Gooberville where we don't have all those carriages and velocipedes jamming up the roads.

RANCID (*Aside*): The sheriff! In the nick of time to see me unmask Tumbleweed! (*He crosses over to the* PROFESSOR) Oh, that marvelous elixir! I have heard much of its rejuvenative properties! Let us try some upon the face of the Old-Timer.

TUMBLEWEED (*Hastily*): Gee, thanks, but, no thanks! I . . . I've just remembered another appointment! (*He starts to hurry off.* RANCID *grabs* TUMBLEWEED *and pretends to rub his face with elixir, removing* TUMBLEWEED'*s false beard in the process.*)

MRS. SOMMERS: It works! The elixir works! Ed, get me a couple of casefuls!

RANCID (*In exaggerated surprise*): Heavens to Betsy! The Tumbleweed Kid! (GUS, SHERIFF *and* PETE *whirl around. Ladies squeal.*)

GUS: The Tumbleweed Kid!

SHERIFF: Gee, it's the outlaw in disguise!

TUMBLEWEED: Oh, I am undone! Methinks Little Bird has a big mouth!

GWENDOLYN: How handsome he is! Oh, be still, my beating heart. Can the gift of a bottle of Professor Dixon's Elixir be the same as a frat pin?

TUMBLEWEED: I stand before you innocent, misjudged . . . the victim of the machinations of the villainous Rancid Naseby.

RANCID: Do my ears deceive me? Such accusations!

TUMBLEWEED: The truth soon will out! According to an anonymous letter I received, there are even now documents in yonder strongbox crudely forged by Rancid Naseby! They will show me to be the rightful owner of the Gooberville Stage!

GWENDOLYN: Oh, suspense! Will the documents prove that

Rancid is indeed the villain? Or is my present girlish fancy for Tumbleweed doomed?

SHERIFF: You have a key to the storeroom, Pete?

PETE: Sure! (*Hands key to* SHERIFF)

SHERIFF: Then I'll just put Tumbleweed in storage for a while. (SHERIFF *exits with* TUMBLEWEED.)

RANCID: All this talk about Mom's cookies has made me hungry. I'll just mosey along to beautiful downtown Gooberville and get a sandwich. Come along, Little Bird. (*They exit.* SHERIFF *re-enters, rubbing his hands together.*)

SHERIFF: Tumbleweed won't get out of there in a hurry! Come on, Delphine, while we're waiting for further developments, let's take your luggage out to the surrey. (*Looking at piles of boxes and carpetbags*) That ought to keep us busy for quite a while! (SHERIFF *and* MRS. SOMMERS *exit, carrying boxes.*)

GWENDOLYN: Professor Dixon, isn't there some way we can help Tumbleweed escape?

CORA: The coast is clear now, Pop.

DORA: Tumbleweed was always our friend—he gave us rides on the stage and everything.

FLORA: If only we had the storeroom key!

PROFESSOR: Why do we need a key? Dixon's Elixir can do anything! (PROFESSOR *exits, carrying a bottle of elixir.*)

GUS: Great! Now, if we only had some disguise for Tumbleweed so he could get away from here. . . .

DORA: No sooner said than done! Here, Flora, Cora, help me get some things out of the trunk. (*They pull open trunk as* PROFESSOR *re-enters with* TUMBLEWEED.)

PROFESSOR (*Looking at bottle of elixir with pride*): It ate right through the lock!

CORA: We've got the perfect disguise for you, Tumbleweed.

GWENDOLYN: Hurry, Tumbleweed. Put on these clothes

before the Sheriff comes back! (GWENDOLYN, CORA, DORA *and* FLORA *put a hat, wig and long shapeless dress on* TUMBLEWEED.)

CORA (*Surveying the effect*): Oh, dear!

GWENDOLYN (*Handing* TUMBLEWEED *one of the large signs*): This will help! (*He holds sign in front of his face.*)

FLORA: That's an improvement. (SHERIFF *and* MRS. SOMMERS *enter.*)

MRS. SOMMERS: Goodness, Professor! Seems to me you've acquired another offspring!

PROFESSOR: Merely a cousin from out of town, Mrs. Sommers. (TUMBLEWEED *waves from behind the sign.*)

CORA: She's very shy!

MRS. SOMMERS: Poor little thing! Maybe I . . .

PROFESSOR (*Hastily*): Show's about to begin! (*He lines up with* CORA, DORA, FLORA *and* TUMBLEWEED *in front of trunk at center.*)

CORA: I'm Cora.

DORA: I'm Dora.

FLORA: I'm Flora.

TUMBLEWEED (*In falsetto*): And I'm Fauna! (CORA, DORA, *and* FLORA *sit on trunk and beat time with their tambourines as the* PROFESSOR *recites.*)

PROFESSOR: What's the tonic that's best throughout the West? (*He shows label to* TUMBLEWEED, *pointing to letters one by one.*)

TUMBLEWEED (*Repeating letters*): D-I-X-O-N-S. Dixon's?

PROFESSOR: Yes, that's right, it's Dixon's! What makes leather supple, and tones up every muscle? (*He gives* TUMBLEWEED *a dig in the ribs.*)

TUMBLEWEED: Dixon's?

CORA, DORA, FLORA *and* PROFESSOR (*Together*): That's right, it's Dixon's! (CORA, FLORA, *and* DORA *do a little dance, still sitting down, keeping time with tambourines and moving their feet as* PROFESSOR *claps.*)

PROFESSOR (*Concluding the number*): It's Dixon's! (*The medicine show company lines up, and headed by* PROFESSOR *begins to file past trunk, each dancing and holding up a bottle of elixir.* LITTLE BIRD *enters, jumps up onto trunk and as* TUMBLEWEED *files past, she lifts off his bonnet and wig. He goes on dancing, not realizing what has happened, then pats his head and gradually comes to a stop.*)

SHERIFF: Tumbleweed! Obviously the storeroom is unsafe. Let us adjourn to the hoosegow.

TUMBLEWEED (*Throwing off long dress*): You can't take me to jail without a wanted poster! It's the code of the old West! (RANCID *enters, munching on a sandwich.*)

RANCID (*Pouncing on a large envelope in pile of mail*): Wanted poster? Look what just came in the mail for you, Sheriff!

SHERIFF: Thanks, Rancid!

GWENDOLYN: Even now all is not lost! Keep a stout heart, Tumbleweed! (*Aside*) Fearful though I am, I shall now try to get the wanted poster first, before the sheriff sees it! (*To* SHERIFF) Allow me to help you, sir. (GUS *and* PETE *bring up two chairs which they place at trunk, center.* SHERIFF *and* GWENDOLYN *sit opposite each other.* SHERIFF *opens envelope, takes out a pile of posters, deals them face down to himself and* GWENDOLYN. *With a dramatic flourish, she takes the top poster from her pile and puts it in the center of the trunk, face up.* SHERIFF *takes a poster from his pile and puts it on top of hers.*)

GUS (*Carried away*): Snap!

ALL (*Together; to* GUS): S-s-s-sh! (GWENDOLYN *plays another poster.*)

GWENDOLYN (*Leaping up*): Goodness, it's a picture of—

SHERIFF: Rancid Naseby!

RANCID: And look at the cheesey reward they're offering for me! Five dollars! Heck, I'll give a hundred.

SHERIFF (*Grimly*): Done!

PRUDENCE: Rancid is unmasked! The time is ripe! Know, then, that I am not really the lowly chore girl around here. I am Prudence Parker, girl detective! Employed by the Pinkerton Agency, Wells Fargo, and others of that ilk. It was I who wrote Tumbleweed that anonymous letter which sent him on his chase after the strongbox.

GUS (*Excitedly*): And now that the mail is sorted?

PRUDENCE: The box can be opened! (*She takes out a key from her pocket and unlocks the strongbox.*)

GWENDOLYN: Dare I hope Tumbleweed will be reinstated into the ranks of the law-abiding?

PRUDENCE (*Taking out a magnifying glass, and looking at the documents which she has taken from the strongbox*): Aha! These documents were indeed forged by the dastardly Rancid Naseby!

SHERIFF (*Looking at documents*): We may now indeed count Tumbleweed again on the side of the innocent, and the rightful owner of the mortgaged Gooberville Stage.

GUS: Gee, that means we get our old boss back!

TUMBLEWEED: Gwendolyn, I lay the Gooberville Stagecoach line, *et cetera, et cetera,* at your feet! May I hope you will be mine?

GWENDOLYN: Oh, happy day which led me to ride the Gooberville Stage!

SHERIFF: As for you, Rancid, we must have a little talk forthwith, down at my office, to determine which of the many states in which you are wanted shall be the first to claim you for its own.

LITTLE BIRD: Oh, Rancid, now that Tumbleweed is unavailable, my loyal Indian heart is drawn to you. I shall wait forever for your return to Gooberville.

RANCID: With such a future ahead of me, can I do aught but reform? A pencil, Little Bird, quickly, that I may write my good resolution down. (LITTLE BIRD *gives him pencil. Unnoticed by others, he starts to work over wanted poster.*)

PROFESSOR: For a wedding gift to Tumbleweed and Gwendolyn, a lifetime supply of my marvelous elixir!

TUMBLEWEED: Oh, goody, just what I always wanted.

SHERIFF: Time to be moving, Rancid!

RANCID: Just a moment, Sheriff. There's been a terrible mistake! This wanted poster cannot, after all, be a likeness of yours truly, Rancid Naseby!

SHERIFF: What? (*He snatches up the poster.*)

RANCID: Do I wear spectacles, do I have a long black beard? (*He hides the pencil behind his back.*)

SHERIFF (*Thoughtfully*): I wonder if Dixon's Elixir can be used as a pencil eraser?

RANCID: Let us fly, Little Bird. Dixon's Elixir can do anything! (RANCID *and* LITTLE BIRD *exit.*)

PROFESSOR: A testimonial from another satisfied customer! (CORA, FLORA *and* DORA *line up behind* PROFESSOR, *shaking tambourines. They begin a snake dance.* SHERIFF, MRS. SOMMERS, GUS, PETE *and* PRUDENCE *join the dance.*)

TUMBLEWEED (*Taking* GWENDOLYN'*s hand*): Let's go ride the Gooberville Stage! (*They exit, followed by dancers, as curtains close.*)

THE END

Hamelot

Royalty on the romp

by Elinor R. Alderman

Characters

KING SIRE, *King of Hamelot*
QUEEN GWENNY, *his wife*
PRINCESS AMNESIA, *their beautiful daughter*
LANCE OF FRANCE, *the King's new valet and suitor to Amnesia*
MERVAC, *the Royal Computer*
LADY PATIENCE, *the Queen's lady in waiting*
LIONEL, *page and train-bearer to the King*
THE GRAND VIZIER, *a villain*
BILLY, *the King's son*
PIPER
JOUSTER
FIVE KNIGHTS OF THE ROYAL POOL TABLE

SETTING: *Throne room of King Sire's castle.*

AT RISE: *The set is empty for a moment and then* MERVAC *enters, followed at a discreet distance by* LIONEL, *carrying a small toy trumpet.* MERVAC *carries a can of air spray and a pool cue decorated with magical signs and symbols. He sprays the air freely, gives the royal throne*

one good squirt, turns smartly toward the audience and steps forward.

MERVAC (*Thumping pool cue*): Hear ye! Hear ye! Hear ye! (LIONEL *gives a small "toot" on the trumpet.*) The Royal Court of His Majesty King Sire, supreme ruler of Hamelot, noble founder of the Loyal Order of Loyal Knights of the Royal Pool Table, sole possessor of the Magical Cue "Excalibrated" . . . (*He runs out of breath.* LIONEL *toots trumpet. He glares at him.*) will-nowbeinsession. (*Gesturing with spray can*) Her Royal Majesty, Queen Gwenny! (QUEEN GWENNY *enters sweepingly. She carries a lap board.*)

QUEEN GWENNY (*In a throaty, deep voice*): Dahling! (*Over her shoulder*) Come along, Pasty! Don't dawdle!

MERVAC: And her loyal lady in waiting, the Lady Patience! (PATIENCE *enters behind* QUEEN, *loaded to the eyeballs with the* QUEEN'*s gear. She carries a feather duster, a cushion for the* QUEEN'*s chair, several packs of playing cards, a box of chocolates, a sweater, a fan, an oversized purse and a small blackboard on legs. On this is printed:* SCOREBOARD, *and, under that,* QUEEN . . . VISITORS. *She has a piece of white chalk between her teeth.*)

PATIENCE (*Bobbing; through the chalk*): 'Morning, Mervy. (QUEEN *has seated herself, lap board in place. Throughout the rest of the introductions she and* PATIENCE *set up for the* QUEEN'*s game of solitaire, which continues throughout the play.* PATIENCE *changes score occasionally.*)

MERVAC (*Gesturing with cue*): Her Royal Majesty number two, the Princess Amnesia! (*Pauses. Nothing happens. He sighs and glances to heavens.*) *Every* time! Every single time! (*Louder*) I *said,* the Princess Amnesia!

AMNESIA (*From offstage; squealing*): Ooh, that's me! (*She enters. She is very beautiful and very friendly. She car-*

ries a large notebook marked SCRIPT, *with a finger between the covers, marking her place. She beams at audience*) Well, hi there! Oh, wow! (*To* MERVAC) That's a *good* house—I thought you said nobody would . . . (*Her voice trails off as he pointedly looks away from her, resolutely staying in character.* LIONEL *toots at her.*) . . . come. Oh, well . . . (*She gives audience a small, apologetic smile and goes sedately to her chair. Opening notebook, she follows the script with one finger and enormous concentration. She does this throughout the play, reading all of her lines.*)

MERVAC: The Loyal Members of the Loyal Order of . . .

AMNESIA (*Leaning forward*): Pss-s-s-s-t!

MERVAC (*Aside, still facing front*): Now what?

AMNESIA (*In a stage whisper*): You forgot *Lance* . . . *again!*

MERVAC: Oh, yes. Him. (*Announcing, flat*) His un-royal, over-rated suitor to the Princess Amnesia, Lance of France. (LANCE *bounds on stage, gives audience a smile and a victory handshake over his head, goes directly to his position behind* AMNESIA. *She lets him hold the hand that she isn't using to follow the script.*) The Loyal Members of the Loyal Order of Loyal Knights of the Royal Pool Table! (LIONEL *does what he can in the way of a fanfare on his trumpet.* KNIGHTS OF THE POOL TABLE *enter in racked formation. Each carries a pool cue flying his number from a pennant attached to the end. They bow formally, in unison, to the audience, and take places around the pool table.*) And *now*— (*To* KNIGHTS) You all ready for this?

KNIGHTS (*Snappily*): Ready, Mervac! (*Pause*)

AMNESIA: Oh! I'm ready, Mervy! (*Stabbing the script*) I'm right there.

QUEEN GWENNY (*Not looking up from her game*): *Really,* dahling—do get on with it. You over-play all this dreadfully, you know . . . (*Sighs, to the cards*) *Where* is that ace. . . .

MERVAC: His Majesty, King Sire! (*Pool cues click,* MERVAC *sprays vigorously,* LIONEL *toots away on the trumpet and everybody stands up. The* QUEEN *holds onto her lap board but cards slide to floor.* PATIENCE *gathers them up as* KING SIRE *enters. He is not very big. He is trailing a small, child's train on a piece of string.*)

KING: Morning, all. At ease. Morning, Mervac—how's the old computer today? Better go warm up your tubes, we have a lot of work ahead of us. (*Rubs his hands together briskly, sending cars of train flying in all directions.*) Oops! Sorry about that, Lionel! But then, that's what I pay you for, isn't it? (LIONEL *tucks his trumpet into a hip pocket and picks up train, taking it offstage and re-entering.*) Good boy, that Lionel. Best train-bearer a king ever had! (MERVAC *goes to his computer equipment and turns dials, etc.* KING *settles into his throne, picking up Excalibrated, which he uses throughout. To the* QUEEN, *reabsorbed in her game*) Morning, Gwenny —how's my little Queen of Hearts this morning?

QUEEN GWENNY (*Offering her cheek, not looking up*): Dahling! (*To the cards*) Ah, *there* it is . . .

AMNESIA (*Brightly, reading her line*): Good morning, Daddy!

KING: Amnesia! The light of my life! (*To audience*) Beautiful, isn't she? (*Looking at the top of her head*) Just beautiful! Look at me, child!

AMNESIA (*In a stage whisper; urgently*): I *can't*—I'll lose my place!

KING: Just keep your finger on it, won't take a second. (*She plants the finger, flashes him a quick smile and goes back to script.*) Lovely! Lovely girl. Now if only our only son, the one and only . . . (*Stops, re-says the line to him-*

self.) Too many "onlys" in that line, Mervac. Make a note of it.

MERVAC (*Back to audience*): Breep?

KING (*Looking*): Sorry. Didn't realize you were turned on . . . (*In turning to look at* MERVAC, *he sees* LANCE *for the first time.*)

LANCE (*With a nervous smile*): Good morning, Your Majesty!

KING: Who's this character? (*Silence*) I *said,* who's this character?

AMNESIA: Oh! (*Reading, carefully*) Why, you remember *Lance,* Daddy. This is *Lance.* He has come to the Court to be your new *var*let!

LANCE (*Brightly*): Yes, Sire! I am Lance, your new . . . (*Leaning over script.*) Let me see that! That's *valet,* stupid. Boy, are you . . . (*Overwhelmed*) beautiful! (*Back in character*) Yes, Sire. I am Lance of France, your new *valet.* I am come to do your bidding!

KING: You am?

LANCE: Yes, Your Highness.

KING: Well, now . . . (*Swinging his legs over arm of throne, playing with Excalibrated*) that's very thoughtful of you. Unfortunately, I always have it sent out . . . what else can you do?

LANCE: Well, Sir—Sire—I mean, King Sire, Sir—

KING: Maybe you'd better show me . . .

LANCE: Yes, Sir. Actually, Your Majesty, I have always been considered more a man of action than a man of words.

KING: I can believe that . . .

LANCE: Yes, Sir. In my native France I was well known for my tilting and jousting, not to mention getting the eight-ball into the side pocket.

KING: Is that so? A jouster, eh? I've always wanted a good jouster in my court . . .

MERVAC (*Clearing his throat loudly*): Ahem!

KING: What is it, Mervac? Transistor trouble?

MERVAC: No, Sir. It's just that I think you should know, we already have a jouster on the agenda.

KING: We have, really? What's he doing out there? Bring him in and we'll give him an audience. (*Looking out*) Not much of an audience . . . go on, son—anything else?

LANCE: Well, Sir, that's about it, I guess. Of course, if you're interested, I sing a good deal.

KING (*Fast*): I'm not . . .

LANCE: And I (*Deadpan*) lance a lot. (*In unison, the* KNIGHTS *groan and droop on their pool cues.*)

KING (*Waving Excalibrated at them*): O.K., boys, O.K. Straighten up. You knew it was coming when you read the cast list. (*They straighten up*) Let's see, now, where were we . . .

LANCE (*Eager to help*): I had just said . . .

KING (*Turning away from him*): Never mind! (*Seeing* QUEEN *again, hard at her game*) My little Diamond! The Queen of Solitaire! How's the game coming, my love? (*Scoreboard now reads* QUEEN 5, VISITORS 0.) Not bad—it's only ten o'clock. (*As he turns away, airily*) Black six on the red seven . . . (*She glares at him.*) Well, back to business. Mervac!

MERVAC: Yes, Your Majesty.

KING: What's the latest bulletin on the Grand Vizier?

MERVAC (*In shock*): The Grand Vizier, Sir?

KING (*Firmly*): The Grand Vizier, Mervac. (KNIGHTS *come to attention. Their pool cues quiver.* LANCE *looks fierce.* AMNESIA *shuts her eyes and goes "eek."* LIONEL *goes toot on his trumpet. The* QUEEN *alone is oblivious.*)

SIR EIGHT-BALL (*Aside to audience*): In case you people out there didn't catch on, this Vy-zeer cat they're rapping about is the *villain* of the piece. We don't have a whole lot of plot, but we have *all* the characters.

MERVAC: The Grand Vizier?

KING: That's right, Mervy—the Grand Vizier. (*He paces floor, speaking to audience.*) Our mortal enemy and chief of the barbaric gypsy tribes that kidnapped our only son, Billy, when he was but an innocent lad of seventeen. The Grand Vizier, against whom we have so valiantly striven these many years, assembling the forces of Purity and Goodness that you see before you: our Loyal Order of Loyal Knights of the Royal Pool Table. (*Relaxing back into his throne.*) How's that for a classy piece of exposition? (*To* MERVAC) What news, O ancient and honorable Computer?

MERVAC (*At his controls, snapping on various switches*): I'll see, Sir. (*Buzzes, squawks, and wails issue from speakers.*)

VIZIER'S VOICE (*From speaker*): . . . so listen, Knights, don't be half safe: use Grand Vizier chalk on *your* cues, and *make* those bank shots. (*Pause.*) On the local front, the Grand Vizier continues to make good progress against the cowardly, scurrilous—but puny—forces of that super-crumb, King Sire! (KNIGHTS *growl and hiss and shake their cues.*) Listen! (*An assortment of terrifying sounds is heard from speakers.*) It has been estimated by an impartial panel of the Grand Vizier's confidential advisors that the Grand Vizier will reach the castle of treacherous, bandy-legged—

KING (*Who has listened serenely up to this point*): Bandy-legged?

VIZIER'S VOICE: Yes, bandy-legged King Sire, *this very day!* (KING *leaps up, flings aside royal robe, checks his legs, climbs up and over back of throne, flails away at speaker with Excalibrated.*) Further developments will be reported just as soon as we can make them uh, ahem, as soon as they come in to us from the front. Stay tuned to your Grand Vizier Network for all the . . . (MERVAC *clicks it off.*)

KING: (*Climbing back onto throne; triumphantly*): I guess I've taken care of that! Mervac! How many knights do I have?

MERVAC (*Counting*): Two, four, six, eight, ten . . . divide by two . . . *five,* Your Majesty!

KING: Five? Only *five?*

MERVAC: Yes, Sir. Five. There they are.

KING: Doesn't look like a full rack to me. What happened to the others?

MERVAC: Sir, all the Odd-Balls have left the Court!

SIR EIGHT-BALL (*To audience*): Hoo-boy! Anybody believes *that* line hasn't been listening! (SIR TEN-BALL *raises his hand.*)

KING: Yes, yes, what is it?

SIR TEN-BALL: Sir, if you'll recall, I was only recruited last night. The dinner bell rang before I could be sworn in.

KING: Not "sworn in," son. Not around here. "Be knighted," that's what we call it, "be knighted."

SIR TEN-BALL: Yes, Sir. That's what I *meant,* Sir.

KING: O.K. Come here. We'd better make it official. (SIR TEN-BALL *goes to throne,* KING *takes his cue from him, holds Excalibrated in the other hand.*) Down, boy! (SIR TEN-BALL *kneels. In bored voice, waving Excalibrated*) I, *et cetera, et cetera,* hereby proclaim you, *et cetera,* to be, *et cetera, et cetera.* (*Whack*) All right, you can get up now. There's your cue. (SIR TEN-BALL *is still reeling but he takes it*) Well?

SIR TEN-BALL: Well what, Sir?

KING: Aren't you going to say something?

SIR TEN-BALL: Say what, Sir?

KING: How do *I* know? It's *your* line—I just gave you the cue! (*Laughs. To* MERVAC) Now what, Brain? How about that jouster you said was waiting on the agenda. He still here? Maybe we could recruit *him* . . . (LIONEL *toots.*) Yes, Lionel—what is it?

LIONEL: He's still here, Sir. And there's another man—I think—with him.

KING (*Expansively*): Good, good. Show 'em in, boy. We'll sign 'em up. (LIONEL *waves toward offstage and* JOUSTER *enters, followed by the* PIPER. *Both are clumsy, and* JOUSTER *carries a bauble.* PIPER *carries a kazoo, with which he pokes the* JOUSTER *toward throne.*)

PIPER (*To* JOUSTER): Move, man, move. You're among Royalty, man. Like the King awaits us and all that jazz.

JOUSTER (*Wiggling*): Don't push! You're crushing my pleats!

PIPER: Yeah? Well, you got lint in my kazoo! (*Tests kazoo, peers into it, wipes it off on his shirt.*) Whoops! (*They arrive at throne, where* JOUSTER *prostrates himself before* KING. *The* PIPER, *busy with his kazoo, stumbles over* JOUSTER *and almost lands in* KING*'s lap.*) Sorry, your Kingship!

QUEEN GWENNY (*Not looking up*): Dahling! Do be careful! I'm almost *out!* (*Scoreboard now reads:* QUEEN 32 —VISITORS 0.)

PIPER: Yes, Ma'am.

KING (*Looking from one to the other*): Knighthood may have been in flower once, but it's certainly going to seed now. (*To* PIPER) What are you supposed to be?

PIPER: Man, your worship-ship, I'm not *supposed* to be *anything!* I *am!* To *be*—that is the answer! Yes, Sir. To *be*—that's *me!* (*Blows kazoo.*) At your service, your highness-ship, man. (*Blows*)

LANCE: Perhaps I can help, Sir . . . Sire . . . (KING *waves it off*) . . . yes, Sir. (*Pulling himself together; to* PIPER) What the King would like to know, my good fellow, is: just exactly what is it that you *do?* (AMNESIA *squeals and almost loses her place because he's so wonderful.*)

PIPER: Oh, *do!* Oh, *that!* I thought all these cats *knew* what I *do!* Man, I *pipe!*

KING *and* LANCE: Pipe?

PIPER: Yessir. Pipe! They call me the Pye-Eyed Piper of Hamelot! (*Blows kazoo flourish*) At your service—which, to tell the whole truth and nothing *but* the truth, hasn't been so hot lately.

KING (*Snapping fingers*): *Now* I remember you! I hired you to be my Royal Exterminator.

PIPER (*Sadly*): Yessir, that's it. That sure is *it.* (*Again to himself, shaking his head*) Just can't figure why they don't *follow* me. (*Blows kazoo, musingly*) I blow and I blow, but they just don't listen. . . . Sometimes I even *call.* I call real *sweet.* Here, I'll show you. . . . (*Takes center stage. Flourish. Gives the kazoo a blast, then leans over from the waist with his hand out in offering*) Here kittykittykittykitty, here kittykittykitty. . . .

KING: Kittykittykitty? For *rats?*

PIPER: Rats?

KING: Rats.

PIPER (*In great relief*): No wonder! I thought you said *cats!* Man, that sure is a relief to me! Here I thought I was a *failure!* (KING *reaches for Excalibrated, stands up, beckons to* PIPER.) *Me,* your manship? (KING *nods.*) Yessir. (PIPER *gets on his knees, carefully sliding* JOUSTER *out of his way.*) What are you going to do with that thing?

KING: Quiet! (*Looks down on them, waving Excalibrated.*) By the power invested in me, *et cetera, et cetera,* I now pronounce you. . . . (*Stops. Shakes his head to clear it. Mumbling*) Start over. . . . I, *et cetera, et cetera,* hereby proclaim you, *et cetera,* to be . . . *et cetera, et cetera, et cetera.* (*Starts to give him the whack, sees that* PIPER *is terrified, ends up just tapping him a couple of times, absentmindedly.*) O.K., that's all . . . (*Hands him cue with number 12 pennant*) Go find yourself a place at the table.

PIPER: What happened?

KING: You were just promoted. You're now Sir Twelve-Ball. Kings these days can't be choosers.

PIPER (*Delighted*): Wow! How about that! (*Moves to pool table, admiring his cue.* KNIGHTS *make a place for him.*)

KING (*Who has been studying the* JOUSTER): All right, boy, your turn! One up and one to go! (JOUSTER *hunches himself back to his original position before throne without looking up.*) Somebody must have told him an army travels on its stomach. (*Leans down*) Hey, Jouster!

JOUSTER (*Mumbling*): Nottajouster—majester.

KING: How's that again?

JOUSTER (*Head up like a turtle*): Mmmnottajouster. Ummajester. (*Head down*)

KING: A jester, you say? You're a jester, not a jouster? (JOUSTER *sits up suddenly and nods vigorously.* KING *leans back.*) That's not so bad . . . I don't have much of a sense of humor myself, but I think we could probably use a little levity around here. (JOUSTER *brightens considerably.*) I don't mean *now,* of course. (JOUSTER *is crestfallen.*) Maybe later . . . say, next year, or the year after. (*He brightens again.*)

MERVAC (*Urgently*): Your Majesty!

KING: Just a minute, Mervac, can't you see I'm busy?

MERVAC: But, Your Majesty! I must tell you . . . (*Whispers in* KING'*s ear.*)

KING: Oh, really? Any minute now?

MERVAC: Yes, Sir. We *must* prepare—at once!

KING: I suppose we must. (*To* JOUSTER) How'd you like to become a Knight?

JOUSTER: A Knight, Sir? Me?

KING: Why not? They're a motley crew anyway. (*Reaches for 14 cue*) Here, take it—I'll hold your dolly. (*Takes bauble, waves Excalibrated*) *Et cetera, et cetera, et cetera.* There you go, boy. (*Crashing sounds are heard from offstage*) None too soon, either. (*Gives 14 cue and bauble to* JOUSTER.)

VIZIER (*From offstage*): Where is that miserable. . . . (*Crashes, sirens are heard from offstage.*)

KNIGHTS: The Grand Vizier!

MERVAC: The Grand Vizier!

AMNESIA: Eeek! (LIONEL *toots trumpet.*)

LANCE: Sees her, seer sire! I mean, he's here, sy sewer! (*Throne room is one grand chorus of confusion and terror.* KNIGHTS *pound their cues.*)

KING (*Standing on throne, waving Excalibrated*): All right! (*Instant silence*) That's better. I'm still King here, and we . . .

VIZIER (*Entering and moving toward throne*): Not any more you're not, Bandy Legs! (KING, *still standing on his throne, flips his robe together to conceal his legs.* AMNESIA *is bent double over her script, in excitement and concentration.* QUEEN *plays cards.*) I will take over now. Get off *my* throne!

KING: Well, now, maybe we should talk this over. Communicate. Have you met my wife? Gwenny, this is the Grand Vizier—you've heard me mention him, I think. *Lovely* fellow.

QUEEN GWENNY (*Not looking up*): Dahling! So good of you to come! (*Scoreboard now reads* QUEEN 162—VISITORS 0) Have a chocolate. (*She reaches for box without looking away from her cards.*) They're divine!

VIZIER (*Disconcerted*): Why, uh, thank you, Ma'am. (*He looks about in bewilderment, scratching his head. A hand pops out from his robe, snatches chocolate from box, disappears back into robe.* VIZIER *looks into box.*) They seem to be all gone, Ma'am.

QUEEN GWENNY (*Not looking up*): Really? How tiresome. (*She drops the box. A cry of pain is heard from inside* VIZIER'*s robe.*)

KING: Say, Grandy, how many men do you have with you?

VIZIER (*Evasively*): I am, uh, well armed.

KING: Yes, I noticed that. (*Getting down from throne, with Excalibrated*) Mind if I take a peek behind the draperies? I think there's something underhanded going on here. (*He gives lower part of* VIZIER'*s robe a poke with Excalibrated.* VIZIER *does a little dance step and wild giggling is heard from inside robe.*) Hm-m-m. Obviously a very ticklish situation. (KING *steps back, Excalibrated at the ready.*) All right, you! (*To lower half of robe*) And you, too, Twinkle Toes! Surrender in the name of the King before I turn you into royal shishkebab.

VIZIER (*Addressing his stomach*): Don't do it, Billy! Run! Get us out of here!

BILLY (*Snapping open robe, his face still concealed by the long beard*): I'm sorry, your Viziership, but I cannot do it.

KING: That voice! That hand! Come to think of it, that name! (*Peering into the beard*) Is that you in there, Billy? (*Beard parts and* BILLY'*s face appears. He and* KING *embrace enthusiastically, dislodging the* GRAND VIZIER, *and the three of them go down in a tangle.*)

BILLY: Father!

KING: My son!

VIZIER: Help! (*He tries to hide inside his robe, which is now miles too long for him.*) I'm ruined, ruined . . . (*He sniffles into his beard.*)

BILLY (*Comforting him*): There, there, Sir. I'm sure my

father will understand when he hears the whole story, won't you, Father?

KING (*Dusting himself off and getting up, slowly*): That all depends, Son. It's been a long day. . . .

BILLY (*Jumping up*): I will be brief, Sir.

KING: Well, that's a good start.

BILLY: This man whom you think of as your enemy is *not* what he seems! There are no mighty armies, no powerful forces, at his command! Even the gypsies have deserted him. Gone, all gone—back to the tearooms and the fortune-telling parlors. (*Aside, to audience*) Tea leaves are very big now, you know. (*Back*) Nor did he have me kidnapped by his men! It pains me to admit it, but fair is fair—I (*Shudder*) ran away!

KING: No! From us? Your loving parents?

BILLY: Forgive me, Dad. I didn't realize what a good, sensible, loving home I had here. Blame it on my youth! And as for the tyrant whom you call the Grand Vizier, look at him! A voiceless, hollow man, lost completely without his electronic equipment!

KING: His what?

BILLY: His tapes, his tubes, his short-wave set and his sound-effects records!

KING: You mean . . . ?

BILLY: Yes, Father. I mean that the Grand Vizier is nothing but a ham! So now you know the whole story. Do you think you can find a place for him in your court?

KING: My boy, for your sake, I will do everything in my power to make him happy here!

BILLY (*Humbly*): Thank you, Father.

KING: There's just one thing . . . I still don't understand why he tried to take over my kingdom.

BILLY: You don't?

KING (*Quickly*): Well, yes, I do, actually, but we need a curtain line, and you're stronger than I am. Tell us, boy

—we're all ears. Tell us why the Grand Vizier wanted my Kingdom.

BILLY (*Facing audience, bravely*): He wanted your kingdom because *here* (*Indicating stage*) is where we're really free . . . to ham a lot! (*He bows, solemnly. Quick curtain.*)

THE END

A Family Affair

by Muriel Ward

Characters

MR. ELLIS
MRS. ELLIS
BARBIE, *16* }
DOTTY, *17* } *their children*
EDDY, *19* }
DICK MARTIN, *Eddy's college roommate*
LILA CARTER, *18, a friend of Eddy's*
JERRY MARS, *Barbie's boy friend*
TOMMY BLAKELY, *Dotty's boy friend*

SCENE 1

TIME: *A summer day.*
SETTING: *The Ellis living room.*
AT RISE: BARBIE *is placing a record on the phonograph. When the record, a brassy jazz number, begins to play, she sighs happily and sits down near the phonograph.* EDDY *enters with a letter in his hand. He grins at* BARBIE.

EDDY: You'll have that record worn out before it's a week old, Barbie.

BARBIE (*Turning her head to look at him*): Then I'll just go out and get a new one.

EDDY: Oh, you wouldn't! The whole family's been forced to listen to it five hundred times already. That should be enough to satisfy even you. (*He relaxes comfortably on the sofa.*)

BARBIE: I wonder why boys always exaggerate so much! You can play a record only about a hundred times before it's worn out, so you couldn't have heard it five hundred times already. And even if you had—this is the most terrific thing that's ever been recorded!

EDDY: Did I hear somebody say something about the way *boys* exaggerate?

BARBIE (*Sidestepping the question*): The trouble with you and the rest of the family is that you don't appreciate what's really good. I can't understand it. I do my best to educate you, but what do I get for my trouble? Dotty can't tell Dave Brubeck from Duke Ellington, Mom and Dad like Lawrence Welk, and you'd rather hear a string quartet.

EDDY (*Affably*): Terrible, isn't it?

BARBIE (*Emphatically*): It sure is! (DOTTY *enters, and sits down next to* EDDY. *She is carrying a book of Shakespeare.*)

DOTTY (*Looking from* BARBIE *to* EDDY): Are you kids doing anything in particular?

BARBIE: I *was* doing something in particular. I was listening to my new record. (*Ironically*) But don't give it another thought—I'd much rather listen to *you,* Dotty. I guess I'd better turn the record off so I won't miss a word you say!

DOTTY (*Pleasantly*): Fine! That's a good idea.

BARBIE (*Turning the phonograph off*): O.K. But this is just temporary. It'll be back on again very soon.

DOTTY: As long as I'm not around I don't mind. (*Noticing the piece of paper in* EDDY'*s hand*) What's that, Eddy, a letter?

EDDY: Yes. It just came.

BARBIE: From anybody we know?

EDDY: No, it's from my roommate at college, Dick Martin. I mentioned him in my letters home, remember? He played with me on the football team. He lives in Maine—Skowhegan, Maine, to be exact.

DOTTY: Oh, sure, I remember your writing about Dick Martin. What's he doing now? Is he working this summer?

EDDY: No, he's on vacation, too, and before school closed for the summer, I asked him to come and visit me if he had a chance. He's a great guy, and I'm sure Mom and Pop will like him, too. This letter says he's coming for a visit.

DOTTY: You mean he's going to stay with us—here in the house?

EDDY: Sure—why not? There's plenty of room. Don't you think so?

DOTTY: Oh, yes—I wasn't worrying about *that*.

BARBIE: Dotty was just worrying about whether he's good-looking.

DOTTY (*To* BARBIE): I was not! Beauty is only skin-deep, as any intelligent person knows. Other things are much more important—a sense of humor, intelligence . . . (*To* EDDY) By the way, *is* your roommate good-looking, Eddy?

BARBIE (*Triumphantly*): Ha, ha!

EDDY: I don't know. He has two eyes, a nose and a mouth, hair on his head and two ears.

BARBIE (*Picking up some of the records strewn around the phonograph and putting them into jackets*): No teeth? That's a wonderful description. I can just see him.

DOTTY: I think you're mean, Eddy. It's only natural for us to be curious about your roommate. You know I'll be nice to him even if he's not good-looking.

BARBIE: You should also know she'll be even nicer to him if he *is* good-looking.

DOTTY: Sometimes I lose all hope for you, Barbara. I'm sure that when I was your age I was never so juvenile. I doubt if I ever acted the way you do.

BARBIE: Can't you remember for certain? After all, it was only a year ago that you *were* my age. You make it sound like George Washington's time!

EDDY: You know, this is one of the things I missed the most while I was away at school: the sisterly way you two carry on.

DOTTY: Oh, I don't believe it. Besides, Barbie and I really do think a lot of each other. You know that. We have our little disagreements, but I wouldn't trade Barbie for a dozen other sisters.

BARBIE: I wouldn't trade you either, Dotty. I've never had any luck on a trade yet!

DOTTY: You see what happens when I do say something nice to her? Let's get back to the subject. When is Dick coming? Is he married or engaged or anything?

EDDY (*Patiently*): He'll get here day after tomorrow, and he's not married, not engaged and not "anything" as far as I know.

BARBIE: Well, he's going to be something when he gets *here*. He'll be beaten down to the sod trying to escape Dotty.

DOTTY: If you don't wear him out first yourself with all your records.

BARBIE: I'm sure he'll like them a lot more than he'll like watching you roll your eyes and bounce your eyebrows up and down while you quote Shakespeare. (*Mimicking her sister*) "O Romeo, Romeo! wherefore art thou, Romeo?"

EDDY (*Laughing*): You both ought to go on the stage, I think. But don't start dividing Dick up between you and making a lot of plans. After all, he and I will have lots to talk about, and I'll be showing him around town.

DOTTY: Of course he's *your* friend, but I don't intend to neglect my duties as a hostess anyhow. When company is in this house, I always do what I can to make them feel at home.

BARBIE (*Grinning*): She sure does—especially if the company's good-looking.

DOTTY: You said that before, remember?

BARBIE: Yes, but "truth is truth to the end of reckoning." That's what your old pal Shakespeare said, wasn't it?

DOTTY (*With dignity*): Let's leave the greatest English poet there ever was out of this.

BARBIE: O.K., but you'd better start practicing up on *Hamlet* so you'll be all ready to give a good performance when Dick gets here. (MRS. ELLIS *enters, carrying bags of groceries. Hearing* BARBIE'*s last words, she immediately joins in the talk as she puts her packages on a table and sits down with the group.*)

MRS. ELLIS: What's this about "Dick"? Who's he?

EDDY: Dick Martin, Mom. My college roommate. I used to mention him in my letters home. We were on the football team together.

MRS. ELLIS: Oh, yes, I remember.

EDDY: He's coming to visit us for a little while. That's O.K. with you, isn't it?

MRS. ELLIS: Why, that's very nice. I wish I could meet all your college friends.

EDDY (*Putting an arm around his mother*): You're a real sport, Mom. I knew you wouldn't mind.

MRS. ELLIS: Of course not. We have room for him, and I'm sure Barbie and Dotty are looking forward to meeting a new fellow.

BARBIE (*Acting casual*): Oh, men are all alike, more or less.

DOTTY: Well, some are nicer than others, I think.

BARBIE: Yes, maybe a few are all right.

EDDY: I'll bet that few includes Jerry Mars, doesn't it? I thought he was a little *more* than "all right" with you. You go to parties and dances with him often enough, don't you?

BARBIE: No more than Dotty goes out with Tommy Blakely. And Tommy won't like it much, I'll bet, if she pays a lot of attention to Dick.

DOTTY: There's no reason why Tommy should be concerned. We're just friends, that's all. Your Jerry is the one who'd probably act jealous. Jealousy is juvenile—and so is Jerry.

BARBIE: Oh, is that so? He has more brains than your friend Tommy. *Anybody* has more brains than Tommy.

MRS. ELLIS (*Calmly interrupting*): All right, girls. Simmer down now. You have so much energy to throw around arguing! I can think of lots of other things you could do with that energy. You could do some dusting or cleaning around here, for example. (*Both girls sit down, suddenly quiet.* MRS. ELLIS *smiles.*) I thought that would take your breath away for a second, at least. (*To* EDDY) Those two are more afraid of housework than they'd be if they went up to their room and found it full of wild animals. Now, when does Dick get here, Eddy? Not today, I hope—I mean, I'd like to be prepared.

EDDY: Oh, no, not today. The day after tomorrow, his letter says.

MRS. ELLIS: Good. That'll give me time to straighten up the guest room.

DOTTY (*Unusually eager to help*): I can do that, Mother.

MRS. ELLIS: Well! I hope my ears aren't deceiving me. That's fine, Dotty. I think it'd be nice if you and Barbie both did it.

BARBIE: O.K., Mom. I'll wipe the dust off the furniture, and Dotty will sweep it under the rug.

MRS. ELLIS: Oh, fine—anything as long as you two stop feuding while our guest is here. (*Looks at her watch*) Oh, dear—it's five already! I'd better start fixing dinner. (*Gathering up her parcels from the table, turning to* EDDY) Why don't you come out to the kitchen with me and tell me a little more about Dick?

EDDY: Sure. Let me take those. (*He takes parcels.*) You'll like him, Mom. Dick's a regular guy. (*They exit, leaving* DOTTY *and* BARBIE *alone.* BARBIE *recalls her interrupted record playing and starts looking through a stack of records.* DOTTY *suddenly remembers the book she brought in with her and thumbs through it to a certain point.*)

DOTTY (*Holding the book up*): Listen to this, Barbie—it's wonderful poetry. (*Reads melodramatically as* BARBIE *pauses and looks at her, unimpressed*)

"Neither a borrower, nor a lender be;
For loan oft loses both itself and friend,
And borrowing dulls the edge of husbandry.
This above all: to thine own self be true,
And it must follow, as the night the day,
Thou canst not then be false to any man."

(*After a short, reverential pause*) *Hamlet*—by William Shakespeare!

BARBIE (*Still unimpressed*): Very interesting. (*Briskly*) Well, now let's hear from Erroll Garner. (*With a quick movement she puts a record on the phonograph and starts playing it.*)

DOTTY: Really, Barbara—you're hopeless!

BARBIE (*Shouting back as* DOTTY *sweeps out of the room*): And vice versa! (*She sits back happily and gives all her attention to the record as the curtain falls.*)

* * *

Scene 2

TIME: *Two days later, in the evening.*

SETTING: *Same as Scene 1.*

AT RISE: MR. ELLIS *is sitting in his favorite chair reading the evening newspaper.* DOTTY *is standing in front of a mirror, giving herself a critical survey and making various faces meant to express different emotions.*

MR. ELLIS (*After watching* DOTTY *for a puzzled moment or two*): What are you doing there, Dotty—playing some new kind of game?

DOTTY (*A little flustered*): Oh, no—no. I was just—just trying to see if my face was clean.

MR. ELLIS: Oh. Quite a process, isn't it? I could have sworn for a minute that I was watching Sarah Bernhardt acting Joan of Arc.

DOTTY: Well, I *am* a member of the Dramatic Club at school, you know. I don't want to get rusty for lack of practice while I'm on vacation.

MR. ELLIS: No, indeed, you mustn't allow yourself to get rusty! (*He watches* DOTTY *as she goes over to the sofa and arranges the cushions fussily before she sits down.*) Where's Barbie, do you know? I haven't seen her since dinner.

DOTTY: She was upstairs soaking herself with my cologne the last time I saw her.

MR. ELLIS: Cologne? Hm-m. Is she going some place special tonight?

DOTTY: No—she's just hoping Eddy's friend Dick will notice her and think she's older than sixteen.

MR. ELLIS: Oh—Dick. Say, he's a nice young fellow. Don't you think so?

DOTTY (*Guardedly*): Yes. He seems very nice.

MR. ELLIS (*Mischievously*): You know, when you crossed

over to the sofa, I thought I noticed a scent of perfume in the air. Were you at the cologne bottle, too, by any chance?

DOTTY: Well, I did put a little on. It's what you and Mom gave me for my birthday—"Heaven Sent."

MR. ELLIS (*Reflectively*): "Heaven Sent." A hard description to live up to, I'd say.

DOTTY: I guess so, but it's a lovely fragrance. I never use more than a drop or two at a time though.

MR. ELLIS: I see. (*Sniffing the air*) It must be powerful stuff then! (MRS. ELLIS *enters and sits in an easy chair.*)

MRS. ELLIS (*Taking some knitting from a nearby sewing bag and starting to work*): Where are the boys—does anyone know?

DOTTY (*Pointedly*): Eddy said they were just going for a little walk and would be right back, but that was a half-hour ago.

MRS. ELLIS: Oh. Well, maybe they met some other friends of Eddy's or stopped somewhere for a Coke.

MR. ELLIS (*To his wife*): I don't recall Dotty's ever having been so concerned about Eddy's comings and goings before, do you, Martha?

MRS. ELLIS: No, I can't say that I do.

DOTTY (*Quickly*): I'm not concerned at all. I'm sure I don't care if he prefers to spend the evening out. (BARBIE *appears in the doorway. Her hair is carefully combed, and she is wearing a necklace of pearls in addition to her usual outfit of sweater and skirt.*)

BARBIE (*Disappointedly*): Hasn't Eddy come back yet?

MR. ELLIS: No. But come in and join us anyhow, won't you? You're not the only one waiting to see *Eddy*. (*He looks significantly at* DOTTY.)

BARBIE (*Entering and sitting on sofa*): I don't want to see Eddy particularly. I was just wondering where he was.

MRS. ELLIS: No doubt he's showing Dick what the neighborhood looks like. I imagine they'll be back soon. By the way, Barbie, those pearls look very familiar.

BARBIE: I hope you don't mind my borrowing them, Mom. I just felt like wearing something around my neck tonight.

DOTTY: You mean something besides the usual ring of dirt, don't you?

BARBIE: Mother! Are you going to let her say things like that? Besides, I'm all clean tonight.

MR. ELLIS: Will wonders never cease! It might be a good idea to have a guest in the house all the time.

MRS. ELLIS: Now let's not tease the girls any more, Harry. I think it's fine that they're looking so neat and ladylike tonight.

BARBIE (*Eagerly*): Don't you think I really look older than I am, Mother?

MRS. ELLIS: To be honest, I don't think so, dear. You look your age—sixteen, but you don't actually want to look older, do you?

BARBIE: Not *real* old—I mean, I don't want to look as if I'm in my twenties, but I would like to look about eighteen.

MR. ELLIS: Now why? (*To himself*) As if I didn't know.

BARBIE: No special reason. It's just that I get tired of being a kid sister sometimes. (DOTTY *is about to answer her back when the sound of the front door being opened is heard.*)

MR. ELLIS (*Putting aside his newspaper*): That must be the boys now. (DOTTY *and* BARBIE *spring up and face the doorway expectantly.* EDDY *and* DICK *enter.* DICK *is a little taller than* EDDY *and is a good-looking boy.*)

EDDY: Well, we're back again. I showed Dick around a little.

MRS. ELLIS: That's nice. I don't imagine it's very much like your home town, is it, Dick?

DICK: There are more people here, but from what I've seen of it so far, I like it.

MR. ELLIS: Good. We want you to enjoy yourself while you're here. Sit down and visit with us for a while, won't you?

DOTTY (*Quickly*): How about trying the sofa, Dick? There's a lot of room, and it's *very* comfortable.

DICK (*After flashing a glance at* EDDY *who, grinning, has taken the one available armchair*): Thanks very much. (*He sits down and the girls sit with him, one on each side. They both give him their most fetching smiles.*)

BARBIE: Isn't this the most comfortable sofa you ever sat on, Dick?

DICK (*Looking uncomfortable*): Yes—it's—it's very comfortable.

DOTTY: You know, Dick, I've always wanted to travel around the world ever since I was a child. (MR. *and* MRS. ELLIS *glance at each other, amused;* DOTTY *does not notice.*) Don't you think it's very exciting, traveling around, meeting people, seeing all the places and things you've heard about?

DICK: I like to travel, too. Someday, when I've finished college, I want to travel all over the country and then to South America.

DOTTY: That would be nice. But I've always particularly wanted to visit Maine.

BARBIE: Really? It's funny you never mentioned it before.

DOTTY: Well, Barbie, with your short memory, you wouldn't remember it if I mentioned it a dozen times a day.

BARBIE: Is that so? I'll bet I can remember plenty of things *you'd* rather have me forget!

MRS. ELLIS (*Quickly*): Would you like some iced tea or a glass of milk or anything, Dick?

DICK: Oh, no thanks, Mrs. Ellis. That was a wonderful

dinner you cooked. I couldn't eat or drink another thing.

EDDY: Besides, Mom, we had sodas when we were out.

MRS. ELLIS (*Smiling*): Oh, I see.

MR. ELLIS: By the way, Dick, I understand there's some good fishing in Maine.

DICK: Yes, sir. There are about 1,600 lakes in the state, with lots of trout, bass, pickerel and salmon. There's good fishing along the coast, too.

MR. ELLIS: Sounds like a fisherman's paradise. We'll have to take a little trip up there someday.

DOTTY (*Dreamily*): I just *know* I'd like to live there for good.

BARBIE (*Eagerly*): How soon can we go, Dad?

MR. ELLIS (*Winking at his wife*): Why, I always thought you liked it here.

BARBIE (*Looking at* DICK): Oh, no. Maine is the place. You said yourself it must be paradise.

MR. ELLIS: Well, even if it is, we could hardly drop everything and leave immediately. But someday—who knows?

DICK: If you folks ever do get a chance to come up that way, I sure hope you'll look us up. I'd be happy to show you around, and I know my mother and dad would, too.

MRS. ELLIS: That's very kind of you. We'll remember. But to get back to right now—you must be feeling rather tired after your trip, aren't you?

DICK: Just a little. I was up pretty early this morning.

MRS. ELLIS: Then I suggest we call it a day. There's always tomorrow, and Eddy's probably making plans for it already.

DICK: Anything you say.

EDDY: Right. Tomorrow's another day. (*They all rise,* DOTTY *and* BARBIE *very reluctantly.*)

MR. ELLIS (*To* MRS. ELLIS): Is the guest room ready for Dick?

MRS. ELLIS: Yes, dear. Dotty and Barbara saw to it.

DOTTY (*To* DICK): I picked some flowers from the garden. They're on the dresser.

BARBIE (*To* DICK): You'll find some copies of *Powerhouse Jazz Magazine* there, too.

DICK (*Overwhelmed*): Thanks . . . thanks a lot. It was very nice of you.

EDDY: Talk about eager beavers!

MR. ELLIS: Well, then, let's go. Women and children first. (MRS. ELLIS, DOTTY *and* BARBIE *start to leave the room, the boys following.*)

MRS. ELLIS: You'll turn out the lights and lock up, won't you, Harry?

MR. ELLIS: Yes, indeed. (*He stands in the doorway, watches the others depart, then comes into the room and starts turning out the lights. To himself*) Ah, life! Well, it could have been a lot more complicated. I might have had *more* than two daughters. What a shivery thought that is! (*He turns out the last light as the curtain falls.*)

* * *

SCENE 3

TIME: *Four days later.*

SETTING: *The same.*

AT RISE: DOTTY *is seated on the couch alone. She is talking on the telephone, frequently looking toward the hallway as though afraid of being overheard.*

DOTTY (*Into phone*): I know, Tommy, I know it's been a week since we've seen each other, but I told you, I'm awfully busy right now. . . . Well, helping my mother with housework. There's a lot to be done around a house, you know. . . . (*Settling herself more comfortably among the sofa cushions*) No, not tonight. I can't make it tonight, Tommy. I have to go to the dentist. . . . No, I haven't said I was going to the dentist *every* night this week. Maybe three or four nights, but not *every* night. Two nights I went baby-sitting, remember? . . . No, of course I'm not trying to get rid of you, Tommy. I've been very busy, that's all. (*Soothingly*) I'd really love to go to a movie with you tonight, but I couldn't break my dentist appointment now. You know how it is. Call me again sometime and—(*She stops suddenly as* DICK *appears in the doorway. Clamping her hand over the receiver*) Hello, Dick—come on in. I was wondering where you were.

DICK (*Entering and sitting on the edge of a chair*): Thanks, but I don't want to interrupt your telephone call. I thought Eddy might be in here.

DOTTY (*Hand still over receiver*): Oh, this is nothing—just a call from—from a girl friend. Wait a minute, and we can both go look for Eddy. (*Into phone*) Hello—Hello, Margaret—are you still there? It was very sweet of you to call, Margaret, but I'm sorry I won't be able to go to that club meeting with you tonight. Just can't make it, but I'll see you soon. Goodbye, Margaret. (*Hangs up hastily. To* DICK) That was Margaret.

DICK: Oh.

DOTTY: Well—it's a beautiful day, isn't it?

DICK: Yes, great.

DOTTY: I've been sitting here thinking of things we could do so you'd have a good time while you're here.

DICK: Oh, I'm having a fine time. But I don't want you going to any extra trouble on my account. I guess Eddy has some plans—(*The telephone rings and he stops and looks toward it.*)

DOTTY (*Paying no attention*): Have you been rowing on the lake yet? There's a lovely lake in City Park, and we have a lot of fun there in the summer. (*Phone continues to ring.*)

DICK: That does sound like fun—but aren't you going to answer the phone?

DOTTY (*Reluctantly*): Yes, I guess I'd better. (*Into phone*) Hello? . . . Oh, it's you again—Margaret. . . . (*Inventing a conversation*) No, I won't be able to go on that picnic tomorrow. I've caught a little cold. (*Gives a few phony coughs to prove it*) Tell the other girls I'll be at the next club meeting, and I'll see you soon, Margaret. . . . Have to sign off now, Margaret. Goodbye. (*Hangs up phone*) Margaret's a sweet girl, but she's a little trying at times.

DICK (*Innocently*): That's too bad. Sorry to hear about your cold. Maybe you shouldn't go out at all today. (BARBIE *enters, energetically humming one of the latest popular songs. She helps herself to some candy on a side table and brings the dish to* DICK.)

BARBIE: You caught a cold, Dotty? That's too bad. I guess you don't want any candy then. You wouldn't be able to enjoy what you can't taste. (*Offers the candy to* DICK, *who takes a piece.*)

DOTTY: It's nothing—I really don't have a cold. You see, I just said that on the phone to—to Margaret because I didn't feel like going some place with her. (*She quickly helps herself to some candy, too.*)

BARBIE: Margaret? Margaret who? We don't know any Margarets, do we?

DOTTY (*Looking sternly at her sister*): *I* do. She's a friend of mine. You don't know *all* my friends, Barbara.

BARBIE: No, I guess not. (*Mischievously, to* DICK) Dotty has a lot of boy friends, Dick. We just get to know one, when she drops him and traps a new one. It's very confusing.

DOTTY: Barbara! How can you say such things when you know they're not a bit true! (*To* DICK) I don't date boys around here much at all. They're either so young or so empty-headed. (*Moving in closer to* DICK, *who looks alarmed*) I like college men. They have so much more sense, so much more poise—and they can appreciate Shakespeare!

EDDY (*Calling from offstage*): Hey, Dick—where are you? (*Appearing in doorway*) Oh, here you are. I've been looking for you. I promised Dad I'd clean the car this morning. Want to come and watch? "Watch" meaning "help," of course.

DICK (*Relieved*): You talked me into it! Excuse me, won't you, girls? (*Before they can answer*) See you later.

EDDY (*To* DICK *as they leave the room*): I'm trying to save up to buy my own car, but it's slow going. I have a friend down the street who has a jalopy. We take it apart and glue it together again about once a week. (*Boys exit, and back door is heard closing as they leave the house.*)

DOTTY: How do you like that!

BARBIE: Eddy has some nerve taking Dick away from us like that. (*Doorbell rings.*)

DOTTY: I'll go—nothing else to do around here now!

BARBIE: No, nothing exciting. (DOTTY *exits.* BARBIE *takes another piece of candy, wanders over to the phonograph and half-heartedly selects a record. She is about to play it when* DOTTY *reappears with* JERRY MARS. *He is in old clothes, and carries a baseball bat and glove.*)

DOTTY: It's Jerry. He's spitting nails about something, so I'll leave you two to fight it out between you. (*She exits.* JERRY *walks into the room, scowling, the baseball bat over his shoulder like a war club.*)

BARBIE: Have a piece of candy, Jerry?

JERRY (*Ignoring the candy*): No. I didn't come over here for candy. I want to find out what's going on around here! And I don't mind telling you I'm pretty sore.

BARBIE: Well, put down that baseball bat at least. You look as though you're about to club somebody to death.

JERRY (*Leaning the bat against a nearby chair, talking loudly*): It happens I feel like socking somebody. We played ball with the Battling Buzzards this morning, and they beat us—20 to nothing. And that's only half of it. I haven't seen you for a week, and when I phone you, you're either on your way to take a clarinet lesson, scrubbing the floor for your mother, or baby-sitting for the neighbors. You always found time to see me before, so what's this "busy, busy" routine all of a sudden? You don't look so busy right now, I notice—just sitting there eating candy!

BARBIE: A girl has to rest sometime. And I don't see what you're getting so huffed up about, standing there shouting as if I were five blocks away.

JERRY (*Shouting*): Who's shouting? I think I'm being very quiet and polite under the circumstances.

BARBIE: Well, I don't. I don't think it's a bit polite of you to come tearing in here, doubting my word and criticizing me right and left. (TOMMY BLAKELY *appears in the doorway.* BARBIE *and* JERRY *stop arguing long enough to turn and stare at him.*)

TOMMY (*Loudly*): Where's Dotty?

BARBIE: I don't know. Around some place. Who let you in?

TOMMY (*Aggressively*): The front door was open. Nobody answered me when I called, and I heard your voices, so I just walked in.

JERRY: Well if you don't mind, this is a kind of *personal* conversation.

TOMMY (*Equally angry*): I don't mind at all. I came to see Dotty, not you, and I'm going to look around till I find her. (*He stalks out, left.*)

JERRY: That Tommy Blakely! Who does he think he is?

BARBIE: Well, he's not one of the Battling Buzzards, so you don't have to be sore at him.

JERRY: I guess I can be sore at anyone I want to. And don't change the subject. You still haven't told me about the big run-around I've been getting this week.

BARBIE: I don't know what you're talking about, Jerry. There hasn't been any "big run-around." I have to practice, and I have lots of other interests, too.

JERRY: For instance?

BARBIE (*Inventing one in a hurry*): I—I'm learning to crochet!

JERRY: You mean you'd rather *crochet* than be with me?

DOTTY (*Entering from right and hearing this*): Better not answer that one, Barbie. He has a baseball bat. (*Wandering around the room, looking in various places*) Have you seen my library book? I couldn't find it up in my room.

BARBIE: I don't know where it is. Look in the bookcase.

DICK (*Appearing in doorway*): Something missing? Let me help look for it. (*He crosses room toward* DOTTY, *as* JERRY *stares, momentarily forgetting his quarrel with* BARBIE.)

DOTTY (*Turning to* DICK *happily*): Oh it's nothing that can't wait. Just a library—(*Gasps, noticing one of* DICK's *fingers is cut and bleeding slightly*) What have you done to yourself? Your finger's bleeding, you poor thing!

DICK (*Putting his hand behind him, embarrassed*): Oh, it's nothing. Just a small cut. I was scraping carbon off the spark plugs of your father's car, and my knife slipped. I was just clumsy, I guess. Eddy said there was some antiseptic in the kitchen.

DOTTY: Let me look at it. (*Firmly takes his hand and examines it.*) Oh, you need antiseptic *and* a bandage on that. I can fix you up in a second. I'll get the stuff, and

I'll be right back. Don't go away now. (*She runs out of the room at full speed, not heeding* DICK'*s protests.*)

DICK: It's nothing, really nothing at all. (*Turns to* BARBIE) Just a little scratch. Your sister shouldn't go to all that trouble.

JERRY (*Still staring at* DICK; *to* BARBIE): Who's he?

BARBIE (*In a low voice*): He's our house guest. Don't be rude!

JERRY (*Beginning to see the light*): House guest! Now I get it. Why didn't you mention him before? Why didn't you come out and say the reason I was getting the big run-around all week was—

BARBIE (*Interrupting, shushing* JERRY): Dick—Dick, I'd like you to meet an old friend of the family. Jerry, this is Dick Martin, Eddy's roommate from college. He's visiting us right now, and Dick—this is Jerry Mars.

DICK (*Smiling*): Glad to meet you, Jerry.

JERRY (*Scowling*) Thanks. (*To* BARBIE, *dramatically*) Baby-sitting! Clarinet lessons! That's not the way I see it now. You're looking at a man who's just had his eyes opened. You're looking at a man who's been heartlessly stabbed in the back!

DICK: Maybe I'd better leave you to finish your talk. I think I'm in the way. (*Starts to exit*) Nice to have met you, Jerry. (*He is kept from leaving by* DOTTY, *who runs back into the room with a bottle of antiseptic, cotton and a roll of bandage.*)

DOTTY: Now, hold out your hand, and I'll have you all fixed up in a minute. (*With a cotton swab she applies antiseptic to the small cut and then wraps a huge, awkward bandage around* DICK'*s finger.*)

DICK: It's very nice of you to go to all this trouble, but— (*He is interrupted as* TOMMY BLAKELY *enters.*)

TOMMY: So! *This* is how you help your mother with the housework. *This* is what's keeping you so "awfully busy."

And you had me so worried, I rushed right over here! I thought you were sick or delirious.

DOTTY (*Flustered*): Oh—Tommy. Where did you come from?

TOMMY: Never mind where *I* came from. (*Indicating* DICK) Where did *he* come from? And why did you hang up the phone *twice* on me this morning after giving me a lot of crazy talk about club meetings and having a cold —and calling me Margaret!

JERRY: Hey, this is *very* interesting!

BARBIE: You keep out of this, Jerry.

DOTTY (*To* TOMMY): I think it's very mean of you to come in here shouting like this, Tommy. If you can't take a little joke over the phone—

TOMMY: A little *joke*? Hanging up the phone on a person twice is a little *joke*?

DICK: Well, if you'll all excuse me, I think I'd better go. Thanks for fixing up my finger, Dotty.

DOTTY (*Warmly*): You're *very* welcome.

DICK: See you later.

TOMMY (*Blocking the exit*): Not so fast, if you don't mind. What's this "see you later" business? Dotty told me this morning on the phone she was too busy to see me!

DICK: If that's what Dotty told you, I'm sure that's what she meant. And if *you* don't mind, I'd like to leave. You're in the way.

TOMMY: Is that so? I have a hunch you've been in *my* way all week. And I have a good notion to take a poke at you!

JERRY (*Eagerly, handing* TOMMY *his baseball bat*): Here— use this.

TOMMY: I don't need that. I can flatten him with my bare hands. (*He squares off like a prize fighter, advances menacingly on* DICK.)

DICK: Look—I don't even know you, so I don't know any reason why we should fight. What's this all about?

TOMMY: Don't act as if you don't know. You're not fooling me. Maybe this'll give you a reason to fight! (*He swings wildly.* DICK *is easily able to sidestep the punch, but* TOMMY *almost falls down as he swings.*)

DOTTY (*Inspired by her sense of the dramatic, gasping loudly*): Oh-h-h! (*She falls gracefully and comfortably across the sofa in a mock faint. Everyone turns and looks at* DOTTY, *surprised.*)

BARBIE: Dotty—Dotty! She's fainted. And I feel dizzy, too! (*With a few wild rolls of her eyes, she collapses into an armchair, feigning unconsciousness.*)

JERRY: Can you beat that! Both of them fainting at practically the same minute! (*As he is saying this,* EDDY *enters with* LILA.)

EDDY (*Casually*): What's the matter with my sisters?

LILA: Oh, dear—shouldn't we do something for them?

TOMMY: They fainted when I took a poke at Dick. It's all my fault, I guess. I lost my temper. I'm sorry.

DICK: It's O.K. Forget it. Just one of those things.

JERRY: Maybe we'd better get some smelling salts or something.

EDDY: Oh, if they don't come out of it in a minute, just get some cold water and pour it on them. That'll revive them. (*Ushering* LILA *over to* DICK) Dick, I want you to meet a good friend of mine. I think you'd get along fine together. This is Lila Carter. Lila, meet Dick Martin, my roommate at college. And these two fellows are Jerry Mars and Tommy Blakely, friends of my sisters, who are indisposed at the moment—(*Indicating*) Dotty on the sofa and Barbie in the chair.

DICK (*Warmly, shaking hands*): I'm very glad to meet you, Lila.

JERRY AND TOMMY (*Simultaneously, disinterestedly*): Hello.

LILA (*To all*): How do you do. (*To* DICK) Eddy just told

me that you're here from Maine visiting him for a few days. When he said you live in Skowhegan, I wanted to meet you because I'm from Skowhegan, too.

DICK (*Excitedly*): You are? That's great. Say, I know some Carters living on Holly Street. You wouldn't be related to them, would you?

LILA: I certainly would. Bill Carter's my uncle. I used to live on Holly Street, too. (*While* LILA *and* DICK *talk,* DOTTY *and* BARBIE *cautiously open their eyes and lift their heads to peek at the newcomer.* EDDY *notices this, and the girls quickly feign unconsciousness again when he glances toward them.*)

DICK: Can you beat that? I live on Edmonds Street, not far from the Baxter Public School.

LILA: Really? I went to the Baxter School till I was twelve and my family moved here.

DICK: I went there, too! I'll bet we even had some of the same teachers. What a coincidence this is!

EDDY: Oh, it's not entirely coincidence. I knew Lila was from Maine, too, and thought it would be a good idea to introduce you.

DICK: I'm sure glad you did. If you're not going to be busy this afternoon, Lila, how would you like to help Eddy show me around town? Say yes, or I'll be very disappointed!

LILA: I'd love to. And maybe you'd come to my house for dinner some night soon. I'd like to have you, and I know Mother and Dad would, too.

DICK: I can't think of anything I'd like better! Shall we go outside and talk it over?

EDDY (*Jokingly*): I'm going in the same direction—if you two old friends don't mind having a stranger walk with you!

DICK: Oh, I guess we won't mind too much, stranger.

EDDY: O.K. Let's go.

LILA (*To* JERRY *and* TOMMY): Goodbye. Nice to have met you. I do hope the girls will be all right.

EDDY: Oh, they'll wake up any minute now. So long, fellows.

JERRY: So long.

TOMMY: Goodbye. (LILA, DICK *and* EDDY *exit.* DOTTY *is first to stage a recovery.*)

DOTTY (*Opening her eyes, looking dazed*): Where am I? What happened? (*She sits up and looks around.*)

TOMMY: You fainted on us! I guess you were afraid of my fighting with that guy, Dick. Well, there wasn't any fight, and I apologized to him. Listen, Dotty, you're not really interested in him, are you?

DOTTY (*Emphatically*): Of course not! If he wants to act silly about the first—(*Catches herself*) I mean, I don't care *what* he does. (*Looks over at* BARBIE) What's she trying to do? Break a record of some kind? (*Loudly*) Barbie—Barbie!

BARBIE (*Pretending recovery*): Is somebody calling me? What happened?

DOTTY: You fainted. (*Aside*) Copycat!

JERRY: Are you feeling all right now, Barbie?

BARBIE: I—I think so. I guess all that excitement was too much for me. (*Smiles at him coyly*) You were so upset when you came in here, I guess I got upset, too.

JERRY: I'm sorry. I never thought you'd get *that* upset. (*After slight pause*) Say, Barbie, you don't have any special interest in Eddy's roommate, do you?

BARBIE: Of course not! But let's not talk about *him.* Sit down. (*Indicates a chair close to her*) You're going to stay awhile, I hope, aren't you? (*Looks around and sees* DOTTY *and* TOMMY *watching interestedly*) Or would you like to take a walk down to the drugstore for a soda? I think the fresh air would be good for me. And I'd like you to tell me about the dance tonight. (*Rising and *steering* JERRY, *with his baseball bat and glove, toward the door*) You know, I'd really *love* to go to the dance. I always have a wonderful time at dances—when I have you for a partner, that is. You're the smoothest dancer I know, Jerry.

JERRY (*Tripping over his own feet, almost falling*): You really think so? Then will you go to the dance with me tonight, Barbie?

BARBIE: I'd love to. I'd really love to, Jerry! (*They exit, smiling happily.*)

DOTTY (*Sorrowfully*): Well, I'm glad everybody else is happy. I guess I'll just sit in my room tonight, all alone, thinking about—life.

TOMMY: I thought you were going to the dentist tonight.

DOTTY (*Remembering her original story*): Oh—yes, I mean *after* I go to the dentist. Then I'll come home and be all alone. Barbie's going to a dance. Mother and Dad will probably go out somewhere . . . but I'll spend most of the evening right here alone, I guess.

TOMMY (*Eagerly*): Well, look, Dotty, if you're not going to be at the dentist's long maybe we could go to a movie tonight after all. How about it?

DOTTY: Why, that'd be fine, Tommy. It's a wonderful idea. You know, I always enjoy going to movies with you more than with anyone else.

TOMMY (*Beaming*): Honest? Gee, Dotty, that goes double! Say, how would you like to take a walk down to the drugstore and have a double chocolate malted or something?

DOTTY: I'd love to. I'd really love to, Tommy! (*They exit, smiling happily, as the final curtain falls.*)

THE END

Enchanted, I'm Sure

by James R. Chisholm

Characters

BEN CANNY, *a book publisher*
GILETTE DE RAIS, *a witch*
DON CHALANT, *a writer*
MISS CHANCE, *Ben's secretary*
WILLIAM, *his office boy*
POLICEMAN

TIME: *Early afternoon.*

SETTING: *The office of Ben Canny, president of Haphazard House Publishing Company.*

AT RISE: BEN CANNY, *a short, middle-aged man, sits behind his desk, talking to* DON CHALANT, *a young writer, who lounges in one of the chairs.* BEN *is reading some papers, then he takes off his glasses and points them emphatically at* DON.

BEN: Don, I'm sorry, but we just can't give you another advance on that book.

DON (*Rising*): But, Ben, this is by Don Chalant! I'm one of your best authors. Why, my last book sold—

BEN: Don, I've been president of Haphazard House for some time now, and you've worked with our company since we took a chance on your first book. Have you ever known me to judge a book on sentiment or on the author's past performance?

DON (*Sitting wearily*): No, Ben. I'll say that for you, you *are* fair. You judge them all on their own merits.

BEN: Then believe me, Don. Your book needs work. As it is, it's not worth the advance. (*Leans back in chair*) Now, I have a book in mind that *will* get an advance. This one can't miss! (*Looks at his watch*) In fact, the young lady who wrote it has an appointment with me in just a few minutes. Stay a minute, Don! I'd like to tell you about her. It may give you some ideas.

DON (*Looks at his watch*): All right, Ben. Just a little while, though.

BEN: That's fine. Excuse me. (*Presses button on intercom*) Miss Chance, could you send the office boy in, please? Thank you. (*To* DON) I have to send for the newspaper. Want to check our ads in the book section.

WILLIAM (*Entering*): Yes, Mr. Canny?

BEN: Oh! You're new here, aren't you? I'm afraid I've forgotten your name.

WILLIAM: William, sir.

BEN: Well, I don't stand on formality. We'll call you Billy, eh? I suppose your friends call you that.

WILLIAM: No, sir—William.

BEN: What, nobody calls a boy your age Willy or Bill?

WILLIAM: No, sir, just William.

BEN: But, why?

WILLIAM: It's my name, sir. (BEN *shakes his head.*)

BEN: Well, William, suppose you go down to the corner and pick up the afternoon newspaper.

WILLIAM: Yes, Mr. Canny. (*Starts off right*)

BEN (*Points off left*): Go this way, through the files. It's shorter. (WILLIAM *exits left.* BEN *turns to* DON.) I like to take a personal interest in my employees, Don. Now, with an office boy (*Gestures toward the departed* WIL-

LIAM) like him—I feel that a youngster like that deserves—well, not only the opportunity but also *encouragement* in being a healthy young American boy. You know—the kind of boy who thrives on give and take, roots hard for the old baseball team. A *real* young man! (*Looks after* WILLIAM *again, shakes his head.*) I don't know what young people are coming to—

DON (*Impatiently*): Look, Ben—if I can't get any money out of you, there are other things I'd like to do. Now, what about this girl and her masterpiece?

BEN: Well, Don—(*Leans forward*) I found her a few weeks ago in the slush pile.

DON: *What?*

BEN: I mean her book. In among the unsolicited manuscripts. I took one off the top of the pile—and there it was: *The Autobiography of a Modern Witch*!

DON: I might have known it. You never could resist that sort of thing. (BEN *rises from his chair and walks about the room as he talks, emphasizing his statements with his glasses.*)

BEN: You know what publishing means to me. It's much more than just a business. It's—it's a *crusade!* Haphazard House is dedicated to waging war on superstition—to eliminating it from the world. Superstition! The lurking enemy of progress—

DON (*In resignation*): Here we go!

BEN: My kids, Don! (*Takes a framed picture from his desk.*) There they are with their little black kitten, Lucky! They're going to grow up unafraid, in a world free of—

DON: What's this got to do with *The Autobiography of a Modern Witch,* Ben?

BEN (*Slapping hand on desk*): That's just it! This girl, this newcomer that nobody has ever heard of, has written the most subtle, the most biting satire on the belief in witches that you could imagine. This Miss de Rais—

DON (*Rubbing back of his neck*): De Rais, did you say? Funny. That sounds familiar. What's the book about?

BEN (*Sitting down*): The heroine is supposed to be a young girl, living today and actually practising witchcraft—right in this city! It's written like an autobiography and it's so delicate and subtle that it almost seems serious. Why, Miss de Rais even has the witch claim—(*Takes a paper off his desk*) well, listen to this passage that I've just been checking over. (*Reads dramatically*) "—and on the thirty-first of October last, the same being the occasion of our annual witches' Sabbat and herbecue cookout, a large number of us did secretly repair to the cellar of Felsenkopf's Delicatessen on Central Avenue, being aware that Felsenkopf had gone on his annual vacation and would not discover us. We did gain admittance to the cellar with the aid of Felsenkopf's store assistant, one Haircut Harrington, also one of our apprentice wizards. There we all spent the night practicing our mystic rites, of which I shall presently speak—" How do you like that for humor, boy?

DON: Sounds pretty gruesome to me. You're sure she doesn't mean it?

BEN: I guess you just don't appreciate—(*There is a knock on the door left. It opens and* WILLIAM *enters. He puts the newspaper on the desk.*)

WILLIAM: There it is, sir. Mr. Canny, after you've finished it, would it be all right if I looked at it? There's something—

BEN: Of course, boy. Want to read the score of the ball game, eh? Well, we all—

WILLIAM: No, sir, the ballet. They're doing *Swan Lake* at the—

BEN: Go! (WILLIAM, *looking rather shocked, exits right.*)

DON (*Taking paper from* BEN's *desk and glancing at front*

page): What do you know? Somebody escaped from the mental hospital. Lady under observation before the police put her on trial. May be dangerous. Seems nice-looking from the picture.

BEN: You never can tell what anybody looks like from those newspaper pictures. They ran one of me once—made me look like an old man.

DON: That's true. (*Excitedly*) Say, get this, Ben! This woman that escaped thinks she's a *witch.* She had some heavy object concealed in her handbag and slugged the attendant when his back was turned. He says that before she escaped she kept muttering, "I must get him out of the way. I *must* dispose of him!" (*To* BEN, *teasing*) You don't suppose it could be your new little author, do you? You'd better watch yourself with her, Ben!

BEN: Suppose you stop being silly, Don. Just how far can your professional jealousy go? (*Sits thoughtfully on the edge of his desk*) I'll tell you something, though—that witch publicity about that woman should help us to put on a big build-up in advertising that book.

DON: You always have an answer, Ben. Well, I'll have to amble along, now. If I get any ideas I might drop back. (*The intercom buzzes.*)

BEN: Excuse me. (*He answers it.*) Yes, Miss Chance? Miss de Rais? Send her right in. (*To* DON) Just a moment, Don. Let me introduce you before you leave.

DON: Sure. (GILETTE DE RAIS *enters. She is tall, slim, and darkly beautiful. She wears black.*)

BEN (*Taking her hand*): Miss de Rais! I'm Ben Canny—it's so good to meet you after communicating by mail and telephone these last weeks. My! I must say your picture will look great on the book jacket. Maybe sell a few more copies. (*Chuckles*)

GILETTE: It makes me very happy to be here, Mr. Canny.

BEN: Why don't you call me Ben? I don't stand on formality. Makes it easier to work together.

DON: Ben, I'm going along now. I'll either drop back or call if I can think of any story changes that will get me that advance.

BEN: Oh, I'm sorry, Don. Don, I'd like you to meet Miss de Rais. Gilette, this is Don Chalant, one of our best authors.

DON: So nice to meet you, Miss de Rais. Gilette? That's a sharp name. I don't believe I've ever heard it before.

GILETTE: It's the feminine for Giles. My father wanted a boy, and Giles is a traditional name in our family.

DON: How interesting! Well, I'm afraid I'll have to leave you two to talk business. Goodbye, Miss de Rais. Think about that advance, Ben. (*Starts to open door*)

BEN: You do some work on that book, Don—then we'll see about it. (DON *waves, smiling, starts out door. He stops, turns for a moment, looking at* GILETTE *in a puzzled manner, shrugs, and exits.*) Fine boy, Don. (*Holds chair*) Won't you sit down, Gilette? May I call you Gilette? You know how I feel about formality.

GILETTE (*Sitting*): Please do—Ben.

BEN (*Sitting at his desk*): Did you read Don's last book? It was a wonderful exposé of superstition—*Inside Santa Claus.*

GILETTE (*Smiling*): No, I don't believe I did. Did you get a chance to read the revised ending to my book, Ben?

BEN: Yes, I did, Gilette. Your style is as subtle as ever—but (*More seriously*), there are several things I'd like to discuss. We may have to make some more revisions. (*Rising, once again he walks as he talks, and punctuates with his glasses.*) You know, Gilette, this book means a great deal to me. I've always had a deep interest in subjects like witchcraft and the Black Arts.

GILETTE (*Startled*): Really! You don't seem the type. Tell me—are you *active* in your interest?

BEN (*Looks at her*): Active? Why, yes. You might say so.

GILETTE: Why, this is fascinating! I must admit that when I came here I hardly expected to meet another—shall we say, devotee?

BEN: Well, yes—you might put it that way. You know, Gilette, I've always *hated* superstition!

GILETTE: Superstition? What does that have to do with it?

BEN: Superstition—the belief in things that don't exist!

GILETTE: Well, *that's* true. I suppose it *is* a waste of time.

BEN (*Slapping hand on desk*): Exactly! Do you see the picture? A world, standing still, wasting its time on unreal things like—oh, witchcraft, for one!

GILETTE (*Shocked*): Witchcraft! Unreal? Oh, I see! Yes, now I understand your interest in it. Yes, I see. (*She laughs, then she sees the newspaper that* DON *has left on the table. She looks at* BEN, *who has turned away, stares at the paper, and hastily turns it over, hiding the headlines.*)

BEN: I'm glad you see, Gilette. I want you to know what it means to me to be able to publish a book such as your *Autobiography of a Modern Witch,* a book which so delicately satirizes belief in such things. (*Whirls to face her*) What do you say to that?

GILETTE: I hardly know *what* to say. Your views are such a surprise to me.

BEN (*Chuckling*): You mean the *strength* of those views. (*Crosses to door, left*) I'll get your manuscript so that we can discuss it carefully, Gilette. It's right here in the file room. (*Exits*)

GILETTE: Take your time. (*She snatches up the newspaper and glances at the headlines. She reads aloud, to herself.*) Woman escapes mental hospital—under observation—claims she is a witch—slugs guard with loaded handbag— Oh, my! (*She hastily folds the paper and stuffs it into her handbag. She sits down and smooths her skirt as* BEN *comes in with the manuscript and sits at the desk.*)

BEN: Here it is. (*There is a knock at the door right, and* WILLIAM *enters.*)

WILLIAM: Excuse me, Mr. Canny—but could I look at the newspaper? Before he left, Mr. Chalant said that a lady had escaped from the mental hospital, and I was wondering if it was Rubashka, the mad ballerina. Of course, I'm too young to have seen her perform, but—

BEN (*Irritated*): Take the paper and go—go!

WILLIAM (*Looking around*): I don't see it, Mr. Canny. (GILETTE *clutches her handbag tighter.*)

BEN: Your *friend,* Mr. Chalant, probably took it with him. Why don't you go back down to the corner and get another one? (GILETTE *winces.*) This time go the *long* way and don't bring it in until you've finished reading it. Now—go!

WILLIAM (*At door right*): Yes, Mr. Canny. This *is* decent of you, sir. (*Exits*)

BEN: Well, Gilette, I guess we'd better get down to business. I don't suppose we have much time to spare.

GILETTE (*Looking after* WILLIAM): *I* don't!

BEN (*Picks up manuscript*): Now about this title, *The Autobiography of a Modern Witch*—we may have to change that. Why, together with the way you used your own name for the witch—(*Chuckles*) people might take it seriously and think *you* were the witch! (GILETTE *gives a forced smile.*) We'll want a name that will sell —something like *Inside Hades* or *Witchcraft Confidential.* (*There is a knock on the door and* MISS CHANCE *enters. She is prim, graying, also wears horn-rimmed glasses.*)

MISS CHANCE: I'm sorry, Mr. Canny, but there seems to be something wrong with the intercom.

BEN: Really? Make a note to have it repaired. Is there anything else?

MISS CHANCE: Yes, there's a call from Mr. Chalant. He seems quite excited about something—

BEN: Oh, that advance! Tell him I'm too busy right now. He'll try to argue, but you just hang up. Can't be polite with someone like Don when it's about money. And, oh, Miss Chance, see if you can get some coffee for Miss de Rais and myself. We may be working on these revisions for some time.

MISS CHANCE: Yes, Mr. Canny. (*Exits*)

GILETTE: So your intercommunication system doesn't work.

BEN: Hm? Oh, no. Well, about this police lieutenant that you have for the secret leader of your coven, or group of witches—what's his name?

GILETTE: Lieutenant Henry Eldritch, a very evil man. He would stop at nothing to prevent the public from knowing what he is.

BEN: We'll have to change that name. Henry Eldritch! Just doesn't sound real, somehow. Now could you explain these revisions on your closing chapters? Why did you decide to change your ending? (BEN, *who has been gesturing with his glasses, puts them down on the desk.*)

GILETTE: Certainly, Ben. (*Rising, she goes to his desk. She opens the manuscript to a certain page, and points it out to* BEN.) There is the original ending. I—the witch reforms when her autobiography is published, because it was her desire for fame and importance that led me—her—into becoming a witch. (*She idly fingers* BEN*'s glasses.*) Having her diary—novel—published, gives her enough fame so that she can be satisfied with being an ordinary girl.

BEN: I thought that was good! What made you decide to change to the blood-and-thunder ending that you have now? (GILETTE *walks while she is talking, and, like* BEN, *punctuates her sentences with his glasses.*)

GILETTE (*Sadly*): Yes, Ben, it would have been a very nice ending. (*Bitterly*) But life is not like that—it could not be!

BEN: I see what you mean—you wanted realism!

GILETTE: Realism? Oh, yes. Yes. We must have realism. I—she would have been so happy, but that horrible Lieutenant Eldritch, the leader of the local witches, could not afford to be unmasked for what he is. Posing as a respectable police official, he learned about the book and knew that he must stop it. First, he had to discredit me. He had me arrested as a madwoman, but I escaped.

BEN: It's easy to see why you're such a good writer, Gilette! You really put yourself into the place of the people in your book.

GILETTE: What? Oh, yes. The book. Her escape gave the witch one last chance to regain the good graces of the coven—the other witches!

BEN: But, Gilette, why do you have her try to kill the publisher of her book? He seems to be a decent enough fellow.

GILETTE: Don't you see? Only he has read her manuscript! If she can destroy him and recover the manuscript (BEN *glances doubtfully at the manuscript in his hands.*) Lieutenant Eldritch will remain undiscovered. He will let her stay free. (*She looks at his desk, puts down his glasses, and picks up the picture.*) This picture! These must be your children. So pretty.

BEN (*Proudly*): Yes, that's young Henry and Penelope—we call them Henny and Penny. Wonderful kids!

GILETTE (*Very curious*): Who is this with them?

BEN: Let's see. (*Looks at picture, chuckles*) Oh, that's Lucky, their black cat.

GILETTE: Hm-m, he looks (*A slight pause, then suggestively*) familiar! (*There is a knock on the door right and* MISS CHANCE *enters, bringing a tray with the coffee. She places it on* BEN'*s desk.*)

MISS CHANCE: Here's your coffee, Mr. Canny. Mr. Chalant called again, more excited than ever. He started to say something about a newspaper, but I hung right up on him.

BEN: Very good, Miss Chance. That's the only way to handle Don! Tell you what, we should be working on this for the rest of the day. I won't be needing you, so you may leave early if you like. William can handle any calls.

MISS CHANCE (*Looking at* GILETTE): Oh, won't that be nice, Mr. Canny! Thank you. (*Exits*)

GILETTE: It's so nice of you, Ben, to treat your employees so well—letting that woman go home early.

BEN: Oh, she deserves it. She's a hard worker. (*Chuckles*) Now, don't you worry, we still have William here as a chaperone.

GILETTE: *I'm* not afraid.

BEN (*Looking through manuscript*): Now, let's see—where's that part that— (GILETTE, *who has crossed behind him, raises her handbag above her head with both hands. At the sound of a knock on the door right, she hastily lowers it and puts one hand on the back of* BEN'*s chair.* MISS CHANCE, *her hat and coat now on, enters.*)

MISS CHANCE: I'm going along now, Mr. Canny. (*Looks at* GILETTE) I thought you'd want to know.

BEN: Yes, yes. Good afternoon, Miss Chance.

MISS CHANCE: Mr. Chalant called again. He started to say something about the police, but I hung right up.

BEN: Good, good. What that boy won't try, to get money! Is there something else, Miss Chance?

MISS CHANCE (*Looking archly at* GILETTE): William will be here, Mr. Canny. I told him what to do—(*Pause*) if Mr. Chalant should call again. Goodbye. (*Exits*)

BEN: She seems to be behaving oddly today. I can't understand it, but then I never was too fast at catching on to people's actions. Books are more in my line. (*Turns back to his manuscript, while again* GILETTE *starts to raise her handbag*) I've lost my place! That part I was looking for should be about—(*Once again there is a knock and* GILETTE *lowers her handbag.* WILLIAM *enters right.*)

GILETTE: Your office is a busy place, Ben.

WILLIAM: Mr. Chalant called again, sir. He started to say something about your not listening to him and that he was warning you. Then I hung up as Miss Chance told me.

BEN: Good! Can you imagine that, Gilette? *He's* trying to warn *me?* Huh! Threats certainly won't get him that advance. (*Shakes his head*) *Him* trying to warn me. Why, I can't get over it!

GILETTE: You won't.

BEN: Huh? What was that? Oh, I won't. You're right there —I certainly won't forget *this* in a hurry. Warn me. (*Looks at* WILLIAM) Well, boy? Is there anything else you want to tell me?

WILLIAM (*Approaching*): Yes, sir. I thought you might be interested. (*Glances at* GILETTE) Did you know that Rubashka, the mad ballerina, could stand on her toes longer than *anyone?* In fact, that's how she went mad. Got up on her toes and they never were able to get her down again. They say that she sleeps that way—

BEN (*Livid*): *Go!* No, wait! There's a stack of envelopes with manuscripts in them on top of Miss Chance's desk.

Put a rejection slip into each one, then go down to the mailbox on the next street. If you don't know where it is, walk around until you find it. The air will do you good. Then mail them.

WILLIAM: But, Mr. Canny, there's a mailbox right in this building.

BEN: I know it. You are a bright boy, but you go look for the other one. Now go! (WILLIAM *exits hurriedly.*) That should take care of him for a while. Now, let's see if I can finally find that passage. Oh, you haven't touched your coffee. Take it, Gilette. I prefer mine rather cool. (GILETTE *takes a cup, starts to sip it while* BEN *looks through the manuscript, looks suddenly at her cup, then at* BEN'*s cup, still waiting at the right hand edge of the desk. She takes a small bottle from her handbag.*) Ah! Here it is, Gilette! (*Points to the manuscript while he reads it intently.*) This part where the witch is trying to kill the publisher. (GILETTE *stands to his right, between him and his coffee.*)

GILETTE: Where? Do you mean the part where I—the witch slips a special potion into his coffee? What's wrong with that part? (*Empties a powder into his coffee*)

BEN: It isn't believable. Excuse me. (*Reaches out for his cup of coffee*) No, honestly—*I'm* a publisher. (*Sips a little coffee*) Do I look like the sort of man who would fall for an old trick like that?

GILETTE (*Backs, facing him, toward the center of the stage*): Well, I—I really couldn't say! (BEN *finishes the coffee all at once, puts the cup on the saucer, pushes both aside, and smugly leans back.*) *Now* I can say. Yes! You not only look like a man who *would*—but in a moment you will look like a man who *did!*

BEN (*Rising*): What! You're joking! I must say—(*He falls back into his seat.*) I can't stand up! You—you've *poisoned* me!

GILETTE: No. Not at all. It will paralyze you for a few minutes, but then you will recover—if you are alive! I doubt if you will be. (BEN *tries to raise his right arm, but it falls back heavily onto the desk.* GILETTE *takes newspaper from her handbag and throws it onto desk.*)

BEN: You witch!

GILETTE (*Laughing*): It's about time you realized that.

BEN: You won't get away with this. You'll be caught!

GILETTE: Can't move at all now, huh? (*Goes to door right, opens it, and peeks out. She closes it and returns.*) Who's going to catch me? Your office boy is gone, probably wandering around the streets down there. You really should have taken an interest in his Rubashka. You so nicely dismissed the motherly Miss Chance. (*Walks to door left, looks out, then closes it*) I'll probably leave this way. By the way, it sounded to me as if your friend, Mr. Chalant, was trying to warn you about me, but I imagine that your poor telephone manners caused him to lose interest. (*Moves toward the desk*) Well, I'll just take the manuscript, take care of you with my handbag (*Feels its weight, tentatively*), and leave! (BEN*'s mouth opens and closes, but no sound comes forth.*) Oh, I see that the paralysis prevents you from speaking. No famous last words to be published after your death—too bad. (*She reaches for the manuscript, when a knock is heard; she hastily drops the manuscript, and looks expectantly at the door right.* WILLIAM *enters.*)

WILLIAM: Hello! I thought I'd take the short cut. I finished mailing the rejections, Mr. Canny. Oh, I almost forgot—Mr. Chalant called *again* just before I left. Said that if you wouldn't talk on the phone he was coming up here! He must want that advance pretty badly! (*Draws nearer to* BEN*'s desk*) Say, Mr. Canny, speaking of that woman who escaped (*He pauses significantly.*), did you know that Rubashka, the mad ballerina almost escaped once? (*He looks at* GILETTE.) She did! One time the attendant brought her something to eat. Well, Rubashka was standing on her toes in the corner of her room, when suddenly she did a perfect *grand jeté* right over the attendant's head and out the door. She waltzed down the corridor (*Demonstrates each move as he describes it*), up the stairs, and out through the front gate. That's where she had her downfall!

GILETTE: What happened?

WILLIAM: She was so happy to be free that she did a mighty *entrechat* (*Demonstrates*)—and when she came down she stubbed her toe. That did it. She was finished without her toes. They caught her easily.

GILETTE (*Pointing to door right*): Go! (WILLIAM *hastily goes to door, stops, then turns to look at* GILETTE)

WILLIAM: You know, this is the first time Mr. Canny has listened to me without interrupting. He must be getting interested in ballet. (*Exits, closing door behind him.*)

GILETTE (*Looking at* BEN *and shaking her head sympathetically*): What a way for you to have to spend your last moments—helpless, listening to *that!* Well, you shouldn't have been so sure that witches weren't real. If I can get rid of you and get this manuscript to Henry Eldritch before I am recaptured—(*Looks over manuscript*) he will be satisfied, use his position as police lieutenant to *prevent* my recapture—and tonight (*Laughs wildly*) I shall have a really wild time at the Witches' Sabbat!

BEN (*Terrified*): The Witches' Sabbat?

GILETTE: Ah! I see you can talk again. The potion is wearing off—I must hurry! (*Puts manuscript down on desk. Lifts handbag over her head.* BEN *winces.*) Now! (*Loud voices and slamming of doors are heard off right. She stares toward the door.*)

POLICEMAN (*From off right*): Which way is it? Get behind me!

DON (*From off right*): Over here! If we're not too late! (*Door right is flung open.* POLICEMAN *enters, followed by* DON CHALANT.) There she is!

GILETTE (*Staring, shocked, lowers the bag*): You! No! No! I won't go with you! (*She casts aside the handbag and dashes out the door left, screaming.*) No-o-o!

DON: Quick, Lieutenant! Don't let her get away!

POLICEMAN: Don't worry, Mr. Chalant. She won't get far —I left two men at every exit. They'll have her waiting for me when I get downstairs. You'd better look after this gentleman.

DON: How are you, Ben? You sure had a close shave with that Gilette.

BEN (*Waving weakly at them*): It's all right, Don. I'll be all right in a moment. (*Breathes deeply*) How did you manage to get here?

DON: You can thank the Lieutenant here for that, Ben. After I left your office I felt that there was something about Miss de Rais that puzzled me, so I bought another newspaper and the picture *did* seem a lot like her. I still wasn't too sure, so I tried several times to call you from a drugstore. (BEN *rises, walks over to* DON *and puts his hand on his shoulder.*)

BEN: I'm awfully sorry about that, Don. (POLICEMAN *wanders over to* BEN'*s desk and sits behind it, leaning back with one foot on the desk.*) Maybe we can even arrange that advance for you.

DON (*Smiling, then clapping* BEN *on the back*): That's what I like to hear, Ben. Well, anyway, the phone calls almost threw me off, and I might have let things drop if I hadn't noticed the Lieutenant here walking by the store. I told him about my suspicions and *he* decided we should look into it—so *he's* the one to thank.

BEN: Lieutenant, I'm Ben Canny, the publisher—and a mighty grateful man. If there's ever anything—

POLICEMAN (*With unusual interest*): Ben Canny! Well, Mr. Canny, it's a real pleasure to meet such an important man. You don't know how pleased I am to *know* you. (*Picks up manuscript from desk*) And I suppose this is a real book manuscript?

BEN: That's right, Lieutenant. I've just finished working on it.

POLICEMAN (*Reading the title of the manuscript*): *The Autobiography of a Modern*—say, I really *am* glad to know you, Mr. Canny.

BEN: I'd like to show my appreciation in a more concrete way, if I may, and if by any chance I can't do that, I'd at least like to know the name of the man who saved my life. What is your name, Lieutenant?

POLICEMAN (*Looking up*): My name, Mr. Canny? My name is Eldritch—Henry Eldritch! (*Curtain*)

THE END

Production Notes

The Whites of Their Eyes

Characters: 9 male; 10 female. The number of cast members in pageant may be increased or decreased, if desired.
Playing Time: 20 minutes.
Costumes: Ordinary, everyday dress. Mr. Krick wears topcoat and derby.
Properties: Roll of green crepe paper, script, costume boxes, broomsticks, American flag.
Setting: The stage of Mr. Krick's theater. The stage is bare except for a few red and white streamers hanging at the back, and a table left, on which are records, record player and a telephone. A pile of broomsticks is on the floor near the table. A few straight chairs at right and left and a ladder at back may complete the setting. Exits are at right and left.
Lighting: No special effects.
Sound: Offstage hoofbeats, patriotic music, telephone bell, as indicated in text.

Professor Countdown Takes Off

Characters: 2 male; 2 female; 3 or more female extras.
Playing Time: 10 minutes.
Costumes: Modern dress. Professor wears a dark suit and Homburg. James wears a chauffeur's uniform. Ladies wear attractive suits or dresses and hats.
Properties: A fake mustache and a tube of glue.
Setting: In Scene 1, two chairs represent a car on a road. In Scene 2, two chairs at left and several chairs at right represent the meeting of the Ladies' Luncheon League. There may also be a speaker's stand at left. The skit may be performed in front of the curtain or in a room without a stage, if desired.
Lighting: No special effects.

Man in the Red Suit

Characters: 9 male; 5 female; 5 boys and girls for carolers; as many boys and girls as desired for Other Martians; boy's voice for TV Announcer (he may be an onstage character, if desired).
Playing Time: 20 minutes.
Costumes: Glog has white hair and wears traditional red Santa Claus suit, with large pockets. When he appears in Scene 2, he has added white beard and bulging tummy. President of Mars has watch. Martians, except for Glog, wear tunic-like costumes; some Mar-

tians have white hair. Earth people wear appropriate everyday dress. Nearsighted Earthman wears glasses; Lady carries change in her pocket or purse; Mr. Kringlehoffer wears wristwatch.

Properties: Toothbrush, toothpaste, box of cakes and cookies, red cap with tassel, electric razor, large and unusual teddy bear, tray with cups and saucers on it, tinsel and other Christmas tree decorations, string of Christmas tree lights, large book.

Setting: Scene 1 takes place on the planet Mars. A small table holding hypno-ray gun is at one side of stage. There may be a painted backdrop showing the planet Earth in the distance. Scenes 2 and 4 take place on a divided stage: stage left is the Krinklehoffers' living room. A Christmas tree stands in one part of room. Front door and window are at center, looking out on stage right. In Scene 2, a table with pile of envelopes on it is by front door. Front door has small steps in front of it, leading toward stage right. Stage right is the yard outside the Kringlehoffers' home. Scene 3 may take place before the curtain.

Lighting: If desired, in Scenes 2 and 4, lights may dim or come up on stage right or stage left, as indicated in text.

Sound: Sound of rocket ship landing and blasting off, as indicated in text.

No Garden This Year

Characters: 2 male; 1 female.

Playing Time: 10 minutes.

Costumes: The men wear sport shirts and slacks. Carrie wears an attractive suit and hat, and carries a purse.

Properties: Golf club and golf ball, for Wilbur; seed catalogues, for Dan; garden tools (rake, hoe, and spade) and hatbox, for Carrie.

Setting: The living room of Wilbur's home. The only necessary furnishings are two chairs and a table with a vase on it. The rest of the stage may be furnished as simply or as elaborately as desired.

Lighting: No special effects.

Ariadne Exposed

Characters: 4 male; 1 female.

Playing Time: 15 minutes.

Costumes: Cretan men may wear long skirts, or sheets worn toga-fashion might be used. Minos should wear a crown, and Ariadne wears a long dress and much costume jewelry. She carries a long-handled mirror. Theseus might wear track shorts, etc., or some other athletic uniform.

Properties: Painted boards for clay tablets, length of twine on a stick.

Setting: The throne room of Minos' palace in Crete. There is a table with chessboard and a chair at center, and a bench down right. There is an exit up center, which may be flanked by pillars.

Lighting: No special effects.

Snow White and Friends

Characters: 4 male; 2 female; 1 male or female for Mirror.

Playing Time: 20 minutes.

Costumes: Appropriate fairy tale costumes. Narrator wears everyday modern dress. Mirror may wear sandwich boards. Woodsman carries an ax.

Properties: Ax, banana, apple.

Setting: Scenes 1 and 3: the Queen's throne room. A throne is at center. Scenes 2 and 4: the forest. A stump is down center.

Teen and Twenty

Characters: 4 male; 5 female.
Playing Time: 35 minutes.
Costumes: Modern, everyday dress. Alice wears a cotton dress and an apron. Jennifer and Dora wear school clothes. Mike wears blue jeans or a baseball uniform. Pete wears school clothes and a letterman's sweater. Tom is dressed in a business suit, and later he appears with his coat removed. Cam wears a sports coat, slacks and a bright bow tie. Madge is also dressed in school clothes, but she must wear a gray skirt. Grace wears a suit and hat and carries gloves and purse.
Properties: Flowers, vase, piece of notepaper, baseball bat and mitt, candy in candy dish, horn-rimmed glasses, *Life* magazine, volume of Shakespeare, letters, briefcase, watch, dress box containing party dress, comic book pages.
Setting: The Waine living room. A modern room, comfortably furnished with sofa, chairs, lamps, etc. There is a coffee table in front of sofa and a small table holding a telephone next to sofa. A large bookcase is placed upstage left. There is an exit at left leading to the front door and an exit at right leading to the kitchen, the patio, and the interior of the house.
Lighting: No special effects.

Miss Frankenstein

Characters: 8 male; 11 female; as many extras as desired for Selected Members of Audience (1 boy and 2 girls minimum).
Playing Time: 40 minutes.
Costumes: M.C. wears formal dress and monster makeup. Mr. Beelzebub wears devil costume; Frankenstein has a Frankenstein mask or makeup; Dr. Jekyll wears cape and top hat, then puts on shaggy wig and long wax teeth to become Mr. Hyde. Mme. Scaremelli wears an elaborate dress. Miss Witch of Witchita's crown is a witch's pointed hat, but heavily decorated with gold and jewels. She wears a long silver cloak, with skull and crossbones design on the back, over a long black dress, and she carries a large jack-o'-lantern. Volunteers, ushers, and members of audience wear everyday dress. The contestants wear costumes described in text.
Properties: Black handkerchief for M.C., skull containing questions, black envelope, stuffed snake, hand mirror, bow, suction cup arrows, target, table, beakers, watch, wallet, scarf for talent performances.
Setting: The stage of the Hauntatorium in Panic City, set for the finals of the Miss Frankenstein Contest. Three chairs are on one side of the stage for judges, and a microphone is on the other side for M.C. For the final judging, a raised throne is placed at center, with four chairs arranged to one side.
Lighting: If desired, spotlight may be used for fashion show, and lights may flicker before curtain reopens for crowning.
Sound: Offstage hoofbeats, appropriate recorded music, if desired for fashion show, talent performances.

Yes, Yes, A Thousand Times Yes!

Characters: 4 male; 6 female.
Playing Time: 30 minutes.

Costumes: In Scene 1, women wear calico dresses. Granny has a shawl. Elegant and Urbane wear top hats, capes, and have long moustaches. Urbane has a cane. Hench and Harry wear jeans, checked shirts, and stetsons. In Scene 2, Nell wears rich gown and wedding band, and Urbane has on dressing gown and cravat.

Properties: Needles, thread, three plain aprons, organdy apron, knitting needles, ball of twine, box, soda crackers, book of clippings, bouquet, box of candy, book, basket of watercress, rope, handkerchief, camera, cookie jar containing deed, dish of bonbons.

Setting: Granny Sweetingood's parlor. A cabinet with cookie jar and box of crackers is up left. Beside cabinet are bucket and dipper and sign reading, DON'T WASTE WATER. There are samplers on the wall. A door is up right, and a window with chicken feed sacks for curtains is up center. A bare kitchen table with chairs is down left, and a rocker is up right. In Scene 2, the table has a lace tablecloth, silver tea service, and candles. Purple drapes hang at the window, and a sampler on wall reads, HOME, LAVISH HOME. A group picture on wall shows girls in organdy aprons and boys in top hats.

Lighting: No special effects.

Junior Prom

Characters: 4 male; 4 female.

Playing Time: 24 minutes.

Costumes: All characters wear evening dress.

Properties: Evening bags for the girls, small coin purse, keys, white handkerchief and red bandanna for Rocky. Girls' bags should contain handkerchief, compacts, lipsticks, and in Marilyn's bag there should be a small ticket.

Setting: The trophy room of the high school. Downstage left there is a settee; downstage right, an easy chair. A desk and chair are up right. Books supported by heavy bookends are on the desk. There are potted palms about the stage, with several in a group upstage left, almost hiding an easy chair. The entrance is upstage center.

Lighting: No special effects.

Note: Dance music should be heard at intervals throughout the play. Offstage records may be used.

Background for Nancy

Characters: 3 male; 4 female.

Playing Time: 25 minutes.

Costumes: Modern dress. In Scenes 1 and 3, Mrs. Bartlett wears housedress, apron, and low-heeled shoes. In Scene 2, she wears evening dress, heels, and long gloves. Mr. Bartlett wears business suit. Aunt Norma and Mrs. Leroy are fashionably dressed. Crane wears suit and carries coat and gloves.

Properties: Coat for Nancy, ironed laundry, plate of rolls, dress box containing evening dress, magazines.

Setting: The living room of the Bartlett home. Comfortable chairs, table, wastebasket, telephone, sofa, lamps, bookcases, etc. make up furnishings. Front door is at the rear; up left is a window which is used as exit. A door at right leads to kitchen, and another at left to the rest of the house. In Scene 2, the lamps are lighted, and in Scene 3, newspapers, books, magazines, opened mail, etc., are scattered on floor and chairs, and the table is lit-

tered with candy bar wrappers and papers.
Lighting: No special effects.

Election Day in Spooksville

Characters: 11 male; 5 female; 2 boys or girls as Ghosts; faculty member (if unavailable, a student leader will do); as many extras as desired.
Playing Time: 25 minutes.
Costumes: Mayor Lucifer is dressed as Satan. Dr. Hyde and Zach wear white lab coats. All monsters and spooks may use stage make-up or masks to create grotesque effects. Monster Frank N. Stein wears rubber mask. Igor has stuffing in his sweater to simulate a hunchback. Mummy wears white pants and shirt wrapped with layers of bandages and white make-up on face and hands. Vampira wears sheath dress, slit at sides, and has long straight black hair (or wig) and long eyelashes, except in Scene 2 where she switches to blue jeans, sweater and pony-tail. Chain Rattlers wear black sweaters and slacks. Ma Cobber dresses as an old hag with blacked-out teeth and oversize shoes. Hairy Mane wears brown wig, brown mohair sweater and brown slacks. Ghosts wear sheets; witches wear pointed hats and black capes. Frank N. Stein, Jr., and Charlie wear street clothes.
Properties: Table, chairs, gavel, crystal ball (goldfish bowl will do), chains, two brooms.
Setting: Scene 1 is set up as meeting hall with table at rear of stage facing audience and rows of chairs set diagonally from table towards front of stage. Speakers are seated behind table. At end of Scene 1 chairs are removed to prepare for Scene 2. Scene 2 is again in Town Hall with computer placed upstage center. (The computer should be painted with dials and knobs, and should have a set of flickering Christmas tree lights.)
Lighting: No special effects.
Sound: Offstage shrieks, rattling of chains.

A Case for Two Detectives

Characters: 6 male; 6 female.
Playing Time: 30 minutes.
Costumes: Modern, everyday dress. Annie wears maid's uniform, and Servants have on appropriate uniforms. 2nd Servant later puts on black mask. Mr. Allen wears a wig. Rivets wears a slouch hat, trench coat with turned-up collar, and bright necktie. Miss Marlowe wears a watch.
Properties: Guns, magnifying glass, cuff link, key, papers, script, armchair.
Setting: The drawing room of the Bartons' Long Island home. French doors leading to the garden are up center. Other entrances are at right and left. A mirror hangs on wall right. Chairs, tables, lamps, etc., complete the setting.
Lighting: No special effects.

The Shop Girl's Revenge

Characters: 4 male; 3 female.
Playing Time: 25 minutes.
Costumes: Dress typical of the end of the gay nineties. Falmouth should be dressed with perfection in every detail. He might wear a swallow-tail morning coat, and certainly a boutonniere. Mrs. Gant can be elegantly overdressed with all the extreme trimmings of high-society—plumes, feathers, etc. She carries a large

purse. Jack's clothes should be very sporty. The shop employees are a little shabby—the girls may wear Gibson-girl blouses and skirts. Gladys must wear a small gold locket.

Properties: Broom, gold watch, cash, apron, purse, a plug of tobacco, a square of chocolate, toothpick, handkerchief, small gold locket like the one Gladys wears.

Setting: The main floor of a department store at the turn of the century. There is a wooden counter with all sorts of notions on it, and on shelves behind it. There must be space behind the counter. Exits are at left and right.

Lighting: No special effects.

Jump for Joy

Characters: 7 male; 7 female.

Playing Time: 30 minutes.

Costumes: Everyday modern dress. Joy Darling should be dressed as a typical movie queen; she might wear a fur piece, costume jewelry, etc.

Properties: Pocket watch for Hobart; purse, envelope with contract, newspaper for Dora; scripts; telegrams; bouquet of flowers.

Setting: The office of Ambrose Bainbridge, a theatrical agent in New York City. There is a desk just right of center. On top of the desk are a typewriter, a telephone, and other office equipment. Behind the desk may be filing cabinets, a clothes tree, etc. There is a door at left. Near the door is a television set, facing the desk at an angle. Between the desk and the door is a row of straight chairs. Theatrical posters are hung on the walls, and, if possible, there should be windows indicated on the upstage walls.

Lighting: No special effects.

The Mystery at Tumble Inn

Characters: 3 male; 5 female; 1 male voice (radio announcer).

Playing Time: 35 minutes.

Costumes: Everyday, modern dress. Opal has on housedress and apron; Duke wears work clothes, and later puts on wet slicker. Girls have wet scarves on their heads when they first enter, and they carry pocketbooks. Mrs. Tushingham wears a traveling suit and carries a purse containing jewel case. She has a small suitcase when she first enters.

Properties: Newspaper, jewel case containing medallion on a chain, larger jewel case wrapped in newspaper (containing diamond necklace), pile of bedding, transistor radio, flashlight, gun, identification card, handcuffs.

Setting: The living room of Tumble Inn. Up center is a desk with a telephone, and down left is a couch. Chairs, tables, lamps, etc., complete the furnishings. All the furniture, except for desk, is covered with sheets. A door up center leads to the outside. Beside door is a window with a shade which can be raised and lowered. An exit at right leads to kitchen and basement, and another exit at left leads to rest of house.

Lighting: Lights go off and come on, as indicated.

Sound: Offstage sound of wind and thunder, loud knocking, voice and music from radio, as indicated in text.

The Gold Mine at Jeremiah Flats

Characters: 7 male; 3 female.

Playing Time: 30 minutes.

Costumes: Costumes of the period.

Patience may be dressed in white. Do-Well may wear bib overalls. Mrs. Allspent has a shawl over her shoulders. Mr. Quickbuck and Mr. Turmoil are very well dressed. Sourdough and the two Miners wear work clothes. The Sheriff should have a large silver star pinned to his jacket.

Properties: Flowers and vase; firewood; sugar bowl; paper money; wooden box; box with fake sticks of dynamite, spools of wire, and plunger generator (this could be a bicycle pump); bag of groceries; tea service; bottle of smelling salts; map of mine, pick and shovel for Do-Well; gun, deed, and pen for Turmoil; deed for Sourdough; 2 cloth-covered gallon jugs for Miners; briefcase containing papers for Miss Truebeauty; paper bag for Patience.

Setting: Scenes 1 and 3: The modest Allspent living room. A door off right leads outside; a door at left leads to the rest of the house. There is a cabinet against one wall, and other furniture, including chairs, a table with vase and flowers at upstage left and a table with a candle at downstage left, is around the room. Scene 2: Near the entrance of the Allspent's gold mine. On the backdrop is painted a boarded-up mine shaft and a sign which reads LUCKY STRIKE MINE pointing offstage right. A wooden box is downstage left.

Lighting: As Scene 1 opens the stage is dark; lights come on gradually. Scene 2 is dimly lighted.

Sound: Sound of gunshots and exploding dynamite.

MUD PACK MADNESS

Characters: 5 female.

Playing Time: 25 minutes.

Costumes: Everyday clothes.

Properties: Nail polish, hair curlers, overnight bag, combs, large jar of green ointment (this may be made with cold starch, colored with green food coloring), mirrors, flash camera, several towels, nail file, bottle of "vinegar," and cosmetic jar.

Setting: The living room of Ginny's house. There are a sofa and a chair. Grooming articles are scattered around the room.

Lighting: No special effects.

Sound: Telephone bell.

SURPRISE PARTY

Characters: 3 male; 5 female.

Playing Time: 25 minutes.

Costumes: Modern, everyday dress. Fran wears a coat and carries a purse when she first enters. James and Ted wear casual clothes. When Rosemary first enters, she wears a robe and slippers and her hair is in rollers. Later she is dressed for the party, with a few rollers still in her hair. Mrs. Taveltite wears a dowdy dress and a shapeless hat. Daisy and Mary Rose wear traveling clothes, and Erskine wears a suit.

Properties: Bobby pin, newspaper, magazines, bag of groceries, bouquet of flowers, suitcases, old-fashioned valise, oversized handbag.

Setting: The Eliot living room. A sofa with pillows is at center, and near it is a magazine rack holding newspapers and magazines. At one side is a small table with a telephone on it. Chairs, lamps, bookcases, etc., complete the furnishings. The exit at left leads to the front door, and beside it is a window. The exit at right leads to kitchen and rest of the house.

Lighting: No special effects.

Sound: Telephone, doorbell.

Miss Cast

Characters: 5 male; 3 female.
Playing Time: 35 minutes.
Costumes: Everyday clothes for all, except Judy, who wears bell-bottomed pants and a bright blouse or poncho. Her hair-do is elaborate, and she always wears sunglasses. In Scene 2, she changes near end to a simple party dress, removes sunglasses and simplifies her hair-do. Margaret, Ray, David, and Bill also change to simple party clothes.
Properties: Carpet sweeper, card table and model airplane parts, watches for Mr. Johnson and Margaret, script, newspaper, knitting needles with sweater in progress, movie magazines, green box of weed killer, tray with coffeepot and cups.
Setting: The Johnson living room. Sofa and chairs are arranged at center; a card table with model airplane parts is up right. A telephone is on an end table. Exits are right, to the outside, and left, to other rooms in the house. There is an open window in rear wall.
Lighting: No special effects.
Sound: Telephone and doorbell, as indicated in text.

Virtue Is Her Own Reward

Characters: 6 male; 6 female. Members of the audience, selected in advance, may cheer or hiss and boo, as indicated in the text, and at other appropriate times.
Playing Time: 40 minutes.
Costumes: Appropriate 19th century dress. Basil has money in his pocket and has a pair of large gloves with him. Members of wedding procession wear appropriate formal dress, and Basil and Roderick add top hats to their costumes and wear carnations in their lapels. Ernest changes to tight pants, loud vest, beads, etc. for last scene.
Properties: Envelope with newspaper clipping inside it, guitar.
Setting: The kitchen of the Candlewicks' home. Up center is a Dutch door with the top half open; other exits are at left and right. A coatrack is at one side of stage; a table and chairs are at center. In Scene 1, the table is set for dinner and there are dishes of food on counters or stove.
Lighting: If possible, lights dim for wedding sequence and spotlight shines on procession. Lights then come up, as indicated in text.
Sound: Recordings of the Wedding March, and the Anvil Chorus, as indicated in text.

Roscoe the Robot

Characters: 4 male; 4 female.
Playing Time: 30 minutes.
Costumes: Everyday dress except for Rafferty, who wears a policeman's uniform. Scotty puts on a robot outfit, as indicated in text. The body can be made from cardboard boxes covered with silver paint or paper. The head is detachable, with a blinking red flashlight fastened to one eye. This can be turned on by reaching through a circular opening at the side of the head. The arms and legs can be made from rolls of silvered cardboard. Silvered gloves can be used for hands, and a pair of oversized silvered boots are used for feet. Bicycle horns are attached for robot's voice.
Properties: Portable electric mixer, old vacuum cleaner, darts, red jacket, magazines, large cardboard

footprint made by tracing boot, handkerchief.

Setting: Scotty's workshop. A long table is at one side, covered with an odd assortment of wires and scraps of metal. A telephone is at one end of it. Several chairs are standing about. In one corner is a large folding screen. A window is in one side wall. Exits are left and right.

Lighting: No special effects.

Ride the Gooberville Stage

Characters: 6 male; 7 female.

Playing Time: 30 minutes.

Costumes: Typical "old West" costumes for all. Women wear long dresses and bonnets, and Little Bird wears a beaded, fringed Indian dress. Cora, Dora and Flora may change to bright dresses for medicine show. Professor Dixon wears a high top hat. Rancid Naseby wears a black suit, cape, top hat, string tie, and mustache. Tumbleweed Kid has a long white beard when he is disguised as Old-Timer, and later he puts on a long dress, wig and bonnet.

Properties: Newspaper, bottles labeled Dixon's Elixir, mail pouch containing letters, postcards, and envelope of wanted posters, carpetbags, boxes, strongbox, hatbox, signs reading DIXON'S ELIXIR, and IF IT'S CHRONIC, TRY OUR TONIC, tambourines, trunk.

Setting: The stagecoach depot of the little Western town of Gooberville. Posters on the walls give the times of arrivals and departures of coaches. One large sign reads, OUR RECORD! NINETY MILES IN NINETY HOURS! There is a counter at right, with pigeonholes behind it for mail, and stacks of tickets on it. A bench is at left, and chairs are placed here and there. Exit is at rear.

Lighting: No special effects.

Sound: Offstage coach sounds, as indicated in text.

Hamelot

Characters: 13 male; 3 female.

Playing Time: 30 minutes.

Costumes: Queen, Amnesia and Patience wear low-budget royal gowns. The Queen wears harlequin glasses on a chain. King Sire wears a large, gilded cardboard crown with fifteen points—atop each point is a numbered circle. He wears an oversized robe edged in mangy fur of some kind; beneath it, a basketball outfit, perhaps in a flashy magenta. Lance and the Knights are dressed as basketball players with their number on the backs of their shirts. Lionel is dressed as a page, and carries a toy trumpet. Mervac has an extension cord tucked into the waist of his trousers, and carries a pool cue decorated with magical signs and symbols, and a spray can. His costume suits a Royal Computer working for a low-budget kingdom. Jouster is dressed as a jester, and carries a bauble. The Piper has long hair, wears a beret, dark glasses, sandals, beads, etc. He carries a kazoo. The Grand Vizier wears a high, peaked magician's hat on a full head of long black hair. His bright orange beard reaches almost to his waist. His robe is long enough to cover himself and the actor playing Billy, since he stands on Billy's shoulders when he enters. Billy and the Vizier, under the robe, both wear basketball suits, without numbers. If possible, the actors playing

King Sire and the Grand Vizier should be short and wiry.

Properties: Excalibrated, an enormous, bejeweled pool cue; seven pool cues, with numbered pennants reading 2, 4, 6, 8, 10, 12, 14; a pool cue with magical signs and symbols, for Mervac; extension cord; toy trumpet; air spray can; jester's bauble; kazoo; lap board; feather duster; cushion; several packs of cards; box of chocolates; sweater; fan; oversized purse; small blackboard on legs, reading SCOREBOARD, QUEEN—VISITORS; chalk; script, labeled SCRIPT, for Amnesia; child's toy train.

Setting: The throne room of King Sire's castle. Up center are an old, overstuffed armchair for the King's throne, a kitchen chair on either side for the Queen and Amnesia. Excalibrated, the jeweled pool cue, leans against the throne; cues 12 and 14 are nearby. Downstage is a large, rickety-looking pool table. Slightly upstage and right of throne is Mervac's equipment: an assemblage of dials, knobs, lights, etc. A speaker system hangs up center, over the throne. Exits are left and right.

Lighting: No special effects.

Sound: Vizier's Voice, crashes, sirens, etc., broadcast through speakers, as indicated in text.

A Family Affair

Characters: 5 male; 4 female.

Playing Time: 30 minutes.

Costumes: Modern dress. Mrs. Ellis has a watch. In Scene 2, Barbie's hair is carefully combed, and she wears a pearl necklace. Jerry Mars wears old clothes.

Properties: Records, letter, book, bags of groceries, newspaper, knitting, candy, baseball bat and glove, bottle of antiseptic, cotton, roll of bandage.

Setting: The living room of the Ellis home. Downstage right is a sofa with several cushions on it. Near the sofa are several armchairs, and a table with a telephone. Upstage center is a table with a phonograph on it; records and record covers are placed around the table. Behind the phonograph is a large mirror. Bookcases, a desk and other chairs and tables complete the furnishings. In Scene 2, Mrs. Ellis' sewing basket is on a table near an easy chair.

Lighting: If possible, Mr. Ellis should turn off the lights at the end of Scene 2.

Enchanted, I'm Sure

Characters: 4 male; 2 female.

Playing Time: 30 minutes.

Costumes: Ben Canny wears a conservative business suit and horn-rimmed glasses. Don Chalant wears slacks and a sport jacket. Gilette de Rais wears a black dress and carries a large black handbag. Miss Chance wears a conservative dress or suit and glasses. The Policeman is in a uniform. William is in slacks, shirt and tie.

Properties: Papers and manuscripts, for Ben; watches, for Ben and Don; newspaper, for William; tray and two coffee cups, for Miss Chance; small bottle, for Gilette.

Setting: The office of Ben Canny. There is a large desk to the left, facing down center, a swivel chair behind it. Up center a small magazine table is flanked by two office chairs, facing downstage. There is an exit up left, and to the right is the door to the outer office. A hatrack stands beside the door right. There is a photograph on the wall.

Lighting: No special effects.

Sound: An intercom buzzer.